Subseries on the History of
Japanese Business and Industry

Japan's rise from the destruction and bitter defeat of World War II to its present eminence in world business and industry is perhaps the most striking development in recent world history. This did not occur in a vacuum. It was linked organically to at least a century of prior growth and transformation. To illuminate this growth a new kind of scholarship on Japan is needed: historical study *in the context of a company or industry* of the interrelations among entrepreneurs, managers, engineers, workers, stockholders, bankers, and bureaucrats, and of the institutions and policies they created. Only in such a context can the contribution of particular factors be weighed and understood. It is to promote and encourage such scholarship that this series is established, supported by the Reischauer Institute of Japanese Studies and published by the Council on East Asian Studies at Harvard.

Albert M. Craig

Managing Industrial Enterprise

Harvard East Asian Monographs, 142

This book is based on a conference sponsored by the Joint Committee on Japanese Studies of the American Council of Learned Societies and the Social Science Research Council with support from the Ford Foundation and the National Endowment for the Humanities.

edited by
WILLIAM D. WRAY

Published by
THE COUNCIL ON EAST ASIAN STUDIES / HARVARD UNIVERSITY
Distributed by the Harvard University Press
Cambridge (Massachusetts) and London 1989

Managing Industrial Enterprise

Cases from Japan's Prewar Experience

The Council on East Asian Studies at Harvard University publishes a monograph series and, through the Fairbank Center for East Asian Research and the Reischauer Institute of Japanese Studies, administers research projects designed to further scholarly understanding of China, Japan, Korea, Vietnam, Inner Asia, and adjacent areas.

Library of Congress Cataloging in Publication Data

Managing industrial enterprise : cases from Japan's prewar experience
/ edited by William D. Wray.
    p.   cm. – (Harvard East Asian monographs ; 142)
    Based on a conference sponsored by the Joint Committee on Japanese
Studies of the American Council of Learned Societies and the Social
Science Research Council with support from the Ford Foundation and
the National Endowment for the Humanities.
    Bibliography: p.
    Includes index.
    ISBN 0-674-54770-5
    1. Industrial management—Japan—History—20th century—Case
studies—Congresses. I. Wray, William D., 1943-   . II. Joint
Committee on Japanese Studies.   III. Series.
HD70.J3M275   1989
685'.00952'0904—dc20   89-7691
                                                                  CIP

THIS BOOK IS DEDICATED TO

Marit Ericson
Kristine Ericson
Megumi Gordon
Catherine ("Katie") Turley-Molony
Anthony ("Anjin") Wray

all of whom were born since the workshop from which this volume emerged.

CONTRIBUTORS

MICHAEL CUSUMANO is Assistant Professor at the Massachusetts Institute of Technology's Sloan School of Management, where he teaches courses on corporate strategy and Japanese technology management. He is the author of *The Japanese Automobile Industry* (Council on East Asian Studies, Harvard University, 1985) and is completing another book on the factory approach to software development.

STEVEN ERICSON teaches modern Japanese history at Dartmouth College. He is currently completing a book on railroad development in Meiji Japan.

ANDREW GORDON is Associate Professor of History at Duke University. The author of *The Evolution of Labor Relations in Japan: Heavy Industry, 1853–1955* (Council on East Asian Studies, Harvard University, 1985), he is currently completing *Imperial Democracy in Japan*, a study of labor and politics from 1905 to 1940.

STEPHEN McCALLION, a graduate of The Ohio State University, did his doctoral dissertation on Meiji Japan's silk-reeling industry. His publications include an article on changes in silk-reeling during the Tokugawa period. He assists regularly in the production of the *Japanese Yearbook on Business History*.

BARBARA MOLONY is Associate Professor of History at Santa Clara University and former director of its International Business Program. She has written several articles on Noguchi Jun and the Japanese chemical industry and has a book in press, *Technology and Investment in the Prewar Japanese Chemical Industry*. Her current research interest focuses on women workers in the prewar Japanese textile industry.

MORIKAWA HIDEMASA is Professor of Business Management at Yokohama National University. Formerly of Hosei University, where he taught for many years, he is the author of *Zaibatsu no keiei shiteki kenkyū* and numerous other books on management and zaibatsu history, including an English-language work in press. He was also co-editor and principal organizer of the *Japanese Yearbook on Business History*.

WILLIAM WRAY is Associate Profesor of History at the University of British Columbia. He is the author of *Mitsubishi and the N.Y.K., 1870–1914: Business Strategy in the Japanese Shipping Industry* (Council on East Asian Studies, Harvard University, 1984), studies of freight conferences, an article on Sino-Japanese economic relations, and a book-length bibliography of Japan's economy. He is presently preparing another book on the N.Y.K. and is conducting research on the electrical industry in Japan.

CONTENTS

This volume emerged from a workshop on Japanese business history held at the University of British Columbia in February 1982. The occasion for the workshop was a planned visit to UBC by Professor Naka-gawa Keiichirō, dean of Japan's business historians. At the time, though a number of North American scholars, most of them relatively young, had begun to work on Japanese business history, there was as yet no cohesive group; nor had any formal gathering been held. The intent of the workshop was to bring together some of these North American practitioners with several leading Japanese specialists. It was hoped that this would lead to some sort of publication and a strengthening of ties, particularly at an institutional level, between Western and Japanese scholars. In retrospect, it is clear that the second of these goals was the more quickly achieved. The best concrete example of the subsequent cooperation has been the appearance of the *Japanese Yearbook on Business History* (1984–), for which some of the contributors to this volume have provided translations.

In the aftermath of the workshop, there was considerable delay in finalizing the roster of participants for this volume. Michael Cusumano, for example, joined the project at a later date. Furthermore, for several of the participants, work on dissertations or books took precedence over revisions to papers.

Conference volumes on Japanese history in recent years can be divided into several different categories. Some have dealt with specific areas or periods, such as the Restoration or the Taishō period, others with themes such as conflict or colonialism. These projects have brought together scholars to relate their different specialties to a common topic. In another type of conference, specialists in the same historical sub-discipline have assembled to treat a particular subject— Tokugawa intellectual history being one such case. Functionally, the present volume is closest to this last category, for all the participants contribute work in the same sub-field, namely, business history (defined to include industry and labor).

All the above types of conferences have contributed, in various ways, to a broader understanding of Japanese history. However, a certain sense of historiographical timing may give the specialized conference like this one a more strategic function in the further development of Japanese history as a field. Today there is no single up-to-date textbook on modern Japan. To write one seems a formidable task. Before it can be attempted, specific sub-fields must be explored in more depth. Indeed, such explorations—which include business, labor, intellectual change, institutions such as the media or government ministries, agrarian social relations, and political history that transcends conventional periodization—probably constitute the mainstream of current historiography on Japan. Together they presage a kind of dynamic tension within the field as a whole. On the one hand, they encourage an increasing differentiation, which can make communication between separate sub-fields more difficult. On the other hand, the textbook writer (a mythical figure perhaps) must not only draw on the recent research in these sub-fields but develop the thematic interconnectedness among them. Though this will prove a difficult undertaking, we may be on the verge of making such connections. The development of sub-fields creates the raw material for them. Furthermore, it is an urgent task. In recent years there has been a rapid growth in the number of world-history textbooks. However, Japan (and Asia as a whole) continues to receive relatively little attention in what are still Western-oriented publications. It is unlikely that Japan can be integrated into the new approaches to world history unless more stimulating and informed syntheses of Japanese history emerge.

These remarks represent a kind of trajectory along which the field is moving and to which this volume can contribute. In a different dimension, though these chapters are closer to research pieces than general essays, they should find a place in teaching, either in assignments to advanced students or in professorial preparation. The scope of their chronology, ranging from the Restoration to World War II, gives the volume a certain utility for modern-Japanese-history courses. For comparative purposes, the volume could be used together with a work like Alfred D. Chandler, Jr., and Richard S. Tedlow, eds., *The Coming of Managerial Capitalism: A Casebook on the History of American Economic Institutions* (Homewood, Richard D. Irwin, 1985), which includes case studies of both business corporations and government policies used in the classroom at the Harvard Business School.

The contributors to this volume are grateful for the comments of other participants in the original workshop, some of whom presented papers being developed for ongoing projects. We should like to thank Alfred Chandler, Mark Fruin, Takeshi Hikino, Nakagawa Keiichirō and Gary Saxonhouse. This project has lasted long enough to encompass the terms of several staff associates at the Social Science Research Council, but Ronald Aqua and Stefan Tanaka performed especially strategic roles for us. Our gratitude goes to the Council for sponsoring the workshop and to the Japan Foundation and the Ōhira Commemorative Fund, administered through the Institute of Asian Research at UBC, for help with transportation and other expenses.

William Wray
Kamakura and Vancouver, 1988

CHAPTER ONE

Introduction

WILLIAM D. WRAY

BUSINESS HISTORY AND ITS APPROACH

A new direction has emerged in the past half-decade in Western writings on Japanese economic history. This development falls under the rubric of "business history" or "industrial history." To some this has often meant "company history," that is, an historical account of an individual firm. The scholars who have pioneered this new trend, however, do not approach their task in that way. Though individual companies have been the subject of many of the recently published works, and of several of the chapters in this volume, the focus of recent business history has been broader, encompassing issues like government-business relations, urban-rural relations, international commerce, technological development, and labor relations. These issues, of course, are also central to the research of economic historians and political scientists. If company history is not its salient feature, how then does the recent business history differ from the work of economic historians and political scientists? Fundamentally, it marks a shift away from aggregate studies by the economic historians, such as analyses of the macroeconomic performance of the Japanese economy, or from the political scientists' principal focus on the role of the state, in favor of a micro analysis of specific institutions such as companies and industries, or specific arrangements in these institutions for matters such as administration of employment, strategies for future investment, and operational ties between firms in different industries.[1] A further characteristic of recent business history is that its central questions are often the reverse of those asked by economists and political scientists. Essentially it is concerned with the interaction between the internal dynamics of the institution under study and the external influences on the institution by the broader economic, social and political context of the time. While an essential part of this history, like the goals of economists, is to show how findings about a specific company or industry affect our interpretation of the economy in general, of equal concern, and having perhaps greater influence over the type of analysis undertaken, is the question of how the general historical context has affected the history of the particular institution.

This approach is rooted in empirical concerns. Fundamentally, it suggests that a new synthesis of modern Japanese economic history cannot be attempted until more research is completed on specific issues. Only then can the "big picture" be painted. But, during the past decade, the individual pieces in this canvas have become easier to draw because of the increased accessibility of primary business records. The gradual accumulation of new interpretations derived from these records will form the basis for new models of Japan's past economy and, in the comparative dimension, for the testing of models based on Western experience.

The shift from macro to micro analysis and the increased use of primary sources in recent business history are by no means new or unique characteristics in the study of Japanese economic history. For over a decade, quantitative economic historians have been using these approaches and methods.[2] But the focus of their work is altogether different. To date it has centered overwhelmingly on the rural economy and has raised questions about demographic change, the standard of living, and the migration of labor, to name a few topics, which are closer to social history than to recent business and industrial history. About issues central to business and industrial history, such as decision making, organizational change, or industrial strategy, it has had little to say. In some respects, older and more sociological work on the rural economy had, in the past, greater influence on business history because of the supposed similarities between social patterns in Tokugawa villages and modern Japanese corporations. In short, there has been little attempt so far to integrate the findings of recent quantitative economic history and business history, though Mark Fruin is one scholar who has in effect crossed over in moving from earlier studies of agriculture and rural migration to business history with an emphasis on industries that emerged from rural settings.[3]

Two specific issues may further serve to differentiate the work of business historians from their counterparts in other sub-disciplines. One of the most hotly debated topics of the Japanese economy in recent years has been industrial policy. Among Western scholars, research on this—and the related problem of industrial structure— was pioneered by political scientists, particularly Chalmers Johnson. They have been followed, and criticized, by economists skeptical of the efficacy of industrial policy, which Johnson and others saw as essential to the successful performance of the postwar economy.[4] Though Japanese industrial policy is an important issue even for the early part of this century, and in some respects for the late nineteenth century, business historians have done only limited work on the subject.[5] It is not yet clear whether they will develop a consensus on the issue that will place them closer to one of the above two positions. In some respects, Johnson's subject is closer to topics studied by business historians, for he treats a specific institution (MITI) and presents his analysis from a historical perspective, beginning his detailed account in the 1920s. Johnson's emphasis on the primacy of the role of the state, however, is met with skepticism by historians concerned with private enterprises and their strategies, a perspective that harmonizes at times with the economists' focus on the functioning of the market. Clearly, however, instead of exclusive attention to state institutions or the macroeconomic effects of industrial policy, the distinctive contribution of business historians to this debate will be to examine the history of specific firms and industries to assess precisely how they have been affected by the government's industrial policy by balancing the government role with other phenomena that provide a context for company decisions and growth.

The postwar zaibatsu dissolution program is another topic where business historians are apt to raise questions that differ from the economists. Most of the economic analysis of this program ("economic," as contrasted with policymaking studies favored by political historians) has been undertaken by specialists in industrial organization.[6] Their central concern has been the impact this program had on the degree of competition within the economy. Business historians would be more inclined to ask particular questions such as how companies responded to production controls and other restrictions on business activity during the Occupation; how the purge affected the management of specific companies; what sort of strategic planning firms engaged in as controls were gradually lifted; how or whether this planning led to substantial transformations from prewar years in the pattern of the company's business operations; and how changes in organization and corporate finance dictated by legal reform affected company planning and investment strategy. Some of these questions have been examined by economists and others from a general or aggregate perspective. In view of the rapid growth of the private sector after the early 1950s, the failure to examine such issues at the concrete level of individual firms leaves a substantial gap in our knowledge of the transition from the late 1930s to the mid-1950s.

THE CHAPTERS

All chapters in this volume examine aspects of industrial enterprise. About half deal with enterprises in their entrepreneurial and mature states; others treat issues of personnel, focusing on managers and workers. The individuals and entities covered include entrepreneurs, stockholders, banks, executives, company boards, government-appointed managers, engineers, university professors, holding companies, government ministries, labor unions, the military, business federations, and particular companies and industries. The chapters examine the interaction among the varied forces represented in the above list. They also affirm the judgment of economist Aoki Masahiko, who favors going beyond the neoclassical view in which the firm is treated like "a technological black box, as summarized by the production function, which transforms combinations of marketed inputs into marketable outputs." Instead he argues that "the modern corporate firm needs to be regarded as a coalitional association of diverse constituents, such as managers, employees, banks, investors, business partners and so on."[7] This perspective is consistent with the approach taken in the chapters that follow.

The contributors have also agreed to focus on the issue of strategy. The topics of the individual studies, however, determine the way this issue has been handled: how unclear goals led to vacillating strategies by government bureaucrats and government-appointed managers (McCallion); how conflict between managers and stockholders some-times led to inconsistent and irrational strategies (Ericson); when salaried managers came to exercise the power of strategic decision making (Morikawa); how conflict between executives within a firm influenced decisions about both ownership and business operations (Wray); how an entrepreneur achieved autonomy in strategic deci-sions through innovative responses to technological change and adroit use of creditors (Molony); how a university professor used his scientific training and business philosophy to build an industrial empire (Cusumano); and how business federations approached specific labor issues in the face of worker demands and pressure from both the military and the social bureaucracy (Gordon).

In addition to their focus on strategy, collectively the chapters cover the whole period from the Meiji Restoration of 1868 to World War II. This introduction provides brief comments on the historical context of each contribution. In the "Afterword," I have discussed some topics not dealt with explicitly in the chapters but definitely suggested.

Finally, a further attribute of the chapters is that, with the excep-tion of Molony's piece on investment in Korea, all focus on domestic enterprise. This was unintentional and resulted from the research projects of the participants when they prepared their contributions. As presented here, they are of two types. Those by Morikawa and Gordon examine managers and workers to make general assessments about business and labor rather than about an individual enterprise. All the others are case studies of particular industries, companies, and enterprises. I discuss them in chronological order.

McCallion's chapter on the Tomioka silk filature is set against a background of crisis in the Japanese economy. Unable to use tariffs to protect domestic industries because of the unequal treaties imposed on Japan by the West, the new government was setting up a series of pilot projects as a program of import substitution. All these projects, which included mines, arsenals, shipyards, cement works, and cotton spinning factories, required substantial Western technology.[8] This was obtained mainly by the direct employment of foreign advisers and partly by Japanese inspections overseas. The heavy expense of such an import-substitution program was financed in large part by export earnings from Japanese silk, the demand for which had grown rapidly in the 1860s because of a silkworm disease in Europe.[9] The need to maintain the quality of silk exports, which was essential for holding on to the market, moved the government to support mechanized silk reeling in the form of the Tomioka project.

McCallion provides an analysis of government policymaking and an assessment of Tomioka's influence. Essentially, he is concerned with what is now called "industrial targeting," in this case, the upgrading of Japanese technology in a strategic industry. The French adviser to the project favored a program that would exploit Japan's strengths, specifically the widespread knowledge of traditional silk-reeling techniques. It would therefore build on Japan's "comparative advantage." The government, however, rejected much of his proposal (as well as suggestions from its own advisers), deciding instead to focus on short-term profit and high-profile technology, a targeting divorced from existing capabilities.

McCallion's account of the problems to which this decision contributed suggests at least three general points about government policy. First, the project was laden with many regulations and requirements often inconsistently applied. While attributable in part to the government's inexperience in such policy matters, this pattern did not soon disappear. Scholars of Japanese industrial policy in the West have tended to contrast the developmental or promotional thrust of Japan's economic policy with regulatory programs in the United States. There has frequently been, however, a strong regulatory component within Japan's developmental policies. Second, Tomioka suffered in its early years because of government vacillation about its principal goal, whether it would turn a profit or introduce a model technology. This indecision soon prompted debate about the project's management, that is, about who should be running the enterprise. This question arose within many of the government's programs of the period, and it was resolved in various ways, most commonly by selling the enterprise to the private sector, sometimes by subsidizing a privately owned firm, and, in later years, by setting up public corporations. Third, McCallion comments that the government's early decisions were made without much debate. This was a pattern repeated for some other industries of the time[10] but one that eventually provoked a reorientation in policy. It is interesting that some leading critics of Tomioka's management, like Matsukata Masayoshi and Maeda Masana, were key figures in shifting the focus of industrial policy toward Japan's comparative advantage in the 1880s.

As an attempt to upgrade an export industry, the Tomioka experiment differed from many of the government's pilot projects of the 1870s which were programs of import substitution. McCallion's treatment of Tomioka is consistent with recent research on both the export and import sides which has turned away from the emphasis on high-profile projects. It stresses instead the strength of certain traditional industrial practices, indirect government financial support, and the effects of government restrictions on foreign merchants. On the export side, McCallion points to continued foreign demand for Japan's traditional hand-reeled silk and even questions the necessity of the Tomioka project. This is consistent with views that stress the staying power of the putting-out system and other small workshops well into the twentieth century.[11] For imports, Sugiyama Shin'ya has argued that the unequal treaties with the West in effect acted as a non-tariff barrier which offered some protection to domestic producers in the cotton spinning industry. This effect developed out of the terms of the treaties, which restricted foreigners to designated ports. Not being able to establish themselves inland, they had to use Japanese merchants as agents, which essentially left them at the mercy of the Japanese distribution system.[12] In contrast to Sugiyama, Ishii Kanji argues that the foreign impact was indeed strong. But he also emphasizes government restriction on foreign investment, as well as the shift to more support for private enterprise after the establishment of the Home Ministry in 1873 and the effects of credit to Japanese merchants supplied through the fledgling banking system. Such measures helped numerous groups of traditional Japanese merchants to recapture the commercial initiative and successfully resist pressure from the large foreign merchant firms.[13] These views, focusing more than most previous accounts on aspects of traditional strength in industry and commerce, differ from earlier interpretations which were more inclined to emphasize large-scale government projects as a kind of last resort against Western commercial invasion.

Changes in industrial and financial policies in the 1880s—the sale of government enterprises, targeting of export products and agriculture, and budgetary retrenchment, for example—coupled with institutional reforms within government ministries and the establishment of the Bank of Japan, led to more economic stability by the latter half of the decade and an upsurge in business confidence. This manifested itself in greatly increased levels of private investment in industry, most of it in the form of joint-stock companies. The most popular industries for this investment were cotton spinning and railways. The latter is the subject of Ericson's chapter.

Ericson examines numerous issues important to mid-Meiji economic history. These include the relationship between ownership and management, the composition of railway stockholding, the business context of the industry's development, and the response to railways by local industrialists and landowners. His principal focus, though, is on the financing of investment. His analysis constitutes a major contribution to our understanding of the role of banks and, in turn, their relationship to the Bank of Japan. His findings suggest that previous scholars have underestimated the importance of banks in the development of the railway industry. Ericson develops his argument through a detailed analysis of the system of stock purchasing and through showing how this system helped conceal the indirect role that banks were playing. His analysis of this system also provides the basis for an assessment of the effects of the financial panic of 1890. Though the stock-purchasing system encouraged speculation, and though speculation itself was one of the causes of the panic, virtually all railway firms survived the crisis. Ericson attributes this partly to the reliance of some railways on passenger traffic, which was less subject than freight to swings in business, and especially to government-formulated credit arrangements for stockholders in troubled railway firms.

This emphasis on the fundamental soundness of Japanese financial institutions during the crisis points to useful comparisons, especially with China. As in Japan in 1890, speculation in China was instrumental in setting off a similar financial panic in 1883, centered on Shanghai. The effects of this panic were strikingly dissimilar, however. The immediate cause of the Chinese crisis was speculation in newly established joint-stock companies, especially in shipping and mining, whose share prices were climbing rapidly. Chinese native banks had made extensive loans, accepting shares as collateral, but, when the share prices collapsed in 1883, many banks and individual industrialists went bankrupt, "nipping in the bud," according to Yen-p'ing Hao's assessment, "nascent Chinese industrial capitalism." More specific effects of the panic included the rise of government-supervised management ("bureaucratic capitalism") and a concomitant discrediting in Chinese eyes of joint-stock enterprise.[14] Here the contrast with Japan is clear. The 1890 panic spurred the Meiji government to develop quickly a legal environment for joint-stock companies and led to the establishment of the first Commercial Code in 1893, which strengthened the Japanese company system.

In contrast to the vulnerability of Chinese institutions to such panics, German States developed arrangements during speculative runs in railway shares in the 1840s that offered more security for their firms than was the case in Japan in 1890. German railways possessed some of the same characteristics in their stock-purchasing system as their Japanese counterparts, but the speculative effects this had in Japan were contained in Germany by business practices of the railway association, which facilitated the sharing of market information, and by government policies of licensing and regulation. These features helped reduce uncertainty and hence the speculative quality of investment.[15] In similar stages of railway development, then, Japan can be seen as somewhere between the vulnerability of Chinese firms and the closely supervised market network in the German States, though, as Ericson's emphasis on the supportive role of the Bank of Japan shows, it was clearly closer to the latter.

Another feature of Ericson's paper relevant to the role of the state is his emphasis on the Fifteenth National Bank in railway development. This bank was established through investment from peers (members of the ruling elite in the Tokugawa period given special new status by the Meiji government), who, along with the Imperial Household Ministry and ex-samurai (*shizoku*), received large grants

from the government. Economic historians in the West have paid little attention to the role of this wealth in specific business institutions, but Ericson's account is part of a renewed research effort in
Japan to develop a broader understanding of it.[16] The Japanese work
on this issue has had three major characteristics: (1) a focus on
specific families or, more commonly, the role of such wealth in
specific enterprises; (2) an attempt to relate it to theories of the development of Japanese capitalism; and (3) coverage limited to the Meiji
period.[17] Some recent work in the specific vein has had a regional
focus. For example, several studies have appeared on the role of
former Chōshū leaders. One work concerns the family of the former
daimyo Mōri and the effects of its loans in transforming Fujita, a mining and construction enterprise, into an industrial zaibatsu. Mōri's
loans to Fujita helped it to overcome the 1890 financial crisis, and
they still remained substantial in the early twentieth century.[18]
Another study examines the Onoda Cement Company, located in
Yamaguchi prefecture (former Chōshū territory) and established in
1881 through the pooling of shizoku funds. The Chōshū financial
connection was a longstanding one, for the Mōri family held a 6.5-
percent share in the firm as late as 1927.[19]

The most recent research on the peers has broadened earlier analyses by uncovering more data on the movement of peerage assets (as
distinct from the simple description of original investment in a
specific firm) and by tracing this investment activity through the
interwar period.[20] A study by Imuta Yoshimitsu is of particular relevance to Ericson's paper, for it provides precise figures on the extent
to which railways attracted peerage money. His analysis of an 1898
survey gives a value for the total stock held by each of twenty-eight
large peers. Among the twenty-eight, the percentage of this value represented by investments in the Fifteenth National Bank and the Nippon Railway ranged from 13 to 100, with a median of 77.[21]

The successful passage of most large joint-stock companies through
the financial panic of 1890 provided a strong base for later industrial
growth. The period between the 1890s and World War I was one of
institutional expansion, leading in some cases to the first stage of
Japan's international industrial competitiveness. Cotton spinning
was the first manufacturing industry to reach this goal by penetrat-

ing markets in China. The period also saw diversification by many zaibatsu into industrial manufacturing, which supplemented their earlier strength in commerce, finance, and mining. What is more, in consequence of the Sino-Japanese War and the indemnity obtained from China, the government again became more directly involved in industrial financing, especially for shipping, for heavy industries like shipbuilding and steel, and for the establishment of special-purpose banks. There were also close mutual ties among separate firms that created links between these numerous developments. The cotton spinning industry, for example, depended on zaibatsu-related firms like Mitsui Bussan for part of its raw-material imports and overseas marketing and the Mitsubishi-related N.Y.K. for shipping services as well as the government-controlled Yokohama Specie Bank for financing.

The enlarged administrative scale and higher technical requirements that were part of this expansion induced company owners (whether zaibatsu families or stockholders) to rely on managers they had hired for their experience, education, or specialized knowledge in a particular industry. These were the "salaried managers" of Morikawa's paper, which analyzes their gradual acquisition of decision-making authority within Japanese companies. It has long been recognized that managers, as distinct from owners, came to play a major role within companies at an unusually early stage in Japan's industrialization. Morikawa's contribution is to demonstrate the scale of this transformation through an aggregate survey of leading companies and to assess its significance by carefully distinguishing between companies that adopted different policies toward the use of salaried managers. Those that refused to delegate decision-making power to such managers, he argues, usually lagged behind competitors in growth or the scale of diversification and, in many cases, went bankrupt.

Morikawa supports his argument with data on the composition of the board of directors, the key decision-making organ in Japanese firms.[22] Especially in postwar Japan, the board is regarded as a distinctive feature of Japan's top management because it contains primarily, and often exclusively, directors who are career managers within their own company. This contrasts with the situation in most Western countries where more board seats are occupied by outside representatives. Though there was no clear linear progression in the development of this distinctive system in prewar Japan, the rise of salaried managers to the board between the 1890s and 1930s represented a strong trend toward it.

Morikawa developed his thesis in reaction to the Marxist emphasis on control by ownership.[23] He argued that it was misleading to focus exclusively on ownership, because it was managers who were making the decisions. Capitalist owners, he states here, lacked the necessary knowledge and expertise to fill that role and, recognizing this, passed on authority to managers. This view is widely accepted among business historians in Japan today, though Yasuoka Shigeaki, in particular, has questioned it on several points.[24] He places more stress on continuity from the *bantō* of Tokugawa times (the head manager appointed by the owner in merchant firms) to the salaried managers of the Meiji period. In both cases, owners were inclined to delegate responsibility. This inclination does not itself prove the case for continuity, for many Meiji owners refused to give managers decision-making authority. Morikawa gives reasons for this hesitation and argues that the key variable in whether or not firms promoted managers to strategic positions was not merchant tradition but the degree of owner "progressiveness," that is, openness to new knowledge and ideas. Yasuoka also emphasizes interference in management by zaibatsu owners, citing in particular the case of Nakamigawa Hikojirō. Mitsui owners eventually came to oppose his reforms as head of the Mitsui Bank in the 1890s, just as stockholders in the San'yō Railway objected to his innovations when he managed that firm, as described in Ericson's paper. Perhaps the key point to make about Nakamigawa, however, is that he trained a large number of followers who later became powerful managers, not only in the Mitsui Bank but in many other companies as well.

As noted above, Morikawa's analysis of the board of directors provides important background to postwar management structure. Another feature of his paper relevant to postwar business is the emphasis on engineers and other technically trained individuals rising to top management positions. The prevalence of engineers at the top level of postwar manufacturing firms in Japan is often contrasted with the large number of lawyers, accountants, and others of non-scientific background at the helm of American firms. From the perspective of Morikawa's themes, two reasons for this postwar phenomenon in Japan would be the pattern established in the Meiji period, which was carried over to the present, and the structure of the company board. Having mostly internal directors on the board allows space for technical personnel that might otherwise be taken by outside financial representatives. The reliance of Japanese firms on technically trained personnel in the prewar period is usually attributed to the need to learn new techniques quickly in view of the relative lateness of Japan's large-scale industrialization. On a more concrete level, around the turn of the century some firms were releasing expensive foreign technicians hired earlier, and people of comparable skill levels to replace them could be found only among university graduates.

The specific case studies in Ericson's chapters and my own provide examples of the themes considered by Morikawa. The dynamics of stockholder-management interaction form the background to Ericson's financial analysis. His general conclusion is that, around 1890, railway management was still dominated by stockholders. Illustrative of the financial concerns of stockholders were the decisions to suspend construction of lines during the panic and, in the case of the San'yō Railway, to sell expensive railway cars purchased earlier by Nakamigawa, a decision taken shortly before the Sino-Japanese War, which soon appeared shortsighted when the war increased demand for such cars. Ericson does show, however, that there were already salaried managers in the middle management of railways at the time of the panic and that some rose to top management a decade later.

World War I constitutes the background to my own study of the N.Y.K. shipping line, which focuses on internal management struggles. The gains achieved by Japan in World War I are well known. Reduced European competition enabled light industry to seize Asian markets, heavy industry expanded in the domestic market with the reduction in machinery imports, and service industries extended their operations on a worldwide basis. Less well studied are company strategies in the transition from wartime boom to postwar recession. How a company planned for this change tended to govern its fate over the next decade.[25] Mitsui Bussan, for example, wisely reduced risky investments toward the end of the war. N.Y.K. leadership, however, failed to grasp the nature of the transition. At the beginning of the war, the N.Y.K. met Morikawa's definition of a "progressive" company in that its board was dominated by salaried managers. During the war, however, the company became the object of heavy speculative investment. As a result, stockholders gained more influence over management, and confrontation soon began over dividend policy. Resignations by key managers over the issue left the N.Y.K. unprepared to plan for postwar changes. Disputes over labor policy shortly thereafter led to more resignations by salaried managers.[26]

Against this background I discuss two individuals. First, Kagami Kenkichi, Chairman of the Mitsubishi-related Tokio Marine & Fire Insurance Company, who was sent to the N.Y.K. to restore order. Kagami personifies several managerial roles described by Morikawa, who notes that some of the salaried managers hired in the Meiji period for their technical expertise were able to acquire such large blocks of stock in their companies that, by the interwar years, they had in effect become capitalists. In his career at Tokio Marine, Kagami became one of the more powerful examples of this trend. His role in the N.Y.K. was that of "financial capitalist," representing the interests of Mitsubishi. The second individual is Ōtani Noboru, the leading career manager in the N.Y.K. The relationship between Kagami and Ōtani typifies the dynamics of the financial owner-salaried manager dichotomy examined by Morikawa. These two differed on matters of fundamental policy, with Kagami advocating horizontal combination with other shipping firms, economizing in ship purchasing, and rationalization of services, and Ōtani favoring maintenance of the company's autonomous identity and expanded purchasing of ships with new technology to upgrade strategic shipping lines. In financial policy there is a clear parallel between this internal N.Y.K. debate and the conflict Ericson discusses between railway executives pushing technical innovation and high-quality equipment over opposition from the financial economizing of stockholders. Morikawa concludes that companies that delegated responsibility to salaried managers were more successful. The next step in aggregate analysis would be to ask questions about possible similarities among these companies in specific policies. For example, the cases mentioned here suggest that, in conflict with owners, salaried managers usually favored the more expansionist investment policy. If this were true in a general sense, it would be interesting to examine the phenomenon in the context of government-business relations in both the 1930s and 1950s when the bureaucracy followed strongly interventionist polices.

Although my chapter is concerned with the zaibatsu, its approach differs from most studies on the subject. Scholars have written extensively about the role of zaibatsu in the economy and about individual zaibatsu, but there have been few studies of intra-zaibatsu issues from the perspective of the individual operating company. I argue that it is important to examine a company's business operations within the context of its industry and its relations with the government, for this context of daily business activity can sometimes give the company a sense of autonomy within its zaibatsu and induce conflict with the zaibatsu leadership.

The years covered by my chapter, roughly the early 1920s to the mid-1930s, correspond to a period of rapid diversification for the firm examined in Molony's contribution, Noguchi Jun's Nitchitsu, Japan's leading electrochemical company. If the era between the 1890s and World War I marked the rise of the textile industry to internationally competitive standards and the beginning of heavy industries like large-scale shipbuilding and steel, it also saw the emergence of industries with a higher technological component. The most important of these were the electrical (including machinery and telecommunications) and chemical industries. Both grew by acquiring Western technology, but they differed in the corporate form which served as the conduit for this borrowing. In the electrical industry, the technology transfer usually led to equity participation by the Western firm (as with General Electric in Mitsui's Shibaura Engineering Works in electrical machinery) or even a joint venture (Western Electric and NEC in telephones). By contrast, in the early chemical industry, as exemplified here by Noguchi Jun, the Japanese firm usually purchased the license for a technology without inviting foreign equity participation. A further difference affected the mode of borrowing. In the chemical industry, what was acquired was a specific technical process rather than a general manufacturing and marketing agreement for a range of products, as with Shibaura.[27]

In Molony's account, Noguchi emerges as an extraordinarily gifted entrepreneur whose main strength was his keen sense of market change coupled with foresight in recognizing how the latest technology could be applied to his manufacturing process. As a fertilizer producer, his added advantage was his control over sources of electric power. This was the basis for his electrochemical investments and his eventual diversification beyond fertilizers to explosives and other military production in Korea. Behind his business strategy was a mentality akin to that of a scientist, always aspiring to higher levels of technology. Never content to remain in one technical stage for long, even if profitable, he frequently sold plants, using older technologies to acquire new processes and stay ahead of his competitors. This gave him a strong position in intra-industry negotiations, such as cartel agreements. Molony shows, too, that his ability to apply this technology depended greatly on his political contacts, which included the Railroad Bureau, politicians in both major political parties of the time, the colonial Governor General in Korea, officials of the Bank of Chōsen, as well as numerous military figures. Like his technical knowledge, these ties gave him an advantage in disputes with zaibatsu that held distribution rights for imported fertilizer.

Noguchi's relationship with Mitsubishi is one of several themes common to both Molony's chapter and my own. By virtue of tradition, personnel, and stockholding, the N.Y.K. had always been regarded as part of the Mitsubishi zaibatsu, though not as a direct subsidiary. Despite financial ties with Mitsubishi (Mitsubishi Bank as creditor and Mitsubishi's owner, the Iwasaki family, as substantial stockholder), Noguchi's firm was not part of the Mitsubishi zaibatsu. His eventual split with the Mitsubishi Bank, in which Noguchi advocated expanded investment in Korea over opposition from the cautious Mitsubishi representatives on his board, recalls both the conflict between the pro-expansionist Ōtani and the restraint-oriented Kagami within the N.Y.K. and the disputes between stockholders and managers in Meiji railways over managers' innovative policies.

Other issues common to the two chapters include company responses to major historical turning points like World War I and the 1932 fall in the exchange rate of the yen. Unlike the N.Y.K., which squandered its resources on postwar dividends, Noguchi managed his firm's more carefully to provide a base for diversification in the 1920s. Also, whereas a postwar expansionist policy proved damaging to the N.Y.K., Noguchi was able to continue such a strategy because of his accurate sense of how much the market would absorb. Finally, the yen's decline in 1932 benefited both companies, not only in making their sales more competitive but in the specific sense of giving them each a stronger voice in their respective cartels.[28]

Noguchi's Nitchitsu has usually been regarded as one of the "new zaibatsu" of the interwar years. A useful companion study to Molony's study is Cusumano's work on another of the new zaibatsu, Riken, founded by Ōkōchi Masatoshi. Riken was much less successful than Nitchitsu, but Ōkōchi embodied some of the major trends in industrial change during the interwar period. Beginning his career as a university professor, Ōkōchi built his industrial empire through his directorship of the Institute of Physical and Chemical Research. Ōkōchi's principal goal was to develop innovative technology in Japan that would be commercialized by Japanese companies, thereby freeing them from excessive reliance on imported technology. His strategy was to establish companies based on patents produced by his institute. In pursuing these goals, he developed a managerial philosophy known as "scientific management," the core idea of which was to give engineers, who had the knowledge to apply the latest technology, responsibility over industrial management. He criticized Japanese businessmen, especially the "old zaibatsu," for allowing "capital" to control investment decisions and for a passive attitude toward technological innovation. Actually, as Cusumano points out, several zaibatsu leaders had adopted strategies consistent with Ōkōchi's admonitions. Furthermore, Ōkōchi's proposals afford a close parallel to Morikawa's account of successful firms that promoted engineers to positions of managerial authority on their boards.

Ōkōchi's efforts at developing Japanese technology place him within the context of a broad movement starting around the mid-1920s to encourage "domestic production" (*kokusanka*). The movement was promoted by various government ministries, such as the Ministry of Commerce and Industry, the Ministry of Communications, and the Ministry of Finance as well as by the military. The measures taken included specific laws that effectively prohibited foreign production in Japan in some industries, substantial tariff increases, government procurement policies that encouraged "national" firms to compete against larger but foreign-affiliated Japanese firms, and "rollback" programs to reduce the share of the foreign partner in certain strategic Japanese companies, a policy accomplished by "discouraging" (through the exercise of the foreign-exchange law) foreign participation in capital stock increases.

Research was one of the goals of the *kokusanka* movement. During the interwar years, most of the research in science and technological development was undertaken by institutes attached to government ministries, special foundations, and technical faculties in universities. Ōkōchi's Riken fits most clearly within this aspect of the *kokusanka* movement. An interesting comparison to its experience can be found in the Electrical Engineering Department of the Engineering Faculty at Tōhoku Imperial University (whose president during the 1930s, as Cusumano notes, came from Riken). This department concentrated on communications technology, and some of the research it inspired, both in its own programs and in those of its graduates, had a strong impact on postwar Japanese electronics technology in fields like television, magnetic recording, and facsimile production.[29] Beyond the specific technologies, the tradition of academic-industrial cooperation that emerged at Tōhoku Imperial has continued to the present and was one of the main reasons why, in the early 1980s, Toshiba established major semiconductor facilities in Kitakami City near the university's base at Sendai.[30]

In contrast to the positive commitment to research at government-related institutions, the large private companies of the time in the heavy and chemical industries were reluctant to invest substantial funds in their own research and development, partly because of their reliance on foreign technology. This barrier confronted Ōkōchi, even before he started his own companies, when he failed to interest Japanese firms in his institute's patents. And, of course, Noguchi, who, in his application of innovative technology, served as a textbook example of Ōkōchi's managerial philosophy, acquired his major technology from Europe. Ironically, too, one of the reasons for Riken's decline in the late 1930s was that its nationally produced technology did not measure up to the foreign imports many Japanese firms still preferred.

The Molony and Cusumano chapters include numerous other themes common to both Noguchi and Ōkōchi. First, though both firms exemplify aspects of the *kokusanka* movement, neither was a major direct beneficiary of industrial policy. Noguchi's government support came mostly in an ad hoc fashion through his political ties and his positioning his firm to meet military needs. Also, the government itself was slow in protecting Japanese fertilizer against foreign competition.[31] Ōkōchi produced for the military and received special favors from it in connection with his "domestic production," but his ideas often conflicted with the precepts of the industrial policy of the time, especially in his opposition to tariffs, which he said reduced the competition necessary for the development of innovative technology. Second, both had similar attitudes toward diversification. The new products Nitchitsu developed always derived from some other product within the firm. Ōkōchi tried to develop by-products from core technologies that would serve not only as the basis for new enterprises but as a means of cutting costs in the original production process. This strategy, notes Cusumano, was known as the "sweet-potato-root" style. This type of diversification resulted in both firms' being vertically integrated, especially Nitchitsu, with its control over electricity. In the workshop at which these chapters were first presented as papers, Alfred Chandler argued that this made Nitchitsu resemble a large vertically integrated American firm more than a Japanese zaibatsu and he thus rejected the "new zaibatsu" label often applied to Nitchitsu.[32] Third, despite the similarity in strategy, structurally Noguchi was much the better manager. Throughout his diversification, at least until the late 1930s, he kept his firm manageable, providing good communications among his subsidiaries and a collegial environment for what Molony calls a "cross-fertilization of ideas" among his scientists. By contrast, Ōkōchi established so many subsidiaries that he lacked a sufficient number of skilled managers to run them. This leads to a fourth and final point. Both leaders, in a sense, went to extremes—Ōkōchi in establishing too many new companies and Noguchi in stretching his investments into too many unprofitable military-related industries, even at times against the advice of his own internal board members.

Though Ōkōchi ultimately failed as a manager, Cusumano suggests that he is a compelling figure, perhaps more for his ideas and his prophetic statements with regard to postwar changes. These include his advocacy of precision technology and machine tools appropriate to it, his emphasis on engineers in management, his comparative analysis of "declining" capitalist states (Britain and the United States), his call for raising wage levels and consumer demand, and his policy of establishing factories in agricultural villages—an early version perhaps of Tanaka Kakuei's plan to disperse industry away from Japan's concentrated centers.

For chronological reasons I discuss Gordon's chapter last, since World War II is an important component in his analysis. I classify it, however, with Morikawa's chapter because both deal with institutional change in the big-business community rather than case studies. In Morikawa's paper, the focus is on companies, in Gordon's on business federations.[33] In a broad sense, both authors are concerned with company decision making or, more precisely, with managerial prerogative. Strictly speaking, this is not a comparison of equivalent categories. Morikawa addresses the question of "who" exercised the prerogative; Gordon of "how" it was exercised, particularly the extent of its applicability. In the broadest terms, Morikawa asks whether it was the owner or the salaried manager who made decisions. The shift from owner to managerial decision making that Morikawa describes sometimes marked an emerging consensus between the two sides; at other times, it developed from specific conflicts. In either case, it represented long-term institutional change in the company as well as market changes that often rendered company administration too complex for ownership alone. The dichotomy that Morikawa posits (owner vs. manager), however, should not obscure the fact that this was a slow process, sometimes over decades. The results, with managers gaining more authority, can be called "informal." Though in some firms they may have led to in-company administrative regulations, they had nowhere near the "force of law."

In contrast to Morikawa's dichotomy, for analytical purposes Gordon treats "management" as an undifferentiated entity which exercised the enterprise's prerogative.[34] His focus is a single issue—labor policy—rather than the totality of decision making, as with Morikawa. His question is how the labor issue posed a threat to management's prerogative, the extent to which decisions affecting it could be removed from its sphere. In his account, the conflicts that threatened to constrict that sphere were initiated by labor and its supporters and by government labor policy. Gordon argues that, by World War II, the latter policy did have the "force of law," but it was tempered by government-business cooperation, by an "informal consensus."

Gordon divides his account of the evolution of this issue into three periods. The first, before and after World War I when labor was a rising threat, was characterized by a lack of organization or unified approach among the interested groups, whether labor unions, political parties, government ministries, or business itself. The year 1930, when business united behind a single organization (Zensanren) to fight a pro-union bill, ushered in a second period. Success in defeating this bill, plus the continued government suppression of the left, made business more confident of its ability to handle labor and more willing to work with the government. In turn, the government tried to formulate policy in terms business could accept. Throughout the decade, an initially adversarial relationship gradually turned more to cooperation. The third period, brought on by war, led to extensive government intervention and regulation in which labor policy was brought under more central control. The government used mobilization legislation and special ordinances, which had the "force of law," to impose standardized labor practices on companies, thereby restricting company autonomy by placing restraints on managerial prerogative within the enterprise.[35] Gordon suggests, however, that this legal dimension was more than counterbalanced by the custom or tradition of government-business cooperation that had emerged in the 1930s and which led business to accept regulation.

The significance of this contrast between law and custom is perhaps best clarified through a comparison with the changes in American labor practices during the wartime period.[36] In Japan and the United States, there were certain similarities both in the bureaucratic background to policymaking and in motivations for the development of new labor policies. In the 1930s, an evolutionary approach was evident in both countries. By the late 1930s, Sanford Jacoby argues, American unions had adapted to the status quo and tried to formulate new demands on the basis of existing company policies. Likewise, after the defeat of the union bill in Japan in 1931, the Social Bureau of the Home Ministry, which was responsible for labor policy, tried to respect existing business practices in promoting new legislation. In American companies, furthermore, the personnel-management section (the seat of corporate labor administration) sometimes conceived of itself as a "third force" between management and labor, and it tended to attract people of reformist orientation (including socialists in earlier years). Its counterpart in Japan, at least in the 1920s, was the Social Bureau, which housed a number of reform bureaucrats who championed moderate labor legislation. While this tendency abated in the 1930s, the Bureau still lent some respect to labor concerns in its negotiations with business over new legislation. More concretely, in each country, the need to mobilize for war led the government to take unprecedented measures to enforce more systematic labor management. Regulation aimed to reduce tensions,

such as the incidence of strikes, and eliminate inequities by standard-
izing policies for wages and labor allocation. Policies to stabilize
employment sometimes even had a similar ring: In Japan, the government imposed monthly salaries for blue-collar workers, while in
America, towards the end of the war, unions demanded annual wage
plans.

Differences, however, were far more revealing than these similarities. The participants in wartime Japan's labor policymaking were
the bureaucracy and big business. Labor itself had generally been left
out of policy formation since 1930. In America, the government
desire to work with unions (backed by Congressional legislation)
often put businesses on the defensive. Consideration of the effects of
these differences highlights the contrast between law and custom. In
Japan, the tradition of government-business cooperation in the late
1930s tempered the degree of intervention in managerial prerogatives and, comparatively speaking, limited the number of precisely
worded codified regulations. In America, law was uppermost. The
government sanctioned an unprecedented expansion of codified and
standardized union rules and practices. Jacoby argues that the war
helped to "forge a distinctively American pattern of internal career
ladders composed of rigidly defined jobs." This contrast is clearly
also useful in assessing the influence of wartime patterns on subsequent decades. Despite major labor gains during the Occupation,
postwar Japanese labor practice has been marked by a high degree of
"informality," that is, the relative absence of a large number of
codified rules. By contrast, though appropriate to mass production in
America during the war, the practices developed at that time, says Jacoby, "have since become outmoded" and are those most open to challenge during the country's recent industrial decline.[37]

Some of the Japanese government-imposed labor policies of the
1930s that Gordon discusses also have specific relevance to Morikawa's treatment of managers. In particular, retirement and severance-
pay policies established in the mid-1930s gave fewer benefits to workers voluntarily leaving a firm than to those fired or retiring after a
full career with their company. The rationale for this was to enhance
stability of employment by maintaining a "disincentive" for leaving.
In this sense, both the Gordon and Morikawa papers are concerned
with stable employment. Similar policies were followed by companies to discourage managers from leaving. These constituted one

factor in the evolution of one-company career managers and the rise of internally promoted managers to company boards.

Gordon's paper also suggests the need for more study of Japanese business federations on issues besides labor, especially as they responded to the problems of economic control in the wartime period.[38] Johnson's work on MITI treats economic control mainly from the standpoint of the bureaucracy. There is no full-scale study of the issue in English that focuses on business.[39] Nevertheless, the periodization Gordon develops can usefully be compared with the dialectic in industrial policy described by Johnson, namely, the three stages of self-control by business in the early 1930s, state-control in the wartime period, and government-business cooperation after the war.[40]

PART ONE

Thematic Overviews

CHAPTER TWO

The Increasing Power of Salaried Managers In Japan's Large Corporations

MORIKAWA HIDEMASA

Beginning at around the mid-Meji period, the scale of operations in Japanese companies underwent a substantial expansion as new technology was applied to production and administration became more complex. Increasingly, leaders of manufacturing firms had to monitor changes in a growing market and negotiate with service firms which supplied them with materials or marketed their products. These changes in the size and scale of business operations coincided with, and then to some extent caused, a reorganization in the form of Japanese companies. Thus, new legal issues were added to operational procedures as fields that required personnel with special skills. The type of functions to be performed in this changing environment can perhaps be broken down into two categories. The first required specialized knowledge in tasks such as compiling manuals, contracts, and government documents; conducting negotiations; translating data; or choosing and installing imported equipment. A second category concerned the need for more general judgment, for the ability on the part of the new personnel to develop policy as representatives of a company's top leaders, as consultants to them, and as managers of many different business units within the organization.

In the period following the Meiji Restoration, Japan was in a situation similar to that of developing countries that suffer from a lack of managerial talent. Japan faced the same challenge. Private companies that promoted industrialization sought highly qualified managers in great numbers but had difficulty acquiring them. Thus, recruitment of such managers is the first problem dealt with in this chapter. A second issue, which forms the heart of the argument here, is the extent to which these managers, whom I call salaried managers, gained influence in decision making after having entered a firm and worked their way up to the top. To measure that influence, I have surveyed their presence in company boards. Although there were several reasons why these managers were appointed to positions of responsibility involving broad policy, perhaps the most important was the degree to which owners recognized the need for new talent. This chapter argues that, at least in a general way, successful business performance depended on the effective utilization of these managers.

The salaried manager can be defined as an employee of the owner-manager in one of the three levels of top, middle, and lower salaried managers. While this chapter concentrates on Japanese salaried managers who have already reached top management or who are advancing into it (that is, from middle management), it also gives attention to salaried managers below these levels. Many scholars are accustomed to using the term *professional manager* as virtually identical to *salaried manager*. I make a distinction, however, because *professional manager* is the term used in contrast to *amateur manager*, whereas *salaried manager* is the opposite of *owner-manager*. Here the term *professional* denotes managers who are full-time, specially trained, and pursuing their own high income while standing aloof from one specific organization. If the term is used only to designate the first two of these criteria then we can find the professional manager both on the owner and employee side, and as a result we cannot clearly separate the owner-manager from the top manager who has advanced from the ranks of employees. At the same time, if we use the term *professional* with the meaning "high-income-seeking and moving between organizations," most of the professional managers in modern Japanese enterprises would be excluded under the lifetime-employment system. For such reasons, I have settled on the above definition of *salaried manager.*

RECRUITMENT OF SALARIED MANAGERS

In the traditional merchant houses of the Edo period, there were many head clerks called *bantō* who, after starting out as apprentices, had accumulated business experience through long employment. This experience, however, proved to be insufficient to transform them into a source of modern managerial talent. The impact of international society and the requirements of modern industrialization exposed them as inadequately educated, limited even in their own field of experience.

Naturally, companies could hire foreign technical personnel (*oyatoi gaijin*) and give them managerial responsibility, but this could be done only at exorbitant wages. The first such foreign technician whose salary is verifiable was a Frenchman named La Roc, employed by the Sumitomo Besshi Mining Company. He received a salary of ¥600 a month during the approximately ten months that he worked in Besshi starting in March 1874. At the time, the salary of the top manager in the Sumitomo family, Hirose Saihei, was just ¥100, or one sixth of La Roc's.[1] This disparity continued for a long time, partly because foreign specialists virtually came to run the departments over which they were given responsibility. When Mitsubishi's Nagasaki Shipyard began operations in 1884, the Englishmen there were paid high salaries. For example, the monthly salary of W. H. Devine, the accountant in charge of the business department, was ¥300 and that of J. F. Colder, a shipbuilder in the manufacturing department, was ¥350.[2] In contrast, after the Iwasaki family relinquished direct management of the shipping business and set up the Mitsubishi Company in March 1886, the monthly salaries of the top managers (*kanji*), Kawada Koichirō and Shōda Heigorō, were both only ¥100.[3]

In a later example, when the Sumitomo Copper Rolling Plant (Sumitomo Shindōjō) established its electrical wire and cable factory in 1906, it hired Henry Goddard, the foreman of an English wire maker, for a monthly salary of ¥1,000. At the time, the monthly salary of the copper-rolling plant's Japanese manager was ¥150 and the starting salary of graduates from the Engineering Department of the Imperial University was only ¥50.[4] The salaries of foreign managers were extremely high, but their effectiveness was often limited by problems of poor communications and negative emotional reactions, the result primarily of linguistic and environmental differences.

Naturally, there was an urgent need for both able managers trained at Japanese universities and for experienced personnel who had acquired know-how at industrial sites and universities abroad. Some companies sent employees abroad at company expense to get the necessary training, but this also was much too expensive. For example, the precursor to Ōji Paper Co., Seishi Kaisha, sent a technician named Ōkawa Heisaburō to the United States in 1879, where for fifteen months, during his on-the-job apprenticeship, the company paid him, in addition to his salary, $50 a month for living costs, travel expenses, and even $250 a year for his tuition.[5] In another case, Yamabe Takeo of Osaka Spinning Co. was sent to England to study cotton spinning techniques on an allowance of ¥1,500.[6] Rather than undertaking the expensive training provided Ōkawa and Yamabe, neither of whom was a university graduate, many companies sought to hire graduates from Japanese universities.

It is well known that, after the Meiji Restoration, the Japanese government supported the establishment of universities on the Western model and promoted the expansion and improvement of university education. This was extremely beneficial for companies seeking to employ graduates who could become managerial personnel. Before World War II, however, and particularly in the early stages of the industrial revolution, the increase in the supply of managerial personnel with university education could not keep up with the growing demand for managers. Moreover, due to the attitude, especially prevalent before World War I, of "esteem of public over private sector," there were many technocrats strongly inclined to seek jobs in government enterprises and the ministries rather than in companies, even after these private firms were well established. For these companies, such employment preferences exacerbated the chronic lack of managerial personnel from the universities throughout the prewar period, and especially in the Meiji era.

To cope with the lack of managers, companies adopted the method of hiring, at high salaries, mid-career personnel who had

already been trained in another line of work. Many former bureaucrats and government-enterprise employees were hired in this way. In
other words, the managers necessary to industrialization were first
pooled in government enterprises and later transferred into the private sector as it developed. The same phenomenon also occurred
when entire government enterprises were sold to capitalists, and the
existing employees became employees of the new private company.
Indeed, in many developing countries, where bureaucratic organizations and government enterprises are organized prior to private corporations, this type of personnel transfer is a common process.

This trend is evident in Meiji Japan if we survey actual examples
of engineers with university degrees who moved from public to private jobs in their careers. By 1890, 68 engineers had graduated from
the Engineering Department of the Imperial University (or its precursor)[7] and, by 1900, they seem to have entered private enterprises.
Of them, 34 engineers, or exactly half, worked in the government sector before transferring to the private sector. Moreover, for the remaining half, records of transfer cannot be verified, and thus it cannot be
stated conclusively that they were employed for the entire period in
private enterprises.

Naturally, hiring personnel in mid-career was only an auxiliary
means of acquiring company managers. The chief method was still to
hire persons straight out of university and train them on the job. It is
especially notable that the Japanese companies that first sought to
hire university graduates were the family-owned companies of the
nouveaux riches whose wealth had been amassed *after* the Meiji Restoration. The family-owned companies of traditional wealth, dating
from long before the Restoration, such as Mitsui and Sumitomo, had
many old-fashioned employees with years of experience, like the
clerks described above. These companies did not fully appreciate that
such employees had reached the limit of their abilities; thus, their
inclination to hire university graduates remained weak.

Among the family companies of newly developed wealth, Mitsubishi was the most determined to recruit university-trained talent.
Starting around 1877, Mitsubishi hired large numbers of new graduates of the Imperial University and Keiō University.[8] They became
the managers of numerous operating units created by the diversification and expansion of shipping, mining, and financing activities, or
they took on the jobs of managing the many new posts necessitated

by modern shipping, such as handling negotiations and communications between the government and foreign trading houses, managing foreign crews, and drawing up legal documents or accounting procedures. Mitsubishi's President, Iwasaki Yatarō, often told his friend Fukuzawa Yukichi (an intellectual leader and founder of Keiō University), that clerks or sales clerks (*bantō* and *tedai*) without higher education, as well as educated intellectuals, had both good and bad qualities. However, he also emphasized that, whereas it was quite difficult to encourage an educated or intellectual spirit in the clerks, it was easy to train the intellectuals to carry on business in the manner of clerks.[9] Thanks to his experience in the shipping business and the influence of Fukuzawa Yukichi, Iwasaki had become more aware of the necessity for personnel with a university education.

Iwasaki did not balk at spending money to acquire personnel. Since the trend of the times was to esteem public over private service, many graduates of the Imperial University's Law Department did not even consider work in the private sector. Successfully countering this trend, Iwasaki sent 4 such graduates to study abroad at company expense, on the condition that they would later work for Mitsubishi.

Although not large in scale like Mitsubishi, other new wealthy family-companies actively sought to employ both new and mid-career university graduates. Such companies as Morimura, Ōkura, Fujita, Yasuda, Asano, Furukawa, as well as Iwasaki's Mitsubishi, also made university graduates into top company managers by eventually marrying them to the founder's daughters or nieces or, in some cases, making them adopted sons. This can be seen as part of the effort to assimilate intellectual talent suitable to the new age by bringing it into the closed sphere of blood relationships. There were also, however, men like Katō Takaaki, a law student who married Iwasaki Yatarō's oldest daughter and studied in England. Upon Iwasaki Yatarō's death, he transferred to the N.Y.K., which took over Mitsubishi's shipping business, but later he became a foreign-ministry bureaucrat, politician, and, eventually, prime minister.

As explained above, traditionally wealthy companies, like Mitsui and Sumitomo, were not as forceful about hiring personnel who had knowledge appropriate to the new age. Many of these enterprises were characterized by *bantō* policies established back in the Edo period, whereby the most senior employee was placed in the position of top management. These clerks, however, did not have knowledge or adaptability suited to the new age, nor the desire to hire new managerial talent. For example, Hirose Saihei, the top manager (*bantō*) at Sumitomo, hired several technicians who had studied in Europe because they were necessary to the modernization of the Besshi mines and ironworks, which used iron sulfide. However, he had no real intention to use these new intellectuals as managers; and he did not hire any other personnel who had received higher education. Although he did hire his two nephews in mid-career to be directors of the head office and the Besshi plant, they were not university graduates. Hirose saw the technicians he hired merely as convenient tools to implement plans he himself dictated; some of them quit the company in opposition to him. While Sumitomo hired technicians because the family business was copper manufacturing, Mitsui, whose family business was banking, did not consider it necessary to employ personnel with higher education.

Not until the failure of relying on uneducated clerks in top management became evident did Mitsui and Sumitomo make strong efforts to recruit personnel with higher education. In Mitsui, the top manager after the Restoration was Minomura Rizaemon, who continued the company's Edo-era dependence on government accounts right into the Meiji period under the new government. Neither Minomura nor the clerks who became his successors had the foresight to develop a strategy for the new age that departed from old-fashioned policy. The dependency on government accounts was accompanied by demands from officials and politicians for inordinately large loans; and, because the clerks felt indebted to these government officials, they hesitated to bill them for loan repayments. As a result, the spiraling increase in the Mitsui Bank's bad loans brought the firm into economic difficulties by 1890.[10] The solution to the problem was reached only by bringing in Fukuzawa Yukichi's nephew, Nakamigawa Hikojirō, from his post as President of the Sanyō Railway. Nakamigawa was a leading businessman of the time, who had graduated from Keiō University, studied in England at Fukuzawa's expense, became a high-level bureaucrat, and gained experience as a newspaper editor. Besides severing Mitsui's dependence on the government and overcoming operational difficulties, he introduced large numbers of Keiō graduates into Mitsui.[11]

Meanwhile, Mitsui Bussan had from early on consistently pursued a policy of hiring graduates of Keiō and the Commercial Business

Training Center (Shōhōkōshūjō), which eventually became today's Hitotsubashi University. Mitsui Bussan had found that such personnel with a higher education were necessary to carry on international trade with foreign businessmen. Also, because Mitsui Bussan was not under the direct control of the Mitsui family, its top manager, Masuda Takashi, could promote his own hiring and training policies.

As indicated above, Hirose Saihei, the clerk entrusted with top management by the Sumitomo family, had autocratic control but lacked a planned and rational leadership. On sheer whim, Hirose refused to found a bank, despite the request of insiders in the organization. He chose instead to continue to invest in the Besshi Ironworks and to disregard both the lack of technological or economic promise in his strategy and the opposition to it. As a result, he impeded successful development of the Sumitomo family enterprises and was eventually forced to resign under the pressure of an internal movement against him.[12] His successor was his nephew, Iba Sadatake, who was not a university graduate. Iba, however, employed persons who had received a higher and more relevant education. Among them, Suzuki Masaya, from the Ministry of Agriculture and Commerce, and Kawakami Kinichi, from the Bank of Japan, proposed new business strategies after being welcomed into top management. Since Iba's time, employing high officials in top or middle management has become characteristic of Sumitomo.

Family enterprises grew out of a closed-ownership system used by the nouveaux riches or traditionally wealthy who eventually formed zaibatsu. In addition to these, however, there were many capitalists or financiers who formed corporations through joint investment that were also important in Japan's economic history. Compared to the West, joint-stock companies were introduced into Japan quite early, at the beginning stage of industrialization. In the 1880s, many joint-stock companies were founded in the fields of banking, rail transport, electricity, and cotton spinning. These enterprises also sought to hire university graduates for management positions.

In both zaibatsu and non-zaibatsu groups, university graduates were first hired in mid-career as technicians in mining and manufacturing companies, and only considerably later as office and business personnel responsible for purchasing and sales (eigyō). For example, Mie Cotton Spinning Co., founded in 1886, was the first in its field to recruit highly educated personnel. Mie hired Saitō Tsunezō, who had worked as an engineer in the Osaka Mint. The following year, Kiku-chi Kyōzō, an engineer in the same Osaka Mint, switched to Hirano Cotton Spinning Co., while Hattori Shunichi, an engineer from the Ministry of the Navy, entered the Owari Cotton Spinning Co. Yamabe Takeo, who started work as a technician at Osaka Cotton Spinning Co. in 1880, with only a half-year's experience working in an English factory, cannot be called a highly educated employee.[13] It was not until the mid-1890s that cotton spinning companies began to hire highly educated talent for their administrative and sales departments.

There are two reasons why the search for university graduates came to have first priority. First, mining and industrial manufacturing companies could not be successful without technology that, in general, could be learned only in universities. Thus, whereas it was difficult to find substitutes for highly educated engineers, administration and sales skills were not taught at university and therefore non-engineers were not deemed to require higher education. Furthermore, engineers were sought after because of their scarcity. Until 1896, there were only two institutions for higher technical education, the Imperial University's Engineering Department (this became Tokyo Imperial University after Kyoto Imperial University was founded in 1897), and the Tokyo Engineering School (or Tokyo Kōgyō Gakko, which became today's Tokyo Engineering University). The total number of graduates from both schools was extremely small. In 1881, there were 48 (all from the Imperial University); in 1886, 50; in 1891, 69; and in 1896, 130 (see Table 1).

The story of Kikuchi Kyōzō, the cotton spinning engineer mentioned above, illustrates the extreme to which companies pirated highly educated engineers because of their scarcity during the early industrial period. Shortly after entering Hirano Cotton Spinning Co., Kikuchi went to England to study technology at his company's expense. Upon his return to Japan after a year of study, the Amagasaki and Settsu Cotton Spinning companies, both in the Kansai area, asked for his services, but were able to hire him only after they had paid a third of the expenses Hirano had incurred for his study. In 1890, Kikuchi thus became, simultaneously, the chief engineer and manager of three cotton spinning mills. He rotated these jobs working at one in the morning, another in the afternoon, and the third the following morning, and received salaries from all three. Eventu-

TABLE 1 The Number of Graduates from Higher Technical Education
Institutions

	Tokyo Imperial University's Engineering Department	Tokyo Engineering School
1881	48	none
1886	26	24
1891	19	50
1896	80	50
1901	97	100
1906	154	153

Note: These figures include the precursors of both schools.

Source: *Tokyo Teikoku Daigaku 50 nenshi* (Tokyo Teikoku Daigaku, 1932); *Tokyo Kōgyō Daigaku 60 nenshi* (Tokyo Kōgyō Daigaku, 1940).

ally he was promoted to the board of directors of both Amagasaki and Settsu (which merged with Hirano), and finally to the position of president of both. At his initiative, these two companies merged in 1918 to become Dai Nippon Cotton Spinning Co., or today's Unitika, and he became the firm's president.[14]

SALARIED MANAGERS AS DIRECTORS

Businessmen and capitalists had high expectations for these highly educated potential managers. After receiving on-the-job training, they were moved up into middle management positions and came to have an increasing influence within the company. However, it was still not easy for them to advance into top management posts. We can provide a fairly precise estimate of the extent to which they penetrated top management by analyzing the composition of the boards of directors.

According to my research on salaried managers in prewar Japan, of the 416 directors of 75 large corporations in 1905, salaried managers, (that is, those that owned little or no stock at the time they became directors) numbered 41, amounting to only 10 percent of the total. Moreover, there were 43 companies with no salaried managers on the board of directors, 22 with only 1, and 6 with 2 or more. (The exact number for the remaining 4 companies is unclear.) In other words, the number of employees who became directors was still small around 1905.

Two things need clarification at this point. First, throughout the history of Japanese corporations, strategic decision-making power has remained in the board of directors. When the number of directors has increased, senior members of the board have formed a high-level team within the board for strategic decision making, but this team has not been a separate entity from the board of directors. Therefore, we can define top management in Japanese companies as the board of directors in corporations and the board of trustees in partnership companies.

Second, aggregate surveys allow us to explain more clearly the role of salaried managers.[15] Using the 1905, 1913, and 1930 editions of the *Directory of Japanese Corporations* published yearly by the Commercial Agency, I chose companies based on the amount of paid-up capital:

- 1905 Over 2 million yen for banks and railways; over 1 million for other companies—a total of 75 companies
- 1913 Over 3 million yen for banks, electric-power, and mining companies; over 1 million and a half yen for others—a total of 115 companies.
- 1930 Over 20 million yen for banks and electric-power companies; over 10 million yen for others—154 companies.

After making a list of the directors (or their equivalent) of these large corporations, I identified as salaried managers those who became directors without also being capital owners or financiers. In addition, there were two types of managers who became directors of large corporations without being large capitalists: (1) salaried managers who represented the parent company or bank where they were employed and (2) directors who came directly from positions in government or politics (so-called *amakudari*). These two types of directors were excluded from the category of salaried managers. This rationale facilitated the aim of this study, to obtain data on the process by which regular employees entered top management.

The 6 companies that in 1905 had 2 or more salaried managers on the board of directors were: N.Y.K. (5 members), Mitsui Bussan (5 members), Dai Ichi Bank (3 salaried managers), Mitsui Mining

(2 members), Osaka Gas (2 members), and Amagasaki Cotton Spinning Co. (2 members). All 6 companies had powerful capitalists or managers who understood the need to employ highly educated people and who enthusiastically supported them. Some examples: in N.Y.K., the Iwasaki family; in the Dai Ichi Bank, Shibusawa Eiichi; and in Osaka Gas, A. N. Brady, President of the New York Gas Co. In the case of Mitsui Bussan and Mitsui Mining, the trend can be attributed to the long-standing influence of Nakamigawa Hikojirō of the Bank, Masuda Takashi of Bussan, and Dan Takuma of the Mining Company, who forced this recruiting policy through, despite the power of the 11 Mitsui families. Moreover, the capitalists among the traditional zaibatsu like Mitsui and Sumitomo, who began as Edo-era merchants, were accustomed to *bantō* policies and did not object to salaried managers as top managers. Of the 3 major Mitsui companies, only Mitsui Bank had just 1 salaried manager on the board of directors, and this was because Hayakawa Senkichirō, the Executive Managing Director who replaced Nakamigawa Hikojirō after his death in 1901, was an ex-government official; he was thus excluded from the list of salaried managers. The case of Amagasaki Cotton Spinning Co. will be treated later.

The diversified enterprises of Mitsubishi and Sumitomo were not incorporated until World War I. In 1905, Mitsubishi's enterprises were departments of Mitsubishi & Co. Ltd., and Sumitomo's were operating units of the Sumitomo head office, which was not yet a legal entity. As a result, the salaried managers of both zaibatsu did not appear in the 1905 survey. The exception is Shōda Heigorō, the General Manager (*kanji*) of Mitsubishi & Co. Ltd., but, since he was married to Iwasaki Yatarō's niece, it is questionable to what extent he can be called a salaried manager. The Sumitomo head office had 3 directors who were not members of the Sumitomo family, but 2 of them were ex-government officials.

The consent of capitalists, whether active or passive, was necessary for salaried managers to advance into top management. Put differently, the reason for the limited participation of salaried managers in top management in 1905 was the strong desire of capital to monopolize top-management positions. This shut out employed personnel from such posts.

I have already discussed the traditional zaibatsu like Mitsui and Sumitomo. Among the newly established houses, in Mitsubishi top management positions were so limited by corporate structure that the advancement of salaried managers was delayed. Nevertheless, during World War I, the company reorganized its management, dividing it into a group of companies, which led to the promotion of a number of salaried managers to top-management posts. Because of this, the assumption that there was resistance to salaried managers must be qualified.

On the other hand, other newly established zaibatsu, like Yasuda, Ōkura, Asano, and Fujita, maintained the custom of keeping top-management positions dominated by the founder's family and relatives. The family would usually also include some highly educated people who had married the founder's daughter or niece. This family exclusiveness stemmed from the absolute authority of the founder, but, after his death, there emerged a more cooperative arrangement between the founder's family and salaried managers. This was true with Mitsubishi after Iwasaki Yatarō's death in 1885, and with Furukawa after Furukawa Ichibei's death in 1903.

Surprisingly, the non-zaibatsu companies, founded by joint investment, exhibited a stronger tendency to shut out salaried managers from top positions. The best example is Amagasaki Cotton Spinning Co., where the major stockholders—mostly merchants and financiers of the Kansai area—continued to oppose the appointment of employees to the board of directors, including such outstanding engineers as Kikuchi Kyōzō. Kikuchi became a director only after the young and progressive President Fukumoto Motonosuke finally won over the firm's major stockholders. When Fukumoto resigned the positions of president and director in 1901, he also appointed Kikuchi his successor as president and selected another employee, Tashiro Jūemon, then sales manager, to assume the vacant post of director.[16]

This type of resistance by capital to salaried managers was not unusual. When major stockholders of Settsu Cotton Spinning Co. opposed Kikuchi as director of Settsu, the appointment was delayed until four years after his Amagasaki appointment.[17] In Osaka Spinning Co., major stockholders strongly opposed the appointment of Yamabe Takeo to the position of director.[18]

In Japan, relative to the level of industrialization, joint-stock corporations had an early start, but the stock market, usually a prerequisite to growth, did not substantially accelerate their development. The fact that there were a limited number of capitalists or financiers available to participate in the formation of corporations caused many wealthy men to spread their investments across a number of companies. Some were trying to enhance their social prestige by gaining multiple directorships in companies where they were also major stockholders. Matsumoto Jūtarō, Osaka Bōseki's second president and an Osaka merchant, was president of 10 companies, director of 1, and auditor for 5 at the same time.[19] Noda Kichibei, also an Osaka merchant, served as president of 6 companies, director of 6 companies, and auditor for 1.[20] Although directorships brought little or no monetary compensation,[21] capitalists competed for the posts of corporate directors because they were symbols of social prestige. Salaried managers, then, were unable to obtain such posts that were valued and fought for by these financiers.

Another motivation for financiers to become directors was to secure their investments. As directors, some were interested only in guarding the safety of their investments and had little desire or intellectual capacity to plan seriously for the company's long-term prospects. Moreover, their multiple duties as managers of their own family businesses and other companies made it impossible for them to concentrate on the management strategy of a single company. Nevertheless, as top managers, their strategic decision-making power enabled them to disapprove plans of middle-management executives and chief engineers. Even highly educated personnel with important roles as middle managers or chief engineers were forced to submit to the power of these investors, based as it was on both status and function.

This domination of financiers in top management changed rapidly after the Russo-Japanese War, with the noticeable advancement of salaried managers. According to my study, of a total of 687 directors in the 115 large Japanese corporations in 1913, 111, or 16.2 percent, were salaried managers, exceeding the 10-percent figure of 1905. The number of companies with 2 or more salaried managers on the board of directors increased from 6 in 1905 to 15, and those with 1 member increased from 22 to 40. Forty-four companies had no salaried managers on the board of directors, basically the same as the 43 in 1905.

Salaried managers generally were not appointed simply as directors but as managing directors (*senmu torishimariyaku*). From the latter part of the Meiji period, there was an increase in the number of corporations that established the post of managing director within the board of directors.[22] The ultimate reason behind the advancement of salaried managers into top-management positions during the eight-year period between 1905 and 1913 was the chronic lack of highly educated potential managers. In order to compete with other firms in attracting and maintaining highly capable managers, the financiers finally had to offer them real promotion from middle to top management. This reasoning, however, may be an oversimplification. In reality, capitalists were divided into progressive types who were aware of the need to employ highly educated personnel in top-management positions and those who continued to shut employees out of top positions. The question, then, is why capitalists, especially of the latter group, finally did turn the top positions over to salaried managers during the short ten-year period after the Russo-Japanese War.

Capitalists who continued to hold top-management positions were simply unable to deal effectively with the various changes in the corporate environment—the depression and management difficulties of large corporations after the Russo-Japanese War; the development of heavy industry; urbanization; new corporate opportunities arising from expansion of overseas resources and markets; reorganization of management structures to expand their scope and create conglomerates; the upsurge in the labor movement; the rise of individualism in society; and the loss of power among wealthy families who lacked management capabilities. In particular, financiers who had no interest in their company's long-term strategy or who concentrated only on maintaining a steady increase in their investment, and those who invested in numerous companies, becoming both directors and major stockholders simply for social prestige, were exposed as totally incompetent managers. On the other hand, there were increasing numbers of middle managers with excellent experience.

Consequently, in some cases, salaried managers of large corporations, whether promoted internally from middle-management positions or recruited from outside, managed to overcome the company's financial and administrative difficulties which had been so insoluble when top management consisted only of investors. Examples of such companies are Tōyō Kisen,[23] Dai Nippon Sugar Manufacturing,[24] Fujimoto Billbroker Trust,[25] Ōji Paper,[26] Mitsukoshi,[27] and Hankyū

Railways.[28] This group includes "innovators" such as Mitsukoshi, which introduced department stores to Japan, and Hankyū, which developed the unique management style of Japanese electric-railway companies, whereby they controlled such diverse businesses as railways, real estate, department stores, and amusement parks. Many of the salaried managers who contributed to the reconstruction of these companies were Keiō University graduates, who were first recruited into Mitsui's middle-management positions during the company's reform period under Nakamigawa Hikojirō, and who had thereby acquired management know-how. These include Fujiyama Raita of Dai Nippon Sugar Manufacturing, Hiraga Bin of Fijimoto Billbroker Trust, Fujiwara Ginjirō of Ōji Paper Co., Hibi Ōsuke of Mitsukoshi, and Kobayashi Ichizō of Hankyū.

As a result, salaried managers came to be increasingly trusted, and capital was forced to depend on them. But actual participation in top management by salaried managers did not always go smoothly. For example, in 1906 in Kanegafuchi Cotton Spinning Co., when speculator Suzuki Kyūgorō bought up stock given up by the major stockholder, the Mitsui family, he clashed with Mutō Sanji, the general manager, regarding plans to increase capital; Mutō ended up resigning. Suzuki's plans, however, eventually threatened financial failure, and, at the request of stockholders and employees, Mutō returned to the company as managing director in 1908.[29] As this case illustrates, there were constant personnel problems between capitalists and salaried managers.

Mutō was another Keiō graduate hired in mid-career by Mitsui during Nakamigawa's reform. He was later offered a position as a middle-level manager of Kanegafuchi. After rising to top management, Mutō attempted to appoint many employees to the board of directors and in later years amended the company rules to permit only those who had five or more years of employment in the company to become top managers.[30] His action arose from his strong criticism of capitalists:

In Japan, there are capitalists who buy up stock for speculative reasons, control the future course of the company, make imprudent plans to increase stock, attempt to raise the market value of stock, and then sell their shares of stock to make big profits. Those who bought stock at high prices not only try to cut operating expenses but even discontinue welfare facilities for employees. Such avaricious capitalists keep the employees in a miserable state and endanger the basis of existence of the company.[31]

A COMPARISON OF COMPANY PERFORMANCE

Rapid economic growth during World War I led to increased hiring of white-collar workers and the creation of additional middle-management posts in large corporations. The challenge of postwar hardships, such as depression, rationalization, the establishment of new industries, and the upsurge of labor movements, on the one hand, proved that financiers were inadequate managers, and, on the other, encouraged white-collar workers and middle-management staff to keep accumulating managerial know-how.

The exposure of capitalists' inadequacies can be explained not only by the aforementioned facts but by the following: (1) problems of succession after the death or aging of zaibatsu founders who had built up a vast fortune in the Meiji era, and (2) overconfidence stemming from the prosperity of World War I. (A good example is Matsukata Kōjirō of the Kawasaki Shipyard.)[32] In fact, in the postwar depression, a number of large companies whose top management posts were dominated by capitalist families went bankrupt. In contrast, companies like Mitsui and Mitsubishi, where salaried managers formed top teams, survived and continued to grow.

The best illustration of this contrast comes from the trading companies. Kuhara Shōji, Mogi Shoten, and Takata Shōkai, run by investors, all went bankrupt. Others in this category included Furukawa Shōji, whose strategy was inadequate despite the participation of salaried managers in top management, and Suzuki Shōten, where old-fashioned head clerks still held absolute authority. Only Mitsui Bussan, managed by the powerful teamwork of capable salaried managers, continued to show high profits even after the war.[33] In the shipbuilding industry, salaried managers in Mitsubishi Shipbuilding Co. teamed up with Iwasaki Koyata (Yatarō's nephew), president of Mitsubishi zaibatsu's head office, to successfully pull through the depression. In striking comparison, Kawasaki Shipyard performed miserably under the personal dictatorship of Matsukata Kōjirō, a major stockholder (see Table 2). The paid-up capital of Kawasaki Shipbuilding Yard was ¥74.25 million in 1930, more than twice Mitsubishi's ¥30 million. But Kawasaki's financial structure was unsound: There were debentures amounting to ¥59 million, ¥50 million worth of notes payable, and borrowings of ¥26 million. By contrast, Mitsubishi had accounts payable of ¥6 million without any debentures or loans.

TABLE 2 The Net Income of Mitsubishi Shipbuilding Co. and
Kawasaki Shipbuilding Yard

	Mitsubishi	*Kawasaki*
1918	¥16.31 million	¥29.37 million
1924	7.37 "	5.63 "
1930	1.57 "	-6.98 "

Source: Mitsubishi Jūkōgyō Kabushiki Kaisha shi (1956), pp. 682–683; *Kawasaki Jūkōgyō Kabushiki Kaisha: Nempyō, Shohyō* (1959), pp. 354–355.

The ratio of salaried managers holding top-management posts increased in large corporations in the early years of the Showa period. My study of 1930 reveals, first, that there were 470 salaried managers in my survey of 154 large corporations, amounting to 37.1 percent of the total of 1,267 directors. This ratio is far greater than the 111 or 16.2 percent figure in 1913. Second, salaried managers were appointed to top-management positions in 135 companies, or 88 percent of total surveyed, whereas 13 companies had no salaried managers on the board of directors. The number could not be verified for the remaining 6 companies. However, in 94 of the 135 companies, the number of salaried managers was less than half the members of the board. This shows that salaried managers still had a long way to go to establish a dominant position in the companies. Third, as shown in Table 3, the number of salaried managers promoted internally to top-management positions increased markedly, exceeding 50 percent in 1930. It can be said that, during the period from World War I to 1930, the pattern of today's business careers in Japan—on-the-job training as a new employee, followed by a middle-management position and a top-management post—was well on its way to being established in large corporations.

The huge zaibatsu enterprises like Mitsui (10 companies), Mitsubishi (5 companies) and Nissan (3 companies) are noteworthy as large companies with a majority of salaried managers on their boards of directors. By contrast, in the Sumitomo concern, only Sumitomo Bank followed this example, with the other companies retaining on the board many former high-ranking government officials and managers sent from parent companies. Overall, though, internally promoted salaried managers were especially notable in large zaibatsu enterprises. There were 15 corporations in which salaried managers

TABLE 3 Comparison of Salaried Managers' Careers in Large
Corporations Over Time

	Total Number of Salaried Managers	Salaried Managers Promoted from Within	Those Employed Mid-Career and Subsequently Promoted	Those Employed as Directors	B/A %
	(A)	(B)			
1905	41	9	26	6	22.2
1913	111	38	53	20	34.2
1930	470	260	160	50	55.3

Source: Biographical data: cf. Morikawa Hidemasa, *Nihon keieishi* (Nihon Keizai Shinbunsha, 1981).

held the majority of directorships, with none or only 1 of them hired in mid-career, and of these Mitsui and Mitsubishi account for 5 apiece. These same companies, it should be noted, stand out for their attempts, from the early Meiji period, to employ highly educated men capable of becoming future managers.

Large companies, especially industries not ruled by zaibatsu, are also among the 41 companies with a majority of salaried managers on the board of directors. The biggest three were Dai Nippon, Tōyō, and Kanegafuchi, but other examples include Nisshin and Naigaiwata in the cotton spinning industry, Dai Nippon and Meiji in sugar manufacturing, Dai Nippon in the beer industry, the O.S.K. in shipping, and Tohō Gas in the public sector. Almost all these non-zaibatsu enterprises had powerful salaried managers as key board members, including Kikuchi Kyōzō of Dai Nippon Spinning Co., Mutō Sanji of Kanegafuchi, Fujiyama Raita of Dai Nippon Sugar Manufacturing Co., Sōma Hanji of Meiji Sugar Manufacturing Co., Magoshi Kyōhei of Dai Nippon Beer, Kita Matazō of Nippon Menka, and Okamoto Sakura of Tohō Gas. These pioneer managers promoted their junior staff members to directorships with the intent of filling top-management positions only by moving up salaried managers.

In both zaibatsu and non-zaibatsu businesses, the increase in the participation of salaried managers in top-management positions of large corporations in Japan was remarkable. One overall observation that holds true is that the financial power and profitability of large corporations created greater opportunities for development of managerial talent, making it possible to compensate salaried managers at the most competitive rates. Another observation is that, because salaried managers, unlike investors, did not see profit making as their main goal, they had more foresight into directing the development of the company, and exhibited extremely competent managerial know-how derived from their long business experience.

Even in 1930, however, in certain areas, the tendency of capital to prevent the advancement of salaried managers into top management remained strong. Among the zaibatsu, this can be seen in Asano and Yasuda. In the latter, the problem was simply the limited number of salaried managers. Likewise, Asano maintained a consistent policy of giving priority to the founding family. In 1930, the founder, Asano Sōichirō, was still in good health, and partly because of this, the board of directors of the head office consisted only of members of the family. Non-zaibatsu joint-stock companies in electric-power generation and electric-rail industries show a clear preference for investors' families, as seen in the composition of their boards of directors. These companies, after growth through mergers, had to offer directorships to the financiers among their merger partners and thus had no room for their own employees on the boards of directors. In Tokyo Electric Light Co., a group of large stockholders from Yamanashi prefecture (the so-called Kōshū zaibatsu) held chairs on the board for a long period, and their capital-centered policies not only worsened the company's financial position but prevented the promotion of managers.

In 1930, salaried managers in large corporations as a whole were highly educated (see Table 4), which indirectly supports the observation stated above that large companies not only sought out educated men with managerial talent, but, as a result, respected their right to speak about policy and encouraged their promotion to top management. Particularly important in this respect were managers with technical training. In 1930, over one fourth of the total number of salaried managers were engineers. When technicians who graduated from the Departments of Agriculture and Science of the Imperial University, higher technical schools, professional schools of technology, vocational schools, and technical colleges abroad are counted with them, the figure increases to 35.5 percent of the total. The fact that engineers accounted for such a high ratio among the total

TABLE 4 Academic Background of Salaried Managers of Large
Corporations (1930)

	Number	% of total
Imperial University		
Law Department	62	
Department of Engineering	122	
Department of Agriculture and Science	7	
Subtotal	191	40.6
Other Institutions of Higher Learning		
Higher Commercial Schools	89	
Higher Technical Schools	26	
Other Professional Schools	11	
Private Universities	69	
Foreign Education	8	
Subtotal	203	43.2
Subtotal of graduates from Imperial University and Other Institutions of Higher Learning	394	83.8
Others	52	11.1
Unclear	24	5.1
TOTAL	470	100.0

Source: See Table 3.

number of salaried managers, including those in financial and commercial fields, also supports the view that engineers were the first among the highly educated to be sought by large corporations.

THE SALARIED MANAGER AS CAPITALIST

The large modern Japanese corporations discussed in this paper can be divided into the following three types: (1) traditionally wealthy family businesses and zaibatsu; (2) nouveaux riches family businesses and zaibatsu and (3) joint-stock corporations established by capitalists. As we have seen, highly educated salaried managers had been appointed in all three types of enterprises and eventually moved into top management. In the first type of company, represented by Mitsui and Sumitomo, highly educated salaried managers took the place of *bantō* salaried managers, who had been entrusted with the role of top management by capitalist families since the Edo period. In the second type, represented by companies like Mitsubishi, highly educated talent cooperated with the founder's family, and, after the latter's death, became top management. Finally in the third type, salaried managers took over directoral posts previously dominated by investors. Notwithstanding some exceptions, there is a general trend from capitalists to salaried managers in the history of top management in large Japanese corporations.

The third type of large enterprise, however, came to exhibit a completely opposite trend. Because stocks were not exclusively owned by investing families as in the first and second types, salaried managers who became directors could gradually increase their share of stock and become major stockholders. In this way, they attempted to enhance their power as top managers. They were also motivated to increase their own personal property, creating a trend that was the exact reverse, by transforming salaried managers into financiers. Table 5 illustrates how Amagasaki's Kikuchi Kyōzō and Fuji Cotton Spinning's Wada Toyoji increased their share of company stock over the years.

The chronic lack of highly educated talent, especially that suitable to top management, is reflected in the fact that a director's compensation in prewar Japanese corporations was quite high, amounting to around 10 percent of corporate earnings. Salaried managers were able to buy company stock because of their high salaries. The amount they could purchase, however, was limited by the high par value of stock. At ¥50 per share, this was equivalent to the starting monthly salary of a pre-World War I Imperial University graduate. Most salaried managers who had purchased their company's shares owned only about 2 to 4 percent of the total stock.[34] Therefore, while there was a trend for salaried managers to become investors, these new capitalists did not necessarily take over the full decision-making power of top management. This limitation, along with the fact that salaried managers in the first and second types of large corporations had no opportunity whatsoever to purchase stock and become investors, reinforced the major trend in all large corporations—what we can call the executive revolution.

TABLE 5 Increase in Share Ownership by Two Salaried Managers

Kikuchi Kyōzō *Amagasaki C.S.C.*			*Wada Toyoji* *Fuji C.S.C.*		
1892	1st half	50	1900	1st half	0
	2nd half	110	(Becomes Managing		
			Director)		
(Becomes Director)			1901	1st half	100
1893	2nd half	138	1902	1st half	154
1894	2nd half	235	1903	2nd half	160
1895	1st half	277	1904	2nd half	200
	2nd half	330	1905	2nd half	600
1896	1st half	403	1906	2nd half	2,500
	2nd half	463 (No. 1 stock- holder)	1909	2nd half	5,000
			1913	1st half	6,000
1901	1st half	(No. 3 ")	1914	1st half	6,800
	2nd half	(No. 2 ")	1916	2nd half	8,000
1908	1st half	2,212 (No. 2 ")	1917	2nd half	9,000 (No. 2 stock- holder)
1909	2nd half	2,484 (No. 2 ")			
			1921	1st half	18,300 (No. 2 ")

Source: Each company's business report (*eigyō hōkokusho*).

Even a 2 to 4 percent ownership, however, guaranteed the right to speak as a major stockholder. In non-zaibatsu corporations, many top-salaried managers thus became major stockholders, combining the rights of both positions, thereby gaining additional power in determining company policy, and in the end regarded the company as their own family company. In time, they also passed the top-management positions on to their sons: Dai Nippon Beer's Magoshi Kyōhei and Kōjirō, Kanegafuchi Spinning Co.'s Mutō Sanji and Itoji, Dai Nippon Sugar Manufacturing's Fujiyama Raita and Aiichirō, Hankyū-Tohō's Kobayashi Ichizō and Yonezō, Fusao, and many more.

In this way, the chronic lack of managerial talent in large modern Japanese corporations increased the power of the salaried manager to the extent that, in its most striking transformation, salaried managers themselves became capitalists.

CONCLUSION

This chapter has examined the rise of salaried managers in Japanese companies through several phases. The first concerned their early recruitment. To a large extent, their initial role was to take over functions that had previously been performed by expensive foreign technicians. These were not just specific, narrowly defined technical duties; they often involved broad managerial responsibilities. Generally speaking, there were perhaps two types of managers who entered companies during this phase of initial recruitment. One was the high-level appointee brought in to bail a firm out of trouble. Nakamigawa Hikojirō was an example of this type. A second type was characterized by appointments to lower levels of the company, sometimes of technical recruits out of the university who would then work their way up, eventually reaching the board. A second phase saw the penetration of salaried managers into the top decision-making echelons of the company. This was a long process, and, as my survey for 1930 shows, though substantial gains had been made by then, it by no means signified full acceptance of salaried managers in top-level decision making. In addition to being long, this process was also uneven. It depended a good deal on short-term circumstances affecting stockholders which could incline them toward intervention in management.

In general, in assessing the performance of companies it is essential to have precise information about matters of personnel in the top decision-making echelon. There were many important turning points in the first few decades of this century. They included the depression after the Russo-Japanese War, the boom during World War I and its subsequent collapse, and the depression starting in the late 1920s. All these events created substantial changes in the market. However, interpretations of company responses to these changes too often lack specificity; sometimes they focus only on the ownership of the enterprise. On the other hand, they may provide only a general explanation, viewing a company's response as a kind of mechanistic reaction to the market. This chapter, however, has shown that the composition of a firm's board was often decisive in explaining what strategies were adopted and whether they were characterized by long-term perspectives. In this sense, assessment of performance is inseparable from analysis of management.

A final point concerns the transition to the post-World War II period. It is acknowledged that the practice of decision making by salaried managers became widespread in Japanese firms after the war. Sometimes, however, in explaining how this system came about, excessive weight is given to the purge during the Occupation, when zaibatsu owners and many top managers were removed from corporate positions. Certainly these measures were of great importance in making way for younger managers. But, it should be clear from this paper that the substantial authority gained by salaried managers by the 1930s constituted a strong precedent for the managerial control of the postwar years.

CHAPTER THREE

Business and the Corporate State: The Business Lobby and Bureaucrats on Labor, 1911–1941

ANDREW GORDON

In Japan, as in the West, businessmen could not monopolize control of factory labor as a capitalist, industrial economy developed. Beginning as far back as the 1890s, labor problems aroused the concern of bureaucrats and politicians, and, in the World War II era, they drew the attention of the military. Because of this widespread interest, a study of the divergent approaches to labor found in the Japanese ruling elite raises larger issues in the history of the Japanese political economy. It illuminates both the cleavages and the cooperation that characterized the relationship of the several elite groups who jockeyed for power in the interwar period.

For much of the pre-World War II era, prominent business leaders disagreed fundamentally with the policies of bureaucrats interested in labor, since they sought to prevent unwelcome "interference" in the management of labor. When a factory law finally became the first major piece of labor legislation to reach the floor of the Japanese Diet in 1910, the All-Japan Cotton Spinning Federation worked with allies in the Seiyūkai Party and forced the government to withdraw the bill. When the Diet approved a watered-down revision of the law in 1911, the organized textile lobby was satisfied; it had succeeded in shaping an acceptably weak law. Two decades later, in 1930 and 1931, a well-organized and more broadly based business lobbying effort achieved a greater victory, defeating a determined attempt by the Minseitō party and elements in the bureaucracy to pass a law granting legal rights to labor unions. Business leaders then consolidated their strength by founding the National Federation of Industrial Organizations (hereafter Zensanren), a powerful group dedicated to presenting a united business front on labor issues.

As national labor unions declined in size and strength in the late 1930s, Zensanren appeared to stand unchallenged. It vetoed crucial provisions of the Retirement Fund Law of 1936, and it took the initiative in making sure the Sanpō labor front did not become a threat to employer authority. By 1940, protection of worker rights and organizations, and even amelioration of work conditions, were no longer legislative issues. Yet, in 1941 and 1942, Zensanren quietly accepted a government regulation that granted the Welfare Ministry explicit authority to dictate company labor policies and intervene directly in labor management at the factory level. Organized business relinquished to government managerial prerogatives it had stoutly defended just a few years earlier, and observers in the press continually referred to the "epochal" character of this regulation.

The major turning point in this story came late in the 1930s, when the mainstream and previously conflicting business and government stands on labor began to converge, and organized business began to work within, and more readily accept, a framework of active state guidance. The extent of change should not be overdrawn; elements of cooperation and common perspectives are found in the earlier era of conflict over labor issues, and antagonism persisted into the 1940s. Yet, an institutionalized adversarial relationship between business and elements of the bureaucratic and political elite had emerged clearly by the 1930s, and this makes the shift of the late 1930s intriguing.

Why did Zensanren begin to lower its voice in 1936 and then contract laryngitis in 1941? The failure to speak out against government intervention had much to do with the pressure of war and the rising strength of the military, whose concerns spread to areas traditionally the preserve of civilian bureaucrats. But in this chapter I shall explore another factor behind the business lobby's change of course: the increasing "corporatization" of interest-group politics and the growing importance of direct ties between business interests and the bureaucracy which bypassed the Diet. A change in the place of business in the state structure was a result of both military pressure and the shift to a species of corporate rule.

PROLOGUE: THE FACTORY LAW

From the 1890s until World War I, a factory law was the most important labor issue discussed in elite circles. Since businessmen and bureaucrats disagreed over the need for such a law, tentative lines of conflict were drawn, which became sharp by the late 1920s. The Industrial Bureau of the Ministry of Agriculture and Commerce and the Health Bureau of the Home Ministry were pitted against a wide range of industrial leaders. The bureaucrats prevailed in appearance in 1911 only by submitting an extremely weak piece of legislation to the Diet.

The government bureaucracy pushed for this law out of a variety of concerns. The Health Bureau forces in the Home Ministry spoke of the need to protect the physical well-being of workers so as to upgrade the quality of both industrial labor and military conscripts. Agriculture and Commerce officials were the most prominent in the drive for a law. Oka Minoru of the Industrial Bureau, "Mr. Factory Law" in early-twentieth-century Japan, told industrialists that poor facilities and overwork caused high turnover inimical to business interests. "This law is necessary to provide for the orderly development of industry," he concluded in 1910.[1] Other official advocates of a law spoke more abstractly of avoiding European "social evils such as strikes" by protecting workers. In all cases, bureaucrats made their case in terms business leaders could be expected to understand. Long-term economic growth and not the rights of labor was the major concern.[2]

Even so, industrialists were unanimously opposed to any law when the topic first came up in the 1890s. They grudgingly accepted the 1911 version only after winning both an ideological and a practical battle over the meaning and content of the law. In the realm of ideas, businessmen by 1911 had convinced most skeptical bureaucrats that "beautiful customs" of paternal care from managers and obedience from workers, rather than legal measures, were the most important tools for avoiding conflict, maintaining order, and using labor effectively. In the consensus of 1911 (which disappeared in the 1920s but re-emerged by the 1930s), social legislation served only as a supplement to paternal welfare measures spontaneously adopted by managers. While such measures were in fact scarce even in the biggest firms at this time, factory law supporters softened their rhetoric by claiming that the law would enforce minimum standards only in smaller factories while allowing big employers to go ahead on their own with further improvements.[3] The final practical battle was fought over clauses in the bill of 1910, which prohibited night work for women and children and directly affected many large textile mills. In the final 1911 version, the Cotton Spinning Federation succeeded in delaying enactment of this clause for fifteen years from passage of the law. Through its Seiyūkai allies in the Diet it also delayed implementation of the rest of the law until 1916.[4]

The businessmen who opposed the Factory Law did so without benefit of any national, multi-industry organization to press their case. Beginning with the earliest factory drafts, considered by the Industrial Bureau of the fledgling Ministry of Agriculture and Commerce in 1883 and 1884, the government sought business input by circulating the drafts to local chambers of commerce and soliciting comment. The response was usually negative, but the chambers of commerce thus consulted offered only scattered, uncoordinated responses.[5] The most effective business representative on this issue was the All Japan Cotton Spinning Federation, formed in the 1880s primarily to combat the pirating of scarce skilled operatives among member firms. The federation worked effectively through the Seiyūkai Party and reduced the law to little more than a minor nuisance for its members. Manufacturers adversely affected by the 1911 law, not surprisingly, were those without strong federations or political clout: small match factories, silk reelers, and silk weavers.[6]

In contrast to their successors in the 1920s, businessmen opposed to the law were relatively unorganized, but, in the context of their times, they coordinated their efforts sufficiently to resist a strong factory law. Close ties to Diet politicians allowed a relatively unorganized business world to prevail over an isolated group of reform-minded bureaucrats. The Seiyūkai, which had a majority in the Lower House at the time, was entirely unsympathetic to reformers not part of its growing clique of party men in the bureaucracy, and it naturally fought on behalf of textile industrialists regarded as important Seiyūkai constituents.[7] While the relative weights of principle and political opportunism are not clear, some anti-Seiyūkai forces in the Diet did support the law, but they were too few to defend the stronger 1910 version.

Several important characteristics of the factory-law struggle were to become more prominent in later years. First, those industrialists of course fared best who were able to organize effectively and mobilize political support. The threat of hostile social legislation spurred these businessmen to join hands and enter political battles. Second, a small group of progressive bureaucrats and intellectuals stood for moderate legal reforms to solve social problems. At this point, they were concentrated in the Home Ministry's Health Bureau and the Industrial Bureau of the Agriculture and Commerce Ministry. They did not represent a consensus for reform cutting across the entire bureaucracy, in 1911, or later, but their strength was to grow. Finally, the shadowy outlines of a policy division between political parties, each with corresponding bureaucratic allies, had appeared.[8] The Seiyūkai stood clearly opposed to social legislation. Anti-Seiyūkai forces, who soon joined in Katsura's Dōshikai, included bureaucrats and politicians in favor of legislative solutions to social problems. The Dōshikai exhibited its commitment to this approach by appropriating funds to finally implement the Factory Law in 1916 under the Ōkuma Cabinet.

ELITE PLURALISM: THE LABOR-UNION ISSUE IN THE 1920s

From the end of World War I until 1931, labor-union legislation replaced the Factory Law as the most significant and divisive issue of labor policy in Japan. The political battle over a labor-union law was far more intense, and the stakes far higher, than the earlier legislative debate, in large part because the "labor problem," so called, indeed had become an issue of paramount importance by the end of World War I. A sharp increase in the number and intensity of labor disputes began in 1917, the union movement proved itself increasingly able to harness the energy released in these actions, and the search for a solution to this labor problem took on an urgent quality among both business and government elites. In this context, the trends evident in the relatively quiet debate over a factory law gained momentum. Progressive bureaucrats centered in the Home Ministry became the leading official force behind a union law, and they cemented a firm alliance with the Kenseikai (later Minseitō) Party. The Seiyūkai continued to oppose reform legislation, relying more heavily on repression, and it built close ties to like-minded bureaucrats, especially in the Justice Ministry. Leading industrialists eventually, if slowly, reached their own consensus on the labor problem and forged a single organized lobby able to defend successfully the business position, but the plurality of approaches to the labor issue, advocated by a variety of political and economic interests, was the most noteworthy feature of the 1920s.

A lack of consensus on the labor problem characterized both the business and government elite when the first serious discussions of a union law took place during Hara Kei's Seiyūkai Party rule, 1918–1921. Bureaucrats and party politicians debated several legislative measures, but Hara and the Seiyūkai eventually rejected the idea of a union law and sought to encourage businessmen to solve their own problems with vertical company unions and works councils. Hara's government would provide a favorable context by harassing any "radical" union efforts which went beyond this narrow "company-union" framework.

Over the following several years, two distinct and opposed approaches to labor unions emerged within the parties and the government.[9] Leaders of the Kenseikai-Minseitō Party and young officials in the Social Bureau of the Home Ministry actively championed labor legislation throughout the 1920s. Within the Diet, the Kenseikai-Minseitō supporters of labor legislation included several forceful, reform-oriented ex-bureaucrats, all familiar with the latest in European social policy, some progressive businessmen active in party affairs, and a substantial, energetic contingent of older Meiji liberals and young "Taishō radicals," mainly journalists, lawyers, or educators such as Nagai Ryūtarō. Within the bureaucracy, ambitious young officials in the Home Ministry, and a strategically placed group of middle-ranked councilors (*sanjikan*) in the Ministry vigorously supported progressive solutions to what seemed increasingly intractable social problems. These "social bureaucrats" combined the traditional elitism, high-powered training, awareness of Western practice, and sense of mission common to all top bureaucrats of the imperial era with a commitment to liberal solutions to social problems particular to the post-World War I decade.

The most progressive versions of the union bill drafted by the Home Ministry's Social Bureau in the 1920s would have tolerated both industrial and general labor federations, protected unions from strike liability, fined companies for union busting, and legalized collective bargaining. The advocates of legal unionism felt that toleration of moderate labor-union activity in a legally structured context would bring order to industry and benefit the economy and society. They looked to England as their model, proposing to wean workers from dangerous radical ideas with legal support for moderate unions.

Several important bureaucratic groups, as well as the Seiyūkai Party, took a different view of the labor question. They opposed recognition of unions and vehemently criticized the policies of the Kenseikai-Minseitō and the Social Bureau. Within the bureaucracy, the Justice Ministry led the fight for a hard-line policy of repressing almost all union or dispute activity. It found a measure of support within both the Ministry of Agriculture and Commerce and even within the Police Bureau of the same Home Ministry which housed the Social Bureau. The Justice Ministry harassed arrested strikers by prosecuting them for a variety of civil or criminal charges: disturbing the peace, sedition, rioting, or slander. The Police Bureau of the Home Ministry supported the Justice Ministry hard line in the early 1920s by arresting strikers when union activity was deemed responsible for a dispute. Although the Kenseikai Cabinet of 1924–1926 explicitly limited this type of repression to disputes at public enterprises or those involving "professional agitators," informal Police Bureau mediation in labor disputes became more frequent in the late 1920s and was generally unfavorable to workers.[10]

Liberals in the Kenseikai-Minseitō and the reform-minded bureaucrats thus faced formidable opponents even within the government as they sought to pass a labor-union law and other social-reform measures after the Kenseikai took power in 1924. They naturally encountered hostility from businessmen as well, but not until passage of a bill granting legal rights to unions appeared imminent did business interests successfully organize a broad-based campaign against it.

In the late 1910s and early 1920s, in fact, business division over how to deal with labor unions equaled the division in government. Businessmen formed several major federations during and soon after World War I, as the Japanese economy grew tremendously and a broad range of economic issues demanded concerted action. These groups all took stands on the union issue in the 1920s, but they spoke with several voices until the end of the decade.

The most important group by far was the Japan Industrial Club (Nihon Kōgyō Kurabu), formed in 1917. Zaibatsu firms dominated the club, which took up the issue of government support of the steel industry as its first major issue. The Club consistently and vigorously opposed any government involvement in labor relations. It was unreceptive to the formation of the Kyōchōkai (Harmonization Society), an organization of business and government leaders founded in 1919 to promote labor-capital cooperation and study solutions to labor problems. It even opposed Seiyūkai legislative efforts to promote factory or works councils as docile alternatives to unions in 1920 and 1921. Finally, it consistently opposed a labor-union law.[11] The Japan Association of Economic Federations (Nihon Keizai Renmei Kai or simply Keizai Renmei) was the second major, national business federation formed in this period. Founded in 1922 and limited in membership to companies capitalized at 5 million yen or more, it too represented the major zaibatsu interests and worked closely with the Industrial Club. Dan Takuma, the Mitsui leader and symbol of the zaibatsu at their peak in the late 1920s, was head of both organizations. The two groups divided responsibility to some extent; the Industrial Club played a greater role on labor issues, and the Keizai Renmei focused more on financial matters.

These two groups did not represent the views of all industrialists in the 1920s. A variety of regional, industry-specific, and informal business groupings indicated willingness to tolerate and deal with labor unions. Business groups in Japan's major industrial centers, Osaka and Tokyo, were prominent among them. This liberal toleration was most common in the early 1920s, when unions were often a force that could not be ignored, but the entire business community did not swing around to a firm anti-union stance until 1930. Further, while usually regional in scope, these groups did not represent only the smaller firms least able to confront unions directly; some leading firms in both light and heavy industry belonged to them. In 1919, a survey of owners of large factories in the Osaka area indicated that the majority would tolerate trade unions.[12] More significantly, the Osaka Industrial Association (Osaka Kōgyō Kai), founded in 1914 and soon the largest industrial federation in the Osaka area, consistently supported a union law from 1919 to 1930. Tokyo federations expressed similar views. In late 1919, the Tokyo Federation of Business Associations (Tokyo Jitsugyō Kumiai Rengōkai) petitioned Hara's government for a labor-union law.[13] Several months later, a group of 74 Tokyo factory owners and managers in the machine industry convened a spur-of-the-moment meeting to discuss the labor problem, just as a wave of strikes had broken across many of their plants. They could arrive at no consensus on how to deal with unions. A significant minority at the meeting favored recognition of unions as the only way to bring order to a confused situation of mutual hostility and ineffective communication with workers.[14] Among industrial associations, the Electric Power Industry Association (Denki Kyōkai) was the most important group to show willingness to tolerate labor unions, again until 1930.[15]

These diverse opinions reflected the uncertainty of industrialists and labor managers faced with the aggressive, at times radical, union movement which had emerged during World War I. By the end of the 1920s, most large factories managed to squash or coopt the unions that had threatened them earlier in the decade, but, in early or even the mid-1920s, not all businessmen were confident they would succeed in their anti-union efforts within their companies. Even the resolutely anti-union Industrial Club opposed the first major Kenseikai drive for a union law, of 1925–1927, mainly by proposing revisions to the government draft, rather than opposing it head on.[16] Many business leaders opposed this union law simply by calling it "premature," much as they had labeled a factory law ahead of its time in the 1890s. Their eventual acceptance of the Factory Law very likely encouraged the Minseitō and Home Ministry to believe that time and "progress" would eventually bring acceptance of a union law as well. In fact, the context of divided business opinion did allow the government to pass both a Health Insurance Union bill and a bill to revise the Factory Law in 1922. The semi-official historian of Japanese business organizations, Morita Yoshio, unhappily acknowledged that business disunity and lack of preparedness prevented effective action in spite of widespread opposition to these measures.[17]

The diversity of business, bureaucratic, and political-party approaches to the labor issues also reflected the pluralistic structure of the political order. Several federations with varied constituencies and opposed positions pressed their cases through the two major parties in the Diet, as did several government ministries with an interest in the labor problem. While this political action centered on the Diet, it was decidedly an elite rather than a democratic pluralism. The workers themselves had no means to participate directly in politics, even after universal male suffrage in 1925. Sōdōmei remained on the fringes of politics, and leftist parties won only a handful of seats in the Diet.

TOWARD CORPORATISM: LABOR ISSUES OF THE 1930s

Business eventually closed ranks on the labor issue. The failure to block the Insurance Bill and Factory Law revision jolted the Industrial Club. It formed a standing committee of company labor managers charged with defending business positions on issues, such as the level of premiums and benefits, which were decided by regulation as the Insurance Law was slowly implemented. The Club also formed an active committee to chip away at the 1925–1926 Kenseikai Union Bill under preliminary consideration in the Home Ministry.[18] In general, the liberal offensive for labor legislation in the 1920s spurred the Industrial Club to more vigorous activities. By the late 1920s, the Club was ready to lead other industrial groups on a concerted drive against labor legislation. In addition, by the end of the decade, the government had destroyed the radical Hyōgikai union, and businessmen were far more confident of their ability to handle labor problems and union organizing on their own. The Union Bill submitted to the Diet twice, in 1926 and 1927, struck some businessmen as a risky but inevitable response to the liberal "trends of the times," but the second major Minseitō Labor Union Bill, proposed in 1930 and 1931, met a different response. Business leaders saw it as a pernicious threat to roll back the measure of non-union stability they had achieved on the shop floor.

With Dan Takuma at the helm, the Japan Industrial Club embarked on a campaign to defeat this Labor Union Bill in the spring of 1930. The rapid conversions of the Osaka Industrial Association and the Electric Power Association were the first major victories. By May, almost all business organizations in Japan were opposed to the government bill, and on this unity the club built an unprecedented effort to force the Minseitō to capitulate. It organized five regional "umbrella" federations of industrial organizations in Tokyo, Osaka, Nagoya, Northern Kyushu, and Hokkaido.[19] In late June, Prime Minister Hamaguchi compromised some; he admitted the possibility of revising the bill before submitting it to the Diet.[20] The bill that finally reached the Diet in late 1930 was in fact a major retreat from the Social Bureau's original draft. It recognized only trade and industrial unions, not more general federations; it made no provision to enforce a clause forbidding union busting; and it retreated from a guarantee of union exemption from strike liability.

In retrospect, the united business campaign of 1930 rendered the defeat of the Union Bill in 1931 a foregone conclusion. Although the Minseitō Party majority in the Lower House held together and approved the bill, Seiyūkai supporters and industrialists in the House of Peers worked together to bottle it up in committee. Factors such as the attempt on Hamaguchi's life and the furor over the London Naval Conference also worked against the Minseitō legislative effort in the 59th Diet of winter 1931. Of greatest importance, however, was continued business lobbying, which mobilized the sophisticated and coherent organization built in the campaign of the previous spring. Business pressure bore fruit in the House of Peers.[21]

The Tokyo Chamber of Commerce, led by chairman Gō Seinosuke, joined Dan Takuma and the Industrial Club in convening a meeting of 31 Tokyo-Yokohama area industrial federations in October 1930. They made a plea for joint action in lobbying the Diet against the Union Bill.[22] These industrialists spurned a last-ditch Minseitō attempt to save the bill with a labor-government-business "summit" meeting in December 1930. They did not attend. Abe Isoo, Matsuoka Komakichi, Nishio Suehiro, and other labor leaders enjoyed a useless chat with Home Ministry officials.[23] The business representatives attended a separate, later meeting and refused to support the Minseitō. On 27 February 1931, just three days after the government submitted the Union Bill to the Lower House, the growing movement of federated industrial organizations held its largest meeting yet, gathering representatives of 175 business groups into a

National Council of Federated Industrial Organizations. Gō Seino-suke was elected chairman, and, in the name of this organization and the five regional federations created the previous spring, the groups resolved to oppose the Union Law. When the bill passed the Lower House in March, council members threw all their efforts into mobil-izing the large business contingent in the House of Peers, which included the leaders of the Industrial Club, to oppose the bill. It never got out of committee.[24]

The defeat of the Union Bill in March 1931 marked a watershed in the history of organized business in prewar Japan. Sentiment among members of the anti-bill federations favored the formation of a per-manent organization to continue to defend business interests on labor issues, and out of this sentiment emerged the National Federa-tion of Industrial Organizations (*Zenkoku Sangyō Dantai Rengōkai* or Zensanren). At an April 21 meeting of the Japan Industrial Club, leaders of the five regional federations created in the Union Bill fight joined to form Zensanren. The first meeting of the new group's exec-utive committee took place in early May 1931.[25]

With the formation of Zensanren, Japanese business reached a new level of organized political coherence. For the next decade (and more), the Industrial Club kept a low profile, serving as a sort of "cloister government" (*oku no in*) of the business world, while Zen-sanren and the Keizai Renmei stood on the front lines, neatly divid-ing responsibility. Zensanren handled labor; the Keizai Renmei acted to defend big-business positions on matters of trade and financial pol-icy (their postwar successors, Nikkeiren and Keidanren, have done the same). Businessmen now spoke with one voice on labor issues, and for a time the government listened and responded respectfully. Zensanren was firmly grounded in its five regional federations, each composed of the leaders of local chambers of commerce and regional organizations in particular industries, such as paper, coal, electric power, textiles, and transport.

The creation of Zensanren marked an ideological as well as an organizational victory for business. Japanese business leaders had also closed ranks behind a vital principle, previously supported by the Industrial Club mainstream and now backed by a far wider spectrum of business leaders. Briefly put, social-policy legislation was not the key to solving the labor problem. At best it was a minor supplement to solutions that businessmen would devise on their own. This had been the stand of the Cotton Spinning Federation and other opponents of a factory law years before. Legislation, they had feared, would undermine the beautiful, ancient, emotional, or paternalistic ties binding owner and worker; it would encourage the worker's awareness of his rights and bring only trouble. Opponents of a union law resorted to a similar impassioned defense of beautiful Japanese customs as a substitute for a union law. They also referred to successful non-union models or trends in the United States or Europe when they opposed the law. In either case, they sought to avoid any government interference in structuring the labor relationship. They would solve their own problems.

After the defeat of the union bill, Matsumoto Gaku, a Home Ministry veteran with experience both in the Police Bureau and as governor of Shizuoka and Kagoshima prefectures, replaced Yoshida Shigeru as head of the Social Bureau. Although neither he nor the Ministry immediately shifted to an anti-union position, Matsumoto's appointment symbolized a change of direction. He was a new face in the Social Bureau, clearly not identified with progressive labor legislation. The Ministry, in fact, never again proposed legal support for unions. In Matsumoto's recollection:

It would have been meaningless simply to follow the path of my predecessor. Whatever our desires, after such a great collection of big shots of the business world had gathered and together crushed [the bill], it would have been a poor policy for the officials to chase after them saying, "How about this version? Or this one?" We had to cool things down. It was out of the question to resubmit a slightly revised version of Yoshida's bill. So we dropped the idea of a union bill entirely, and I decided we should consider something like an "Industrial Peace Movement" as [a way to get at] the more basic problem.[26]

Under Matsumoto and his successors in the early 1930s, the Home Ministry nurtured ties with union leaders willing to eschew strikes and cooperate with management, and it gently pressured managers to respect such unions. This policy does not seem to have met significant Zensanren disapproval; for business, it was certainly an improvement over Ministry support for a union bill.

Yet, an adversarial relationship continued in the 1930s between the newly united business world, led by Zensanren, and the government, represented in labor matters by the Social Bureau of the Home Ministry. These bureaucrats still did not trust businessmen to handle labor issues properly on their own. The Ministry's initiative that led Zensanren to flex its newly developed muscle between 1932 and 1936 was the Retirement and Severance Pay Law (*Taishoku tsumitate kin oyobi taishoku teate hō*). The law passed through several progressively weaker versions before gaining Diet approval in 1936. As finally enacted, it required all enterprises with 50 or more employees to set up a fund out of which retirement or severance-pay lump-sum allowances would be paid. The law set minimum levels for recipients in accord with seniority and the reason for leaving (quit, fired, retired).

The law was a child of the Depression. In 1932, the Home Ministry created an advisory Committee on Unemployment Policy. A subcommittee of this group discussed legislative measures to deal with unemployment. The makeup of the committee is of interest. In addition to numerous Social Bureau officials, and a few representatives from other ministries, the committee enlisted the services of two of Japan's most prominent business spokesmen, Ikeda Seihin and Fujiwara Ginjirō. Fujiwara had been one of the founders of Zensanren, and Ikeda was a leading figure in the Mitsui zaibatsu. Also appointed at the outset was the socialist leader, Abe Isoo, and Matsuoka Komakichi of Sōdōmei joined the committee in 1935, but the debate over a law boiled down to a struggle between the Social Bureau and Zensanren, despite this labor participation. Labor representatives naturally called for a comprehensive and generous law, but, in Japan in the 1930s, they did not have the power to make demands of business or the state. The critical issue was whether the Social Bureau could force or persuade the business lobby to accept any law at all. After several years of discussion in a rapidly shifting political context, this subcommittee approved a draft of a Retirement Fund Bill in 1935.[27]

Why did the Social Bureau take the lead in advocating this law? Its reasoning is worth noting. Japan had come out of the Depression quite rapidly, and, by 1933 or 1934, most of the unemployed of the Depression era had been absorbed into a rapidly expanding labor force. Even so, Social Bureau officials felt the military-led nature of the recovery somehow "abnormal," and they sought to create a system to soften the impact of an expected future collapse or recession. They acted in anticipation of a possible future social problem more than in response to immediate pressure from organized labor or from unemployed workers. They deemed unemployment compensation too foreign; it was too much a "translation" of Western social policy. The impact of Zensanren philosophy and strength is evident in this reasoning. If social legislation were to have any chance at all, it must respect existing business practices. The custom of granting lump-sum payments to fired regular workers was one such practice. It was already fairly common among large firms by the 1930s. In many cases, these payments rose with seniority and became, at the top of the scale, a retirement payment to a worker leaving after a full career with the company. The Social Bureau decided to promote a law that would systematize and extend existing practice. It was particularly eager to extend this benefit to workers at smaller firms, which rarely offered such payments, and to guarantee all workers their payments. As matters stood prior to the law, most companies granted only one-third or none of the full benefit to voluntary leavers, although these workers had generally contributed to the company fund out of their wages. Finally, under the existing, customary system, companies in financial trouble could and did abandon their commitment to such payments, using retirement funds to meet other obligations.

Zensanren opposition centered on protecting several customary business practices: A law would end management ability to be selective about recipients; it would make a previously benevolent gift into a dangerous worker right; and it would destroy many small businesses. Zensanren forcefully raised its objections as the subcommittee worked on a draft of the proposed law, and the Social Bureau, determined to pass a law but wary of Zensanren strength, modified its version in hopes of satisfying business interests. The compromise draft, which raised from 10 to 30 employees the size of enterprises covered by the law, and gave employers considerable new latitude in administering the funds, finally gained the approval of the subcommittee in December 1935. The new version still displeased Zensanren, which made plans to take its case to the Diet, set to open in January 1936, but, as expected, the session was short; the Diet was dissolved before it considered the matter, and an election set for 20 February 1936.

By the time the Diet reconvened, finally to consider the Retirement Fund Bill, a major political event had placed Zensanren at a considerable disadvantage. The abortive coup d'état of 26 February 1936 placed the business establishment on the defensive. In the public eye, capitalists were one cause of the illness afflicting Japanese society and producing such outbursts. Zensanren even felt moved, two months after the incident, to issue an unusual public statement defending Japanese industrial leadership, explaining its goals, and practically apologizing for the current misunderstanding of business intentions. It even stated willingness to accept "appropriate" social legislation that respected the special Japanese industrial spirit. In a slightly hasty conclusion, some observers in the press called this statement the Zensanren "conversion" (tenkō).[28]

The Social Bureau therefore approached the Diet session of spring 1936 with some hope, but Zensanren continued to lobby actively against objectionable features in the law. After a complicated month of political maneuvering, a once-more revised, joint Minseitō-Seiyūkai version of the bill gained easy Diet approval in June. It also met the major Zensanren objections. The business lobby succeeded in further limiting the scope of the law to enterprises of 50 or more employees, and it gained the right to give voluntary leavers less than fired or retiring workers. Perhaps most important, Zensanren won a provision allowing companies with existing retirement-fund programs deemed sufficient merely to set up an emergency reserve fund while administering the company program as before.[29]

While Zensanren and the Social Bureau, or, more generally, business and government, were clearly at odds in this important case, the result of the conflict indicates that, after the political turmoil of February 1936, bureaucratic power increased slightly relative to the business world, at least on labor issues. To be sure, businessmen rationalized acceptance of the law without admitting defeat; this law, unlike the Union Bill, was social policy of an appropriately Japanese style. It certainly did reinforce existing practice rather than impose a new foreign structure of unemployment compensation. The Social Bureau had also weakened the law to meet Zensanren objections. Even so, Zensanren would have preferred to defeat this labor legislation rather than to accept even a weak new law.[30] The business lobby certainly was anxious and able to defeat the weak 1931 Labor Union Bill, even after forcing a government retreat from stronger earlier drafts. And the Retirement Fund Law did force some large firms to initiate new retirement funds. Others had to expand their existing funds by offering higher benefits to fired workers and extending benefits to temporary employees.[31] Bureaucratic ability to intervene on labor matters had received a boost from the young officers' rebellion.

In addition to offering signs of increased bureaucratic power, the struggle over this law suggests that a closer, less antagonistic relationship was emerging between organized business and reformist bureaucrats, and perhaps labor. Business and labor representatives sat on two other Home Ministry Advisory committees in the 1930s, as well as the Unemployment Committee. Central figures in Zensanren (Isomura Toyotarō, Miyajima Seijirō, Shiraishi Genjirō, and Gō Seinosuke) joined labor leaders Matsuoka Komakichi, Hamada Kunitarō, Kagawa Toyohiko, and Suzuki Bunji on either a Labor Insurance Committee or a Central Employment Exchange Committee during these same years. These very businessmen were among those who had spurned a three-way dialogue in 1930 during the Union Bill dispute, but, over the following several years, they seemed to be joining labor in discussing a range of social-policy issues under bureaucratic auspices. Of course, the participation of a weakening labor movement had less impact than did business and Zensanren involvement with the bureaucracy. In addition to placing business leaders on these committees, the Social Bureau dealt directly with Zensanren, passing along to the Zensanren staff preliminary drafts of *all* pending labor bills and regulations, or revisions of earlier laws. Zensanren would study each draft and offer its opinion, and a significant dimension of cooperation crept into the relationship of the two groups. We can discern compromises and shifts on the part of both Zensanren and the bureaucrats.[32] The convergence centered on the notion of "appropriate," "Japanese-style" social policy. Zensanren moved from outright opposition to any union bill in 1931 to acceptance in principle, by 1936, of social legislation that reflected the "Japanese situation." The Social Bureau, for its part, responded to Zensanren pressure with a series of major concessions on the scope and content of the Retirement Bill, and it accepted from the start the notion that the unemployment problem be approached through a "Japanese-style" law built on existing practices.

The bureaucrats who formed these committees and presided over their deliberations appear to have been nurturing a political relationship of a corporatist nature. Direct negotiations between the state and *organized* business and labor interests suggest the emergence of an unofficial tripartite structure of consultations, co-existing with

Diet politics. In fact, however, the labor presence reflects a bureaucratic desire for symmetry more than real labor strength. The emergence of Zensanren and its central role in weakening the Retirement Fund Law suggest that the elite pluralism of the 1920s was giving way to an equally elite Japanese version of a corporate political order.

Corporatism is a slippery term, but it seems apt in this case. Two characteristics of labor policy formation in the early-to-mid 1930s define it in its prewar Japanese context. In place of a multitude of scattered interest organizations, there emerged an autonomous but hierarchic, all-inclusive business lobby with a single function—to deal with labor problems. Also, in place of Diet politics, direct negotiation between Zensanren and the bureaucracy took on increasing importance in deciding labor issues. These characteristics fit Philippe Schmitter's interesting definition of a "societal" (rather than "state") corporate political order with remarkably little stretching.[33] The "societal" adjective is used to indicate that the corporate tendency in Japan in the early 1930s was not chiefly the result of state intervention or direction. The state did not create its corporate counterparts out of whole cloth; rather, "society" produced them. Zensanren, that is, emerged because businessmen themselves felt the need to direct their political efforts into narrower, more structured channels. It took nearly a decade before Zensanren and the state bureaucracy began to cooperate more than they disagreed. The neatly structured corporatist pattern embodied in the monopolistic, direct relationship of Zensanren with the government had evolved out of the rather pluralistic political scene of the 1920s.

TOWARD STATE CORPORATISM

The trend toward business-government cooperation, or at least the blunting of the sharp adversarial relationship of earlier years, continued as the Industrial Service or Sanpō (contraction of *sangyō hōkoku*) movement evolved between 1937 and 1940. While Zensanren and the government continued to differ on significant issues, they now resolved these differences in private meetings and discussions. The floor of the Diet and the pages of major newspapers were no longer their battlegrounds.[34] In addition, the state, represented on labor matters by the Welfare Ministry, began to intervene more aggressively in directing the course of labor policy. Zensanren gradually was forced into a defensive, then a subordinate position, and the signs of some semi-official labor participation of the early 1930s diminished between 1938 and 1940, and then vanished.

A sharp rise in disputes in small factories in 1936 and 1937 brought the Sanpō movement to life. In the absence of unions or other worker organizations, mediation was extremely difficult; a dispute rarely involved two distinct, organized parties. From late 1937 through the summer of 1938, government, business, and right-wing Japanist labor-union representatives reached agreement on a program that became the core of the Sanpō approach to labor problems: Councils serving as forums for labor-management discussion and composed of both workers and managers would be formed in factories throughout the nation, and they would be linked into a hierarchy of regional and national "Sanpō" organizations.

The first plans for creating such councils came from prefectural police departments, part of the Police Bureau of the Home Ministry. The interest of the police emerged from its stance as mediators on the front line in many labor disputes. The best known of these plans, put together by the Aichi Prefectural Police Department between October 1937 and February 1938, called for binding arbitration in cases where factory-level councils were unable to resolve a dispute. This plan did not specify whether worker representatives were to be elected or chosen by management, but many others called for elections and gave councils authority to *decide* matters of treatment, not just offer advice. These plans gathered support at higher levels in both the Home Ministry and the new Welfare Ministry. The latter was formed in January 1938 and absorbed the Social Bureau of the Home Ministry. It subsequently became the central-government agency involved in labor issues.

The Zensanren response was rapid and adroit. While binding outside intervention in disputes, councils with real authority, and elected worker representatives were all unacceptable to business, Zensanren sought immediately to join and indeed lead the movement in a safe direction, rather than fight it. Nearly a dozen businessmen, all top Zensanren officials, joined and sought to dominate an influential Kyōchōkai subcommittee formed in February 1938 to deal with wartime labor problems. Numerous officials from the

Home and Welfare Ministries also sat on the subcommittee. This Kyōchōkai group became a semi-official forum to consider various versions of the Sanpō idea.

The Welfare Ministry participants sought real authority for factory-level councils, empowered to deal with significant issues and composed of representatives elected by workers as well as labor managers and white-collar employees selected by the company. They also envisioned fairly tight central control and authority over the councils. The Zensanren vision was quite different. Total management control over labor within the enterprise was not to be violated. If existing in-company organizations, such as the fairly popular factory councils, were deemed sufficient, they would serve as the Sanpō councils. Each company was to retain freedom to design (or indeed refuse to create) the type of council it felt appropriate. Zensanren favored councils of appointed worker and management representatives which would seek to build a spirit of harmony and cooperation, under strong management control, rather than discuss work conditions or wages. Finally, the central Sanpō organization would coordinate activities among company units, but it would have little authority to direct them. The two sides really agreed only on the need for councils of some sort. Their conceptions of the role of Sanpō factory units were entirely different.

In the spring of 1938, the Kyōchōkai committee, with full Zensanren cooperation, held meetings in industrial centers throughout Japan to promote the weaker version of the Sanpō movement among businessmen. Although, even in June, the Welfare Ministry wanted to give a more active role to freely chosen councils, officials decided to back the Kyōchōkai initiative rather than provoke an open confrontation and risk destroying the movement.[35] Very likely, the Ministry was content to accept a fairly weak Sanpō as a foot in the door, in hopes of later controlling and directing more active councils. By July, business, government and right-wing Japanist labor leaders, centered on the Kyōchōkai committee, formed the Sanpō Federation (Sangyō Hōkoku Renmei) to promote company-unit councils throughout Japan. Sanpō advocates compromised on continued points of disagreement by leaving to each company the question of electing worker representatives (a gain for Zensanren) while empowering councils to discuss treatment and wage (*taigū*) issues (a Welfare Ministry gain).

In December 1940, this semi-official federation was superseded by the Sanpō Association (Sangyō Hōkoku Kai), an official government organization controlled by the Welfare Ministry. If, at any point along the way, the Sanpō councils had functioned as conceived by initial advocates in the Welfare Ministry or the Police Bureau's local departments, they would have indeed placed constraints on business authority within the enterprise. In the event, Zensanren carried the day. Throughout the transition from movement to Federation to government-run Association, Zensanren continued its close involvement in leading Sanpō and keeping the factory councils powerless.

Zensanren and Welfare Ministry behavior during the early days of the Sanpō movement stands in contrast to business and bureaucratic action during the Union Bill or Retirement Fund struggles. In all three cases, a struggle for control of a major initiative in labor policy clearly took place between a business organization and the government, but the tone and character of the struggle was different in 1938. Zensanren leaders had gained over six years' experience dealing with government bureaucrats, and they were sensitive to any appearance of unpatriotic selfishness in a time of perceived national crisis. They accepted Sanpō from the start, although it was not a business idea in origin, and they moved carefully and effectively, in close consultation with the Welfare Ministry, to keep Sanpō from becoming a threat. The Ministry, as well, was more amenable to compromise than in the earlier cases. It needed business cooperation in other areas as well. The result was agreement on a watered-down Sanpō.

Similar caution, combined with a firm defense of fundamental business interests, characterized Zensanren's response to the public, official, and intellectual enthusiasm for the vaguely defined New Economic Order championed by the second Konoe Cabinet of 1940. This plan to mobilize the economy effectively and equitably for the war effort posed at least a theoretical threat to the independence of Japanese capitalists. Zensanren gave a lukewarm welcome to the call for a New Order in late 1940. The plan for a New Economic Order will be vital to building a new Japan, it declared, but the private sector must be the creative force, taking responsibility and vigorously running its own enterprises. The government role should not be direct involvement in managerial affairs but general economic leadership. In particular, Zensanren strongly affirmed both the right of private enterprises to autonomy and the need to seek profits. It defended profit seeking as necessary for a strong state. It also maintained that economic controls, if inevitable in wartime, should not interfere at all with the operation of the enterprise.[36]

Yet, just one year later, in the fall of 1941, Zensanren and the business community meekly accepted a labor regulation that contradicted the essence of this forthright stand. The Ordinance on Labor Management in Essential Industries (*Jūyō jigyōjo rōmu kanri rei*) explicitly denied management the right to autonomous control over labor, in theory and in practice, but no struggle took place. The Zensanren response to this ordinance does not compare to its active leadership of the Sanpō movement. An important shift had taken place in the relationship of this business lobby to the government.

The regulation, first publicly discussed in August 1941 and promulgated in February 1942, began with a bold statement of political philosophy: The primary obligation of both workers and managers (in designated essential plants) was to the state; the worker-manager relationship was no longer one of private, voluntary contract between two parties. The regulation implemented this philosophy by giving company work rules and management orders the force of law, while simultaneously placing legal restrictions on management. The government sent "labor management inspectors" to all designated plants and gave them authority to issue orders concerning virtually any matter involving labor: hiring, firing, hours, punishments, rewards, bonuses, welfare facilities, hygiene, safety, disputes, and wages.[37]

An elaborate series of piecemeal regulations enacted over the previous two years under authority of the National General Mobilization Law had already given government some control over most of these matters. Even so, this regulation had special significance. It consolidated previously scattered authority over a variety of matters into a single reform. More important, many previous regulations merely set general standards for all factories in an industry or region. Wage controls, for example, specified hourly wage standards for an industry in a particular region, and these levels rose with age, but in practice individual companies retained a fair amount of freedom. So long as the entire wage bill of the company remained under a government ceiling, actual distribution of pay need not conform neatly to the standard scales. Under provisions of this new regulation the government could intervene extensively and treat each company as a separaate case. The Welfare Ministry would collect from individual companies written wage regulations, work rules, and pay-raise regulations, review these, and order any changes it felt necessary. The state, in the person of the Welfare Minister, was now an active partner in the labor management of hundreds of major companies, mainly large firms in heavy industry producing products for the military.

Informed observers at the time recognized the importance of this regulation. They referred to its "epochal" character, stressing above all the new "statist" (*kokkateki*) concept of labor embodied in the regulation. The General Manager of Japan Steel, in September 1941, remarked that the regulation repudiated the capitalist concept of labor as a commodity. Labor and capital were no longer two independent entities interacting in the marketplace; both were under the control of the state.[38] A highly placed Sanpō official wrote in February 1942 that the great significance of this regulation lay in the transfer of ultimate power over company labor policy from the enterprise to the Welfare Ministry.[39]

In accepting this "transfer of power," Zensanren seemed to retreat from its policy of opposition to, or manipulation of, Ministry initiatives. The emergence of the military as a major actor in labor policy late in the 1930s is a major part of the explanation for business behavior. Military involvement promoted a new level of integration between Zensanren and the civilian government, and helped the Welfare Ministry to emerge as the dominant partner in labor matters. Military concern with private industrial production in Japan dated back to the first orders for a warship or a cannon placed with a domestic manufacturer. Both the Army and the Navy created bureaus of inspection to oversee ship and arms production and insure that standards were met. By the early 1930s, the naval inspection apparatus included 11 well-staffed regional offices, 7 of which were located within major private companies, including the Mitsubishi Shipyard, Uraga Dock Co., and Muroran Steel. Until the China War, however, the inspection focused chiefly on technical specifications, and the military rarely sought to control overall management strategy or policy toward labor.[40]

Military concern with labor issues reached a new level in the fall of 1937. The invasion of China proper changed the political and social climate in Japan, and the military moved to mobilize the entire nation for war. A long dormant piece of legislation, the Munitions

Industry Mobilization Law passed in 1918 (inspired by the European experience of World War I), provided a rudimentary structure for economic mobilization. It enabled the government to gather information preparatory to the designation of factories for possible "mobilization," should such prove necessary.[41] Two decades later, the Diet agreed with the military that mobilization was in order. In September 1937, it authorized the Navy and Army to activate the law and place designated military producers under their supervision. The following January, the military also created a new Munitions Inspection System. Then, in May 1938, one of the first regulations promulgated under the Mobilization Law was a Factory Enterprise Administration Act which reinforced and extended the Munitions Industry Law by putting it under the umbrella of the National General Mobilization Law, then before the Diet.[42]

In early 1940, the military finally exercised the authority it had gained two years earlier to supervise private firms. The war in China was dragging on, confrontation with the United States and Britain seemed more likely each month, and the domestic economy was showing signs of strain, with inflation and labor shortages frustrating the mobilization drive. In this context, the military ministries designated firms in shipbuilding, steel, engineering, and the like as either Army or Navy Inspection Factories, and they dispatched inspectors to oversee operations at each plant. The mandate of the inspectors went far beyond that of the earlier technical observers to include "supervision" of matters such as "hiring, firing, training, punishment, rewards, wages, salaries, and hours." It appears, however, that inspectors promoted no particular labor policies beyond exhortation to produce quickly and cheaply.[43]

As problems with the supply, distribution, and control of labor became issues for Cabinet-level discussion in 1940 and 1941, the military had this apparatus in place, potentially able to back its claim for a voice in determining and implementing labor policy. When a Cabinet meeting of 29 August 1941 produced an 8-point "Emergency Labor Policy," the Welfare Ministry feared it might lose control of labor policy to the military. In the event, it managed to increase its authority at the expense of the Naval and Army inspectors in the implementation of the emergency policy.[44]

An ambitious cohort of young officials, anxious to further their own careers by protecting or expanding the powers of the Welfare

Ministry, apparently led the Ministry's battle to retain jurisdiction over labor matters. They included Ōhashi Takeo, the head of the Ministry's Wage Section in the Labor Division in 1941. Ōhashi was a survivor who went on to ally himself with Yoshida Shigeru (the diplomat/Prime Minister), serving as his Justice Minister at the time of the 1950 Red Purge and filling the posts of Labor Minister in 1962 and Transportation Minister in 1966.

He and other Welfare officials argued that problems with productivity and the distribution of skilled labor to areas of critical need demanded a concerted overhaul of the entire labor-control apparatus, which it alone was qualified to administer.[45] In winning the bureaucratic struggle to control labor policy, the Ministry gained responsibility for the implementation of the emergency plan, including Point 5, the "reform of labor management." This soon emerged as the Essential Industries Labor Management Ordinance. Welfare Vice-Minister Kodama told the press that the Ministry would create a special "guidance system for labor management in strategic industry." It would draft the several regulations called for in the Cabinet decision and enact them under the authority of the National General Mobilization Law, upon gaining approval of the Mobilization Law Council.[46]

The subsequent quiet acceptance of the Essential Industries Ordinance by Zensanren is puzzling when viewed against the background of the business lobby's defense of the need for private enterprise independence and autonomy as late as 1940. It is less of a riddle as we recognize that, for Zensanren in late 1941, the likely alternative to Welfare Ministry control was not freedom from all control but closer direct scrutiny from the military inspectors already on hand in many plants. Zensanren as an organization, and many businessmen as individual managers, preferred civilian to military oversight, for the Welfare Ministry was a familiar entity, already in transition from opponent to partner of Zensanren by 1941.

Increased state intervention to control labor was thus one major domestic development in 1941. A second was increased integration among the agencies with an interest in labor, and businessmen themselves. The Welfare Ministry maintained intimate contact with the military and the Ministry of Commerce and Industry as it drew up and implemented the Essential Industries Ordinance, and, through dealings with Zensanren and the Mobilization Law Council, it could assure business leaders of its good intentions and seek their cooperation.[47]

This council was born of a compromise forced on Prime Minister Konoe in 1938 by Diet men uneasy over the powers handed over to the bureaucracy in the sweeping National General Mobilization Law. In exchange for political-party support for the Mobilization Law, which gave the bureaucracy power to act through regulations on many matters previously subject to Diet approval, Konoe agreed to set up an advisory National General Mobilization Council of 50 members, and he promised that a majority would be Diet men. Konoe followed through on his promise; the Council members appointed in July 1938 included 30 Diet men, 15 Cabinet ministers or vice-ministers, and 3 prominent business leaders, Yūki Toyotarō (Bank of Japan), Kagami Kenkichi (Mitsubishi), and Ogura Masa-tsune (Sumitomo). Yūki and Kagami were both directors of the Japan Industrial Club, while Ogura was a founder of Zensanren and an adviser to Sanpō.[48]

Beginning in summer 1938, the Council functioned as a sort of advisory, miniature Diet. It reinforced the image (if not the reality) of an elite consensus behind policies to mobilize the nation and pursue the war, and in so doing served to legitimize these policies. The government felt it necessary to gain the approval of the nominally powerless Council for any regulation promulgated under the Mobilization Law. While the Council never came out directly against a proposed regulation, members did engage in parliamentary stalling tactics such as relegating a controversial proposal to a subcommittee, a sign the group was not an entirely symbolic entity. One such case occurred in August 1941 over a proposed regulation concerning control of electric-power distribution.[49]

The lively debate over electric power came just before consideration of the Essential Industries Labor Management Ordinance. It suggests that debate and dissent would have taken place had the ordinance been seen as a grave threat, but that, in fact, Zensanren was not disturbed by extensive state intervention. The *Asahi* announced in early September that the next Council meeting would focus on labor regulations, and businessmen were reportedly quite interested in the upcoming meeting.[50] However interested, they were not upset. The Essential Industries Ordinance sailed through the short afternoon committee meeting of 11 September together with several other labor measures. While 12 Council members directed questions to Welfare Ministry officials present to describe and defend the regulations (in a capacity analogous to that of government ministers at Diet interpellations), none of the business members spoke out. This stands in sharp contrast to the meeting over electric-power regulation one month earlier, which ran until late in the evening and had to reconvene for a second, all-day session the following day. The *Asahi* had described these August debates as "enthusiastic" and "active" (*nesshin, kappatsu*) exchanges of opinion, with "serious questioning" and even a "white hot," "boiling" discussion.[51] It used no such adjectives the following month.

The lack of response was not for lack of awareness. The version of the regulation considered by the Council, and published in major newspapers the following day, was almost identical to that finally promulgated in February, and the *Asahi* editorial of 13 September, as well as a lengthy explanatory article, stressed that this regulation signaled a "major shift" in labor policy.[52] Over the following months, the Welfare Ministry polished its version of the regulation and made complex arrangements to hire, train, and deploy 62 labor management inspectors to oversee nearly 400 factories. Some were recruited from the personnel offices of major companies.[53] In view of the pattern found in responses to previous government initiatives on labor policy, we would expect Zensanren at least to have lobbied for a favorable version of the regulation, and the group did keep abreast of developments concerning the measure. On 7 November, Ōhashi Takeo spoke about the pending Essential Industries Labor Management Inspection Ordinance, as it was then called, to a major gathering of 270 labor managers sponsored by Zensanren.[54]

Yet, while Zensanren historian Morita Yoshio apparently regarded the regulation as the most important new labor policy since the inauguration of the Sanpō Association in 1940, his work makes no mention of dissent on the part of the organization.[55] Several Welfare Ministry officials involved in drafting the regulation recalled no business resistance or criticism prior to promulgation when queried in 1980 and 1981.[56] A survey of major periodicals sympathetic to business supports their recollection. Only one article, in the 1 October 1941 issue of *Daiyamondo*, hints at some unhappiness. It remarks in connection with the regulation that "labor controls come as an external pressure against management in various cases, and these are not welcomed or supported positively by management, because such regulation infringes on management's total authority in an enterprise."[57] In fact, Zensanren calmly accepted the ordinance.

The quiescence of organized business on this issue in the autumn of 1941 stemmed from the changed relationship among business, the bureaucracy, the military, and organized labor. A relatively close working relationship had emerged out of nearly a decade of interaction between the leadership of Zensanren and its formerly open bureaucratic opponents, especially as organized labor declined in strength, and the military gained. The Sanpō movement signaled one major step in the evolution of this relationship. Perhaps of necessity, bureaucrats in 1938 went along with the business insistence on a "weak Sanpō," while business made a concession of sorts just by cooperating in the formation of these potentially threatening councils in their factories. Yet, at this point, businessmen still distrusted bureaucratic intentions; they acted to prevent bureaucrats from creating the sort of councils that could sanction a labor interest in the factories. The subsequent dissolution of the nation's few remaining independent labor unions into the Sanpō structure in 1940 eliminated entirely this longstanding threat to business authority. Then, by late 1941, the intensifying pressure of an overheated war economy and the threat of direct military involvement further altered the relationship between business and bureaucratic elements of the ruling elite, who moved, within a decade, from outright opposition to wary cooperation to, finally, the embrace of an elite marriage of necessity and mutual convenience. By 1941, businessmen were the subordinate partners in this marriage. Like many Japanese housewives, who control the purse strings of the family economy, the businessmen retained substantial real control in the national economy, but they were formally subordinate. Initiatives and policies usually came from the state, and business could only respond and manipulate.

Hattori Eitarō, professor at Tōhoku Imperial University, offered an excellent picture of this more intimate relationship in an essay of 1942 on the new Labor Management Ordinance. One should not fear business resistance to this regulation, he assured his readers. Even among leading labor managers and industrialists, reservations about the existing system of labor management, and support for greater state involvement, have been growing spontaneously. In addition to placing restraints on managers, regulations promised to mobilize and distribute labor more efficiently. In fact, he noted, the Kantō-area Zensanren committee recently requested government action to maintain a balance of wages and work conditions among enterprises within a single industry, so as to retard job switching in the context of tremendous labor scarcity. Hattori found this request from Zensanren striking, for government steps to balance or standardize wages and working conditions had long been anathema to Japanese industrial leaders, and Zensanren itself had long stood in the forefront of this opposition, as in its resistance to the standards imposed by the Retirement Fund Law. Yet, now the same industrialists were calling out for government standardization.[58] In a similar vein, a labor manager for an Osaka manufacturer of rolling stock noted in December 1941 that the Kantō Zensanren committee had recently called for creation of a public manpower corporation (*eidan*) to replace the current system of competitive labor recruiting in an open market.[59]

While neither of these Zensanren requests specifically called for or welcomed the more sweeping Labor Management Ordinance, a similar perspective doubtless informed the business response. Despite the loss of once treasured and stoutly defended independence, in the new wartime context there was much to gain from the regulation. It specifically exempted designated essential enterprises from existing limits on a company's total wage bill, which had prevented managers from competing for scarce labor by raising wages. This was a gain for many firms. Also, the Welfare Ministry justified the regulation as necessary to raise productivity and output through "stronger labor management." While to Ministry officials this meant insuring "livelihood wage" levels and limiting hours of work to prevent utter exhaustion, in the non-union context of 1941 such "worker protection" was no longer a threatening affirmation of worker rights. This was also an important factor inducing Zensanren to hand over authority to write work and pay regulations (the latter previously top-secret rules closely guarded by the company personnel office) to a government ministry seen as a dangerous threat several years earlier. In the absence of an organized labor interest, or even the potential threat of one, indeed in the wake of the voluntary dissolution of this labor "interest," business leaders did not fear the government as before. They could reasonably expect that the Ministry and its labor management inspectors would only help them direct workers to produce to meet the continual flow of profitable war orders.

Over the next several years, it turned out that businessmen had miscalculated Welfare-Ministry intentions. One year after the Labor Management ordinance took effect, a Welfare-Ministry official writing for *Daiyamondo* magazine hinted at this. "At the time it was promulgated, many people saw the regulation as exempting strategic industries from controls entirely. In fact, this ordinance provides, in a sense, stricter control or regulation of wages than earlier regulations."[60] The Ministry used its authority to rewrite company rules to force Japanese managers to offer semi-annual pay raises to all workers meeting minimal attendance standards. It thus imposed the seniority wage, now a cornerstone of Japanese labor-management practice, upon managers who previously had offered small "seniority raises" only inconsistently to a select minority of skilled workers.[61] The government also used this regulatory lever to force payment of family allowances, and it finally mandated monthly salaries for blue-collar workers, in place of variable combinations of day and output wages, in the closing days of the war.[62] One outraged personnel manager in the wage section of the huge steelmaker Nippon Kōkan stormed into the office of Kaneko Yoshio of the Welfare Ministry soon after the regulation took effect to protest the manner of its implementation. Regular raises guaranteed to all would destroy motivation and the free-enterprise system, he complained—to no avail.[63] On the whole, however, businessmen accepted government orders which, as in 1936, broadened and systematized existing customs rather than entirely overhaul the wage system.

The dissolution of Zensanren several months after the ordinance on Labor Management in Essential Industries took effect closed the book on independent organized business activity concerning labor in wartime Japan. Welfare Ministry officials felt that organized business, in fairness to labor and in cooperation with the new statist order, ought to follow the labor lead and dissolve itself. Welfare proposed that Zensanren first join, and then dissolve itself into, a labor-management research organ within the Sanpō structure. This new organization would be called the Labor Council (Kinrō Kyōgikai). In October 1941, Zensanren leaders decided that their special role and the integrity of their positions would be respected in this new structure, and the Kantō Zensanren regional committee participated in a February 1942 meeting of the Labor Council. Several months later, in May 1942, Zensanren leaders overrode the objections of one powerful member, Gō Seinosuke, and dissolved the group as an independent organization. This was a step Zensanren had explicitly refused to take in 1940, immediately after the Sōdōmei union had disbanded and joined Sanpō, despite urgings from the Welfare Minister at that time.[64] By early 1942, the marriage of convenience and necessity stood on firm ground; business no longer feared government intentions concerning labor enough to justify maintaining a distinct institutional presence.

CONCLUSION

Business and bureaucratic leaders had sparred over a factory law, but they were able to reach a reasonably amicable agreement after exchanging a few sharp blows. By the 1920s, they were fighting in earnest for high stakes. Businessmen, bureaucrats, and the political parties were all divided between and among themselves over the union issue. A species of elite interest-group pluralism had evolved in Japan. This structure changed by the early 1930s. Pressures from the Minseitō and reformers in the bureaucracy led businessmen to close ranks and form a single labor lobby in 1931. The result was movement toward a corporatist political economy, where an autonomous and spontaneously formed, but exclusive, hierarchic, single-issue business lobby bargained with the state over labor policy. As in the 1920s, the absence of an effective labor representative distinguishes this system from some of those called corporatist in Europe.

A second shift took place between 1937 and 1941. The state bureaucracy sought firm control of this evolving corporatist structure, and the pressure of war and an overheated economy forced elite opponents to cooperate. New institutional arrangements emerged as a result. On a macroscopic level, one symbol of this shift toward a new level of state control and elite integration was the National Mobilization Council. Businessmen, Diet men, and both military and civilian ministers of state together met in council to discuss and approve measures to control the economy and society, which they worked out in prior and subsequent consultation. Our worm's-eye view of the labor issue has uncovered a similar shift at the grimier level of day-to-day policy. First came the Sanpō structure, born of consultation and the complex manipulations of Zensanren and the Welfare Ministry. Until 1941, state control was more apparent than real. By the eve of the Pacific War, however, businessmen had lost the initiative over labor. They suffered no great economic loss as a result, but their decision-making authority was severely compromised with the Essential Industries Ordinance and the Labor Management Inspectors, who eventually imposed some unwelcome policies. The state was now in the driver's seat, acting through the Welfare Ministry to direct private-sector activities for "public" (although certainly not popular) ends. As the initiative shifted from the private sector to the military-dominated state, the integration and cooperation among these several elites intensified at the ground level as well as in the distinguished Mobilization Council. In implementing the Essential Industries Ordinance, the Welfare Ministry hired some of the new labor inspectors from the personnel offices of private firms. It also appointed several of the military's factory inspectors and a few of the Ministry of Commerce and Industry's industrial inspectors to serve simultaneously as Welfare Ministry labor-management inspectors.

The dynamics of change at work in this shifting process suggest three concluding points. First, the emergence of corporatist structuring of economic interests (here, the Welfare Ministry link to Zensanren) is compatible with, and may in some cases depend upon, prior development of plural interest groups. Interestingly, Schmitter suggests this dynamic pattern to be a defining feature of what he calls societal corporatism.[65] Zensanren drew its strength from the initially spontaneous coalition of dozens of regional, local, and industrial federations. Indeed, the emergence of a coherent business lobby in opposition to progressive bureaucrats allowed and encouraged the subsequent submersion of independent-interest politics. Not all businessmen approved of Sanpō even in its weak, Zensanren-approved version, but Zensanren was the only voice able to represent business interests on labor effectively at the highest political levels.[66] The extremely effective aggregation of business interests in regard to labor served to squelch dissent in this case, paving the way for a further transformation of the Japanese political economy in the crucible of war.

Second, ideology does not appear to have been of critical importance in motivating bureaucrats to seek to dominate an increasingly authoritarian, corporate structure. The Welfare Ministry bureaucrats were pragmatists out to help Japan win the war. Ōhashi Takeo, the man most responsible for imposing the Essential Industries Ordinance, later became a close confidant of Prime Minister Yoshida Shigeru. He was no "closet red," no state socialist in wartime disguise.

Finally, the elaborate integration of military men, bureaucrats, and businessmen in the system of labor controls by no means indicates that the Japanese had developed an effective labor or economic policy as the nation moved inexorably to war. The labor policy imposed by these men was not only harsh; it was riddled with contradictions. It caused suffering and wasted talent. Integration at the top, or at the level of policy implementation, was not harmonious. Even before Japan started losing the war, this system was clearly a failure. Manpower policy robbed strategic factories of skilled workers and replaced them with inexperienced, unmotivated students, women, and Korean and Chinese laborers. The early wage controls ironically made peacetime employment more attractive than work in regulated strategic factories. Throughout the war, wage controls worked at cross-purposes with the anti-turnover regulations; workers would illegally switch to employers who, legally or not, were able to pay higher wages. Even before the American bombing raids led many to flee to the countryside, morale in the tightly controlled and regulated factories was low. Absenteeism was rising, and productivity fell.[67]

The validity of this picture of a shift toward an active partnership of business and the bureaucracy, and movement from elite pluralism to a species of corporate organization of the economy, will be affirmed only as it is found useful in the study of other areas of the economy. The relationship between the various Industrial Control Associations, headed by business leaders, and the Ministry of Commerce (later Munitions) comes to mind as a major parallel to the labor story, in which the other exclusive business lobby, the Keizai Renmei, played a significant role, although it appears that, in this case, the zaibatsu lost little, if any, autonomy to the economic bureaucrats. Whatever labels are used, the evolution of a close working relationship between organized business and bureaucratic elements of a single ruling elite would seem to be a general phenomenon of wartime Japan. This system eventually collapsed under the weight of its own contradictions and the American military, but the contemporary relationship of business, government, and political parties in Japan bears the imprint of both the elite pluralism of the 1920s and the statism of the wartime order.

PART TWO

Case Studies

CHAPTER FOUR

Trial and Error: The Model Filature at Tomioka

STEPHEN W. McCALLION

The ability of Japan's Meiji regime to achieve the ambitious modern-ization it had espoused shortly after taking power depended, to a con-siderable degree, on the performance of the nation's silk-reeling industry. From the time trade with the West began, in 1859, the value of raw silk exported through Yokohama had consistently dwarfed that of all other commodities; in 1868, the year of the Meiji Restora-tion, it accounted for almost 40 percent of the value of all exports, and 45 percent of all tax revenues from exports.[1] No other product even remotely approached raw silk as a source of the foreign capital so desperately needed by the new government.

Despite the healthy revenues generated for the public treasury by the silk trade, the industry was plagued with problems which, it seemed, the government could ignore only at its own financial peril.

The commencement of trade with the West had prompted an immediate and unprecedented increase in demand for raw silk, and an extraordinary rise in the price one could expect to receive for the commodity. As silk producers rushed to cash in on the new, apparently unlimited market, the quality of their output began to decline. The Tokugawa Shogunate had instituted some half-hearted measures to reverse the trend, but to no avail. At first, this did not matter much: A silkworm blight in Europe and the Taiping Rebellion in China sharply curtailed production by Japan's major competitors and put an artificial premium on Japan's output. But, by the end of the 1860s, the silk-reeling industry in both those areas was beginning to recover, while the quality of Japan's output continued to deteriorate. As a result, prices for silk thread on the Yokohama market at last began to reflect these changes. Prices fell by one-third in 1868, the first decline since trade with the West had begun; and, though they rose in 1869, they resumed their downward trend throughout 1870 and 1871.[2]

The Meiji government responded, as the Tokugawa government had, by requiring that all silk thread bound for export be certified at officially designated inspection centers. The results were no more felicitous than they had been before 1868. In February 1870, the Ministry of Civil Affairs took up the matter in a lengthy directive on sericulture which it had distributed throughout the nation, and which stated, in part:

Japan's raw silk is of poor quality solely because the nation has no good machinery. It therefore behooves us to build European-style machines. People at present are worried only about exporting as much as possible to get the highest profit; they do not care if their silk is good or bad and pay little heed to production methods. There has been so much bad, dirty thread this year that much of it cannot be exported and has to be used at home; the result has been substantial losses for many, including Japanese merchants. Merchants therefore should consider these problems carefully. If they can distribute good machinery around the country, the quality (of thread) will improve substantially. Also, if foreigners are hired as instructors, the necessary skills can be learned in a short period; such people will not have to be employed for very long, and the quality and price of silk thread will go up, thereby making it easy to defray the cost of the machinery.[3]

Although the Ministry's directive did not exclude the possibility of improving traditional silk-reeling techniques, the emphasis clearly was on the acquisition of Western techniques and machinery as the ultimate solution. As clear as the government's diagnosis of the problem was its insistence that the responsibility for corrective action lay in the hands of businessmen, not public officials. This is not surprising: The government was not in a position to direct, much less to finance, any major program of mechanization; and merchants, particularly those who dealt with Western companies in Yokohama, were probably best able to obtain information about Western production methods. Yet, in the same month the directive was issued, the Ministry of Civil Affairs began plans for a huge model filature at Tomioka, which it considered, at least in the beginning, the cornerstone of the effort to modernize the silk-reeling industry.

Tomioka Filature was one of the Meiji government's more financially ambitious exercises in model building, a silk-reeling factory whose scale and sophistication were far above any other such operation in Japan.[4] But the apparent contradiction in government policy that existed at its conception hardly boded well for the filature's future, or for the government's willingness to remain committed to the success of the venture; and this contradiction was only the first of many problems that were to beset Tomioka during its period of public ownership. Though public officials went to great lengths to see that the filature employed the best technology the West had to offer for the silk-reeling industry, they spent little time formulating in precise terms the functions the filature was to play in the industry, or determining how it ought to be managed in order to perform those functions. Precisely because such issues were not addressed at the start, because it was not determined what kind of "model" the operation ought to be—specifically, whether it was to serve as a showcase for new technology, a demonstration of the profitable use of this technology, a training center for those who reeled silk, or all three—Tomioka's performance was an object of almost constant criticism, and its management was dictated less by the need to achieve clearly stated objectives than by the need to satisfy the whims of the government at any particular time.

Rashly conceived, Tomioka Filature became, by turns, a source of prestige and a financial albatross for a government that could ill afford it and that persistently demanded that it show a profit. Tomioka's ability to perform with any degree of effectiveness was seriously compromised as long as its proper function, and therefore the way to carry out this function, remained in dispute—a situation that obtained until the government sold the operation. The controversy that surrounded Tomioka during the late nineteenth century was in large measure due to this confusion. This same lack of precise definition underlies much of the historical debate concerning the efficacy of the filature, a debate that seldom considers what, under the circumstances, Tomioka Filature ought to have been able to accomplish, and what in fact it did accomplish.

TOMIOKA FILATURE: THE MAKING OF A MODEL

In 1869, the head of the Dutch commercial office in Yokohama contacted Itō Hirobumi, then the Vice-Minister of Finance, and offered to build a model silk-reeling operation in Japan that would, he said, transform the industry and bring substantial profits to all parties concerned. When Itō turned down the offer, the merchant suggested that the Japanese government assume directorship of the operation, while he supplied the capital and technology. Itō again turned him down, but, intrigued by the merchant's apparent conviction of the profitability of such a venture, initiated discussions between the Ministries of Finance and Civil Affairs about the advisability of a project along the lines suggested by the merchant. The result was a decision by the government to hire foreign advisers and set up a model filature.[5] Itō and Shibusawa Eiichi, then head of the Finance Ministry's Taxation Bureau and the only high official with any background at all in the silk industry, were assigned the task of securing the necessary Western assistance. On the advice of French businessmen, they engaged Paul Brunat, a young Frenchman with experience in the silk trade in Lyon and Yokohama, to oversee the operation. A provisional contract was drawn up, and, at the government's request, Brunat submitted a prospectus on the project shortly thereafter.[6]

It is apparent from this prospectus that Brunat viewed the proposed filature as a business venture, to be run at a profit. He therefore advised against a wholesale importation of Western machinery and techniques and suggested instead that European reeling methods be adapted to circumstances peculiar to Japan's silk-reeling industry so that the results might be copied more easily. In addition, he stressed the need to select for training women with substantial experience in traditional silk reeling, and recommended that at least some of the equipment be made in Japan. With regard to scale, Brunat recommended that the operation have 300 reeling frames, which would require, according to his estimates, about 460 Japanese employees, including managerial and supervisory personnel, and a Western staff of at least 3 supervisors and 6 female instructors. To reduce the cost of the proposed filature, he suggested that some of the Western technical personnel be brought in temporarily from the French-assisted shipyard at Yokohama, and that a waterwheel rather than steam be considered as a possible source of power.[7]

The government reacted favorably to Brunat's prospectus. Tomioka was selected as the site for the filature shortly thereafter and, on 29 November 1870, a final contract was signed by Brunat and representatives of the Ministry of Civil Affairs. Much of the contract accorded with suggestions Brunat had made in his prospectus; but no mention was made of adaptation to existing reeling methods, and all machinery needed for the filature was to be imported from France. The contract reserved the ultimate decision-making authority for the appropriate Japanese officials, though, at the same time, it gave Brunat considerable latitude in the selection and supervision of the Western employees, the acquisition of raw material, and the assignment of duties for Japanese working at the filature. Brunat's period of employment was set at five years beginning January 1871; other foreign employees were to serve at the government's discretion for at least two years but for no more than four. Finally, the contract stipulated that, in the event that the filature was operating at a loss at the end of 1873 and that there was little likelihood of improvement in the foreseeable future, the government could, if it so chose, release all foreign employees, including Brunat, with pay up to that time and passage home.[8]

The French employees were crucial to Tomioka's success, at least for a while. That being the case, the stipulation that their tenure be tied to the filature's financial performance reflects (as do the circumstances under which the proposal for the filature was made and adopted) the government's desire that Tomioka be not only an example for others to follow and learn from but also a source of public profit. Left unresolved was the question of how, or indeed whether, both objectives could be achieved simultaneously. Apparently without much debate, the government had agreed to appropriate a large sum of money to set up the operation, and it gave a rather free hand to a French adviser no one really knew, altering his proposals only by making them potentially less adaptable to the Japanese context.[9] The plans for Tomioka were nothing if not ambitious; but this was hardly enough to guarantee success, and the government would soon have to make very specific managerial decisions that would unalterably affect the performance and fate of what was seen, at first, as the place that would turn the silk-reeling industry around.

On the same day Brunat's contract was signed, the government appointed 5 officials from the Ministries of Finance and Civil Affairs to supervise construction of the filature. These included Shibusawa Eiichi and his cousin Odaka Atsutada, who was de facto head of the group, and who would eventually become Tomioka's first director.[10] Before departing for France in January 1871 to buy the equipment and hire the necessary personnel, Brunat went to Tomioka with Odaka and several others to choose the construction site for the filature. On their way, the group stopped in Maebashi to discuss the project with Hayami Kenzō, the local government's silk-reeling expert and the founder of Japan's first Western-style filature. To the undoubted dismay of Odaka and his coterie, Hayami expressed strong reservations about the advisability of the project and Brunat's qualifications to oversee it, and he insisted that the proposed filature would be too large, its technology too complex and expensive, to be of any immediate benefit to Japan's silk-reeling industry. For the first time, someone had challenged the very nature of the project.[11]

The reaction to the project in the Tomioka area was no more reassuring, though for different reasons. When the site for the filature was finally chosen, Odaka and the other officials went to great pains to minimize local opposition and obtained a statement signed by all local residents declaring that they would not obstruct the construction or operation of the filature.[12] But, though Odaka was able to obtain the consent of Tomioka's residents to have the filature built, he could do little to arouse their enthusiasm. Tomioka had had a long and profitable history of reeling silk by hand, and was doing rather well at it on the export market; local producers therefore had great difficulty understanding why such an operation as the government planned was even necessary, especially in their area. No one took the project seriously; most, in fact, seem to have greeted it with derision.[13]

Nor was popular skepticism the only obstacle Odaka faced. The sheer problem of constructing the buildings was a monumental one, compounded by the fact that Tomioka was (and remains to this day) difficult of access, approachable only in a roundabout way over secondary roads. Brunat had arrived back in Japan in the summer of 1871, bringing with him the reeling equipment and some of the French personnel.[14] The machinery had to be transported from Yokohama over often difficult terrain. In addition, the blueprints for the filature, drawn up by a French architect employed at the government's Yokohama shipyard, had specified that the exterior of the buildings be of brick—an item practically nonexistent in Japan outside of Yokohama and Tokyo, and unheard of in places like Tomioka. Odaka and Brunat hired traditional tilemakers who, after some experimentation, managed to produce a reasonable facsimile to brick.[15] When finished, the entire complex of buildings was, for its time and especially for its place, huge. In retrospect, what is most impressive here is the speed with which everything was done, despite all the obstacles: Construction began in March 1871 and was, for the most part, completed in July of the next year. The filature was ready to begin production in early autumn.[16]

Still to be decided, however, was the question of how Tomioka ought to be run. As the prospective director of the filature and the man most intimately connected with the mechanics of getting it built, Odaka Atsutada took a distinctly less cavalier approach to the project than others seem to have, and he broached the unsettled issue of management to the government shortly before Tomioka was to open. The terms of the contract with Brunat had implied that the entire operation—from obtaining raw materials to selling the final product—was to be in government hands; this meant that the government would be solely liable for any losses incurred. But Odaka suggested that this would not necessarily be the best approach and offered two alternatives: that Tomioka reel silk thread on contract to others, thereby avoiding the hazards involved in purchasing raw material (that is, cocoons) and in transporting and selling the finished product; or that the government enter into a partnership with a (necessarily) wealthy private producer for half the output and produce the other half on contract.[17]

Odaka's introduction of possibilities other than that suggested in Brunat's contract indicates, at the very least, that he had reservations about a purely state-run enterprise. His suggestions seem to have had no influence on the government, however: According to Odaka, the government ultimately decided, on the basis of a survey of cocoon prices which had shown little flux over the preceding thirteen years, that it could make the filature a going concern even if it handled everything itself.[18] Once again, then, the government clearly indicated that it wanted, and expected, to reap profits from the operation; but it also wanted Tomioka to be a model. Odaka's memorandum points, however obliquely, to the possible incompatibility of these two objectives by suggesting that, if Tomioka were an exclusively public enterprise, it might entail more financial risk than the government was really willing to bear. The issue was bypassed at this point, but it could not be ignored indefinitely.

The other major problem that had to be dealt with before the filature could open was the recruitment of employees, and the solution the government adopted here was to have a decisive influence on the nature and effect of what was done at Tomioka. In February 1872, the Finance Ministry, which had assumed jurisdiction over Tomioka upon the elimination of the Civil Affairs Ministry in 1871, sent a notice to the prefectural governments informing them that the filature would soon be ready to begin production, and asking them to recruit women to work and train there.[19] Understandably, there was virtually no response to this. Tomioka was, as noted above, remote, even from other areas in the same prefecture (Gumma), and it should not have been expected that people would be willing to send their daughters to such an isolated place, particularly since the central government, rather shortsightedly, had not offered to pay their transportation expenses. But the crux of the matter here was not the location or even, it seems, the fact that the filature represented something completely new; these were incidental compared with the fact that Tomioka was to be supervised by Westerners. Rumors abounded as to the strange and dangerous behavior of Tomioka's French employees and had far more persuasive impact on most people than the government's request for prospective trainees.[20]

Recognizing the problem, the Finance Ministry issued a second announcement in June, sent it to all city and county offices, and instructed them to distribute copies to villages under their jurisdiction. The announcement was actually the government's first detailed public statement with regard to the filature and its purpose. It cited problems associated with poor production techniques, declared that Tomioka was meant to remedy this by producing raw silk which would be of the finest quality, and invited everyone, regardless of status, to visit the place, examine its technology, and send their daughters there for training. The announcement denounced as absurd the rumors about the French personnel and denied the apparently widespread suspicion that the aim of the filature was to obtain profits for the public treasury; rather, it said, Tomioka was intended to enable people to learn how to reel silk thread by the most modern Western methods, transmit the skills they acquired throughout the nation, and thereby "enrich the entire citizenry."[21]

The June announcement had no more effect than the earlier one had had; by October, Tomioka was ready to begin reeling operations, but the government had managed to round up only 100 or so women, most of them the daughters of the Bakufu's hapless direct vassals, sent to Tomioka under duress.[22] With barely one-fourth the necessary work force, the Finance Ministry sent a notice to 5 prefectures, in effect ordering them each to produce at least 10 trainees as soon as possible. Even with this, only 2 prefectures came up with the required number, and 2 failed to send any women at all.[23] As a last resort, Odaka brought his own 13-year-old daughter to Tomioka and then persuaded others—mostly fellow samurai—near his home to do the same.[24] Samurai in general were much more susceptible to the kind of patriotic appeal the government was making, so that the pattern set by Odaka was ultimately repeated elsewhere, and, by January 1873, Tomioka had a work force of 404 women.[25]

The government had finally managed to surmount the recruitment hurdle, but the solution actually created other problems for the filature. For one thing, since most trainees came from within Gumma or from neighboring Saitama, Tomioka's immediate effect, if any, would be extremely localized. Thereafter the pattern shifted slightly, but there was no appreciable representation from, for example, the Kinki area until 1876.[26] Of even greater effect on the filature's ability to function as expected was the fact that almost all the women were "refined" and "city-bred"—hardly the sort to have had much, if any, silk-reeling experience behind them, and altogether a far cry from the kind of trainees Brunat had in mind when he wrote his prospectus.[27]

The government had not intended this eventuality. It had gone through a number of schemes aimed at recruiting a reasonably representative and capable work force; it had made it clear, especially in the June 1872 announcement, that Tomioka was to be open to all, regardless of status; and it had on no occasion asked specifically that daughters of samurai be sent as trainees. Part of the problem was certainly beyond the government's control; the fear of working under foreign supervision was quite genuine, as was the reluctance to send young women to a location far from home. But the government compounded the problem by, among other things, neglecting to provide for the trainees' transportation and requiring that the women stay at Tomioka for at least one year—a useless rule that was to prove impossible to enforce.[28] Indeed, that Tomioka Filature ended up with about 400 genteel and inexperienced young women of patrician rather than peasant birth reflects the lack of planning and foresight that characterized preparations for the project in general. The government put much time and money into construction, machinery, staff, and the like, but gave relatively short shrift to the more fundamental aspects of running the operation. Even before the filature opened, Odaka Atsutada and Hayami Kenzō had expressed misgivings over this lack of foresight. Both men were ignored on these points, but the issues they raised remained unsettled.

TOMIOKA UNDER FRENCH TUTELAGE: THE UNEASY ALLIANCE

With the arrival of the necessary number of trainees, Tomioka finally began operations in earnest in January 1873. Along with Brunat, the French staff consisted of his 2 assistants, a coppersmith, a doctor, a machinist and 4 female instructors.[29] The women had, of course, more direct contact with the trainees than the other French personnel, but, even in their case, contact, in the form of instruction, was limited: They explained the reeling techniques to 4 trainees, each of whom then instructed 5 other employees, and so on. Techniques were therefore transmitted down the line, as it were. The process was a sensible one, considering the large number of trainees involved and the fact that the French women could not speak Japanese to any appreciable extent; it had the additional advantage of averting potential problems arising from contact with the Western personnel, though, in fact, there seems to have been little trouble in this regard, despite all the initial apprehension. The French instructors were strict, but no more so than their Japanese counterparts.[30] There is no evidence to suggest any serious conflict or rancor between the Western employees and the trainees; the two extant accounts by trainees in Tomioka's first years treat the French women, in particular, in almost incidental fashion, suggesting that, in time, the trainees simply accepted the presence of the Westerners as a matter of course.[31]

The same cannot be said of officials connected with Tomioka or of the government in general, and no effort was made to keep the French at Tomioka any longer than absolutely necessary, if that long. Part of the problem was, simply, money. Relative to the Japanese staff at the filature, the French employees received extraordinarily high remuneration: In 1873, their salaries and expenses accounted for 46 percent of Tomioka's budget.[32] The government was paying dearly for the French employees' services and obviously could not continue to do so indefinitely. In addition, relations between the French and Japanese staffs do not seem to have been particularly harmonious. The Japanese no doubt resented the princely salaries the French received, as well as the implication that they were somehow less qualified than the Westerners. At one point, Odaka Atsutada referred, with understandable indignation, to an opinion common among Western merchants that Tomioka was able to produce good raw silk only because the French were there; as he saw it, practically the opposite was true, and the first two years of Tomioka's existence were a time of "almost complete commotion," during which nothing substantial could be accomplished, all because the French advisers were there.[33] Odaka's criticism was exceptionally harsh, and almost certainly overdrawn, since it is difficult to conceive how Tomioka could have operated had the French not been there at least in the beginning. But he was the official most directly responsible for the French employees, and it was he who had to attend to their needs, respond to their requests or demands, and mediate between them and the Japanese staff. Under the circumstances, it is not surprising that he tended to view their presence as a nuisance rather than an asset.

Odaka did not really have to complain for very long. Though Brunat's contract had specified that the French advisers were to stay for at least two years, in fact almost all of them left early—some almost immediately. By the end of 1873, all French personnel except Brunat, the doctor, and 3 instructors had left Tomioka.[34] The remaining instructors left in March 1874; though they departed nine months before the expiration of their contracts, the Ministry of

Home Affairs, which oversaw Tomioka at the time, observed when they left that "their absence will present no difficulty."[35] This suggests that the process of transmitting Western reeling techniques had gone more quickly than either Japanese officials or Brunat had originally anticipated and that, whatever problems the French presence had created, it paid off in the end.

Yet this French presence was still not to everyone's satisfaction. A report by the Ministry of Home Affairs in July 1874 said that expenses were so high at Tomioka that the filature could not afford to bring in enough women to work, could not buy a sufficient quantity of cocoons, and could not run its equipment at full capacity. The report also accused Brunat of agreeing in principle that spending had to be reduced in certain areas but of balking whenever specific proposals were brought to him. Because of this, and because Japanese officials and workers at Tomioka were considered sufficiently well versed in their duties that they could get by without Brunat, the Ministry recommended that he and the French doctor be dismissed.[36] In the end, both Brunat and the doctor stayed at Tomioka through 1875, but only because stipulations in Brunat's contract would have made his dismissal as costly as keeping him on.[37]

Still, the very fact that the government had come close to dismissing Brunat less than two years after Tomioka opened is significant in view of the enthusiasm with which the project had initially been approached; clearly, officials in Tokyo had very quickly become impatient with the filature. Their rather abrupt change in attitude was not due to any problems with what Tomioka had produced. This was the one area in which Tomioka was manifestly successful so far: The first raw silk from the filature sold extremely well in Lyon and Milan, and won second prize at the 1873 International Exposition in Vienna.[38] The issue was, as the Brunat episode suggests, one of finances. Quite simply, the government had expected Tomioka to turn a profit—immediately—and, however unreasonably, showed considerable irritation when it did not. As early as the summer of 1873, official patience with Tomioka's financial problems began to wear thin; in July, the government authorized emergency funding for the filature, already in debt, but at the same time Ōkuma Shigenobu, then a high official in the Finance Ministry, was sent to Tomioka to talk with Brunat and others and make them reduce expenditures.[39] Whatever effect the funds and Ōkuma's powers of persuasion had in the short run, they did nothing to stem the flow of red ink; Tomioka operated consistently at a loss through fiscal 1875, by which time it registered a massive ¥220,000 deficit.[40]

TOMIOKA UNDER BUREAUCRATIC MANAGEMENT

Even before the figures for Tomioka's first three years were in, officials at the Ministry of Home Affairs realized that losses would be substantial and, alarmed at this prospect, sent Hayami Kenzō to the filature to find out what was wrong. Hayami, it will be recalled, had set up Japan's first mechanized silk-reeling operation in 1870, and, since that time, had won increasing renown for his expertise in the field. Appointed to the Ministry of Home Affairs in early 1875, he functioned in effect as the central government's troubleshooter for the silk industry, and it was in this capacity that he went to Tomioka almost immediately after taking up that post. Hayami had opposed the Tomioka project from the start, and, though the report he submitted was therefore predictably critical, it was also the first sustained analysis of the filature since its opening. He began by citing the most obvious reasons for Tomioka's problems: the filature's remote and inaccessible location, its scale, the expense involved in maintaining its imported equipment, its reliance on only the most expensive raw material, and its inability to maintain a stable, well-trained work force.

Hayami reserved his sharpest criticism, however, for the public officials who ran Tomioka and who, in his estimation, were largely responsible for the above problems as well as a host of others. They were, he said, concerned mostly with their bureaucratic careers and regarded Tomioka less as a model to enhance the national welfare than as a step to a higher position in officialdom. They performed tasks for which they had no technical competence and were so inept in their handling of Tomioka's workers that the women often left before acquiring the skills for which they came or, if they had acquired them, thereby depriving the filature of trained personnel. Finally, Hayami said, the officials who ran Tomioka were so trapped by red tape and by bureaucratic duties that they could not run the place efficiently even had they been so inclined.[41]

The government undoubtedly got more than it bargained for here. It had expected Hayami to analyze Tomioka's finances; he did that, but in the process he also challenged the very notion that the state ought to run the place. This was an idea that had never really been questioned from the start, except indirectly by Odaka Atsutada; even when Hayami had expressed his misgivings to Odaka and others in 1870, he had not disputed the merits of a state-run enterprise. The general assumption all along had been that a model operation, by nature, should be at least initiated by the government. Hayami did not explicitly reject this in his report, but it would have been almost impossible for anyone to read his analysis and not see the gist of his criticism: that state ownership and management were fundamental weaknesses in the way Tomioka operated.

Nevertheless, the government took no action in response to Hayami's critique—this despite the fact that, less than one month later, it received an equally disquieting report from a French merchant in Yokohama who had been instrumental in the selection of Paul Brunat. Hayami, in his report, had not really touched on Tomioka's effectiveness as a model (he would do that later), but the French observer went right to the heart of the matter: Although, he noted, Tomioka's raw silk was the equal of what Europe could produce, "the standards (of quality, scale, and sophistication) set by the filature could not be duplicated by the average Japanese producer for years to come."[42] One might reasonably suppose that the cumulative effect of the two reports would have been to force the Ministry of Home Affairs to adopt a consistent and clearly defined policy with regard to Tomioka, aimed, at the very least, at putting the filature on a sound financial footing. But this was not the case, as events in 1876 were to show. In that year, Odaka managed, by shrewd speculation on the cocoon and raw-silk markets, to erase Tomioka's debts and show a profit for the first time. The Ministry responded by reprimanding him for conduct unbecoming a public official, whereupon the exasperated Odaka resigned. He had acted as he had, Odaka later recalled, because he considered Tomioka a business enterprise, one where progress and improvement could not be achieved without the pursuit of profit, which, in turn, required close attention to the purchase of raw material and the sale of the finished product.[43]

By rebuking him, the government clearly indicated that it did not agree; but, in the same year, the Ministry of Home Affairs stated that Tomioka's functions were "to test reeling machinery, make clear the advantages of careful production, promote improvements in the quality of raw silk, and show the way to true profits."[44] All noble sentiments indeed; but the Ministry neglected to explain how (or if) Tomioka was to achieve them simultaneously, or what "true profit" (*shinri*) amounted to. In 1877, the Ministry set Tomioka's annual appropriation at ¥200,000, but, without specific (or consistent) direction, the filature continued to run into trouble.[45] Odaka's successor, Yamada Yoshiyuki, introduced economizing measures aimed at making Tomioka profitable once and for all; he was able to generate a profit of ¥100,000 in 1877, but at a rather drastic cost in other ways. His exacting methods alienated almost everyone employed at Tomioka, and even Hayami Kenzō complained that Yamada's parsimony was creating more problems than it solved.[46] Worse still, when Matsukata Masayoshi, then head of the Ministry of Home Affairs' Agricultural Promotion Bureau, attended the Paris Exposition the following year, he was confronted with complaints that the quality of raw silk from Tomioka had deteriorated and found to his chagrin that it was now rated far below European thread.[47]

Alarmed by this turn of events—for if Tomioka had been a financial headache, it had at least, until that point, been a source of prestige—Minister of Home Affairs Itō Hirobumi approached Hayami about taking over as director. Hayami demurred at first and said directly what he had only implied before: that the government had no business running Tomioka. Itō finally persuaded him by guaranteeing complete freedom of action, and Hayami succeeded Yamada in March 1879. For all his expertise, though, even Hayami was unable to effect any real change for the better. He did manage to improve the quality of the thread produced, but only marginally—and only by putting the place back into deficit, so that Hayami, of all people, had to request a supplementary appropriation of ¥50,000; frustrated by the seemingly unavoidable choice between quality and profit and convinced, as before, that Tomioka should be sold, Hayami resigned in November 1880.[48]

In only five years, then, Tomioka had gone through three directors—a rate of turnover almost as bad as for the filature's trainees. The departures of Odaka, Yamada, and Hayami were not the result of specific shifts in managerial policy on the part of the Ministry of Home Affairs, but rather of the Ministry's continual failure to articulate precisely what it expected Tomioka to do, and how the filature was to do it. In the absence of such guidelines, Odaka and Yamada acted on their own, under the assumption that what the government wanted most was for the operation to show a stable record of profit. The measures they took are understandable; everything the government had said until then indicated that financial concerns were paramount. Yet the Ministry of Home Affairs did not agree with what they had done, and therefore Hayami Kenzō renewed the stress on production quality, only to put Tomioka back into debt again. By its very indecisiveness, the government produced the kind of managerial instability that made it almost impossible for Tomioka to accomplish any of its objectives.

Tomioka's lackluster performance did enable Hayami Kenzō to succeed in at least one respect: He finally managed to convince Ōkuma Shigenobu and Matsukata Masayoshi to dispose of the filature, and, when the terms of disposal for government factories were announced in November 1880, Tomioka was among those up for sale. According to the announcement, the factories had accomplished their original objectives and were all in healthy shape.[49] In Tomioka's case, the latter was not at all true, as an official report on the filature, issued the following month, made glaringly apparent. The report was by far the most critical to date; it accused those in charge of careless management, of failure to institute any real reforms despite their obvious need, and of causing the work force to become "dispirited"; furthermore, it concluded that Tomioka's raw silk was no better than the best hand-reeled thread produced in nearby Maebashi.[50] Not surprisingly, the government found no takers for Tomioka, a situation it rather lamely attributed to the filature's size.[51]

This first attempt to divest itself of Tomioka having failed, the government was left with the problem of what to do next. In March 1881, Hayami Kenzō, who lacked nothing in the way of hubris, offered the government a solution of sorts by suggesting that it lease the filature to him for five years. Nothing came of this, and, when the Ministry of Agriculture and Commerce, which had assumed control of Tomioka in the middle of 1881, formally requested that the government continue its annual appropriation for the filature, it was told that Tomioka had already fulfilled its purpose and that, if no one wanted to buy the place, it should be shut down rather than be allowed to continue running up losses.[52] The Ministry did manage to keep the filature open and, in December 1881, tried again to have it leased to Hayami, this time with a far stricter provisional contract.[53]

The government formally rejected this second attempt in May 1882 and opted instead to maintain the status quo, particularly because the filature's financial position (profits in fiscal 1880, anticipated profits in fiscal 1881) was better than it had been for some time. It declared that the decision to try to sell Tomioka in 1880 had been premature—implying that it considered disposing of Tomioka less a problem of scale or price than simply a matter of time.[54]

With this, Tomioka's fate was settled, at least for the moment. But the government had chosen the easiest solution by deciding to do nothing to change the situation and, that being the case, the filature continued to be plagued by the problems it had had before, and some new ones besides. As predicted, Tomioka made profits in 1881, but the next three years saw substantial losses. One reason for this was a worldwide decline in silk prices; another was Tomioka's heretofore heavy dependence on sales to France. Demand, and prices, on the Lyon market fell steeply throughout the early 1880s, thus greatly reducing receipts.[55] The filature was able to extricate itself, more or less, from the situation by beginning exports to the burgeoning American market, which, from 1882, consumed a steadily higher portion of its wares.[56]

But other factors behind Tomioka's difficulties were less susceptible to easy solution. The filature's scale continued to be a problem on several counts. By the middle of the 1880s, maintenance and repair costs were mounting rapidly, a trend aggravated by the sheer amount of equipment and by its European origin; and, because Tomioka required such a large supply of cocoons, it had to rely heavily on shipments from throughout the country rather than on what was produced in the immediate area, so that it was impossible to produce thread of uniform weight, thickness, and sheen.[57] In addition, the location remained as inaccessible as before, and transportation costs made the price of cocoons and other necessities higher in the Tomioka area than almost anywhere else in Japan.[58] Officials in Tokyo, who by this point probably regretted the decision not to lease to Hayami, had no sympathy for Tomioka and its problems and routinely turned down requests for supplementary appropriations for the filature.[59]

The government was obviously wearying of Tomioka and its woes, and was becoming less and less inclined to improve the situation. At the same time, since 1881, no one seems seriously to have

considered selling or abandoning the filature. The bruising experience of the 1880 disposal attempt precluded selling, at least for a
while; and the government's perception of Tomioka's utility as a
source of prestige rendered abandonment unattractive.[60] The government therefore retained the place, but kept it at arm's length; surprisingly, Tomioka managed to do rather well in this situation. Hayami
Kenzō was persuaded back to the filature in early 1885. His second
tenure as director was considerably more successful than the first had
been: From 1885 until its disposal in 1893, Tomioka consistently
showed a profit, however modest, despite the persistence of conditions that had led to trouble in previous years. But Hayami was able
to effect a financial turnaround only by taking steps, some of them
rather Draconian, that substantially altered the way Tomioka operated. The government had ordered that costs be cut, and Hayami did
this with a vengeance. Operating expenses were reduced by more
than half in 1886, yet, in the same year, production rose by over
17,000 pounds.[61] Hayami accomplished this impressive feat by slashing worker's wages in half, lengthening the work day (by as much as
two hours per day during some months), and, as of 1887, reducing
the number of workers employed.[62] The emphasis in these years was
clearly on increasing output and lowering costs as much as possible;
for most of the time, Hayami achieved both.

The change was significant, but probably least of all because it
made Tomioka profitable at last. Reduced wages, extended hours, a
stress on quantity over quality—none of these is the stuff of a
"model" operation designed to train instructors. They smack of commercial enterprise, which is essentially what Tomioka had become.
The fact that the government, or parts thereof, consistently
demanded that Tomioka yield a profit meant that the impetus to run
it as a factory, pure and simple, rather than as a model training center
was always there, even if in latent form; and it became stronger as
time went by. In this sense, Hayami simply completed a process that
began well before 1885. Tomioka's role as a model was dubious from
the start, and, although officials, both at the filature and in Tokyo,
never explicitly disavowed this notion, it assumed less and less importance as time went by.

In any case, the changes Hayami put into effect made Tomioka
infinitely more salable than it had been in 1880; and the government
had never abandoned that idea. Nor had Hayami, and, by 1890, both

he and officials in Tokyo concluded that the time had come to dispose of the filature. The relatively healthy state of Tomioka's finances was certainly a factor here, since it made it much more likely that a suitable buyer, one capable of maintaining the place, could be found. But the main reason appears to have been political. Hayami, predictably enough, initiated the process by sending the Ministry of Agriculture and Commerce a furious letter of protest against new regulations instituted in accordance with new budgetary procedures necessitated by the opening of the Diet. Complaining that "these rules . . . take so much time and trouble that they have become, in effect, my job, and I have no time to do what I ought to be doing," and warning that the progress he had achieved at Tomioka could be nullified overnight by the new situation, Hayami asked to be relieved of his post, and recommended that Tomioka be sold as soon as possible.[63] The Ministry ignored Hayami's request to be relieved; but the opening of the Diet and its assumption of budgetary powers posed problems, quite apart from those Hayami presented, which could not be ignored. Tomioka would henceforth be subject to public scrutiny on an annual basis— something that could, the Ministry concluded, vastly complicate matters. With this, the Cabinet, after first considering and rejecting a proposal to attach Tomioka to the Imperial Household as a way to avoid parliamentary interference, decided to put it up for sale once again.[64]

The Cabinet also specified that Tomioka be sold at public auction, despite vigorous opposition from Hayami on the grounds that the filature might thereby fall into the hands of someone unable to manage it properly or—even worse—a foreigner using a Japanese as a proxy. In June 1891, two silk producers from Nagano prefecture submitted bids, but, because neither one met the minimum set by the government, Tomioka remained unsold.[65] In May 1893, the government announced that it would again accept bids, and, in September, received them from five interested parties, including Mitsui Bank. The government had set an undisclosed minimum price of ¥105,000 this time; only Mitsui's bid of ¥121,460 exceeded this, and thus Tomioka went into Mitsui's hands.[66] Mitsui took over Tomioka in October 1893, and the last of the public officials assigned there left in February of the following year.[67] Tomioka's era as a model state enterprise had ended. In the end, the government actually made a profit on the venture: By 1890, the filature had repaid all prior debts, and

Mitsui's payment enabled it to recover establishment costs, and to provide the public treasury with a modest ¥13,000 surplus.[68]

TOMIOKA FILATURE: AN ASSESSMENT

The Ministry of Agriculture and Commerce's last financial report on Tomioka, drawn up in late 1893, took proud note of the filature's ultimately solvent position, and concluded that "directly and indirectly (Tomioka) has been an asset to our nation."[69] This laudatory assessment was not shared by most of those concerned with the filature during its period of public management. Once it opened, Tomioka's purpose and utility were the objects of almost constant debate. Indeed, even now the controversy continues, one school of thought seeing Tomioka as a crucial element in the development of Japan's modern silk-reeling industry, another dismissing it as of no substantial importance.[70] That the contemporary debate is rather reminiscent of the controversy that surrounded Tomioka while it was in government hands is due, in large measure, to the fact that the criteria on which Tomioka has been evaluated have never been defined with much precision. To say, for example, that Tomioka failed (or succeeded) as a model does not mean much unless one considers what kind of model it was intended to be, and what kind it actually was. Similarly, to call it a technological success or failure requires that one consider how it succeeded or failed; but most observers of the filature have not done this.

The lack of precision is apparent from the start. In the announcement it issued in June 1872, the government said that Tomioka's purpose was to train instructors and to serve as a technological model, using modern machinery to produce the finest raw silk and inspiring others to do so. Privately—for example, in its contract with Brunat—the government also expected it to operate at a profit. Odaka Atsutada was the first to suggest that Tomioka might not be able to do all of these at once, that it might be more than the place could handle. He was right, but he was ignored, because to deal with the issue at that point would have required defining Tomioka's purpose in more explicit terms than the government was then willing to accept. As a result, there was no lack of agreement that Tomioka ought to be a means through which the mechanization of the silk-reeling industry was accelerated, but there was confusion as to how this should be done, or even how important it was. The issue came to a head in 1878 in a conversation between Itō Hirobumi and Hayami Kenzō prior to the latter's first appointment as Tomioka's director. Itō ventured the idea that, because Tomioka had the burden of instructing people in new production methods, operational losses were inevitable; its role, he suggested, was to teach people how to produce, not how to manage. Hayami responded with the assertion that Tomioka would be of virtually no beneficial influence on the silk-reeling industry if it were run that way because "what people look for in a model factory are its profits and losses."[71] Hayami predicted that he could train people, produce thread of high quality, and make a profit, but his years as director of Tomioka belied this, and his second term showed that the only way to make profits was at the expense of Tomioka's educational functions.

Hayami's point, at any rate, was a legitimate one; Tomioka might be a showcase of new technology, but that would matter little if it lost money, because producers would simply assume that technological innovation entailed operating at a deficit; thus his insistence that Tomioka yield profits. The government also wanted it to be profitable, but not out of consideration for any theoretical niceties; it simply needed the money. This insistence on profits is the one consistent note in an otherwise labile official policy toward the filature. It explains the government's rejection of Odaka's alternative management proposals in 1872; its decision to try to sell Tomioka in 1880 and then, when the financial picture brightened, to keep it; and its insistence on cutbacks in the 1880s, which undermined the filature's ability to pursue its other functions. Finances took priority in the scheme of things, at the expense of Tomioka's role as a center for technical training and for the dissemination of new technology. This was particularly true in the 1880s, when Finance Minister Matsukata Masayoshi abandoned the rather freewheeling fiscal approach of the previous decade for a policy of severe budgetary restraint. But, even before then, official correspondence reveals little concern for matters other than the balance sheet. When, therefore, the Ministry of Agriculture and Commerce pronounced Tomioka an asset in 1893, it did so only after noting, in the previous sentence, that Tomioka finished up with a net surplus.[72] The order here is not fortuitous.

The government placed an overriding priority on the pursuit of profit, but did not explicitly disavow Tomioka's other functions. Nor could it have, given the filature's ostentatious beginning, and given its apparent value as a source of prestige overseas. As long as it was under public management, therefore, Tomioka was open for inspection to anyone interested in improving his own silk-reeling operation, and young women trooped to the place to learn how to reel silk thread on sophisticated machinery, after which they would, in theory, return home to teach others the skills they had mastered. That things were not quite turning out this way was implied by Hayami in his 1875 report, and stated clearly in the French merchant's report of the same year. The government's preference for profit, and its tolerance for the ill effects this had on Tomioka's ability to instruct, was to some degree an attempt to salvage what it could out of the project. There were some—Shibusawa Eiichi, for one—who clung to the myth that Tomioka's purpose was primarily educational, and that profits were consequently of secondary concern; but these were not the people who made the decisions.[73] Those who did thought otherwise. They never renounced Tomioka's educational role, but they also did nothing much to further it, or to correct circumstances that made pursuance of this role difficult. Tomioka operated, then, under serious external constraints, and this must be borne in mind when evaluating its performance as a training center and as a technological model.

As originally conceived, Tomioka was supposed to train young women recruited throughout Japan in the skills necessary for mechanized reeling, so that they might pass on those skills to others. It is impossible to know exactly how many women actually received training at Tomioka between 1873 and 1893, but extant records from the filature as well as prefectural and other documents indicate that over 5,000 women spent time at Tomioka before it was sold to Mitsui.[74] Since, as of 1884, there were about 1,100 mechanized filatures in the entire country,[75] it would seem logical to assume that the women from Tomioka played an important role in many of these places. That, at least, is what was supposed to have happened. But for several reasons it was not the case.

Tomioka Filature began operations with a work force of women who were almost all the daughters of samurai. This was not, as we have seen, intended; nor was it intended to continue, but it did. Prefectural documents dealing with the dispatch of women to the filature generally mention that they were from samurai families and were expected to work in silk-reeling operations set up by, and for, samurai in their area.[76] The predominance of these women at Tomioka was not without its political benefit, since it meant that they could learn a skill with which to help their families get through the difficult post-Restoration years. But it also meant that Tomioka was burdened with trainees who had little or no experience, who consequently took longer to train than the kind of trainees originally envisioned, and who therefore compounded the filature's financial problems. Furthermore, the fact that many of these woman, upon completion of their training, simply returned home to work in filatures (most of which ultimately collapsed) run by others of samurai background makes it highly unlikely that their role as diffusers of new techniques was at all extensive. There is little to indicate that diffusion here went much beyond the confines of their own place of work.

Partly as a result of this dependence on samurai women, Tomioka was never able to achieve the kind of broad geographical representation among its trainees that was at first expected. This in itself was not a problem. It would have been more prudent, in fact, to recruit women mostly from those relatively few areas that either had a well-developed tradition of silk reeling or were mechanizing rapidly. Indeed, Tomioka as a site made sense only to the extent that this was done, since most such areas were not far from Gumma. But it was not done. Between 1873 and 1884, the period for which information on geographical background is available,[77] women from Gumma accounted for the highest number of trainees, fully 20 percent. But more than half were in and out of Tomioka by 1876, after which Gumma's proportion fell drastically. Even more important, they appear to have had virtually no effect on their prefecture's flourishing silk-reeling industry. Gumma's silk producers hardly mechanized at all until very late; the women were at Tomioka, it seems, simply because the filature was nearby. Shiga prefecture had the second highest representation, 17 percent. But again, the trainees were of no apparent influence. An 1879 report on silk reeling there noted that women back from training at Tomioka could not find suitable employment; and, as late as 1893, a Shiga delegate to a national silk-producers' conference aptly described the industry in that area as "still in its infancy."[78] Women from Nagano accounted for 10 percent of the total, but most of them left Tomioka well before producers in their area began to build mechanized filatures to any significant degree. Saitama also contributed a substantial number of trainees, most during the first three years of Tomioka's existence; yet, as of 1879, silk thread from that prefecture was judged among the worst in Japan, and there was little mechanization.[79]

These examples reflect a general trend: Either women returned home from Tomioka long before anything in the way of mechanization was done in their own areas or—and this was more common—they came from regions that never had, and never would have, much of a silk-reeling industry. The latter case was especially true during the 1880s, when most of the women at Tomioka were from Shiga, Aichi, Niigata, Oita, and other prefectures that were, and continued to be, of no importance in the silk-reeling industry. Thus, geographical representation at Tomioka was not only limited; it was increasingly limited to areas irrelevant to the filature's avowed purpose. As time went by, Tomioka served, in effect, less to train potential instructors than to be a repository for the daughters of unemployed samurai.

Another factor that limited Tomioka's effectiveness as a model training center was the length of time women actually underwent training. There were two contrasting trends here, neither of them salutary. In the 1870s, few women stayed for as long as three years, and most stayed for a much shorter period. Precise statistics are available only for Saitama and the Nagano prefectures, most of whose trainees went to Tomioka before 1880, but the trend they indicate is revealing. In both cases, one-third of the women worked at Tomioka for six months or less, over half for less than a year. Only 10 percent of those from Nagano, and 7 percent of those from Saitama, remained for three years or longer.[80] Obviously, most woman did not stay at Tomioka long enough to acquire the skills they were sent to master; this is especially apparent when one considers that most of them had never done this kind of work before, and that they were expected to learn not only silk reeling but all other aspects of thread production (cocoon culling, rereeling, and thread binding, among other things) as well.[81] Many of the women left Tomioka without having become very skilled at anything; they certainly were not qualified as instructors.

In late 1875, the government changed its policy with regard to training at Tomioka by requiring that women stay for at least three years, and up to five.[82] Ostensibly aimed at correcting the aforementioned situation, the new policy was actually part of Tomioka's attempt to economize: It could never hope to cut costs without a stable, reasonably well-trained work force. The measure had no appreciable effect at first; women continued to come and go at about the same rate as before. But, by the next decade, they began to stay longer—far longer, in fact, than could conceivably have been necessary for them to acquire the appropriate skills. The trend reflects the fact that, largely in the interests of economy, Tomioka had become less a training center than a factory whose aim was to operate at a profit. Thus, hours were lengthened, something Brunat had specifically opposed on the grounds that it would render training less effective; women were recruited from areas that were of no significance to the silk-reeling industry but that contained large numbers of samurai who welcomed the opportunity to have their daughters employed; and the filature began hiring, on a significant scale, local women who either commuted daily or worked on a day-to-day basis.[83] This last trend is especially indicative of how Tomioka had changed: It made no sense to hire local women on any basis, since, by the 1880s, it was clear that Gumma's silk producers were not mechanizing their operations and were doing rather well anyway—unless, of course, the women were hired simply to work rather than to be trained.

In any case, the significance of Tomioka's ability, or lack thereof, to turn out competent instructors depended largely on the degree to which it fulfilled its other function—namely, to serve as a model for other mechanized silk-reeling operations. Such training as the women received would have been of no real value had they not been able to apply what they learned in a work situation reasonably close to their experiences at Tomioka. Yet here, too, the results were not at all up to original expectations. Tomioka's very scale and sophistication meant that it was impossible to duplicate what was done there, or even to follow it very closely. The government had invested ¥200,000 just to build and equip Tomioka; no private producer could spend that kind of money. In Gumma itself, Tomioka evoked virtually no response at all.

The filature that most resembled what the government had done was Rokkusha, set up in Nagano prefecture in 1874 by a group of samurai who had invested, on a per reeling-unit basis, less than one-tenth of what had been put into Tomioka, and with one-fifth the work force.[84] The filature was built under the supervision of a man who had studied Tomioka's technology, and its instructors had spent over a year at Tomioka. But, though it adopted Tomioka's reeling methods and tried to imitate its technology, Rokkusha was a vastly simpler, more primitive filature. One of the instructors later recalled that her associates complained about Rokkusha's inferior cocoons and crude equipment, and she herself observed that Rokkusha was "as different from Tomioka as earth is from heaven. What had been copper, iron, and brass was now wood; glass was wire; and brick was mud."[85]

The women were correct: Compared with Tomioka, Rokkusha *was* primitive. But, whatever its flaws, Rokkusha was a veritable replication of Tomioka when compared with other operations. Many silk producers did visit Tomioka, especially in the 1870s; but, if they subsequently mechanized at all, they ended up modeling their filatures on a mixture of what they had seen at Tomioka and at other much less sophisticated operations.[86] Others who imitated Tomioka never even saw it, but based what they did largely on hearsay.[87] For most, imitating Tomioka usually meant adopting its *tomoyori* method of connecting cocoon strands into a line of thread, and using steam to heat the basins in which the cocoons were boiled. Most places were extremely small, some with as few as 6 workers; none used steam for power, relying instead on waterwheels or human labor to turn the reeling frames. Many closed within a year or two. In some cases, people who had visited Tomioka returned home and, lacking either the means or the incentive (or both) to do otherwise, began reeling silk by hand.[88]

Mechanization in the silk-reeling industry was most rapid in Nagano prefecture. Nagano is adjacent to Gumma and, as we have seen, many woman from the prefecture went to Tomioka; the government's filature ought, therefore, to have had considerable effect in the area. To some extent it did: In the 1870s, at least 69 filatures were established which were based, in one way or another, on Tomioka's technology, or which adopted the technology some time after they opened. Some of them also hired instructors who had worked at Tomioka. But, like Tomioka spin-offs elsewhere, they were largely, as Hayami Kenzō remarked after going through the area in 1877, imitations in name only.[89] Over half of them had no more than 20 employees; only 7 had more than 40. And they were not, on the whole, notably successful: A prefectural survey taken in December 1883 showed that 32 of them had closed in the interim, 10 had been forced to retrench, and only 13 had been successful enough to expand beyond their humble beginnings.[90]

This high rate of failure was not a phenomenon unique to Nagano; at least through the 1870s, it was common to the industry as a whole. Mechanized operations were particularly susceptible to collapse; those based on Tomioka were even more so, because, no matter how simplified they were, they required a greater capital outlay for establishment and maintenance than operations that reeled by hand, or even other mechanized places. Unlike Tomioka, none of them had the benefit of an annual appropriation from the central government to tide them over during the crucial period of the year when cocoons had to be purchased, but when receipts from the sale of their thread were often late in coming. That so many filatures modeled after Tomioka failed is not, then, surprising. But it meant that Tomioka's effectiveness as a model for the silk-reeling industry was, at best, limited. Imitation means nothing in practical terms if it ends in failure.

Tomioka Filature had been expected to train women as instructors, to serve as a standard upon which mechanized silk reeling was to be based, and to deliver a profit to the public treasury. In retrospect, it is clear that it could not do all of these at the same time. Ironically, Tomioka received the most intense official scrutiny and criticism with regard to its ability to operate at a profit; in the end, this was the one area in which it clearly performed as expected. The filature's ability to function as a source of new technology was severely circumscribed by its size and sophistication, and by the way it was run. But this is precisely what a model factory is normally expected to do, and, in this context, it is necessary to consider whether Tomioka was of any significance at all to Japan's silk-reeling industry; whether it was largely a failure, or whether it actually accomplished anything.

Writing on Tomioka in 1909, Shibusawa Eiichi observed that most people decided that they could never hope to imitate very closely what the government had done, if for no other reason than that they had none of the financial security that Tomioka, as a public enterprise, enjoyed. But, Shibusawa said, Tomioka was an impetus to silk producers, encouraging them to set up filatures, which, though nothing on the order of the original, were at least mechanized.[91] In this limited, rather cautious appraisal of Tomioka's significance,

Shibusawa was correct. Tomioka's economic travails are now a matter of public record, but they were not in the late nineteenth century. Few silk producers knew of the difficulties the operation had; to most, it was Japan's silk-reeling factory par excellence. That Tomioka's position in the public eye was therefore mostly symbolic, and based more on myth than on fact, is not of much consequence here: Myths and symbols often have considerable power of their own, and they did in this case. Thus, we find producer after producer going to Tomioka to find out what its technology was about or sending his daughter there to learn how to reel silk thread by machine, or hiring instructors specifically because they had trained there. No place based on Tomioka actually matched its scale; few did so in the quality of their output. But that their owners decided to mechanize at all, at a time when the success of their efforts was by no means assured, can often be accounted for by the fact that Tomioka Filature offered them something toward which they might strive.

Mechanization unquestionably proceeded with considerable rapidity in the silk-reeling industry: By 1900, there were about 2,000 mechanized filatures in Japan, whereas only 1 had existed thirty years earlier.[92] But, though Tomioka frequently served as an inspiration of sorts, most mechanized operations were very modest undertakings. Even in the Hirano area of Nagano prefecture, the single most intensely mechanized silk-producing region in Japan, investment per reeling unit in 1885, for example, was only 5 percent of what the government had put into each of Tomioka's units.[93] Tomioka was far too sophisticated for the silk producer of ordinary means to copy closely, and, in any case, trying to copy it with any degree of exactitude was not a realistic solution to the need for increased production of raw silk as long as labor was so plentiful and capital so scarce. The simplified adaptation of Western reeling technology that prevailed during the late nineteenth century was therefore largely the result of economic necessity. Eventually, the economic advantages of mechanization became more substantial, especially as producers improved their initially crude operations. By the early 1890s, mechanized reeling units were almost twice as productive as traditional equipment, though production costs per pound were only marginally greater.[94] It is ironic that, by this time, when the silk-reeling industry had developed to the point where Tomioka might have been copied with some accuracy, the filature itself was out of date.[95]

Factors other than the sheer impossibility of matching its scale and complexity limited Tomioka's ability to function as a model. The central government could have taken steps to increase the filature's influence on the silk-reeling industry in general. Trainees could have been selected from those areas that were obviously mechanizing their operations most rapidly; the training period could have been shortened without reducing the degree of skill required; and organized attempts could have been made to ensure that silk producers willing to mechanize were given access to Tomioka's technology. None of this was done. The government's disillusionment with the filature, already apparent less than two years after it opened, meant that no real effort was made to see that Tomioka accomplished its original lofty objectives. Except for Odaka Atsutada and Hayami Kenzō, no officials with any control over Tomioka appear to have considered seriously what its functions ought properly and practically to have been and how they ought to have been accomplished. That being the case, financial concerns took precedence, and from the start, Tomioka was expected, above all, to operate at a profit. It is difficult to conceive of a more unrealistic expectation, especially if the filature was to fulfill its educational functions, and the overriding importance attached to finances made it impossible for Tomioka to function effectively as a technological model. In retrospect, Tomioka Filature reflects the hubris of a new government bent on making Japan the equal of the West and confident that, at least in the silk-reeling industry, the process would be quick and simple. It soon found otherwise.

The government's lack of interest in Tomioka's effectiveness as a technological model was, in large measure, due to the fact that the problem that had prompted the filature's establishment very quickly ceased to exist. Tomioka had been planned because of an alarming decline in raw-silk prices on the export market. This decline was attributed to a deterioration in output quality, and the Meiji government initially concluded that permanently arresting the price decline was possible only by converting to Western production methods. The qualitative problems that had caused this decline persisted to one degree or another throughout the nineteenth century, but in fact had no long-range effect on the export market. Western buyers complained loudly about the quality of Japan's raw silk, and then gave the lie to their complaints by purchasing ever-increasing amounts of the commodity, despite the lack of substantive qualitative change and regardless of the method of production. Raw-silk exports to the West increased substantially between 1868 and 1899, and the average annual price went up during all but thirteen of these years.[96] These concurrent trends meant that silk revenues from the West increased almost every year; for a government that desperately needed foreign capital for its ambitious industrialization plans yet preferred not to borrow the funds, this was what mattered. It mattered much less, if at all, how raw silk was produced as long as revenues from the export trade continued to go up. As a result, the government was able to take no more than cursory interest in the silk-reeling industry's technological development; as far as it was concerned, mechanization was a means rather than an end. In this sense, Tomioka Filature proved to be not only a technological anomaly, but an unnecessary one at that.

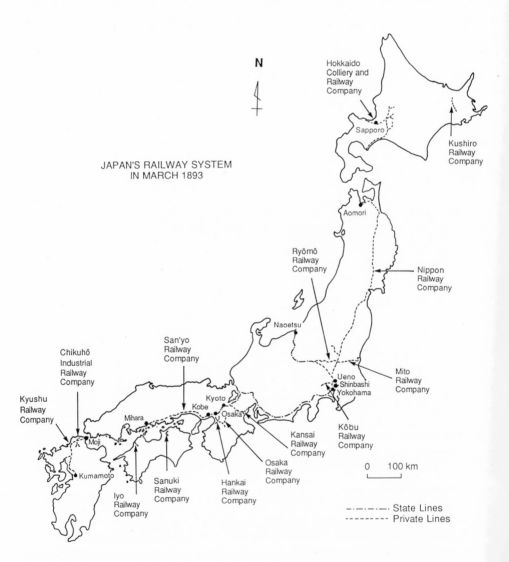

N

JAPAN'S RAILWAY SYSTEM
IN MARCH 1893

Hokkaido
Colliery and
Railway
Company

Sapporo

Kushiro
Railway
Company

Aomori

Ryōmō
Railway
Company

Nippon
Railway
Company

Naoetsu

Chikuhō
Industrial
Railway
Company

San'yo
Railway
Company

Mito
Railway
Company

Kyushu
Railway
Company

Ueno
Shinbashi
Yokohama

Kyoto
Kobe

Mihara

Osaka

Moji

Kansai
Railway
Company

Kōbu
Railway
Company

Kumamoto

Osaka
Railway
Company

Iyo
Railway
Company

Sanuki
Railway
Company

Hankai
Railway
Company

0   100 km

—·—·—·— State Lines
- - - - - - - Private Lines

Railroads in Crisis: The Financing and Management of
Japanese Railway Companies During the Panic of 1890

STEVEN J. ERICSON

The nature of joint-stock company finance and decision making constitutes a central yet unresolved issue in the study of Meiji business
history. Much of what we do know about this problem rests on analyses of the cotton spinning industry, one of the leading sectors of
Meiji industrialization. Kozo Yamamura, for example, supports his
argument for deemphasizing the role of banks in industrial financing
during the Meiji period by citing, in particular, the case of cotton
spinning firms.[1] And Nakamura Takafusa contends, mainly on the
basis of the spinning industry, that control over management decisions in Japanese companies remained largely in the hands of owner-
capitalists until late in the Meiji era.[2] Using Alfred Chandler's
schema for the evolution of modern business enterprises, this configu-
ration would place the modern sectors of the Meiji economy at

the initial stage of entrepreneurial capitalism, wherein owner-entrepreneurs act as the top decision makers in the dominant firms, which are free of dependence on outside capital and therefore of interference from the financial institutions that normally provide such funds.[3]

In these discussions, however, scant attention has been paid to the other industry that spearheaded Meiji industrial development, namely, private railways. In view of the relatively low capital requirements and small scale of management of spinning companies, it is no wonder that generalizing from such firms should result in the conclusion that Meiji business concerns relied little on external funds, whether from banks or from the government, and moved only slowly in the direction of separating management from ownership. It would not be surprising to find significantly different patterns of financing and control in more highly capitalized and operationally complex businesses such as railway companies.

This chapter focuses on the important but neglected field of private railway enterprise in order to determine whether the experience of that industry calls for revisions in current generalizations on joint-stock company funding and management during the Meiji era. The time frame I have chosen is the early 1890s. During those years, the Japanese economy was gripped by a serious recession, triggered by the financial panic that had broken out in the wake of the enterprise boom of 1886–1889. Private railways, the oldest of which dated back to 1881, had led the company boom, and, by 1890, they had surpassed the state railways in total length of line open, a position they were not to relinquish until the nationalization of the principal railway companies in 1906–1907 (see Table 1). But the Panic of 1890 and the ensuing recession, by disrupting the capital-raising mechanism of the boom years, presented railway firms with their first real test. Forcing the companies to develop alternative means of access to funds, the crisis placed in sharp relief the patterns of both railway financing and decision making on financial and related matters. Moreover, the array of capital-raising strategies to which railway concerns resorted in trying to cope with the crisis, together with the measures they had adopted during the preceding boom period, offered a model of corporate finance to Japanese joint-stock companies in general. Thus, besides illuminating the funding and control of private railways, issues significant in their own right—after all, railway firms accounted for

TABLE 1 Length of Railway Line Open, 1872–1907 (in miles)

Year	State (A)	Private (B)	Total (A+B)	B/A+B (%)
1872	18	0	18	0
1874	38	0	38	0
1876	65	0	65	0
1878	65	0	65	0
1880	98	0	98	0
1882	171	0	171	0
1884	182	81	263	30.8
1886	265	166	431	38.5
1888	506	406	912	44.5
1890	551	849	1,400	60.6
1892	551	1,320	1,871	70.6
1894	581	1,537	2,118	72.6
1896	632	1,875	2,507	74.8
1898	768	2,652	3,420	77.5
1900	950	2,905	3,855	75.4
1902	1,227	3,011	4,238	71.0
1904	1,461	3,232	4,693	68.9
1906	3,116	1,692	4,808	35.2
1907	4,453	446	4,899	9.1

Source: *Meiji shijū nendo Tetsudō Kyoku nenpō,* ed. Teishin Shō Tetsudō Kyoku (Tetsudō In, 1909), pp. 30–31.

fully one fourth of all the paid-up capital of joint-stock ventures in the early to mid-1890s[4]—this case study in "crisis management" has implications for patterns of financing and decision making in other fields as well.

The first section of this inquiry explores the nature and impact of the 1890 Panic itself, regarded by many as Japan's first modern financial crisis. The study then examines the response of the railway companies in terms of the main groups that had a say in management decisions concerning financial and construction policies. An attempt will be made to characterize those groups, whether they consisted of major stockholders, top managers, local residents, or government officials, and to determine the influence each had on the key decisions made by the railways in seeking to deal with the crisis. Following that analysis is an investigation into the actual outcome of those decisions—the variety of steps taken by the railway firms to raise construction funds during the panic and recession—and its significance for the emergency and long-term financing of those companies. In conclusion, I shall return to the broader questions raised in this introduction, as seen in light of the experience of private railways during the financial crisis of the early 1890s.

THE PANIC AND ITS AFTERMATH

The Panic of 1890 was basically a reaction to the excessive promotion and speculation accompanying the enterprise boom of the late 1880s. Ever since the beginning of the Meiji period, investment in joint-stock companies, both speculative and sound, had hinged on an installment system of stock payment, supported by the stock-collateral lending of commercial banks. Prior to the implementation of the Commercial Code in 1893, there were no legal regulations concerning the proportion of the par value of corporate shares that subscribers had to pay up at the time of a company's establishment, and fairly lenient requirements thereafter. As a result, until the practice was legally abolished in 1948, almost all joint-stock enterprises, including railway concerns, used an installment system for the payment of subscribed stock whereby shareholders would initially pay up only a portion of the par value of their shares, gradually paying up the rest as the business developed. This method enabled a company to collect payments commensurate with its immediate need for funds, thereby avoiding idle capital and reducing the weight of dividend payouts; it also lightened the burden on stockholders of paying up high-denomination shares. Moreover, commercial banks underpinned the whole system by actively lending funds to stockholders on the security of the paid-up portion of their shares.[5]

The installment-payment system and stock-collateral lending by banks greatly facilitated the founding and expansion of joint-stock companies, particularly under favorable business conditions such as prevailed after the Matsukata financial reform of the early 1880s. In so doing, these practices played a crucial role, not only in giving rise to the enterprise boom of the late 1880s, but also in bringing about its collapse. In the absence of legal provisions governing the ratio of subscribed capital that a newly established firm had to raise forthwith, the installment method of stock payment allowed companies to be set up with only a fraction of their stock actually paid up. The result was a proliferation of joint-stock ventures, many of them unstable or purely speculative. Furthermore, payment by installment and borrowing on shares made it possible for investors to oversubscribe to newly issued stock in terms of their personal resources. Such over-extended holding was masked so long as the boom continued, but any significant decline in stock prices had the potential for disrupting the supply of share capital to corporations by causing banks to balk at making further loans on shares and stockholders to default on their payments.

As calls on share capital multiplied during the course of the boom, a growing proportion of available funds became tied up in the financing of joint-stock companies, much of it in the form of fixed investment that would remain unproductive for some time to come. Private railway firms, as proponents of their nationalization would argue in 1891, represented the leading "culprits," for railways had on the average the largest capital requirement and one of the longest gestation periods among joint-stock enterprises. In fact, railway concerns accounted for nearly a third of the increase in authorized capital, and probably for an even greater share of the rise in paid-up capital, for joint-stock companies as a whole between 1887 and 1889.[6]

During 1889, the pressure exerted on the money market by the paying up of corporate shares rose sharply, as the installment payments for companies founded during the enterprise boom fell due in growing numbers that year. This heightened demand for share capital, combined with the issuance of ¥11 million in government bonds and an increase in the price of rice owing to the poor harvest of 1889, produced a tightening of the money market. As a consequence, interest rates climbed, triggering a decline in stock prices. That decline, in turn, prompted banks to stop lending on the security of shares or to insist on more collateral. As early as 4 July 1889, the *Chōya* newspaper reported a sudden increase in stock payments and a suspension of stock-collateral lending by banks "fearful lest a panic should break out among the public." These trends intensified at the very close of the year, setting off the dreaded crisis with a panic on the Tokyo Stock Exchange in early January 1890. Stock prices plummeted. By increasingly refusing to make loans on shares, banks simply added to the financial stringency and the rise in interest rates, which further depressed stock prices.[7] Caught in this vicious circle, many joint-stock companies were thrust into a serious financial crisis. A number of the speculative ventures went bankrupt or dissolved, and even solid enterprises faced difficulties in raising capital. The panic itself lasted until March 1890, after which time the money market began to ease, but the ensuing recession let up only in 1893.

Thus, the major cause of the Panic of 1890 was the speculative mania of the late 1880s, which generated a flood of unsound firms and put heavy pressure on the money market. Inasmuch as the panic represented the collapse of the mania, it did not deal that severe a blow to established companies. Yet, in view of the standard emphasis on the speculative nature of private railway enterprise during the boom, one would expect railway companies to have been hard hit by the crisis. A close examination of the data, however, reveals a more complicated picture.

Scholars who stress the speculative character of railway investment during the enterprise boom are apt to cite the critical observations of Railway Bureau Chief Inoue Masaru, who, as an outspoken advocate of state railway development, obviously had his own ax to grind. In March 1887, for example, Inoue depicted private promoters as wild-eyed speculators who had "contracted the railway disease, which has been epidemic of late," and two years later he was still harping on "the want of substantiality in the plans of railway projectors" and the prevalence of "capitalists whose sole object is to gain money by speculating in the sale and purchase of shares."[8] Certainly, speculative investors abounded during the boom, as the currency of the term *railway mania* in contemporary newspapers and journals attests, and undoubtedly they furthered a number of questionable schemes. Indeed, 20 of the 37 promoters' groups that applied for licenses to establish railway companies during the years 1886–1889 failed, 14 because their applications were rejected by the government and the rest because they were forced to disband at various stages prior to commencing construction.[9]

The important fact, however, is that nearly half these groups did succeed in establishing railway firms and that the majority of the firms already had lines open to traffic by 1890. Moreover, most of these railways, despite relying on direct and largely public stock subscriptions, managed to sell all their shares on schedule during the boom.[10] They did so by capitalizing on the very outburst of stock speculation that was giving rise to so many bubbles during that time. As M. C. Reed observes of early Victorian railways in a passage equally applicable to their mid-Meiji counterparts, speculation played an important part in "widening and deepening the sources from which railways were able to draw their capital. . . . The very possibility of speculative gains . . . attracted investors who in a more quiescent market would not have been prepared to accept the risks involved."[11] That such investors were enlisted in large numbers is suggested by the fact that, by the end of fiscal-year 1889, 62 percent of the operating railway companies' total authorized capital stock of roughly ¥45 million had been paid up.[12] As a whole, therefore, railway companies during the enterprise boom were far from the fragile schemes that some observers have made them out to be.

By the time the panic struck, private railways had made solid progress in the construction of lines. Twelve companies, all but 3 of them still in the process of extending their lines, had track open by March 1890 for a total length of 586 miles compared to 551 for the state railways.[13] The fact that these private firms were already operating lines indicates that they were by no means speculative ventures. Nevertheless, many had just recently been set up and were still in the early stages of construction. Having yet to show much in the way of profits, these companies were still struggling to win the confidence of lenders and investors. Thus, the panic found them in a much more precarious position than the older and more established firms.

Insofar as the speculative mania had markedly promoted private railway investment during the enterprise boom, the reaction to that mania had at least some impact on all the railway concerns. In particular, the decline in stock prices and the tight money situation made it extremely difficult for many of the companies' shareholders to meet payments on the outstanding portions of their subscribed stock. The plight of railway stockholders is vividly described in a petition urging the nationalization of private railways that brokers on the Tokyo Stock Exchange submitted to the Diet in late 1891:

Although their stock prices have fallen, railway companies have been steadily moving ahead with their construction work and have been urgently calling for stock payments. Even if the shareholders wish to comply with their demand, however, they are not free to do so because of the tight money market. As the enterprise mania has subsided, stock prices have dropped daily, and, even if shareholders wish to sell on the stock market and sever their relationship with the companies, they can by no means make use of the exchange when a company has given notification and payment is unfinished, the market having strict regulations to that effect. Therefore, shareholders have increasingly rushed to liquidate their holdings by incurring debts and paying up their shares; stocks have flooded the market, and prices have dropped even further, with the result that selling at a loss has become more and more frequent. Circulating capital has poured into railway shares . . . With the money market tightening all the more, almost everyone shows signs of panic.[14]

The statistical data show that the current prices of most railway shares did indeed fall, some precipitously. In February 1890, the average monthly price of San'yō Railway shares on the Osaka exchange dropped below the paid-up value of the shares, remaining there throughout the recession (see Table 2). Similarly, in March 1890, the average monthly price of Kyushu Railway shares on the Osaka exchange fell below their paid-up value, equaling or surpassing that value in only one of the remaining months that year. In December 1890, these two kinds of shares hit their lowest point for the year, San'yō shares dropping 23 percent below their paid-up value and Kyushu shares, 18 percent. Data on the average annual prices of railway shares give a rough indication of the same trend. Of the 11 kinds of railway shares listed on the Tokyo or Osaka stock exchanges or both in 1890, the prices of 8 either fell or remained below their paid-up values that year. Five of those 8 did not recover their paid-up values until after 1892.[15] Naturally, banks were reluctant to extend loans on the security of such depressed shares. The upshot was that a number of the more recently established railways were forced to suspend construction work owing to the inability of stockholders to pay up.

Several scholars have played down the difficulties railway companies as a whole faced in raising construction capital at this time. Nakanishi Ken'ichi, for example, argues that the panic had little impact on the expansion of private railways: "Overall one can see no marked decline in the pace with which capital was paid in or lines were extended."[16] The data, however, suggest otherwise. In 1889, the total paid-up capital of railway firms in operation had risen 86 percent over that of the previous year. The figure then dropped sharply during the panic and recession, falling below the 10-percent mark during the years 1892–1893 (see Table 3, Column 3). The comparable figures for length of line open show basically the same trend, albeit with a slight lag. Allowing for building time, one can see from Table

TABLE 2 Average Monthly Quotations for San'yō and Kyushu
Railway Shares, Osaka Stock Exchange,
July 1889–December 1890

Year	Month	San'yo Railway	Kyushu Railway
1889	July	¥42.19 (40)[a]	¥24.79 (20)
	August	19.65 (20)	22.80 (20)
	September	20.00 (20)	24.40 (20)
	October	20.03 (20)	24.10 (20)
	November	21.25 (20)	26.15 (20)
	December	20.75 (20)	24.40 (20)
1890	January	20.20 (20)	21.70 (20)
	February	18.10 (20)	20.05 (20)
	March	17.25 (20)	24.70 (25)
	April	16.08 (20)	23.70 (25)
	May	17.40 (20)	25.20 (25)
	June	15.80 (20)	23.85 (25)
	July	17.95 (20)	24.00 (25)
	August	17.23 (20)	22.75 (25)
	September	16.70 (20)	26.65 (30)
	October	15.55 (20)	26.05 (30)
	November	15.60 (20)	24.60 (30)
	December	15.43 (20)	24.55 (30)

Source: Takizawa Naoshichi, *Kōhon Nihon kin'yū shiron* (Yūhikaku, 1912), pp. 248–250.

Note: [a]Figures in parentheses represent paid-up values.

3, Column 2, that little new construction was undertaken during the recession.

The panic also had a noticeable effect on the profit and dividend rates of several of the operating companies. The aggregate figures reveal a definite drop in the profit rate at the time of the panic, followed by a gradual recovery during the recession years. The overall dividend rate, however, remained fairly stable through this period, with government subsidies playing a critical role in maintaining that rate, particularly in 1890 when they accounted for 44 percent of all railway company dividends (see Table 3, Columns 5, 7, and 9).

The impact exerted by the panic on railway dividends as well as profits can be characterized more precisely through analysis of the

TABLE 3 Private Railway Development and Business Results, 1888–1894

Year	Number of Operating Companies (1)	Length of Line Open (miles) (2)	Paid-up Capital (C) (¥1,000) (3)	Profit (P) (¥1,000) (4)	P/C (%) (5)	Dividend (D) (¥1,000) (6)	D/C (%) (7)	State Subsidy (S) (¥1,000) (8)	S/D (%) (9)
1888	6	406	14,997	1,127	7.5	1,342	8.9	311	23.2
1889	12	525 (29.3)a	27,943 (86.3)	1,427	5.1	1,927	6.9	648	33.6
1890	12	849 (61.7)	38,493 (37.8)	1,630	4.2	2,612	6.8	1,147	43.9
1891	13	1,166 (37.3)	43,441 (12.9)	2,122	4.9	3,099	7.1	1,017	32.8
1892	13	1,320 (13.2)	46,737 (7.6)	2,659	5.7	2,782	6.0	955	34.3
1893	15	1,368 (3.6)	48,870 (4.6)	3,470	7.1	3,725	7.6	887	23.8
1894	20	1,537 (12.4)	59,177 (21.1)	4,648	7.9	4,564	7.7	779	17.1

Sources: Tetsudō Kyoku nenpō (1909), Appendix, pp. 22–46 passim, 102; Nihon teikoku dai jūsan-dai jūshi tōkei nenkan, ed. Naikaku Shokikan-shitsu Tōkei-ka (By the Editor, 1894–1895), pp. 703 (1894), 712 (1985).

Note: aFigures in parentheses represent percentage increase over previous year.

rates of individual companies. The extent to which the crisis affected a given railway depended not only on its level of development but also on its primary source of revenue. Railways such as the Hokkaido Colliery that derived their income mainly from the conveyance of goods, especially coal, sustained a sharp drop in profit rates, as the coal-mining industry was hard hit by the recession. Also experiencing a decline or at least stagnation in their rates of profit were trunk-line firms in the early stages of construction, including the San'yō and Kansai. On the other hand, the returns of small interurban railway concerns fell little, if at all, since the demand for passenger transport, on which companies of this kind heavily relied, was much less influenced by business fluctuations than the demand for freight transport. Indeed, railways like the Kōbu and Hankai enjoyed a steady increase in their rates of profit in spite of the panic and recession. These trends are also reflected in the companies' dividend rates, with the interurban railways generally raising their rates throughout the period and most of the trunk-line firms either cutting theirs or keeping them at a low level.[17]

The financial crisis placed in a far more serious predicament unsubsidized concerns that had yet to begin operation and hence were unable as yet to offer investors any returns whatsoever to induce them to pay up their shares. The Sangū and Sōbu railways of the Kansai and Kantō areas, respectively, both came to a standstill during the early 1890s due to their inability to collect stock payments. Licensed in December 1889, the Sōbu Railway, despite having "completed arrangements to start construction,"[18] was compelled to postpone work in 1890 when a number of stockholders defaulted on their payments. The normal practice in such instances was for the company to confiscate and put up for resale the shares of delinquent stockholders, but apparently the firm was too recently established for this step to be taken. On 25 December 1890, the *Chōya* newspaper reported that "the company is planning not to adopt such an extreme measure, but to supplement [its capital] by specially inviting new stock subscriptions through a broker." This course of action notwithstanding, the firm was unable to begin construction work until 1893.

Companies with lines open to traffic were not immune to such difficulties. This was particularly true of the Kyushu and San'yō railways, which, as recently founded truck-line firms, had massive capital requirements and heavy construction loads, but nonetheless received relatively little assistance from the government. The crisis dealt these concerns a severe blow in the form of delays in both stock payments and construction work. Significantly, however, the enterprise boom immediately following the post-panic recession would again center on railway firms, reflecting the fact that, during the early 1890s, as one journal subsequently noted, "even if they did not reach their anticipated goals, relatively few companies had the misfortune of failing badly and then dissolving."[19] In fact, only one railway that had obtained a full license—the prerequisite for issuing shares in the company's name and for starting construction work—namely, the Kōshin Railway, folded on account of the financial problems it experienced during the crisis.[20] Yet, apart from the Mito Railway, which merged with the Nippon in 1892, no railway enterprise with open track disbanded during the early 1890s. Cotton spinning companies actually did not fare much worse in this regard—just two of them went bankrupt during the crisis—but they were clearly much harder hit than railway firms in terms of difficulties raising capital and sustaining profit and dividend rates.[21]

Sound enterprises to begin with, operating railways were, for the most part, never in grave peril during the crisis and, with passenger-oriented profit structures, government subsidies, and the like, managed to come through in comparatively good shape. Still, many railway firms reacted to the panic and its aftermath as though the latter did constitute a life-threatening situation. To understand fully the behavior of private railways at this time, one needs to examine the impact not only of the financial crisis itself, but also of the various groups that influenced railway-company decisions. We now turn to what was perhaps the most important such group, a railway's principal shareholders.

DECISION MAKING DURING THE CRISIS: INFLUENCES AND CONSTRAINTS

Major Railway Stockholders

THE LEADING GROUPS OF INVESTORS. During the Meiji period, private railways on the average raised about 80 percent of their financing through stock issues. This high ratio of equity capital gave shareholders a sure basis for affecting, if not determining, the business strategies of railway enterprises. By analyzing stockholders' lists, one can identify the major classes of railway investors as a first step toward elucidating the nature and degree of their impact on railway-company decision making. Unfortunately, there are few such lists available prior to 1894, but, by extrapolating backwards from the more complete record of later years against the fragmentary data for the early 1890s, one can obtain a fairly accurate picture of the principal categories of railway capitalists during the panic and recession.[22]

In analyzing the data, however, one should bear in mind certain pitfalls associated with nominal stockholding during the Meiji period. As Hoshino Takao points out, stockholders' lists often fail to indicate the real owner of a given interest or the actual size of a given investor's holdings.[23] First of all, national banks, although they purchased stock in various companies, do not appear on the stockholder's lists of those firms. The reason is that national banks evaded the prohibition against their holding corporate stock by investing in companies in the form of stock-collateral loans to their own directors and employees. In October 1890, for example, the Fourth National Bank of Niigata owned stock in the Ryōmō Railway in the name of one of its directors, Nishiwaki Kunisaburō. Nishiwaki's nominal and personal holdings in the company, amounting to 4,678 shares, made him the railway's largest shareholder with over 15 percent of its entire stock.[24]

Second, portions of the stock owned by principal shareholders were frequently held under the names of others. Under the articles of incorporation of many joint-stock companies founded during the Meiji era, restrictions were placed on the number of votes major shareholders could cast at general stockholders' meetings. In order to increase their voting power, therefore, such investors would often transfer some of their shares to associates, who would then ask the real owners to exercise their votes by proxy. In the San'yō Railway, for instance, the maximum number of votes to which an owner's holdings would entitle him was 300. Consequently, Mitsubishi, the largest stockholder in that railway with 25,490 shares, or nearly 10 percent of the total, under Iwasaki Hisaya's name in September 1891, sought to strengthen its hand in the company by distributing part of its stock among Mitsubishi executives such as Shōda Heigorō and Teranishi Seiki.[25] In this case as well as that of the Fourth National, it is difficult, if not impossible, to determine precisely the number of shares held by the owner. Not only must one identify the nominal stockholders; one must also disentangle their personal investment, if any, from their nominal holdings.

Though these questions complicate exact quantification, one can at least indicate the dominant groups of railway stockholders in the early 1890s. Probably the leading group in terms of both number of investors and total investment consisted of bankers. One is struck by the extent to which lists of major stockholders at this time are studded with bank executives. Takechi Kyōzō, in his study of railway stockholding primarily in the years 1895–1896, has found that directors of companies and chambers of commerce formed the largest class of principal railway owners, accounting for nearly 30 percent of his sample of 369 stockholders, of which bankers represented the major subcategory.[26] Available stockholders' lists for the recession years also point up the importance of bank officers as railway capitalists. In the October 1890 list of leading stockholders in the Ryōmō Railway, for example, bank executives constituted the largest group of investors whose occupations could be determined, accounting for at least 14 of the 80 holders of 100 or more shares. These 14 bankers possessed 25 percent of the railway's total stock issue.[27]

Admittedly, many railway investors who were engaged in banking were concurrently involved in other fields of activity, such as stockbroking, shipping, or manufacturing. Such was the case, for example, with Tanaka Ichibei, Imamura Seinosuke, Matsumoto Jūtarō, and Hara Rokurō, who together held over 5 percent of the San'yo's 260,000 shares in September 1891.[28] One can assume, however, that, in many instances, sizeable portions of the shares held by bank officials represented nominal holdings on behalf of the banks with which they were associated. Institutional investors, especially banks and life-insurance companies, generally begin to surface on railway stockholders' lists only in the latter half of the 1890s; national banks do so after their conversion to ordinary bank status, at which time they were able to make public their holdings of railway stock.[29] Until then, many private banks and insurance companies as well as national banks appear to have owned railway stock under their officers' names. In 1891, for instance, the Mitsui Bank apparently held 1,012 shares of San'yō Railway stock under the name of its Kobe branch manager, and the Meiji Life Insurance Company, 1,000 shares under the name of its president.[30]

The most clearly documented case of bank investment in railway stock is that of the Fifteenth National Bank's involvement in the Nippon Railway Company, Japan's first successful private railway.[31] Hugh Patrick and Kozo Yamamura have rightfully pointed out the uniqueness of this so-called "Peers' Bank," established as an investment organ for the nobility by Iwakura Tomomi and showered with special privileges by the government, and Yamamura claims that one should therefore exclude this institution from discussion of the role of banks in industrial financing during the Meiji period.[32] Yet, as Hoshino has shown, the Fifteenth National, like the Nippon Railway with which it was so closely tied, gradually lost the favored status it had enjoyed at its founding. In particular, following the revocation of its most important privileges with the revision of the National Bank Act in 1881, the bank came to operate by and large under the same constraints as the other national banks. Moreover, although the Peers' Bank was apparently exempted from the prohibition against corporate stockholding by national banks, it nevertheless complied with this regulation and, like other national banks, invested in railway stocks under the names of its directors and employees.[33] Regardless of the bank's degree of uniqueness one simply cannot omit from consideration of bank financing at least of railway companies an institution that, through its investment in the Nippon Railway alone, accounted for a minimum of 9 percent and more likely 15 percent of the total paid-up capital of private railways in the early 1890s.[34]

According to Hoshino, at the time of the establishment of the Nippon Railway in 1881, the Fifteenth National Bank accepted 26,000 shares in the company with a par value of ¥1,300,000, or 22 percent of the railway's first stock issue, making it the Nippon's largest stockholder.[35] Because of the ban on corporate stockholding by national banks, however, the Fifteenth National concealed its investment in the Nippon Railway by having its shares held under the names of former daimyo and samurai who were directors and employees of the bank. It then advanced stock-collateral loans to these individuals in order to finance installment payments on its shares. In 1881, the Nippon Railway required stockholders to make an initial payment of 1 yen per share. The nominal holders of the shares owned by the Fifteenth National thus had to pay in ¥26,000, which was precisely the amount of stock-collateral loans made by the bank in 1881. The same correlation held at the end of the following year, when the sum of installment payments on Nippon Railway stock that the bank's nominal holders had to have met—¥260,000—equaled the total amount of funds lent by the bank on the collateral of corporate shares. Thereafter, the Fifteenth National began to make loans on shares other than those it possessed in the Nippon Railway, so that, by the end of 1892, the minimum amount that the bank had to have paid in on its share of Nippon Railway stock, assuming that it had continued to pay up its initial subscription and had accepted all three of its capital-increase allotments since then, had declined to about one fourth of its outstanding stock-collateral loans.[36]

In May 1897, however, when the Fifteenth National became an ordinary bank and made public its ownership of Nippon Railway stock, it held some 260,000 shares in the railway—about a third of the total—with a combined paid-up value of around ¥10 million.[37] That is over one and a half times the minimum investment the bank had to have made by the middle of 1897 under the aforementioned assumptions. This fact indicates that the Fifteenth National had increased its equity participation in the Nippon Railway by purchasing additional shares beyond its capital-increase allotments. It further suggests that, in 1892, the proportion of the bank's outstanding stock-collateral loans that actually represented investment in Nippon Railway shares owned by the bank was in fact closer to one half than to one quarter. The Fifteenth National thus maintained its position as Japan's leading railway shareholder, despite the proliferation of railway companies during the Meiji era.[38]

A second major group of railway stockholders, significant in terms not of their numbers but of the level of their investment, comprised the future zaibatsu builders, particularly Mitsubishi and Mitsui. Mitsubishi was the second largest shareholder in private railways throughout the period until the nationalization of 1906–1907. By the early 1890s, it had considerably narrowed the gap between its holdings of railway stock and those of the Fifteenth National Bank. In 1891, whereas the Fifteenth National held at least 79,000 shares in the Nippon Railway, Mitsubishi had over 28,000 shares in the San'yo, more than 11,000 in the Nippon, and possibly over 22,000 in the Kansai, Kyushu, and Chikuhō Industrial railways combined.[39] (All these shares had par values of 50 yen.)

Mitsui embarked on large-scale investment in railways somewhat later than Mitsubishi, although, by 1893, it had surpassed the Imperial Household to become the third largest stockholder in railway companies, a position it held until the 1906–1907 nationalization.[40] Mitsui did enter the recession with roughly a 1-percent interest— 3,000–4,000 shares—in the Nippon Railway and a 3-percent interest in the Ryōmō.[41] But, as for the two companies that would eventually be the primary targets of its railway investment activities, Mitsui under the names of its representatives fails to appear on an 1894 list of leading stockholders in the Hokkaido Colliery and Railway and barely does so on the 1891 list for the San'yō Railway.[42] On the other hand, Mitsui in the early 1890s may have had as many as 8,125 shares in the Kyushu Railway, a number second only to Mitsubishi, and, by 1893, it had also become the second largest stockholder in the San'yō, with 17,399 shares compared to the 32,220 held by Iwasaki Hisaya.[43]

Another major class of railway stockholders was composed of former daimyo and aristocrats, including members of the Imperial Household Ministry. Such investors, together with politicians and government bureaucrats, constitute the second largest group in Takechi's sample, representing 11 percent of the total.[44] With a 10-percent interest in the Hokkaido Colliery and Railway, approximately a 2-percent interest in the Nippon, and minor holdings in one or two smaller companies, the Imperial Household was the third largest shareholder in private railways during at least the first two years of the recession.[45] Railway financing by members of the nobility likewise centered in the heavily subsidized Nippon and Hokkaido Colliery. In the Nippon Railway, besides the huge sums of money based on daimyo commutation bonds that were channeled through the Fifteenth National Bank, nobles sank in personal funds around 900,000 yen, equivalent to about 16 percent of the company's total stock issue, at the time of its establishment.[46]

A fourth category of major railway stockholders encompassed industrial capitalists, exclusive of bank and emergent zaibatsu executives. Members of this group, men who invested in railways funds derived primarily from mining and manufacturing, fall into several of the categories set up by Takechi, so it is difficult to use his typology to make any estimate of their probable numbers. These investors hailed chiefly from the Tokyo and Osaka areas, although local industrialists, such as the Kyushu coal-mine operators who helped finance the Chikuhō Industrial Railway, figured prominently in certain lines. Of the big-city capitalists, Fujita Denzaburō, who was involved in shipping as well as in various industrial enterprises in Osaka, had motives for investing in private railways that were more in tune with those of local businessmen than of his metropolitan colleagues. Like the Kyushu mining entrepreneurs, who poured money into railways mainly to secure improved transport and enlarged markets for their coal, Fujita was principally interested in the indirect benefits resulting from his railway investment, specifically, in the railway-building contracts that would accrue to his construction firm.[47] More typical of the big-city industrial capitalists was Amenomiya Keijirō. A diversified entrepreneur in the Tokyo area, Amenomiya took a strong interest in railway finance mainly out of a desire to reap direct returns in the form of stock dividends. By the early 1890s, with substantial holdings in the highly profitable Hokkaido Colliery and Kōbu railways, he was well on the way to earning his eventual sobriquet of "private railway king."[48]

A final group of leading railway shareholders consisted of capitalists who financed their purchases of railway shares using income drawn primarily from the more traditional activities of land ownership, trade, and moneylending. Some 7 percent of Takechi's sample comprises stockholders whose sole occupation was landholding, although the addition of large landlords who were at the same time bankers, industrialists, and the like raises the figure to over 20 percent.[49] Perhaps the biggest railway stockholder among the pure landlord capitalists was Moroto Seiroku of Mie prefecture, who invested heavily in Kyushu railways. Merchants and moneylenders together constitute 12 percent of Takechi's sample; again, however, major railway investors who were involved concurrently in trade or money lending and other fields come under several other of Takechi's categories.[50] The leading railway capitalist among traders at this time—and eventually one of the top investors among all groups—was Tanaka Shinshichi, a Yokohama cotton-yarn merchant.[51] A related field of activity widely engaged in by railway investors, although one might quibble with its inclusion under the rubric "traditional," was the stock- and commodity-exchange business. Takechi identifies 26 stockholders in his sample as having been involved exclusively in brokerage activities. Broadening the category to encompass brokers and exchange directors who, like Tanaka Shinshichi, were at the same time active in other fields results in a near doubling of this number.[52] The prominence of this group of shareholders, almost half of them stockbrokers, bespeaks the speculative character of a good portion of railway investment.

Major railway stockholders engaged in the brokerage business naturally tended to come from Tokyo and Osaka with their relatively developed markets in commodities and securities. So did those involved in trade and, to a much less extent, in land ownership. Yet the landlord-merchant category represents another group, in addition to that of industrial capitalists, in which one would expect to find fairly extensive participation by local investors eager to reduce transport costs and to expand markets for locally produced rice, raw silk, and so on. Indeed, descriptions of the sources of railway share capital during the Meiji period commonly list capitalists residing along the projected routes of railway lines as forming one of the principal classes of railway investors, especially in the case of smaller companies serving local markets. Sugiyama Kazuo, for example, states that "most local railways were established and planned by local notables (*meibōka*) such as landlords and merchants."[53] Certainly, such investors played an important role in the promotion not only of local companies such as the Ryōmō and Chikuhō Industrial, but also of trunk-line firms such as the San'yō and Kyushu. Moreover, local landlords and merchants did on occasion become major stockholders of railways that ran through their communities. For instance, Onishi Shin'yuemon, a large landlord and sake brewer of Hyōgo prefecture, helped promote as well as finance the San'yo Railway, in which he was the tenth largest stockholder with almost a 1-percent interest in September 1891.[54] In the Ryōmō Railway, which traversed the textile manufacturing districts of Gumma and Tochigi prefectures north of Tokyo, local merchants connected with the textile industry were represented by at least 8 of the company's top 80 stockholders in October 1890. Together, these 8 traders held nearly 6 percent of the railway's total stock.[55] Meanwhile, "local" merchants were naturally heavily involved in the financing of the Osaka and Kōbu railways, since parts of these companies' lines lay within the city limits of Osaka and Tokyo, respectively.

Yet, looking more closely at the geographical distribution of investors and expanding the field of vision to encompass small and medium shareholders, one obtains a very different picture of local invest-

ment. In the Kōbu Railway, for example, in March 1891, textile manufacturers, raw-silk dealers, and other investors from the Santama
region, at the western end of the line opposite Tokyo, accounted for
less than one quarter of the total number of stockholders and barely
8 percent of all the shares.[56] In the case of the Ryōmō Railway, a prefectural breakdown of the stockholders in 1890 reveals that Tokyo prefecture held first place with almost half the total, followed by Tochigi
and Gumma, the prefectures in which the line was situated, together
with over one quarter. In terms of percentage of total stock
accounted for, Tokyo again topped the list with some 39 percent;
Tochigi and Gumma, however, came a distant fourth and fifth, respectively, with only 18 percent of the total combined.[57]

These examples point up the need to qualify the notion of the
importance of local investment in smaller railways, at least for the
early 1890s. Takechi presents data indicating that, by the mid-1890s,
local financing of such railways had increased substantially, especially
with the proliferation of local lines during the second railway boom.
Even in the established Ryōmō Railway, 19 of the top 45 stockholders hailed from Tochigi and Gumma in 1896, whereas only 10 had
done so in 1890.[58] Sugiyama suggests that this trend continued into
the mid-1900's, by which time there was "extensive participation [in
railway finance] by local men of wealth, particularly landlords and
capitalists residing along railway lines."[59] However, practically all of
the evidence for the panic and recession years as well as for the preceding boom period attests to the limited scale of local investment,
even though most railways established during this heyday of trunk-
railway incorporation were actually local in character. In the late
1880s and early 1890s, whether because of the shortage or timidity of
local capital, railway stockholders living along the line in which they
invested rarely held enough shares as a group to give them majority
ownership in the operating company.

Even in cases where local capitalists did take the lead at this time
in the promotion and initial financing of railway firms, the companies concerned tended to draw increasingly on sources of capital
outside the areas served by their lines. For example, the local coal-
mine owners who founded the Chikuhō Industrial Railway in July
1889 faced serious financial problems with the outbreak of the 1890
Panic. According to an employee of the railway, "Since the majority
of stockholders were all having difficulty meeting the expenses of

their main business—coal mining, they could not possibly afford to pay up their shares in the railway, which was from the beginning [only] a side business"; consequently, the company "could not avoid changes among its stockholders."[60] At the end of September 1889, residents of the Chikuhō region accounted for 48 percent of the total number of stockholders in the railway. By the end of March 1890, this figure had dropped to 37 percent, at which time most of the investors holding 200 or more shares in the company were nobles and other capitalists from Tokyo.[61] The relative decline in local investment occasioned by the financial crisis may have been just a temporary departure from the trend suggested by Takechi and Sugiyama, though this certainly was not the case with the Chikuhō Industrial, whose connection with the coal-mining industry made it a prime target of investment by Mitsubishi in the 1890s and hence something of an anomaly among local railways. Nevertheless, the general tendency of railway companies to rely heavily on capital from distant urban centers, especially Tokyo and Osaka, had, as we shall see, serious implications for railway business strategy during the panic and recession.

STOCKHOLDER INFLUENCE ON RAILWAY COMPANY POLICY. This overview of the occupational and geographical distribution of railway stockholders during the early 1890s points to the conclusion that private railways had attracted investors who were by and large cautious and risk-avoiding. To be sure, as a result of the mania preceding the panic, railway investment included a significant risk-taking component in the form of short-term, speculative finance, as suggested by the large number of stockholders in Takechi's sample from the second railway boom. Risk taking in a far different sense from such passive, impersonal investment was that of local capitalists and many non-local merchants and industrialists, including the emergent zaibatsu. Presumably, these investors were more concerned with the external economies of railway building than with the rate of direct return on their investment.

The vast majority of railway share capital, however, represented an investment attitude that fell in between these two extremes. Like the speculators, investors of this persuasion—bankers, nobles, and most other big-city capitalists—had their eye primarily on profits, though in the form of steady dividends rather than capital gains; yet, generally, they also had a long-term commitment to the interests of particular companies and, as we shall see, frequently took part in their management. On the other hand, to the extent that such capitalists were from distant urban centers and were unlikely to share in the external benefits accompanying railway development, their vested interest in the companies they helped to finance, except for the few who made railways their career, was rather qualified and their sense of ownership closer to that of speculative investors than of local capitalists.

Railway companies drew bankers and nobles, in particular, by offering safe and remunerative investment opportunities. One reason railways had such attraction (aside from government subsidization in the case of the large, trunk-line firms) was that most of them centered their operations on passenger transport, and therefore business cycles exerted relatively little impact on their revenues and dividends. As indicated earlier, this was especially true of interurban lines such as the Kōbu and Hankai railways, whose dividends were stabilized at a comparatively high level because of the constant or rising demand for passenger transport in the more densely populated parts of the country. In the case of the Kyushu, San'yō, and Kansai railways, however, the passenger orientation of their business was of little advantage to them at the time of the panic when they were still far from completing their lines and received only moderate or no subsidies from the government. For these companies, the expectation that, once the lines were finished, shareholders would enjoy stable but high dividends, though based increasingly on freight income, seems to have been the operative factor in drawing cautious yet profit-seeking investors. Such capitalists had good reason, therefore, to push for completion of railway construction work; nevertheless, when faced with a choice, as Sugiyama puts it, "they naturally sought security rather than positive growth in the enterprise."[62]

The tendency toward risk avoidance and profit maximization on the part of railway investors had several consequences for railway company policy during the panic and recession. First, railway firms were increasingly pressed by shareholders to economize. Such retrenchment involved cutting back, not only on operating outlays so as to increase net income, but also on capital investment so as to reduce immediate demand for stock payments. One form of the latter economy was curtailment of construction costs. Albert Fishlow, writing of antebellum American railways, offers a positive appraisal of such economizing. In the United States, according to Fishlow, cheap construction methods constituted one of several procedures that served to maximize the rate of return on railway investment and hence to make railway projects more attractive to private investors. Fishlow states that "engineering considerations always ranked second to early completion, as the small extent of tunneling and double tracking, among other characteristics, bear witness"; these and other building practices enabled railway firms not only to foreshorten the gestation period, but also "to economize on the absolute quantities of capital needed. Durability was sacrificed for lower capital costs."[63] In sum, these methods helped reduce the huge capital requirements of railway construction, thereby easing railway companies' access to needed funds. Much of what Fishlow says here of American private railways applies equally to their Japanese counterparts during the Meiji period. In Meiji railways as well, the use of high gradients, single tracking, and the like represented efforts to lessen the difficulty of raising construction capital by minimizing expenditures on plant. Such practices, which began before the 1890 Panic, were to a large degree simply ways in which railway firms coped as best they could with an underdeveloped capital market.

Nevertheless, during the crisis years of the early 1890s, economy measures of this sort appear at times to have been carried to such an extreme that they ultimately proved detrimental to the companies concerned. Such was the case, for instance, with the Kyushu Railway. A committee appointed to investigate the company's business affairs in 1899 reported that, from its founding in 1888 until the Sino-Japanese War of 1894–1895, the Kyushu Railway had been compelled by stockholders "to make its policy the curtailment of construction expenses to the fullest extent possible."[64] As another observer put it, "The Kyushu Railway was dominated from the beginning by the vulgar view that it should economize on construction expenditures"; such economizing reached a peak during the recession, when the company left various facilities in an "excessively makeshift" state and employed extremely steep gradients in building its line.[65] The 1899 committee remarked that Hermann Rumschoettel, the German engineer employed as an adviser by the railway, "knew from the start that the [company's construction] plans were inadequate and predicted that the firm would some day regret it"; under pressure from its shareholders, however, the railway was in the end forced to proceed "as if it were carrying out temporary construction work."[66] And, just as

Rumschoettel had anticipated, the company in later years had to put out enormous sums of money in order to offset the shortcomings of its original plans.

Meanwhile, the San'yō Railway witnessed another form of stockholder-induced retrenchment of capital expenditure, namely, a lowering of fixed investment in rolling stock. In anticipation of future demand, President Nakamigawa had imported large quantities of passenger and freight cars from Britain, especially during 1890–1891, when the number of cars rose from 270 to 684. Nakamigawa's policy was to spare no expense in order to obtain rolling stock of the highest quality. Accordingly, all the cars he purchased featured state-of-the-art vacuum brakes, making the San'yō the first private railway to use such equipment.[67] Once Nakamigawa resigned in October 1891, however, the company was "dominated by the Osaka school of economization."[68] Osaka capitalists, who together held a majority interest in the railway and had long been clamoring for retrenchment, prevailed on the firm to sell off much of the rolling stock that Nakamigawa had imported. Thus, in 1892, the company sold to the government Railway Bureau and the Nippon Railway about a third of its freight and passenger cars on the grounds that the previous management "had made unnecessary purchases."[69] As with the Kyushu Railway and its cheap-construction policy, though, the San'yō would eventually pay for its decision to economize on rolling stock. For, during the post-Sino-Japanese-War boom, the company faced a shortage of cars and had to buy back for over twice the sale price those it had unloaded only a few years earlier.

A second result of the cautious investment behavior of railway shareholders was that, once the recession set in, they were quick to demand suspension of installment payments and construction work alike. In early 1891, for instance, over 100 stockholders in the Kyushu Railway petitioned the company to that effect. The firm's officers agreed to accept their demands in view of the financial crisis. Finance Minister Matsukata Masayoshi, in reporting his approval of the company's application for an extension of its construction deadlines, quoted Kyushu Railway President Takahashi Shinkichi as explaining:

One after another, the majority of principal stockholders from Tokyo, Osaka, and so on have requested suspension of the construction work because of the tight money market and the difficulty of paying up shares. Since the circumstances are unavoidable, the board of directors has voted to postpone [the deadlines].[70]

Later that year, however, stockholders pressured the railway to apply for a second extension. In his application, which the authorities approved in April 1892, President Takahashi again suggested that big-city capitalists represented the driving force behind the railway's decision for postponement:

Since finance is still not smooth and the value of the stock continues to decline, the principal stockholders from Tokyo, Osaka, and so on have one after another requested suspension of the construction work, citing the difficulty of paying up their shares, and, because raising construction funds . . . would only give rise to various complaints, there is no prospect of proceeding smoothly.[71]

Another consequence of the conservative character of railway investors, and perhaps the clearest expression of stockholder domination of railway firms, was the tendency for profits to be paid out almost completely as dividends. In the Kyushu Railway, for instance, dividends accounted for all the profits and subsidies for 1889 and apparently for 1890 as well. In the following year, ¥3,000, or 1 percent of the profits and subsidies, was applied to directors' bonuses, ¥45 to carryover, and the rest to dividends. The year 1892 was the first in which the company put profits into reserves, although the amount allocated for that purpose—¥3,400—represented only 1.5 percent of the railway's net income. Beginning in 1893, the company raised the reserve rate to a more substantial 4–5 percent of annual profits.[72] Nonetheless, the overwhelming majority of those profits continued, as before, to be paid out as dividends.

Other railways experienced a similar pattern of profit distribution; for example, the Osaka and Kansai, both founded in 1888, did not begin to put profits into reserves until 1891 and 1893, respectively, and other firms generally allotted only nominal amounts for that purpose in the early 1890s. The major exception was the Nippon Railway, which routinely allocated for reserves around 5 percent of its profits and subsidies during the recession. The Nippon, of course, was a well-established company with a healthy cash flow, thanks in part to generous government subvention, and it could well afford to build up its reserves. By contrast, younger firms could spare little, if any, of their profits other than for dividends, what with the need to attract investors and encourage them to meet installment deadlines during the critical early stages of construction. Moreover, as Patrick points out, the railways had to satisfy the demand of stockholders, who relied to a great extent on bank loans to pay up their shares, for "dividend payouts at least sufficient to cover the interest charges on the loans"; most companies at this time had profit rates that were just equal to or less than the loan interest rate, "so profits tended to be paid out fully."[73]

The railways were also constrained in their dividend policy by the conservative attitudes or, as Patrick puts it, "the relatively short-run time horizons of many investors, . . . who preferred to receive profits as income rather than plow them back as retained earnings."[74] Such attitudes were slow to change. Whereas in 1890 the combined reserves of railway companies amounted to 1.3 percent of their total paid-up capital, in 1900, after a decade of growth in profit rates, the figure had risen to only 2 percent.[75] The comparable figure for spinning firms in 1900, following an equally remarkable period of business expansion, was about 9 percent.[76] As a proportion of equity and debt, however, the reserve rates of railways and spinning companies were somewhat closer, owing to the latter's substantially heavier dependence on borrowed capital. Thus, cautious investment behavior characterized both of the leading sectors of Meiji industrialization well beyond the early years of relatively low profitability. This fact strongly suggests that, during the early 1890s, stockholder conservatism was no less important than were stagnant profit rates in determining railway company policy on dividend payout.

Railway Managers

The extent to which the risk-avoiding and profit-seeking proclivities of investors affected railway-company decision making during the early 1890s was a function not only of the strength of those attitudes but also of the degree of overlap between management and ownership. The earliest available set of roughly contemporaneous lists of top managers and major stockholders of private railways established prior to 1893 dates from the year 1896, when, if anything, one would expect to find fewer principal owner-capitalists among company officers than there were during the recession. Analysis of these lists suggests that the separation of management from ownership and the rise of a professional managerial class were still very much in their early stages during the first half of the 1890s.[77] Most top managers at that time appear to have been drawn from the aforementioned groups of major stockholders and hence shared their cautious views on business strategy. In fact, almost every one of the individuals cited above in illustration of those groups served as a senior executive of one or more railway companies during the early 1890s. This helps explain why, with one or two notable exceptions, there was surprisingly little tension between managers and owner-capitalists over corporate policy during the crisis and, more specifically, why shareholders were able to influence that policy to the point of dominating it, as revealed in corporate decisions on installment payments, dividend payouts, and the like.

Admittedly, to be eligible for a directorship in a joint-stock company during the Meiji period, one generally had to be a shareholder with a specified minimum interest in the enterprise, such as 50 or 100 shares. Railway firms were no exception. The articles of incorporation of the Nippon Railway, for example, stipulated that its directors be elected from among holders of 100 or more shares in the company; the cutoff was raised to 200 shares in 1900.[78] The San'yō Railway made this same change much earlier, obtaining government approval to increase its officers' minimum holding requirement from 100 to 200 shares in June 1889.[79] This revision meant that the company's directors were ipso facto included on its 1891 list of "major stockholders," broadly defined. Although this roll covered less than 15 percent of the railway's total number of shareholders, there was still a vast difference in holdings even within this list between a director like Fujita Denzaburō with 300 shares or a 0.1-percent interest in the firm and one like Ōtsuka Osamu, the third largest stockholder with 4,935 shares or a 1.9-percent interest in the company.[80] Indeed, President Nakamigawa, who held 64th place on the list with 803 shares, is described by the recent compilers of his biographical materials as "just a minor stockholder," on which point, among others, "he was an exceptional and remarkable figure as a manager of the Meiji era."[81] In addition, his successor, Matsumoto Jūtarō, the San'yō's 18th largest shareholder in April 1892 with 1,400 shares, is represented by Sugiyama as a top manager whose "character as an owner-type president was extremely weak."[82]

Whether these men had uncommonly small holdings for railway

executives at the time is debatable. Four of the 9 directors of the San'yō Railway in September 1891, for instance, possessed fewer shares than Nakamigawa, while, in October 1890, President Nara- hara of the Ryōmō Railway was only the 55th largest stockholder in that company with all of 100 shares.[83] Nonetheless, judging from the data for 1896, one can probably assume that over a third of the pres- idents and directors of private railways during the early 1890s num- bered among the top 10 shareholders in their firms; over half of them, among the top 30. This distribution would mean that Matsu- moto was fairly typical of railway-company officers in terms of his stockholder rank in the San'yō, but one might question from the standpoint of the absolute, if not of the relative, magnitude of his share the claim that his interest in that company was in fact weak.

Nakamigawa, for his part, may not have been unusual among rail- way managers in the size of his holdings either; however, he definitely was unique both in the progressiveness of his policies and in the amount of friction his pursuit of those policies generated between management and ownership in the San'yō Railway. As sug- gested earlier, Osaka led all prefectures in terms of the number of shares it accounted for in the San'yō in 1891, with Hyōgo prefecture occupying third place after Tokyo. Five Osaka investors and two from Hyōgo counted among the railway's top 10 shareholders that year.[84] The Kansai capitalists had originally intended that a local gov- ernment official, Murano Sanjin, become president of the company. In addition, they had initially planned to lay the line only from Kobe to Himeji, a section equivalent to one tenth the railway's eventual mileage, and one that "would be easy to build and certain to bring profits."[85] The government, however, set as its condition for licens- ing the railway the extension of the proposed line to Shimonoseki. In order to meet this requirement, the promoters solicited a major investment from Mitsubishi, which, in turn, appears to have made its participation contingent on the appointment of its candidate for the presidency, Nakamigawa.

Duly elected president of the railway in April 1888, Nakamigawa introduced management techniques that were highly innovative for the times; in Tsunehiko Yui's view, "his activities as manager were idi- osyncratic and epoch-making."[86] Of particular interest here are Nakamigawa's positive investment policies. Besides purchasing sufficient land for double-tracking and importing the most up-to-date rolling stock from England, Nakamigawa insisted on building the line to exacting engineering standards. Specifically, he required that curves be no more than 15 degrees and gradients, 1/100 or less, the latter stipulation for which he earned the epithet "One Hundredth (*wan handoretsu*)" from his beleaguered engineers.[87]

Nakamigawa adhered to these policies even at the height of the recession, despite pressure from many stockholders to retrench on construction expenditures. The financial crisis served only to sharpen the differences between Nakamigawa and these investors, as the tight money market, combined with the railway's poor business results, made shareholders all the more unwilling, if not unable, to support the president's expansionary programs. Criticism of those programs mounted, especially among the major Osaka investors, who were openly dissatisfied with the low dividend rate as well as the princely salaries enjoyed by Nakamigawa and his staff. In October 1890, these owners managed to secure the appointment of one of their number, Ōtsuka Osamu, to the board of directors. No sooner had he joined the board than Ōtsuka, according to one observer, "voiced opposition to President Nakamigawa on everything."[88] In the end, he and his fellow "Osaka-style economizers," in the words of another contemporary, "conspired with the [other] stockholders to set up an investigative committee and intervened in the internal affairs of the company." As this commentator put it, the "mediocre men" on this committee "concluded that the pay of the staff was too high and decided that, with the exception of the engineers, the salaries of office workers earning ¥50 or more a month should be curtailed."[89]

Nakamigawa himself proved to be the prime target of this retrenchment drive. A San'yō employee later recalled that, while Nakamigawa was in Tokyo on company business in 1891, the directors held a special meeting, attended by Vice-President Murano San-jin, and moved to cut the president's monthly salary from ¥400 to ¥250.[90] As Yui notes somewhat understatedly, "This was obviously tantamount to an expression of non-confidence in Nakamigawa."[91] Finding it increasingly difficult to carry out his programs in the face of stockholder interference and personal attacks, Nakamigawa finally resigned from the presidency in October 1891 to become full-time director of the Mitsui Bank. Following his departure, the Osaka investors gained control over the San'yō board, increasing their representation from 2 to 4 of the 9 directorships.[92] Murano took charge of the management until the appointment of a new president in April 1892. Reversing Nakamigawa's course, he "adopted an extremely conservative policy," one more in keeping with the cautious views of the major stockholders, under which he "raised passenger fares, abolished the biennial bonuses for employees, and reduced the staff in the head office."[93]

Nakamigawa was clearly ahead of his times in his aggressive championship of strategies for business expansion, for both the nature of his programs and the intensity of stockholder resistance to them were unparalleled at the time. Yet, two factors suggest that one should not attribute the progressive features of San'yō management solely to Nakamigawa's genius and foresight, as an uncritical reading of his biographical materials might lead one to do. For one thing, Nakamigawa was probably not alone in his advocacy of expensive construction methods. At least on that score, he no doubt received strong backing from one of the founders and directors of the railway, Fujita Denzaburō. For, although a colleague of the Osaka "economizers," Fujita, as the chief building contractor for the line, stood to gain immensely from large construction outlays. Second, the San'yō faced far greater competition from alternative forms of transport than any other railway. Specifically, the firm was at the outset "constantly overwhelmed by steamship companies"[94] whose vessels plied the Inland Sea routes adjacent to the course of the railway. In order to vie with these shipping firms, the San'yō was compelled from the first to offer rates substantially below those set by the government; many of the other aspects of Nakamigawa's program, such as the use of cars equipped with vacuum brakes, can be seen as attempts to provide superior service and thereby to draw traffic away from the company's formidable rivals at sea. Long after Nakamigawa's resignation, competition from shipping remained a powerful impetus for innovation in the San'yō, as the railway continued to be the industry leader in the introduction of dining and sleeping cars and the like.[95]

Yet, despite the rather unusual set of circumstances affecting the management of the San'yō Railway, the fact remains that it was Nakamigawa who first established the kinds of policies necessitated by those circumstances. Moreover, the adoption of those types of policies, in the short run at least, was by no means a foregone conclusion, as evidenced by the sudden turnabout in strategy immediately following Nakamigawa's departure. At any rate, his programs contrasted sharply with those of an owner-executive like Imamura Seinosuke, who in terms of his attitudes was much more representative of top railway mangers in the early 1890s. As a director of the Kyushu Railway, for example, Imamura appears to have played a key role in that company's adoption of a retrenchment program in 1891. According to Kyushu President Takahashi Shinkichi, Imamura from the beginning urged him "to try to curtail expenditures and to raise the dividend."[96] Once the panic struck, his biographer notes, Imamura stepped up his pressure and, "as a temporary expedient, advised President Takahashi to reduce the company's operations, to take a very conservative policy, and to endeavor to maintain the status quo."[97] His biographer further claims that Imamura was also behind the stockholders' petition demanding a second postponement of the railway's scheduled construction work in late 1891. As this source puts it, the director privately persuaded his acquaintances among the owners to come out with the petition, suggesting that management's decision to suspend construction was by no means forced upon it by recalcitrant shareholders. On the other hand, Imamura himself was apparently a leading investor in the company. In this capacity, he would have had a strong personal motive for desiring an increase in dividends as well as a delay in the collection of stock payments, his own disavowal of self-interest notwithstanding.[98]

Imamura exemplified senior railway executives in mid-Meiji, not only in the kinds of policies he supported and in his dual status as director and principal stockholder, but also in his primary occupation. As a banker with experience in the stock-exchange business, he fits into the mainstream of top managers, who, as we have noted, came largely from the predominant classes of major railway investors. By contrast, Nakamigawa was an exceptional figure in this regard as well, having as he did a background in journalistic management. A more significant category of senior railway officers not included among the dominant investor groups consisted of former public servants, specifically, government bureaucrats and state-railway engineers. Among the top executives with experience in state administration were Narahara Shigeru, president of the various companies in the Nippon Railway network, who had served as a prefectural governor and a secretary in several government ministries, and Takahashi Shinkichi, who resigned his post as head of the Commerce Bureau in the Ministry of Agriculture and Commerce to become the first president of the Kyushu Railway.[99]

The prominence of such managers at this time reflected the necessity, especially marked in the case of trunk-line firms, of obtaining state assistance and cooperation in the early stages of the enterprise and thus the desirability of securing a chief executive with connections in the central bureaucracy. No doubt railway companies also recruited government bureaucrats as a way to make up for the shortage of qualified administrators in the private sector. From the authorities' standpoint, the placement of public officials in the companies as top managers was a means of exercising influence and ensuring accountability during the period of state subvention. In fact, the government itself appointed several of the ex-bureaucrat executives in the private railways. Takahashi, for example, owed his position to a request by the promoters of the Kyushu Railway that the authorities select the company's president.[100] In the case of the Hokkaido Colliery and Railway, which at the outset was almost as closely tied to government policy as the Nippon, the state reserved for itself the power to appoint and dismiss for the duration of the government subsidy not only the president but the vice-president and directors as well.[101] Under this authority, the government named as the first president Hori Motoi, who had worked as a department head in the Hokkaido government office.[102]

State railway engineers, with their virtual monopoly of railway technology in the early years, were active from the beginning in private railway companies as technical advisers or chief engineers. While some were on loan from the railway bureaucracy, others, in *amakudari* fashion, resigned from their official posts to enter private employment. It was generally not until later in the 1890s, however, that former government engineers like Minami Kiyoshi and Sengoku Mitsugu moved into managerial positions, as a new generation of engineers emerged to take their place as technical functionaries in the companies. Two government engineers who did make the transition to private railway manager in the early 1890s were Hirai Seijirō and Mōri Jūsuke. Originally an employee of the Hokkaido state railways, Hirai had left government service in 1888 to supervise the construction successively of the Osaka, Sanuki, and Hokkaido Colliery railways; in January 1892, he was appointed a director of the Hokkaido Colliery.[103] Mōri, on the other hand, had overseen the construction of a section of the Nippon Railway while in the employ of the Railway Bureau in the early 1880s. He resigned from the Bureau in 1885 to become chief engineer of the Nippon and was promoted to vice-president in April 1892.[104] A unique variant on the engineer-to-manager pattern is provided by Shiraishi Naoji, an engineering professor at Tokyo Imperial University from 1887 to 1890. During his tenure at the university, Shiraishi served as chief engineer of the nascent Kansai Railway, then resigned his faculty position to become the third president of the company in October 1890.[105]

As full-time salaried managers with little share in their companies' ownership, ex-government officials like Shiraishi brought a degree of professionalism to the top management of private railways. For the most part, however, such senior executives had to concentrate on the routine administration of their firms, since railway companies in general had yet to achieve a scale of operation such as to require extensive managerial hierarchies. The result was that investors continued to dominate top-level decision making. To be sure, the railways were beginning to develop a professional middle management in the early 1890s. Indeed, by 1896, when complete information on lower-level executives becomes available, superintendents (*shihainin*) or general superintendents (*sō-shihainin*) were coordinating the activities of various functional managers in 10 of the 18 railway companies founded prior to 1893 that were still in existence.[106] The exceptions to this pattern were significant, though, including as they did 3 of the 5 largest railways. Furthermore, 1 of the 2 firms that had by then established the position of general superintendent, namely, the San'yō Railway, did not do so until February 1894. At that time, Ushiba Takuzō, a former Finance Ministry bureaucrat, was appointed to this newly created post under President Matsumoto Jūtarō, Nakamigawa's successor and concurrently president of the Hankai Railway and 130th National Bank.[107]

In reporting the establishment of this position by the San'yō Railway, the *Jiji shinpō* suggested that the office of superintendent had already become a commonplace among business enterprises, but that in any given company the holder of that office "managed the business under orders from the president, directors, and the like."[108] On the other hand, the need for a general superintendent, implying an executive with a greater say in top-management decisions, had only recently arisen, especially in railways that were just completing their lines or beginning to work them on a large scale. As the journal explained:

The office of general superintendent is most indispensable to a company. In particular, once a firm has been completely established, its foundation settled and its stockholders stabilized, and it enters the age of operation when it becomes necessary solely to consolidate and expand the business steadily, the company must have the most competent general superintendent.

The need was particularly acute, the journal continued, when "as at present, the directors of the various companies are all connected with several firms, and pressed with work, are unable to devote themselves entirely to one company." In retrospect, therefore, Ushiba appears as a harbinger of the full-time career managers who in the late 1890s came to play an increasingly important role in the top-level decision making of railway companies.[109] Yet it seems doubtful that, in the early 1890s, a man like Ushiba, who upon his assumption of office could hardly be termed a professional railway manager, would have had the influence, knowledge, or experience to "take part in the high command."[110]

Dominating the top management of railway firms during the crisis, then, were the major stockholders who filled most of the directorships and some of the presidencies, assisted by the former state officials appointed to many of the chief executive posts. A corollary to the overlap between principal owners and top managers was the limited involvement of local investors in railway management. Admittedly, local entrepreneurs invariably participated in the promotion and early administration of railway companies. In fact, in the case of the Nippon Railway, a provision was written into the articles of incorporation expressly calling for local representation on the firm's initial board of directors.[111] The Tokyo investors who dominated the company, however, were required to observe this concession to interests along the route of the railway only until the first section of line, that between Tokyo and Maebashi, had been completed.

In smaller railways serving narrower markets, one might expect to find a fairly strong local presence on the companies' boards, and indeed this was often the case, at least at the outset. Yet, as in the Nippon Railway, local participation in the management of such firms was largely tied to their need to obtain cooperation from the localities in raising construction funds and purchasing rights of way. Once majority ownership had passed into the hands of non-local investors as capital demand exceeded local supply, or the companies had finished their construction work, the tendency was for local influence over management to diminish markedly in railways where it had originally been significant. In the Chikuhō Industrial Railway, for example, the sharp decline in the local share of the company's ownership from 1889 to 1890 was followed in April 1891 by a management shake-up that left an auditor as the sole remaining officer from the Chikuhō region.[112] Meanwhile, the Ryōmō Railway Company, commonly regarded as the quintessential local railway, initially had two local men, one of whom was the vice-president, on its 6-member board of directors. From 1889, when the company's line was completed, until 1890, however, there was no local representative on the Ryōmō's board and, thereafter, only one.[113] With local shareholders having such a weak say in the operation even of railways with a local character, it is no wonder that the communities served generally had little control over railway-management decisions during the panic and recession.

The inability of local interests to influence corporate policy directly was clearly evident in the Kyushu Railway. That company's decision in 1891 to suspend construction provoked area residents to flood the firm with petitions demanding a reversal of the decision.[114] Despite the local uproar, the railway went ahead with the postponement and in fact, as we have seen, secured a second extension of its construction deadlines the following year.

External Constraints: Local Communities and the Government

Railway firms could not ignore local importunities indefinitely, however. This was particularly true after the opening of the national legislature in 1890. From that date, if local communities lacked representation on the companies' boards, they did have their spokesmen in the Diet, which, through its legislative power, could vitally affect decision making in the railway enterprises. The capacity of local residents to exert pressure on railway management in this indirect manner appeared most strikingly during the nationalization movement of late 1891. Railway companies, many of which were putting off construction work, confronted the possibility of the Diet's enactment of a railway nationalization bill enthusiastically supported by impatient local interests. Especially vocal in their backing of such legislation were communities along the route of the San'yo Railway, which had repeatedly delayed extension of its line since mid-1890. The Hiroshima Chamber of Commerce and City Assembly and groups of residents from Okayama and Yamaguchi prefectures were among those petitioning the Diet to pass the nationalization bill proposed by the Cabinet in December 1891.[115] The Hiroshima Chamber of Commerce spoke for all these groups when it singled out the San'yō Railway for special criticism. The Chamber complained:

Despite the fact that its railway is a nationally indispensable trunk line, the San'yō Railway Company has applied for postponement of its prescribed completion date either because it has actually resolved to discontinue permanently construction of said line under the guise of suspension, owing to the difficulty of raising share capital, or because it has decided to embark on a long-term policy of waiting for an opportunity [to begin construction work again].[116]

In view of "the pressing need for completing the San'yō Railway," there seemed no alternative but for the government to buy out and finish the line. Local demands of this kind undoubtedly contributed to the sense of urgency with which the San'yō's new management sought to resume construction after April 1892.

The localities, of course, were attempting, through the Diet, to prevail on the central government, and it was ultimately with the central government that the railway companies were more concerned. The parties in the Diet, eager to reduce government expenditures and hence the tax burden on their constituents as well as to increase their power vis-à-vis the oligarchs, were adamantly opposed to the Cabinet's nationalization proposal. For their part, government leaders were less committed to nationalization than to the other half of their legislative program, railway construction. They were thus willing to forgo the purchase bill in exchange for passage in June 1892 of a compromise measure for state railway extension, an item upon which both sides could readily agree.[117] Indeed, top decision makers like Matsukata Masayoshi and Inoue Kaoru were generally quite supportive of private railway enterprise, and, for the most part, government policy had a positive, enabling impact on railway-company strategy and planning. The state helped the railways to weather the financial crisis, for example, by granting subsidies to the principal trunk-line companies and easing access to bank funds by investors in virtually all the operating railway firms.

Nevertheless, inasmuch as the government had to balance a number of competing interests, its actions could not always be favorable to the railway companies. In particular, a change in official policy on the acquisition of private land by public utilities that occurred just before the panic broke out resulted in the imposition of a severe constraint on private railway development during the recession. Until July 1889, the government had aided railway companies in buying rights of way by expropriating whatever private land they had required and then selling the land to them. This administrative practice had received legal confirmation in Article 15 of the 1887 Private Railway Regulations. Then, on 30 July 1889, the government promulgated the Compulsory Land Purchase Law, which included provisions protecting landowner interests. Under this law, the private land expropriation provision of the Private Railway Regulations was repealed, and railway companies were thenceforth compelled to negotiate for the acquisition of private land directly with the owners.[118]

The railway companies were none too pleased with this development. In a petition to Prime Minister Kuroda Kiyotaka, dated 31 August 1889, President Nakamigawa of the San'yō Railway complained that, lacking the coercive powers of the state, a railway enterprise would face endless difficulties in attempting to buy the land it needed from "hundreds and thousands of owners" and asked that the government continue its practice of expropriating right of way on behalf of his company. Otherwise, he warned, "in the future, plans for further construction are liable to collapse in a moment."[119]

In his written opinion on Nakamigawa's petition, Railway Bureau Chief Inoue Masaru was surprisingly sympathetic. Inoue asserted that, "in light of our experience, the request of the San'yō [Railway] Company is entirely unavoidable" and urged that the government grant the request.[120] Yet government leaders had other priorities in mind. In its decision of 5 November, the Cabinet denied the San'yō Railway's application on the grounds that making an exception for private railways would go against the purpose of the new law, namely, "to remove the danger of causing resentment among landowners,"[121] whose land taxes still accounted for the majority of state tax revenues and whose votes would be deciding the first Diet elections the following year. Nevertheless, the Cabinet recognized that the law would indeed pose hardships for railway companies; as a way of averting such hardships, one that was "in tune with the objective of protecting and encouraging public utilities," it resolved to have the Home Minister instruct local officials to assist private railways in purchasing the land they needed.

The San'yō Railway was by no means the only railway firm to voice its displeasure with the change in procedure for land acquisition. In fact, concern that the new land-purchase law would deal a severe blow to private railways sparked a concerted movement by railway managers to have it amended. In September 1889, the presidents of 9 other railway companies joined Nakamigawa in a second memorial to Prime Minister Kuroda requesting reinstatement of the previous system of land purchase. In their petition the railway executives protested that, under the new system, "there is hardly any hope of completing construction work within a reasonable period of time," what with "the delays and obstacles" that were expected to attend the companies' compulsory purchase of land.[122] In November, the government rejected this request as well, on the basis that it was "identical to the petition of the San'yō Railway Company President."[123]

With the onset of the tight money situation in late 1889, the timing of the government's enactment of the Compulsory Land Purchase Law could not have been worse for the railway firms. By early 1890, at the height of the panic, the companies' worst fears concerning the impact of the law, assistance from local officials in the acquisition of land notwithstanding, seemed to be materializing. In May 1890, the *Japan Weekly Mail* offered the following details on the problems private railways were experiencing as a result of the law:

Railway companies desirous of acquiring land for carrying on works [have] to deal directly with the landowners, who in some cases number from 120–130 per mile. These people cannot all be assembled together with the view of obtaining their opinions, and yet the process of negotiating with them severally leads to almost interminable delay, while the prices they require are most extravagant. Persons owning land lying on the route of the Kyushu Railway demand figures ranging from 8 to 130 yen per *tsubo* [approximately 36 square feet]. The trouble and inconvenience resulting from the present state of matters have at length driven the railway companies to devise concerted action.[124]

The newspaper reported that the railways were continuing to petition the government for a reinstatement of the previous practice of land expropriation. Their campaign apparently had some effect, for, in July 1890, the government issued regulations establishing a formal mechanism for land-purchase negotiations between businessmen and landowners.[125]

The measures implemented by the authorities to facilitate acquisition of land by public utilities, although they undoubtedly eased the burden on railway companies, were nonetheless a far cry from the previous practice. And for several railways they were simply not enough to prevent dreaded construction delays. As the following examples suggest, difficulties in purchasing land were perhaps just as responsible for setbacks in private railway-building programs during the recession as were problems in collecting stock payments.

The Kyushu Railway was the first company to put off construction on account of difficulties in buying right of way. In late 1889, the railway obtained permission from the government to postpone the deadline for completing the last section of the Hakata-Moji line, for which land acquisition had not gone smoothly.[126] In the case of the Chikuhō Industrial Railway, a whole series of disasters, including an outbreak of cholera, a heavy rainfall, and a major flood, impeded construction work from 1890 to 1891.[127] Then, problems in acquiring land and raising capital began to take their toll in 1891. In May of that year, the company petitioned the government for a year's extension of its deadlines for finishing two sections of line, explaining:

There are various difficulties with respect to the company's negotiating directly with the landowners. Few of them readily comply with the expropriation [of their land], and the majority appeal for a decision by the Compulsory Land Purchase Committee of Inquiry; furthermore, interested parties raise many objections regarding the construction plans, and we are not yet ready to begin work [on the sections in question]. Such being the case, business has slumped badly; in addition, with the current tight money situation, it has been extremely difficult to make headway on the construction work [in progress], and at present we have only completed half the entire line. Under these circumstances, there is absolutely no hope of finishing by the deadlines . . .[128]

The government granted the company's request on the grounds that its predicament was, in Railway Bureau Chief Inoue's words, "beyond its control."[129] Even a year's extension proved insufficient, however, as the work continued to stall in the face of exacting landowners and severe flooding. Accordingly, the railway was forced to apply in May

1892 for yet another one-year postponement of its completion dead-lines.[130]

Difficulties in acquiring land often had less to do with the techni-cal problems of negotiating with landowners than with outright opposition to railway construction from communities along the route of a projected line. At times, such resistance appears to have resulted from the residents' involvement in competing forms of trans-portation. The Sōbu Railway, for instance, set out to build and oper-ate a line through Chiba prefecture, which boasted an extensive and well-developed river network. Although founded in December 1889, the company was not able to complete its first section of line, a 25-mile stretch, until July 1894 partly because of the opposition of peo-ple engaged in inland water transport along the route.[131]

Railway companies were thus forced to make difficult adjustments in purchasing right of way just when they were least able to do so. From the government's standpoint, the railway construction delays occasioned by its change in policy represented a necessary trade-off in its attempt to placate the nation's landowners. Yet, the authorities went to considerable lengths, short of reinstating the old expropria-tion system, to lighten the increased load on the railway firms, show-ing that they were by no means unsolicitous of the railways' plight. Not only did the government readily grant extensions to the com-panies, but it sought to facilitate their negotiations with landholders and directed local officials to help them in that task. The latter activ-ity came naturally to prefectural authorities, who had enthusiasti-cally participated in the planning and promotion of such railways as the Kyushu and San'yō, actively soliciting private investment and state subvention on their behalf. In short, central and local govern-ment continued to cooperate with the private railways in the acquisi-tion of land, though in a fashion that was less generous, if more evenhanded, than before.

Of potentially greater impact on railway-company decision mak-ing, and more suggestive of a real shift in government attitudes towards private railway enterprise, was the Railway Construction Law, the aforementioned compromise act passed by the Diet in June 1892. This law called for a systematic program of railway building by the government, encompassing nearly all the trunk and branch lines yet to be constructed; it also provided for the nationalization of pri-vate railways in cases where it was deemed necessary for completing the projected state lines. The act, therefore, seemed to foreclose both the establishment of new main-line companies and the expansion of the old, not to mention place in jeopardy the continued existence of the latter. In fact, Noda Masaho contends that the law had the effect of limiting private railway building to lines other than those scheduled for construction by the government under the act. Consequently, the second railway boom, which followed the post-panic recession, centered mainly on relatively small companies that were local in character.[132]

What Noda fails to point out, however, is that the law contained a crucial provision allowing for private building, subject to the approval of the Diet, of any projected line on which the state "has yet to begin construction." The result, as Aoki Eiichi notes, was to give legal confirmation to the policy the government had theretofore carried out in practice of promoting parallel state and private construction of the trunk-line network.[133] To be sure, local railway companies proliferated and state railway building accelerated under the construction act. Yet, the government never put into effect the nationalization provision of the law and actually permitted private companies to construct many of the scheduled lines, including those that formed parts of major arteries. On the one hand, the law recognized the preferential right of established firms such as the San'yō and Kyushu to build lines nominally slated for construction by the government under the act for which the companies had already obtained licenses prior to the promulgation of the Railway Construction Law.[134] On the other hand, the government exercised the private construction option for many of the remaining scheduled lines, repeatedly securing Diet approval for the licensing of such new main-line firms as the Hokkaido, Hokuetsu, and Hankaku.[135] As one popular account aptly puts its, "A construction law for state lines had in no time become a construction law for private railways."[136]

The pragmatic, economy-minded leaders of the government had sought legislative affirmation of the principles of state construction and ownership, primarily at the urging of Railway Bureau Chief Inoue Masaru. Inoue, who was naturally eager to enlarge his bureaucratic empire, was one of the few consistent advocates of national ownership within the government. Those in the top-decision-making positions, however, were concerned less with the form of railway ownership and control than with the speed and cost of railway construction. Their real goal was the rapid completion of the basic rail network, though at minimal expense to the state treasury. Under the enterprise boom beginning in 1893, they simply found it unnecessary to uphold the cherished principles of the railway bureaucracy in order to achieve that objective.

As implemented, therefore, the Railway Construction Law did not in fact mark a decisive shift in official views and treatment of private railways. In practice, it imposed few, if any, new restrictions on the establishment and growth of railway enterprises. Granted, the carrot and stick embodied in the private-construction and state-purchase provisions of the act may well have spurred the companies to get on with their construction work, and in that sense the law may have exerted a strong positive influence on the management of the firms. With regard to line selection at least, the law did place the companies under greater state control. Still, the Cabinet had exercised strict supervision in this regard, if in a less structured manner, even before the passage of the act.

What was different was that the construction law introduced into the licensing process two checks on the government bureaucracy in the form of the Railway Council, an advisory body set up under the Cabinet with broad representation and authority, and the Diet. This broadening of the decision-making arena had the potential for making it much more difficult for railway companies to obtain licenses, what with the heightened possibility of political disagreements and attendant delays. Nonetheless, by giving the localities a voice in the process via their representatives in the Diet and by establishing a clear procedure for the licensing of railway firms, the Construction Law in the long run facilitated the founding and extension of private railways. In sum, the law basically left intact the cooperative relationship between the railway companies and the state, a relationship reinforced by the crossover of government personnel to the companies and by the continued favorable attitudes of government leaders toward private railway enterprise.

PATTERNS OF FINANCING DURING THE CRISIS

Government Subsidies

Such attitudes found their clearest expression in the forms of financial assistance the authorities granted railway companies during the panic and recession. The railways resorted to a variety of emergency measures in order to gain access to funds in the tight money situation and thereby to avoid the more drastic steps of suspending construction work, merging with larger concerns, or selling out to the government. Given the generally supportive nature of state policy and the conservative outlook of the dominant investor groups, it was only natural that the companies should have turned first to the government for relief from the financial crisis. And state officials obliged them with subsidies and indirect loans from the central bank.

During the early 1890s, four railway firms—the four largest, to be exact—enjoyed government subventions. The state offered annual interest subsidies prior to the opening of their lines, and profit guarantees for specified periods thereafter, of 8 percent to the Nippon Railway and 5 percent to the Hokkaido Colliery and one-time payments of ¥2,000 per mile of completed track to the Kyushu and San'yō railways.[137] Actually, all four companies had applied for their subsidies, and all but the San'yō had won government approval of them, prior to the outbreak of the panic. The San'yō, however, had made its subsidy request on the very eve of the crisis, at a time when business enterprises were already feeling the squeeze of a tightening money market. Moreover, all the subsidized railways, except for the Hokkaido Colliery, obtained their largest subventions during the period 1890-1891, the only years in which total railway subsidies exceeded ¥1 million.

Nevertheless, the Nippon and Hokkaido Colliery railways benefitted from government subsidies during the crisis to a much greater degree than did the Kyushu and San'yō. The state subvention supplied the former two with a vital cushion against business fluctuations, inasmuch as the government subsidized them before the opening of their lines and guaranteed their profits for substantial periods thereafter. Thus backed by the state, the Nippon Railway had little, if any, difficulty in collecting payments on two new stock issues floated just before and during the panic for construction of the two relatively unprofitable sections north of Sendai. Those issues were both paid up, and the sections completed, by 1891.[138]

Similarly, government subsidies made it possible for the Hokkaido Colliery and Railway to continue construction work during the recession, despite the slump in the coal market. As one of only three railway companies in operation during the crisis years that derived their income primarily from freight traffic, the Hokkaido Colliery naturally experienced a sharp drop in its profit rate at this time, heavily dependent as it was on coal transport. Yet, thanks mainly to the state subvention, the firm was able to offer a dividend of over 7 percent throughout the recession. In consequence, it too had relatively little trouble calling up shares, which, in turn, enabled the company to finish its railway net by 1892.[139]

By comparison, the subvention granted the Kyushu and San'yō railways left their building programs far more vulnerable to disturbances in business activity, for their subsidies were relatively modest lump-sum payments, contingent on the completion of designated sections of line. The two companies did receive large amounts of this state money at the start of the recession. The subsidy played a key role in allowing both firms to offer a dividend of 6 percent during each semester of 1890 and 1891 (see Table 4). But, with the recession keeping their profits and the collateral value of their stocks at depressed levels, the government subsidy was just not enough to prevent their shareholders from demanding, before long, postponement of both installment payments and construction projects. Forced to heed the shareholders' demands, the two railways had practically no increase in paid-up capital or mileage during the years 1892–1893. During that period, as neither firm was able to finish a designated section of line, the state subsidy ceased to be awarded to either of them. The dwindling of government support was, in turn, largely responsible for the drop in the companies' dividend rates beginning in 1891. Hence, the San'yō and Kyushu railways, like many of the unsubsidized firms, were caught in a bind between the necessity to complete sections of line in order to raise their income and dividends and the difficulty of procuring construction funds owing to the tight money market and their own poor business results. In the end, therefore, the government subsidy simply did not enable these companies to avoid major setbacks in their building programs.

TABLE 4 Development and Business Results of San'yō and Kyushu
Railway Companies, 1889–1893

			San'yō Railway				
Year	Length of Line Open	Paid-up Capital (C)	Profit (P)	P/C	State Subsidy	Dividend	Div. Rate
	(miles)	(¥1,000)	(¥1,000)	(%)	(¥1,000)	(¥1,000)	(%)
1889	44	2,915	85	2.9	0	77	3.28 [a] 3.00
1890	91 (106.8)[b]	5,720 (96.2)	110	1.9	172	–	6.00 6.00
1891	140 (53.8)	7,010 (22.6)	200	2.9	36	226	4.10 2.76
1892	145 (3.6)	7,020 (0.1)	280	4.0	0	257	3.33 4.00
1893	145 (0)	7,020 (0)	354	5.0	0	312	4.50 4.50
1894	192 (32.4)	7,794 (11.0)	652	8.4	0	453	5.50 7.00
			Kyushu Railway				
1889	23	2,991	62	2.1	92	154	6.00 6.00
1890	55 (139.1)	5,036 (68.4)	105	2.1	140	–	6.00 6.00
1891	137 (149.1)	5,663 (12.5)	243	4.3	41	281	6.00 4.25
1892	137 (0)	5,700 (0.7)	230	4.0	4	228	4.00 4.00
1893	137 (0)	5,700 (0)	329	5.8	0	293	4.74 5.53
1894	146 (6.6)	6,481 (13.7)	506	7.8	0	424	7.00 7.50

Sources: Tetsudō Kyoku nenpō (1909), Appendix, pp. 23–24, 41, 79, 97; *Nihon teikoku dai jū-dai jū-shi tōkei nenkan,* ed. Naikaku Tōkei Kyoku or Naikaku Shokikan-shitsu Tōkei-ka (By the Editor, 1891–1895), pp. 330 (1891), 680 (1892), 673 (1893), 703 (1894), 711 (1895); *Tei-koku tetsudō yōkan,* 3rd ed. (Tetsudō Jihō Kyoku, 1906), pp. 128–129, 160.

Notes:[a] per semester
[b] Figures in parentheses represent percentage increase over previous year.

Central Bank Discounts

The other principal form, albeit an indirect one, of state assistance to private railways during the crisis was the extension of stock-collateral lending by the Bank of Japan. Affecting a much larger number of railway concerns than did subsidization, this measure proved absolutely crucial to the financing of such hard-hit firms as the San'yō and Kyushu in the first year or so after the panic. Prompting its adoption in May 1890 was a vigorous campaign mounted by private business for government intervention to defuse the crisis. No sooner had the panic broken out than businessmen began to inundate the authorities with a variety of general relief proposals. Chambers of commerce in Tokyo and elsewhere organized special committees to investigate the causes of the tight money situation and to recommend measures for alleviating it. Some of these bodies urged the government to float a foreign loan; others, to establish an industrial bank. The business-oriented journal *Jiji shinpō* even called for the setting up of a national lottery.[140] The Finance Ministry initially responded to these demands by redeeming ¥8 million in commutation bonds and authorizing the Bank of Japan to exceed its note-issue limit by ¥5 million. But, at the continued prodding of private businessmen, the authorities took their most far-reaching step: the broadening of the central-bank policy of discounting bank bills using corporate shares as collateral.

In May 1885, the Bank of Japan had begun accepting the shares of certain "sound" (*kakujitsu*) banks and companies, including the Nippon Railway, as security for term loans and discounts on bills. The government had approved this course of action in spite of Article 12 of the Bank of Japan Act, which prohibited lending by the central bank on the security of corporate stock. In the wake of the 1890 panic, then, as a financial-relief measure, the authorities expanded the list of companies whose shares the Bank of Japan would accept as collateral for discounts on bills. All ten of the firms added to the list were private railways.[141]

Significantly, it was not the railway companies themselves, but the Tokyo and Osaka bankers' associations that together proposed this measure and pushed for its adoption. The fact that these two groups came forward with a relief plan calling for the acceptance of several additional kinds of railway stock as security for central-bank loans simply underscores the extent to which the city banks had tied up their capital in stock-collateral loans as well as the degree to which the latter had centered on railway shares. Both these tendencies can be measured quantitatively, at least in part, using the available data. According to an 1890 report by Finance Minister Matsukata, at the end of 1889 some 64 percent of the funds advanced by 61 national banks in Tokyo and Osaka were stock-collateral loans. At ¥17 million, the latter accounted for roughly 15 percent of all loans and advances made by commercial banks that year.[142] The ratio of stock-collateral to total loans made by the national banks of Tokyo and Osaka remained virtually the same in 1891, when the figure stood at 0.63. The ¥20 million lent by those banks using shares as collateral represented about 16 percent of total commercial bank loans that year.[143]

In addition, a survey of 38 out of the 42 Osaka city banks conducted by a committee of the Osaka Chamber of Commerce revealed that, in July and August 1891, railway shares accounted for over half of the more than ¥5 million in stock collateral held by those banks.[144] If one can assume that this proportion held for national banks (exclusive of private city banks) in Tokyo as well as in Osaka, then the national banks of those two cities alone would have indirectly contributed to the financing of private railways at least ¥10 million, or just under one quarter of the total paid-up capital of railway companies, in 1891. All this evidence suggests that, around the time of the panic, the city banks had become heavily involved in lending on the collateral of railway shares. With the liquidity of their capital reduced mainly because of the loans they had made on the security of such shares and with their assets adversely affected by the decline in value of many of the railway stocks they held as collateral, it is no wonder that members of the Osaka and Tokyo bankers' associations should have singled out railway shares in their relief proposal.

The implementation of the enlarged discount system proved a tremendous boon to those commercial banks that had tied up large sums of money in the form of loans secured by railway shares, since the banks could thenceforth, in turn, use those shares to borrow extensively from the Bank of Japan. In its report on the banking industry for 1890, the government's Audit Bureau described the impact of this measure as follows: "Every bank, as if receiving rain after a drought, has raised idle capital and become active, . . . and all

TABLE 5 Discounts on Domestic Bills by the Bank of Japan,
1890–1896

Year	Discounts on All Domestic Bills (A)	Discounts on Bills with Collateral (B)	B/A
	(¥1,000)	(¥1,000)	(%)
1890	56,983	15,897	27.9
1891	56,769	30,318	53.4
1892	43,454	23,638	54.4
1893	57,856	33,381	57.7
1894	93,295	49,776	53.3
1895	115,009	62,212	54.1
1896	178,546	79,528	44.5

Source: Tsuchiya Takao, "*Nihon Ginkō hanki hōkoku* kaidai," in *Nihon kin'yūshi shiryō: Meiji Taishō hen*, ed. Nihon Ginkō Chōsa Kyoku (Ōkura Shō Insatsu Kyoku, 1956), VIII, 71.

are once again enjoying the benefits of the financial community, which had long been dried up."[145]

Banks clearly made heavy use of the system. Of all discounts on domestic bills by the Bank of Japan, discounts on bills with collateral jumped from 28 to 53 percent between 1890 and 1891 and exceeded 50 percent every year thereafter during the first half of the 1890s (see Table 5). At the end of March 1893, railway shares served as collateral for ¥1.8 million out of ¥2.6 million in outstanding central-bank discounts on bills with collateral, or approximately 70 percent of the latter (see Table 6). Applying this percentage to discounts on collateralized bills for fiscal-year 1892 as a whole yields an estimate for central-bank discounts on bills using railway shares as collateral that year of ¥16.5 million, an amount equivalent to over one third the total paid-up capital of railway companies in 1892. In view of the evidently short-term nature of these discounts, however, the 16.5 million figure is less meaningful than the ¥1.8 million in discounts outstanding at the end of the fiscal year; the latter amounted to some 55 percent of the increase in paid-up capital for private railways as a whole between 1891 and 1892.

During its first year or so in operation, the extended discount program also seems to have greatly benefited the designated private railways by making it easier for their shareholders to borrow funds from commercial banks in order to meet installment payments. But from

TABLE 6 Discounts Outstanding on Bills with Collateral by the
Bank of Japan, 31 March 1893

Type of Collateral	Total Value of Discounts
	(¥1,000)
Hokkaido Colliery and Railway Shares	505
Kyushu Railway Shares	473
San'yō Railway Shares	260
Kansai Railway Shares	231
Nippon Railway Shares	189
Ryōmō Railway Shares	92
Kōbu Railway Shares	65
Osaka Railway Shares	25
Total Railway Shares	1,840
N.Y.K. Shares	440
Osaka Railway Bonds	200
Public Bonds	121
Grand Total	2,601

Source: "Kashidashikin teitōhin shuruibetsu hyō," 31 March 1893, *Matsuo ke monjo*, Vol. LXIX,
no. 28, Finance Ministry Archives, Tokyo.

1891 to 1893, the program generally appears to have been of much
less advantage to the companies, in view of the sharp drop in the rate
of increase in their total paid-up capital and the problems experienced by the San'yō and Kyushu railways, among others, in collecting stock payments during those years. Nonetheless, the fact that the
railway firms enjoyed any increase in paid-up capital at all under the
prevailing recession and tight money situation was due in no small
measure to the central-bank discounting system.

The financial authorities initially intended the expanded discount
policy to be just a temporary relief measure. In fact, the government
approved the policy on the condition that a special bank eventually
be established to take over the program.[146] In November 1892,
Finance Minister Watanabe Kunitake, in granting the Bank of Japan's
request that the corporate bonds of the companies covered under the
program be accorded the same treatment as their stocks, felt constrained to add the following reminder: "Because the collateral system originated as a temporary expedient at the time of the tight

money market in 1890, be advised that, once financing has returned to normal, said collateral system will gradually be abolished."[147] The government finally did move to terminate the program in June 1897 as part of the central-bank reform that year. Nevertheless, on the grounds that suddenly to abolish a system that had been in existence for several years would have serious repercussions on the nation's financial markets, the authorities decided essentially to continue the discounting program under a different name.[148] Meanwhile, the plan to set up a special bank to assume discounts on corporate shares never materialized. The Bank of Japan thus remained, in Noda's words, "an ex-post-facto bearer"[149] of stock-collateral loans from commercial banks to railway shareholders right up until the nationalization of all the railways in question in 1906–1907.

Financial Retrenchment

In many cases, official assistance, whether in the form of state subsidies or central-bank discounts, proved insufficient by itself to enable the railway companies to satisfy even minimum funding requirements during the recession. In order to secure needed financing, most firms were compelled in their own right to adopt various emergency measures. One of these steps was financial retrenchment. We have already described how some railways, under pressure from economy-minded shareholders, cut back on fixed investments in order to reduce capital demand itself. A number of firms also responded to the crisis by slashing operating expenses so as to raise dividends and thereby to encourage or enable stockholders to meet at least their immediate installment payments.

In April 1891, for example, the officers of the Kyushu Railway decided voluntarily to cut the president's salary by a quarter and the directors' pay by half. They also resolved to lower the salaries and extend the working hours of the staff as well as to reduce its size. During fiscal-year 1891, the company dismissed almost one fourth of its employees, who had numbered 1,482 in March 1891. The deterioration in the firm's business results the following year prompted management to approve another round of economies in September 1892. Salaries were again curtailed, President Takahashi agreeing to a one-third cut in his own pay, and the number of company employees was further reduced by some 13 percent in fiscal-year 1892.[150]

Meanwhile, the San'yō Railway, forced by its owners to carry out a similar program of personnel retrenchment, also sought to economize by reducing the operating speed of its trains. On 19 July 1891, for instance, the *Tōkyō nichinichi* reported that, beginning 1 August, the railway's Kobe-Himeji run would take 23 minutes longer than it had at its opening. Consequently, the paper declared, "although San'yō Railway trains have been called the fastest in the country, henceforth we shall see quite the opposite result."

Pathbreaking Strategies: Preferred-Stock and Corporate-Bond Issues

Railway firms also took more positive steps to cope with their financial problems during the crisis. In fact, at this time they pioneered the use by Japanese joint-stock companies of two of those measures, namely, the issuance of preferred stocks and of corporate bonds. From 1890 to 1892, five railway companies sought to raise capital by issuing new shares. Prior to the revision of the Commercial Code in 1899, it was common for joint-stock enterprises to increase their authorized capital stock before their old shares had been fully paid up; such was the case with three of the five railways. Yet four of these firms—the Nippon, Hankai, Osaka, and Iyo—were relatively unscathed by the crisis and had little apparent difficulty in disposing of their additional shares. The Chikuhō Industrial was the only hard-hit railway to issue new shares during the recession, and it managed to do so in 1892 only by offering the shares as preferred stocks. Moreover, it was the first business in Japan to offer such shares and, until the revised Commercial Code authorized for capital-increase purposes the issuance of preferred stocks, which had in the meantime been prohibited under the 1893 code, the only company so to do.[151] At the railway's special stockholders' meeting in December 1891, it was decided to finance new construction by issuing ¥1,500,000 in new shares with a preferred dividend rate of 8 percent. The firm was to allot these shares to the existing stockholders, but, owing to the continued tightness of the money market, it was actually forced to discontinue the offer after the owners had subscribed to less than half the shares involved.[152]

The depressed financial and economic environment plainly limited the effectiveness of both government and corporate measures aimed at enabling private railways to raise sufficient share capital to

TABLE 7 Aggregate Capital Structure of Private Railway Companies, 1888–1894 (Unit: ¥1,000)

Year	Paid-up Capital (A)	Reserves (B)	Bonds (C)	Loans (D)	Construction Costs (E)	$\frac{A+B}{E}$	$\frac{A+B+C+D}{E}$	$\frac{D}{E}$
	(1)	(2)	(3)	(4)	(5)	(%) (6)	(%) (7)	(%) (8)
1888	14,997	231	0	165	11,834	128.7	130.1	1.4
1889	27,943	367	0	30	20,366	139.0	139.2	0.1
1890	38,493	511	269	1,162	33,816	115.3	119.6	3.4
1891	43,441	649	1,494	843	44,062	100.1	105.4	1.9
1892	46,737	775	1,710	580	47,508	100.0	104.8	1.2
1893	48,870	518	5,680	703	52,050	94.9	107.1	1.4
1894	59,177	1,322	5,778	877	60,794	99.5	110.5	1.4

Source: Tetsudō Kyoku nenpō (1909), Appendix, pp. 44–45.

meet their funding needs during the crisis. Indeed, with the precipitous drop in the rate of increase in paid-up capital for railway companies as a whole in the years following the panic, the sum of the
railways' total paid-up capital and reserves barely matched their overall construction costs in 1891 and 1892 and fell significantly short of
the latter in 1893. To cover the difference, several firms resorted to outside capital by negotiating bank loans or issuing corporate bonds (see
Table 7, Columns 6-7).

For railway companies in general, borrowing from banks was
strictly a stopgap during the recession. Between 1890 and 1893, six
operating railways had outstanding bank loans; only two of them carried those debts for more than three years running, including the
years before and after that period, indicating that the loans were for
the most part relatively short-term and probably renewed, if at all,
but once or twice.[153] Moreover, the percentage of aggregate construction costs represented by these bank loans in any given year during
the early 1890s was never very significant, ranging as it did from 1.2
percent in 1892 to 3.4 percent in 1890 (see Table 7, Column 8). Furthermore, one company, the San'yō Railway, accounted for the vast
majority of bank funds advanced to railway enterprises in operation
during the period 1890–1892. And, in 1891, the only one of those
years in which the San'yō's share of the total fell below 90 percent,
the equally distressed Chikuhō Industrial was responsible for most of
the remainder; it also had over half the loans outstanding in 1893, by
which time the San'yō had liquidated the bank debts it had begun
contracting soon after the panic.

The San'yō had taken its loans from such banks as the Yokohama
Specie, Mitsui, and Mitsubishi-owned 119th National. As a trade journal suggested in June 1890, the railway had intended this borrowing
merely as a temporary expedient to make up for arrears in stock payments and thereby to avoid delays in construction work.[154] In October 1890, the Chikuhō Industrial had likewise borrowed ¥250,000
from the First National and other banks in order to offset overdue
installment payments and thus enable the railway to meet its initial
building expenses.[155] The company had paid back this loan by 1892.
In the short run, direct bank loans did make a substantial contribution to the financing of certain railway firms: In 1890, for example,
banks lent the San'yō Railway the equivalent of 22 percent of its construction costs. But this method of capital procurement was clearly a

makeshift. Playing a far more important role in the long-term financing of the San'yō and other private railways were corporate-bond issues, to which a number of companies turned heavily in the 1890s.

The issuance of corporate bonds represented the second form of joint-stock-company finance that owed its introduction into Japan to the difficulties experienced by railway enterprises in the aftermath of the 1890 Panic. The Osaka Railway held the distinction of being the first Japanese business to float corporate bonds. In April 1890, that firm's stockholders voted to issue bonds totaling ¥268,500, "in order that this company might, for the time being, compensate for the shortage of [construction] capital."[156] The bonds were to pay 10-percent interest and to mature in five years. Other railways soon followed the Osaka's lead. Besides the Osaka Railway, the four largest railway firms and the Chikuhō Industrial all issued bonds in the early 1890s. All but the Nippon and Hokkaido Colliery did so to cover shortfalls in construction funds resulting from the companies' inability to collect installment payments or to sell new shares. The percentage of building costs represented by outstanding corporate bonds for each of these four concerns during the years 1890–1893 ranged from 14 percent in the case of the Osaka Railway in 1891 to 40 percent in the case of the Chikuhō Industrial that same year. In 1893, both the San'yō and Kyushu issued bonds equivalent to nearly a fourth of their respective construction costs.[157]

The Osaka redeemed its bonds in their entirety after only two years, but the other three railways left most or all of their bonds outstanding for extended periods. In April 1893, the San'yō floated ¥2,000,000 in 6-percent corporate bonds redeemable for a period of 10 years after May 1898; in fact, after that date the company liquidated only a portion of those bonds, redeeming them at the leisurely rate of ¥50,000 a year.[158] In July 1893, the stockholders of the Kyushu Railway decided to issue 5-percent bonds totaling ¥1,500,000 with a 10-year term of redemption.[159] However, in 1906, on the eve of its nationalization, the company still had outstanding bonds in the same amount. In the meantime, by 1904, the firm had fully redeemed the high-interest bonds it had issued in exchange for those outstanding of the Chikuhō Industrial when it bought out the latter in 1897.[160] At the time of the merger, the Chikuhō had yet to recover ¥395,000 out of the ¥600,000 in corporate bonds it had floated by

1893. In short, there is no question as to the long-term nature of these bonds.

On the other hand, the issuance of corporate bonds was clearly an emergency measure prompted by the financial problems these railway companies faced during the panic and recession. Like the San'yō, for example, the Kyushu "took into consideration the difficulty of raising share capital"[161] when it decided to procure construction funds by floating corporate bonds instead. Accordingly, the railways stopped issuing bonds altogether at the height of the ensuing boom, when stock subscriptions as well as installment payments were once again proceeding smoothly.

The four largest companies accounted for a growing majority of the bonds issued by railway enterprises prior to 1898. By 1895, they were responsible for over 90 percent of the outstanding bonds; the San'yō and Kyushu alone, for more than 60 percent. The tide turned dramatically, however, during the Panic of 1897–1898. The strained financial situation at that time triggered a revival of bond issuance among railway companies, but those responsible for virtually all of the private railway bonds floated during those years and most of those issued thereafter were small to medium-sized firms, especially those founded during the second railway boom. Consequently, the share of total railway bonds represented by the big four dropped to 50 percent in 1898 and had further declined to 31 percent by 1904.[162] During the panics and recession that followed the second railway boom, the total owned capital of the smaller companies, unlike that of the major railways, fell substantially short of their aggregate investment needs.[163] As a result, after 1897, firms in the small to medium range accounted not only for most of the bond issues, but also for the majority of the bank loans and all the preferred-stock issues floated by railway companies.

Meanwhile, with the four largest railways having a total of only three bond issues after 1895, corporate bonds represented, on the whole, a progressively smaller share of the financing of those firms. Moreover, the Kyushu and San'yō, each of which floated one of those three issues, did so not to raise construction funds during the succession of financial crises around the turn of the century, but rather to finance the purchase of another railway company.[164] Their issuance of bonds for that purpose testified to the stability they had by that time acquired as business enterprises.

The bond issues these two concerns floated in 1893, however, played a vital role in enabling them to reach a position of soundness in the first place. At a time when stock payments had come to a dead halt for both firms, the Kyushu and San'yō owed their ability to resume construction work in 1893 almost entirely to the successful flotation of those issues. The two companies actually sold the latter to a comparatively small number of individual and institutional investors. Unlike the Osaka Railway, which had distributed its bonds among its shareholders, the Kyushu and San'yō offered theirs to the general public, as did the remaining bond-issuing railways. Nonetheless, the companies had relatively few takers. At the end of fiscal-year 1893, for instance, the Kyushu Railway, with an authorized capital stock of ¥7,500,000 and an outstanding bond issue of ¥1,500,000, had 1,858 stockholders, but a mere 218 bondholders.[165] Moreover, because the government requirement that corporate bonds be registered reduced their negotiability, the bonds tended to remain concentrated in relatively few hands.

Noda asserts that, from 1891 to 1892, banks and insurance companies, seeking safe investment opportunities for their deposits, "emerged as large-scale subscribers" to railway and other corporate bonds, and, owing to the comparatively low transferability of the latter, "most of the corporate bondholding by institutional investors in effect became nothing but a variety of long-term lending."[166] The available data for railway companies appear to corroborate Noda's claim, with insurance firms and banks figuring prominently in a 1905 list of bondholders in the Kyushu Railway and insurance companies in an 1895 list for the Chikuhō.[167] In any event, the issuance of bonds proved to be a crucial alternative means of private railway finance, an innovative expedient that enabled companies like the San'yo to catapult from the recession into a second round of expansion in the mid-1890s.

CONCLUSION

On the whole, therefore, railway firms managed to deal resourcefully with the Panic of 1890 and its aftermath. Together with government support, the emergency finance provided by commercial banks played a significant part in making it possible for them to do so. The crisis also brought into focus the banks' vital contribution to the supply of ordinary share capital to private railways through the making of loans to railway stockholders on the security of their shares. Kozo Yamamura has made several important observations on the difficulty of interpreting the available data on stock-collateral lending by banks during the Meiji period. As Yamamura points out, the data are often unclear as to whether the corporate shares accepted by banks as loan collateral were industrial or non-industrial; whether the loans secured by these shares were long- or short-term and, if short-term, whether or not they were renewed; and whether these loans were put to industrial or to non-industrial uses. Such ambiguities, Yamamura contends, make it impossible to draw any definite conclusions concerning the role of banks in providing industrial capital during the Meiji era.[168]

In the financing of railway companies, however, there seems to be little doubt as to the importance of bank participation. Around the time of the 1890 Panic, railway shares probably accounted for over half the stocks held as loan collateral by Tokyo and Osaka banks, which together supplied the great majority of all bank loans made on corporate shares. It appears that these loans were mostly short-term, but so long as railway shares remained relatively stable in price, the loans for which they served as collateral were readily renewed. Moreover, the Bank of Japan's policy of discounting commercial-bank loans secured by railway shares gave liquidity to those loans, further encouraging the banks to renew them. These circumstances had the effect, therefore, of converting what were ostensibly short-term loans into long-run investments.

The thorniest problem is to ascertain the purposes for which railway shareholders used these loans. The only positive evidence we have that money lent by commercial banks on railway shares was actually invested in private railways involves the Fifteenth National Bank and the Nippon Railway Company. As noted earlier, the Fifteenth National had its shares in the Nippon Railway held under the names of its officers and employees, to whom it made stock-collateral loans to finance payments on those shares, as a way of circumventing the prohibition against corporate stockholding by national banks. The Fourth National Bank of Niigata also appears to have adopted this strategy in connection with the Ryōmō Railway, and, in view of the prominence of national as well as private bank executives on railway stockholders' lists, the practice may have been widespread.

Unfortunately, we lack data on the use of bank funds borrowed on the security of railway shares by non-bank-affiliated stockholders. Nevertheless, even if such borrowers applied most of their loans to purposes other than paying up railway shares, those loans were still, as Yamamura admits, "important in releasing the [borrowers'] funds for long-range investments,"[169] in this case, in railway enterprises.

Yamamura shows, however, that, regardless of their exact composition and use, stock-collateral loans as a whole represented only a small portion of the overall financing of joint-stock companies. According to one set of data cited by Yamamura, in December 1894 "the ¥43 million in bank loans secured by shares amounted to less than 25 percent of the total share capital paid in."[170] Yet, our evidence on stock-collateral lending by banks around the time of the panic suggests that it may not be unreasonable to assume that loans made on railway shares accounted for about one-half of all loans collateralized by shares in 1894. Making that assumption, one can say that bank loans secured by railway shares represented some two-fifths of the railways' estimated total paid-up capital of ¥57 million in December 1894. Hence, banks were clearly an important factor in supplying capital to this key area of the Meiji economy.

This conclusion in no way controverts Yamamura's contention that, in aggregate quantitative terms, bank participation in industrial financing during the latter half of the Meiji period "has been significantly overstated."[171] It does indicate, however, that one ought to modify that assertion by pointing out the qualitative importance of the industrial financing that banks did provide, much of it centering as it did on one of the leading sectors of Meiji industrialization. In illustrating his argument with case studies of individual enterprises, Yamamura omits from consideration private railway firms, apparently because of what he views as the upward bias imparted to bank funding of railways by the Fifteenth National, which accounted for perhaps a third of all bank loans made on railway shares in 1894 and which, he argues unconvincingly, ought to be excluded from any discussion of the role of banks in supplying capital to Meiji industry.

Instead, Yamamura focuses on companies representing the cotton spinning industry to demonstrate "the much less than dominant participation of the banks"[172] in industrial financing during the Meiji era. Sugiyama has written that, in the 1880s, spinning firms relied heavily on short-term bank loans for their operating capital, but, during the 1890 Panic and recession, banks became reluctant to continue lending them money, owing to the managerial difficulties the companies were experiencing at the time. Thereafter, trading firms gradually replaced commercial banks as the major suppliers of short-term credit to spinning concerns.[173] Whether the panic produced a cautious attitude among banks toward the provision not only of operating funds to the spinning companies, but also of investment capital to their shareholders in the form of stock-collateral loans, is unclear. Certainly, after 1890, banks would far and away have preferred the shares of private railways over those of spinning firms as security for loans, since the special treatment accorded railway shares under the central-bank discount system placed them among the items most attractive to banks as loan collateral. Thus, to appreciate fully the contribution of banks to industrial financing during the Meiji period, one can ill afford to ignore such an important sector of the economy, and an obvious target of industrial investment by banks, as private railway companies.

These observations do not, however, mean that German-style investment banking dominated the financing of Meiji railways. To the contrary, the patterns of capital raising among railway companies in mid-Meiji Japan, as Yamamura asserts of Meiji industry in general, seem to have approximated those in England much more than those in Germany during the nineteenth century. Like their British counterparts, Meiji railway firms depended largely on ordinary share capital supplied by individual investors and turned to borrowing primarily as a means of obtaining emergency finance.[174] The importance of individual shareholders in providing railway capital in Meiji Japan contrasts noticeably with the leading role of investment banks in financing private railways in Germany.[175]

Nevertheless, banks in Japan, in addition to furnishing emergency funding directly to railway enterprises, played a vital indirect part in the provision of railway share capital through the practice of lending money on the collateral of shares. Moreover, by the turn of the century banks had emerged as prominent stockholders in their own right, as various institutional investors such as the Fifteenth National and Mitsui Bank made public their direct holdings of railway stock previously held under the names of representatives, and other commercial banks began to invest extensively in railways.[176] The concealment of equity participation by banks around the time of the panic, therefore, made the patterns of railway financing in mid-Meiji Japan appear to be much more similar to those in Victorian England than was actually the case. By the late 1890s, it had become evident that the Japanese experience was in fact more of a hybrid between those of England and Germany. At least in the case of private railways, "true industrial banking" seems to have begun much earlier than suggested by Yamamura.[177]

If railway firms anticipated the emergence in Japan of investment banking on the German model, which Yamamura sees as occurring no earlier than in the 1920s, they also prefigured the rise of professional managers in the nation's joint-stock enterprises. Yet railway companies gave little indication of doing so in the early 1890s. Indeed, the high degree of influence exercised over the management of railways by owner-capitalists at that time presents a striking contrast to the "freedom of managers from interference in their programs by corporate stockholders"[178] in Japanese companies today. In view of the fact that the principal owners and top executives of railway companies overlapped considerably in the early to mid-1890s and that the extent of their coincidence remained virtually the same a decade later,[179] one would have to say that the experience of private railways supports Nakamura Takafusa's assertion that even late in the Meiji era "the clear separation of ownership and management was to come only in the distant future."[180]

This lack of division does not necessarily mean, however, that shareholders continued to dominate the top management of railways to the same degree they had in the early 1890s. In fact, by the turn of the century, a significant number of full-time salaried managers had risen from middle-level administrative or technical posts to positions in the high command. Nakamura notes that in the case of spinning companies a similar trend became apparent in the late 1890s.[181] This tendency was, if anything, even more pronounced during those years in the case of railway firms. Certainly, individual railways varied as to the timing and extent of the emergence of career administrators as decision makers. The San'yō Railway, for example, was moving, however haltingly, in the direction of professional management from the start, whereas the Kōbu Railway, with owner-entrepreneurs like Amenomiya Keijirō monopolizing most of the senior posts, had the character of being what Chandler calls an "entrepreneurial enterprise"[182] throughout its existence. Nevertheless, the general trend toward greater professionalism in private railway administration is unmistakable. The case of railway concerns, therefore, suggests that Nakamura understates the shift of control over companies from major stockholders to career managers when he asserts that "this shift had barely begun in the Meiji era."[183]

Many railway firms began as "entrepreneurial enterprises," initiated by local capitalists such as the Fukuoka coal-mine operators, Nada sake brewers, and Tochigi textile merchants who helped to establish, respectively, the Chikuhō Industrial, San'yō, and Ryōmō railways. Before long, however, the magnitude of their financial requirements compelled these and many other railways to look to major non-local providers of capital. As we have seen, railway companies obtained from financial institutions, particularly city banks, a substantial proportion of the funds they secured from such sources. We have also noted that these institutions, besides lending stock payment money to railway shareholders, supplied financing directly to railway concerns through stock purchases, made mostly under the names of institutional representatives until the latter part of the 1890s and, secondarily, through bond purchases and loans.

Along with this investment came participation in the management of the railways. The financial crisis of the early 1890s proved to be decisive in this regard. Banks and similar institutional investors, many of which had become engaged in private railways prior to 1890, solidified and extended their influence over those companies during the panic and recession. It is perhaps not unreasonable to group Mitsubishi and Mitsui with banks and other financial institutions with respect to their involvement in railway enterprises. To be sure, the emergent zaibatsu's interest in developing railways to serve their coal-mining and other operations meant that their motives in financing railway firms resembled those of entrepreneurs, while, on the other hand, Mitsubishi and Mitsui were a leading force in the eventual rise of professional railway managers. Still, Mitsui channeled its railway investments largely through its bank, and the generally conservative investment behavior of both zaibatsu was not unlike that of banks and other financial houses. As did the latter, the zaibatsu also placed part-time representatives on the boards of the railway concerns they helped to finance. Thus, Japanese railway companies in the early 1890s seem to fit Chandler's definition of the "financial enterprise," in which entrepreneurs and salaried managers have to share top-management decisions with the agents of investing financial establishments.[184] If by the end of the panic, then, most private railways had moved from the "entrepreneurial" to the "financial" stage of modern business evolution, by the turn of the century several were well on their way to becoming what Chandler terms "managerial enterprises."

The patterns of financing and management of railway firms around the time of the panic had significance for those of joint-stock companies in other fields as well. In pioneering such measures as preferred-stock and corporate-bond issues, private railways offered other kinds of joint-stock enterprises a model of both emergency and long-term funding, especially after legal restrictions on the use of those measures were relaxed later in the Meiji period. And railway concerns would continue to lead the way after the turn of the century by becoming the first Japanese corporations to float bond issues abroad.[185] As for management, railways in the early 1890s were perhaps unique in the extent to which local residents and government authorities were able to influence corporate decision making. Yet, as the rights of way were purchased and the lines completed, as the terms of state subsidies expired, and as railway executives of government stock became more professional in outlook or were replaced by career managers, the administration of railway companies gradually lost its special character, becoming much like that of other joint-stock ventures. In fact, the relatively early professionalization of railway management, particularly in the case of the San'yo Railway under Nakamigawa and Matsumoto, suggests that in Japan, as in the United States, railway firms were also pacesetters in the introduction of modern administrative practices among joint-stock enterprises.[186]

Nevertheless, the contribution of private railways in this regard had little to do with their actual experience in coping with the Panic of 1890 and its aftermath, except insofar as that crisis accelerated the railway's transition to the intermediate phase between entrepreneurial and managerial capitalism by heightening their dependence on financial institutions. With respect to modes of financing, however, that particular experience clearly played an important role in the development of joint-stock companies in general during the latter part of the Meiji era.

Kagami Kenkichi and the N.Y.K., 1929–1935: Vertical Control, Horizontal Strategy, and Company Autonomy

WILLIAM D. WRAY

Several of the largest shipping firms in modern Japan, especially those that emerged in the early Meiji period, have been members of the zaibatsu. Compared to other zaibatsu enterprises in fields like banking, trading, or manufacturing, which became direct subsidiaries, shipping companies enjoyed considerable managerial autonomy and were less subject to intervention or vertical control from their zaibatsu. There were at least two reasons for this. First, the zaibatsu had only a small equity participation in shipping companies, which were therefore considered affiliates in contrast to the direct subsidiaries whose stock was held wholly or primarily by the holding company. Second, in normal business operations, shipping firms developed extensive ties outside their own zaibatsu, especially with trading companies, manufacturers, and banks. Business operations which include purchasing, financing, manufacturing, insuring, shipping, and marketing are usually termed vertical if they are carried on within a single firm or zaibatsu. Generally, the activity of the shipping firms studied here cannot be characterized this way. In view of this and also because my principal focus is managerial dissension rather than business operations, I have used the term *vertical* in a slightly different way, namely, to refer to the pattern of control or the type of relationship that existed between zaibatsu leadership and individual companies within the zaibatsu, particularly the shipping firms. In examining autonomy, I am concerned primarily with the capacity of the individual company to make decisions independently or to ward off interventionist policies from zaibatsu leadership that would result in a fundamental change in the identity of the company.[1] In this chapter I emphasize the phenomenon of company autonomy within a zaibatsu, as illustrated by the relation between the Mitsubishi zaibatsu and the N.Y.K. (Japanese Mail Steamship Company).

The Mitsubishi-N.Y.K. relationship was essentially ambiguous. On the one hand, Mitsubishi's close financial and personnel ties to the N.Y.K., established at the N.Y.K.'s founding in 1885, had greatly diminished by the end of World War I. Furthermore, Mitsubishi was not a major shipper for the N.Y.K. On the other hand, by functioning as a market for ships, the N.Y.K. provided the basis for Mitsubishi's diversification into heavy industry prior to World War I. This strategic role sometimes prompted Mitsubishi to intervene in N.Y.K. affairs, even though the N.Y.K. was only an affiliate with a largely independent business operation.

Western historiography on the Japanese shipping industry has long been influenced by official views. Both the British Imperial Shipping Committee of 1938 and the reports and policies of the American Occupation generally exaggerated the extent of the business connections between shipping firms and the zaibatsu, often assuming that shipping, as described above, was just one part of the vertical operation within a zaibatsu, and thus emphasizing, for example, the close ties between Mitsubishi and the N.Y.K.[2] As opposed to these views, Japanese shipping executives have strongly argued that firms like the N.Y.K. enjoyed autonomy within their own zaibatsu. For example, Terai Hisanobu, N.Y.K. president from 1942 until he was purged in 1946, argued:

The N.Y.K. is a Mitsubishi-related firm, but in fact the N.Y.K. was established when Mitsubishi withdrew from the shipping industry [in 1885]. Just as the N.Y.K. received no special treatment from Mitsubishi-related firms in shipbuilding, banking, and warehousing, so too it gave no special treatment to the freight of Mitsubishi Shōji (Mitsubishi Trading) and other Mitsubishi firms. In my 30 years service with the N.Y.K., I have never heard of any case where the company was subject to managerial intervention from Mitsubishi. The relation between the O.S.K. (Osaka Commercial Shipping Co.) and Sumitomo has probably also been similar. Since Mitsui Senpaku (Mitsui Shipping Co.) and Mitsubishi Kisen (Mitsubishi Steamship Co.) [established respectively in 1942 and 1943 as spin-offs from trading companies] are under direct zaibatsu management, they are not germane to this discussion. There are no other zaibatsu-related companies in the shipping industry. In this situation, I do not believe we can say that Japanese shipping is under the vertical (*suichokuteki*) managerial organization of the zaibatsu.[3]

Terai enjoyed a reputation as something of an intellectual, and after the war he wrote several candid and perceptive accounts of Japanese shipping history. His views cannot be dismissed simply as self-serving defense against American policy toward the zaibatsu during the early Occupation. Insofar as it applies to normal business activity, Terai's statement can be accepted. But it also ignores the fact that, during the Depression, the company was indeed subject to financial pressure from other Mitsubishi firms dependent on a healthy N.Y.K. and anxious because of its plummeting fortunes. In particular, it overlooks the role of Kagami Kenkichi, N.Y.K. president from 1929 to 1935. Though Kagami was principally an insurance specialist who had built up the Tokio Marine and Fire Insurance Company to world rank, he also became the most influential financial figure within the Mitsubishi zaibatsu during the 1930s. His presence in the N.Y.K. ensured a strong Mitsubishi influence.

Zaibatsu vertical control and individual company autonomy in the shipping industry can be thought of as two extremes between which a pendulum swung according to the state of the economy. When times were good (from 1912 to 1919), it swung toward autonomy; when times were bad (from about 1920 to 1933), it swung toward vertical control. Added to this vertical pressure, applied by the zaibatsu leadership, was the horizontal tendency toward cartelization within the shipping industry, prompted by the long recession of the 1920s and the shipping crisis of 1929 to 1932.[4] In the early 1930s, this tendency all but reached its ultimate limit when negotiations took place for a merger between the N.Y.K. and the O.S.K. The

O.S.K., Japan's second largest shipping firm, was linked to the Sumitomo zaibatsu through Sumitomo's role in the company's establishment in 1884 and through personnel ties in the inter-war years.
Though the O.S.K. was not a formal Sumitomo affiliate, Sumitomo
officials eventually entered negotiations with Mitsubishi regarding
the proposed N.Y.K.-O.S.K. merger. This attempt at merger, though
abortive, is a good subject for a case study because it cuts across the
normal categories of company, industry and zaibatsu through the
interaction of vertical pressure (Mitsubishi's effort to rescue the
N.Y.K.) and horizontal strategies (the proposed merger). I have
briefly summarized the economic and financial pressures that
prompted the merger negotiations and concentrated instead on the
views of certain managers. I have drawn these views from various
reminiscences, newspaper reports, interviews, and, most important,
the diary of Ōtani Noboru, N.Y.K. vice-president during the course
of the negotiations.

It is often said that Japanese companies do not keep detailed
records, and thus it is difficult for historians to analyze the process of
decision making. However, Ōtani's diary, N.Y.K. documents, and
accounts and statements by the principals make it possible to construct in unusual detail the events and decisions surrounding this
abortive merger. These sources provide insight into the nature of
intra-zaibatsu relations from the perspective of a member firm, a
topic that has received little attention from scholars either in Japan
or the West. They also help to elucidate an aspect of industrial organization, specifically the issue of mergers and cartels. It is generally
assumed that inter-zaibatsu cooperation increased during the Depression and the 1930s. From a longer-term perspective, though, membership in a zaibatsu often acted as a disincentive toward merger or the
strengthening of independent industrial cartels. In the case under
study, however, Mitsubishi, in the person of Kagami, strongly encouraged the N.Y.K. to merge. In the end, I argue, company autonomy
and the existence of cartel agreements in the shipping industry
proved to be stronger than this pressure for merger.

THE HORIZONTAL DIMENSION: PROBLEMS OF THE
MAJOR SHIPPING COMPANIES IN THE 1920s

During the most of the two decades from the start of Japan's trans-oceanic shipping in the mid 1890s down to World War I, the N.Y.K. had been the only Japanese shipping firm operating beyond East Asia. Through government subsidies, effective business alliances with trading companies like Mitsui Bussan and cotton spinning firms, and skillful negotiating with the international freight conferences dominated by Europeans, the N.Y.K. had established an integrated network of lines to Shanghai, London, Seattle, Bombay, Calcutta, and Melbourne. Though its share of Japan's steamship tonnage had declined from 77 percent at its birth in 1885 to 23 percent in 1913, it still held a nearly 2 to 1 edge over the O.S.K., its nearest Japanese competitor, on the eve of World War I.[5]

During World War I, the N.Y.K. earned enormous profits from the increased demand for Japanese shipping. Despite this, its business performance was sub-par compared to that of other Japanese firms. These results were shaped in part by a conservative strategy, dating from about 1907, of specializing in regular transoceanic lines and shunning new opportunities in tramp shipping. The N.Y.K. responded slowly to the new demand, even after the outbreak of the war. Kondō Renpei, company president since 1895, expected a short war and an ensuing recession, and was at first reluctant to undertake extensive ship purchasing.[6] Furthermore, during the war the government controlled freight rates on regular overseas lines where the N.Y.K. did most of its business. N.Y.K. thus exploited the war less effectively than the operators of irregular lines. These were the tramp shippers, mainly operators engaged in chartering, like Mitsui Bussan, Yamashita Kisen, Kawasaki, and the newly formed Kokusai Kisen. They were the principal beneficiaries of the war.[7] Even among shipowners, the N.Y.K.'s growth rate was slow. By 1920, the ratio of N.Y.K. to O.S.K. tonnage had fallen to 1.2:1.

Whereas the N.Y.K. lost its dominance over the industry during the war, its failure to plan adequately for postwar changes brought on many of its problems during the 1920s.[8] In 1919, thinking of renewed British competition in Asia, Kondō unveiled a plan to double the size of the company's fleet. Although this was not carried out, between 1920 and 1922, when the shipping boom ended, the

N.Y.K.'s tonnage grew by 13 percent compared to a more prudent 8 percent for the O.S.K.[9] This left the company with a huge excess capacity as it faced increased competition from the O.S.K. and the new shipping enterprises.

Labor disputes and managerial dissensions in the N.Y.K. exacerbated these business problems in the early 1920s. During the war and postwar boom, sea employees had achieved major gains in both pay and rank. Some had even been promoted to executive positions in shore-based offices. To combat what they saw as favoritism toward seamen, land employees formed their own group, the Dōkōkai. Itō Yonejirō, the pro-seamen's president who had succeeded Kondō in 1921, responded to the Dōkōkai's demands by firing 11 high-ranking employees. This action precipitated the mass resignation of over 700 shore employees, split the ranks of N.Y.K. directors, most of whom resigned, and culminated in Itō's own departure in October 1924.[10] By mid-decade the N.Y.K.'s business was in decline and its management in shambles, with most of its first-rate executives gone. At this point, Mitsubishi's President Iwasaki Koyata intervened to appoint as the new N.Y.K. President Shirani Takeshi, head of the government-owned Yawata Iron and Steel works.[11]

Shirani's regime saw continued labor problems. He did, however, bring greater calm to management, presided over the amalgamation of the N.Y.K. with Tōyō Kisen's deficit-plagued Pacific operations, and led the company into an era of huge ocean liners to upgrade the passenger business on its San Francisco line acquired from Tōyō Kisen (Oriental Steamship Co.).

Shirani also began to tackle a major financial controversy left over from the war. During the peak of the boom, management had paid out dividends of more than 100 percent. As the recession set in, the company continued to appease stockholder demands. As shown in Table 1, from 1920 to 1925 dividends greatly exceeded profits in every year. The N.Y.K. has been singled out for criticism because it allowed its assets to flow out of the firm by using reserves to pay the dividend.[12] However, a comparison with Table 2 shows that, from 1921 to 1923, in relative terms, the O.S.K. was even more guilty of this practice than was the N.Y.K. A second misunderstanding about the O.S.K. is that its business performance was better than the N.Y.K.'s in the 1920s. On the contrary, a comparison of Tables 1 and

2 shows that it was indeed worse, as measured by profit in terms of assets and income, in every year but 1925.[13]

The truth, it seems, is that the O.S.K.'s planning during the 1920s was more farsighted. This does not show up in the business results for the postwar decade, but it did enable the company to outperform the N.Y.K. by a wide margin during the recovery from the Depression. By 1930, the O.S.K. had become a formidable opponent, which presented the N.Y.K. with the unpleasant choice of wasteful competition or horizontal cooperation.

Table 3 suggests that the turning point in the O.S.K.'s fortunes relative to those of the N.Y.K. came in the mid-1920s. The reasons for this turnaround can be summarized briefly. First, the O.S.K. began to rely on debt capital and bonds to upgrade its fleet three years earlier than the N.Y.K. (1924 vs. 1927). Second, as shown in Table 4, in a reversal of prewar trends, the O.S.K. maintained a consistently high freight-to-passenger income ratio, whereas the N.Y.K., especially after the merger with Tōyō Kisen, greatly increased its reliance on passengers. Along with the excess capacity inherited from Tōyō Kisen, these delays and strategic changes left the N.Y.K. with 130,000 tons of laid-up ships in 1933 compared to almost none for the O.S.K.[14] Third, the O.S.K. had greater continuity of managerial expertise, as seen in the rise of specialists like Murata Shōzō, who led Japanese shipowners in introducing diesel engines. Fourth, the O.S.K. benefited from its geographical base in Osaka, the center of the textile industry, which constituted Japan's fastest growing export trade. By contrast, the N.Y.K. continued to rely heavily on its European line even though Japan's overall trade with Europe was declining relative to the increasing share enjoyed by Asia and North America.

The N.Y.K. felt the impact of O.S.K. growth in two ways. The Osaka firm became a competitor on virtually all the N.Y.K.'s overseas lines, and the consensus by which the two firms had managed their subsidiaries tended to break down, leading to a struggle for control toward the end of the 1920s. The O.S.K. had been established in 1884 as an amalgamation of many small shipowners. During its first decade, it was confined mainly to regional shipping in western Japan. Following the Sino-Japanese War, it started lines to Chinese and other East Asian ports. Just prior to World War I, it began to challenge the N.Y.K. in transoceanic routes, first with a regular line to

TABLE 1 N.Y.K. Business Results, 1919–1934
(¥1,000)

Year	Assets (A)	Income (I)	Profit (P)	Dividend (D)	Dividend Rate (%)	Profits as % of			Dividend as % of Profit D/P
						Assets P/A	Income P/I	Paid-up Capital	
1919	232,134	216,755	50,180	43,500	50 100	21.6	23.2	86.5	86.7
1920	177,154	153,548	26,385	20,300	40 30	14.9	17.2	45.5	76.9
1921	166,448	91,828	8,872	13,050	25 20	5.3	9.7	15.3	147.1
1922	151,729	79,505	5,396	8,700	15	3.6	6.8	9.3	161.2
1923	143,159	74,766	3,659	7,250	15 10	2.6	4.9	6.3	198.1
1924	136,696	68,453	3,532	5,800	10	2.6	5.2	6.1	164.2
1925	140,208	68,244	3,067	5,220	10 8	2.2	4.5	5.3	170.2
1926	125,623	73,099	5,397	4,831	8	4.3	7.4	8.4	89.5
1927	139,637	78,470	5,836	5,140	8	4.2	7.4	9.1	88.1
1928	187,507	80,742	6,320	5,140	8	3.4	7.8	9.8	81.3
1929	187,859	82,475	6,386	5,140	8	3.4	7.7	9.9	80.5
1930	177,677	74,512	-5,865	1,606	5 —	-3.3	-7.9	-9.1	—
1931	173,529	62,866	-728	—	—	-0.4	-1.2	-1.1	—
1932	172,634	61,788	175	—	—	0.1	0.3	0.3	—
1933	177,871	76,319	1,926	—	—	1.1	2.5	3.0	—
1934	159,576	77,822	4,247	1,927	3	2.7	5.5	6.6	45.4

Source: NYK 70 nenshi, pp. 701–707. Where two figures appear under the dividend percentage, different amounts were given in the two halves of the business year. The N.Y.K.'s paid-up capital was ¥58 million from 1919–1925 and ¥64.25 million from 1926–1934.

TABLE 2 O.S.K. Business Results, 1919–1934 (¥1,000)

Year	Assets (A)	Income (I)	Profit (P)	Dividend (D)	Dividend Rate (%)	Profits as % of			Dividend as % of Profit D/P
						Assets P/A	Income P/I	Paid-up Capital	
1919	126,345	127,169	20,824	15,369	30 30 / 10 10	16.5	16.4	55.7	73.8
1920	131,625	89,716	11,052	9,937	15 5 / 10 10	8.4	12.3	17.7	89.9
1921	118,799	59,335	2,030	6,250	10 7	1.2	2.4	3.2	307.9
1922	107,978	53,038	1,255	5,313	10 7	1.2	2.4	2.0	423.3
1923	104,734	52,065	1,206	4,375	7	1.2	2.3	1.9	362.8
1924	112,616	58,246	2,840	4,375	7	2.5	4.9	4.5	154.0
1925	121,939	64,893	3,623	4,375	7	3.0	5.6	5.8	120.8
1926	125,024	70,335	4,161	4,375	7	3.3	5.9	6.7	105.1
1927	125,026	70,065	3,851	3,750	6	3.1	5.5	6.2	97.4
1928	133,983	70,406	4,107	3,750	6	3.1	5.8	6.6	91.3
1929	140,820	72,200	4,099	3,750	6	2.9	5.7	6.6	91.5
1930	125,560	61,628	-41	—	—	-0.0	-0.1	-0.4	—
1931	124,326	57,814	-112	—	—	-0.1	-0.2	-0.2	—
1932	125,312	60,471	677	—	—	0.5	1.1	1.1	—
1933	119,882	74,384	2,326	1,562	— 5	1.9	3.1	3.7	67.2
1934	115,078	84,799	5,747	3,152	5	5.0	6.8	9.2	54.4

Source: OSK *80 nenshi*, pp. 798–813; O.S.K. *50 nenshi* (Dōshahen, 1934), pp. 474, 855; OSK business reports (*eigyo hōkokusho*).

Note: In 1919–1920, the dividend rate varied with the degree to which shares were paid up. See note 30 below.

TABLE 3 Gross Income Per Ton Owned

Year	N.Y.K.	O.S.K.
1913	78	91
1921	177	143
1924	132	133
1925	130	146
1926	120	154
1927	131	148
1928	132	148
1931	86	114

Source: OSK 80 nenshi, pp. 764–765; NYK 70 nenshi, pp. 675; and Table 4.

Tacoma in 1909 (later called the Puget Sound line) and then to Bombay in 1913. During the years of plenty, from 1914 to 1920, it started lines to Europe, New York, South America, Australia, and Calcutta, eventually gaining admission to the respective conferences. Though the N.Y.K. and O.S.K. signed a freight-rate agreement in 1922 to cover some of these parallel routes, they began to encroach upon each others' traditional spheres in domestic waters.[15] This competition soon spilled over into the battle for subsidiaries.

In early 1927, without first informing the N.Y.K., the O.S.K. approached the former's Kinkai Yūsen (Near-Seas Mail Steamship Co.) subsidiary with a proposal for a share swap that would have given the O.S.K. control over the Kinkai Yūsen and the N.Y.K. control over the O.S.K.'s Kita Nihon Kisen (North Japan Steamship Co.). The swap would have eliminated duplicate services of the two subsidiaries and enabled the O.S.K. to rationalize its East Asian lines. The N.Y.K. rejected the idea, fearing that the O.S.K. would thereby threaten the N.Y.K.'s dominance over the Chōsen Yūsen Kaisha (Korean Mail Steamship Co.). This was a joint subsidiary of the O.S.K. and N.Y.K., but the N.Y.K. had the larger number of shares and by consensus appointed its president. The N.Y.K. Board decided that, "in order to support the Chōsen Yūsen's operations, it is absolutely necessary for us to hold a majority interest in the company. In future, care must be taken to buy up floating shares when they become available."[16] The following year, the consensus over the Chōsen Yūsen collapsed, despite attempts by the colonial administra-

TABLE 4 Freight-Passenger Ratio (Based on Income)

Year	N.Y.K.	O.S.K.
1913	5.31	3.07
1921	6.28	4.45
1924	5.69	4.45
1928	4.15	4.17
1931	2.79	4.11

Source: *OSK 80 nenshi*, pp. 798–800; and *NYK 70 nenshi*, pp. 702–703.

tion in Korea to preserve it. The N.Y.K.-affiliated president, Onda Dōkichi, had to hold back on his intended resignation when the O.S.K. rejected an N.Y.K. nominee for the presidency and put forward its own man.[17] This seems to have been part of a deal whereby the N.Y.K. relinquished the presidency of the Nisshin Kisen (China-Japan Steamship Co.), which it had held since 1914, to an O.S.K. man. This firm was also a joint subsidiary, with the O.S.K., holding 49 percent of the shares compared to the N.Y.K.'s 44 percent.[18]

The duplicate services on the transoceanic lines and within East Asia had been established during prosperous times. As the country plunged deeper into the recession, the two firms could no longer afford this competition. Rationalization was called for.

THE VERTICAL DIMENSION: MITSUBISHI AND N.Y.K.

The N.Y.K. was established through a merger between Mitsubishi's shipping operations and a government-sponsored firm, the Kyōdō Unyu Kaisha (Union Transport Co.). Initially, Mitsubishi was the N.Y.K.'s largest single stockholder with 45 percent of company shares, but, over the next fifteen years, it sold most of these shares to finance the purchase of mines and real estate. Though the new Mitsubishi did not have extensive business relations with the N.Y.K., it did retain its influence through its personnel who transferred to the N.Y.K.. Beginning in the late 1890s, the business connection between the two became closer, as protectionist subsidy legislation gave the N.Y.K. incentive to buy its large ships from Mitsubishi's Nagasaki shipyard.

During the boom of World War I, Mitsubishi had set up most of its operation divisions as separate joint-stock companies under the control of Mitsubishi Gōshi Kaisha (Limited Partnership), owned by the Iwasaki family. There is no space here to describe the many subsequent stages in the evolution of Mitsubishi's management, but several key trends can be noted.[19] First, as shown in Chart 1, the principal firms can be divided into three categories:

1. Direct subsidiaries	— Normally Mitsubishi had a majority interest. — Management was subject to regulations imposed by the head office of the holding company (that is, Mitsubishi Gōshi).
2. Affiliated companies	— Most were founded before the establishment of Mitsubishi Company in 1886 (following the withdrawal from shipping). — Mitsubishi had only a minority interest. — Mitsubishi had one or two Board members but did not generally intervene in business operations.
3. Associated companies	— Stock was held directly by the Iwasaki family.

Changes in Mitsubishi's management structure during the interwar years were prompted in large part by the uneven performance of its subsidiaries. The poor results of its mining and shipbuilding enterprises, which had formed the basis for early diversification, forced the company to advance into fields like electrical manufacturing, for which private demand was expanding outside the shipbuilding sector, and aircraft manufacture, for which there was a steady military demand. Mitsubishi's financial enterprises—banking, real estate, and insurance—also experienced rapid growth. But, with profits down in mining and shipbuilding, growth was uneven. As a result, the head office found it difficult to impose uniform standard procedures on all subsidiaries. In 1929, then, new company regulations were issued. They allowed subsidiaries more flexibility in personnel matters and granted them autonomy in budgeting, in accounting, and in the acquisition and use of capital. These changes in company organization brought to the fore a new type of

CHART I Mitsubishi's Business Structure, 1931

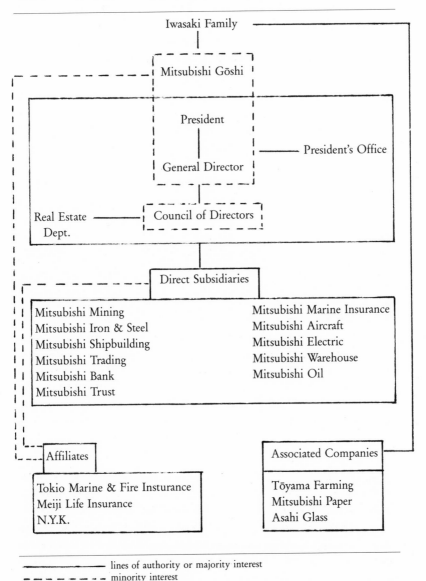

Iwasaki Family

Mitsubishi Gōshi

President

President's Office

General Director

Real Estate Dept.

Council of Directors

Direct Subsidiaries

Mitsubishi Mining
Mitsubishi Iron & Steel
Mitsubishi Shipbuilding
Mitsubishi Trading
Mitsubishi Bank
Mitsubishi Trust

Mitsubishi Marine Insurance
Mitsubishi Aircraft
Mitsubishi Electric
Mitsubishi Warehouse
Mitsubishi Oil

Affiliates

Tokio Marine & Fire Insturance
Meiji Life Insurance
N.Y.K.

Associated Companies

Tōyama Farming
Mitsubishi Paper
Asahi Glass

——————— lines of authority or majority interest
— — — — — — minority interest

Source: Mishima, ed., *Mistubishi*, pp. 100–101.

manager. The growth and increased autonomy of the subsidiaries expanded the authority of their specialized managers within the top leadership group of the whole zaibatsu, making a shift away from the more exclusively presidential leadership that had prevailed until the mid-1920s. Also, Mitsubishi's policy of opening the stock of its subsidiaries, which culminated in the incorporation of the head office in 1937, placed a premium on the utilization of financial experts. Managers of this type came to hold the largest number of concurrent directorships within Mitsubishi in the 1930s.[20]

Kagami Kenkichi was the major example of the reliance Mitsubishi placed on specialized managers and financial experts. Without an awareness of these managerial preferences it would be hard to understand how Kagami, despite his success at Tokio Marine, could have become so influential within Mitsubishi. Until the last stage of his career he remained outside the formal leadership posts of the head office, clinging until the 1920s to the principle of "one industry per man" (*ichinin ichigyōshugi*).[21] As a career insurance man, Kagami had managed a Mitsubishi affiliate rather than a direct subsidiary that might have put him closer to the head office at an earlier stage. Suzuki Mosaburō notes that Kagami ran his insurance trust in such a way that he was not subject to intervention from Mitsubishi. During World War I, Mitsubishi set up its own marine insurance company, Mitsubishi Kaijō (Mitsubishi Marine Insurance Co.). However, in 1933, through an exchange of stock, Mitsubishi Kaijō became a wholly owned subsidiary of Tokio Marine, while Mitsubishi Gōshi gained a larger share of Tokio Marine.

This deal brought about a closer relationship between Mitsubishi and Kagami's insurance empire, and, as I shall note later, it was similar to the new ties secured between Mitsubishi and the N.Y.K. during the early Shōwa years. It is also said that Kagami's relationship to Mitsubishi in his management of Tokio Marine was like that of a *tozama* (outside) daimyo to the shogun, except that Kagami was more powerful. Drawing analogies between the Restoration and the developments in the 1930s was a common habit of intellectuals in the early Shōwa. In this case, the analogy is suggestive, especially if we draw a parallel between the samurai bureaucrats in *tozama* domains who carried out the Restoration and the specialized managers in financial companies who gained influence within Mitsubishi as a whole during the 1930s.[22] In short, Kagami rose to power through his specialized expertise, which gave him control over a vast number of financial institutions. In 1937, he finally became a director of Mitsubishi's new holding company, his influence having grown rapidly since he took control of N.Y.K. in 1929.

Kagami brought impressive credentials on his mission to the N.Y.K. Long experience in London prior to 1900 (as noted in Chart 2) had given him a thorough familiarity with the international economy. Domestically, the event that catapulted him to fame, bringing recognition from the business world for his great ability, was the Kantō Earthquake of 1923. In its aftermath, insurance companies faced a crisis because of the enormous claims against them, but Kagami rescued the industry by negotiating with the government for long-term low-interest loans for fire-insurance companies.[23] In addition to his managerial expertise, Kagami had impeccable family ties, having married a niece of Iwasaki Yatarō, as shown in Chart 3. This helped him amass a vast personal fortune, some of it held outside the Mitsubishi zaibatsu.[24] With Tokio Marine's control over many other insurance firms, as well as with the N.Y.K.'s control over its subsidiaries, Kagami's position transformed him into a virtual institution, akin to a holding company.[25]

As Kagami's political influence grew during the 1930s, especially after his appointment to the Cabinet Deliberative Council in 1935, he was often cast beside Mitsui's Ikeda Seihin. The comparisons between these two were favorable to Kagami. Ikeda, it was said, had grace and refined bearing, whereas Kagami was more headlong, forceful, and direct. His combative nature was regarded as the equal of Ikeda's, and he was the only Mitsubishi executive with the real power and influence to rival the Mitsui leader. Kagami thus became Mitsubishi's representative to the outside world. Mitsubishi saw him as a "great man" (*ketsubutsu*) and the one most likely to bring credit to their zaibatsu in his role as emissary.[26]

Kagami's influence as N.Y.K. president derived not only from his power base in the insurance business and from his government appointments but also from his long experience with the N.Y.K. itself. After World War I, he had foreseen the coming recession earlier than most. In 1919, as the representative of Tokio Marine, the N.Y.K.'s third largest stockholder, Kagami had clashed angrily with Kondō Renpei over the latter's fleet-doubling plan. Although Kondō backed down, Kagami felt that the N.Y.K. had over-expanded and

CHART 2 Greatly Abbreviated Chronology of
Kagami Kenkichi's Career

Institution	Position and Dates	
Tokio Marine Insurance (later Tokio Marine & Fire)	Entry	1892
	London (Studied insurance business)	1894–99
	Head, Business Dept.	1899
	Marriage	1901
	General Manager	1906
	Director	1917
	Chairman	1925–39
Mitsubishi Trust Co.	Chairman	1927–36
	Director	1927–39
N.Y.K.	Director	1924–39
	President	1929–35
	Chairman	1935–39
Kinkai Yūsen	Director	1924–36
	Chairman	1931–35
Mitsubishi Bank	Auditor	1929–39
Nisshin Kisen	Director	1929–36
Yokohama Dock Co.	Director (merged with Mitsubishi Heavy Industries)	1932–35
Mitsubishi Co. (holding company)	Director	1937–39

Industry-Wide & Government

Japan Shipowners Association	Chairman	1929–32
Japan Industrial Club	Director	1930–37
Industrial Consultative Council	Member	1930
Temporary Industrial Rationalization Bureau, Shipbuilding Committee	Member	1930
Temporary Shipping Investigative Council	Member	1930
Cabinet Deliberative Council	Member	1935
Advisory Council on Mobilization	Member	1938

Source: Iwai, *Kagami,* pp. 268–271; Suzuki, ed., *Kagami,* pp. 263–279.

CHART 3 Kagami's Family Ties

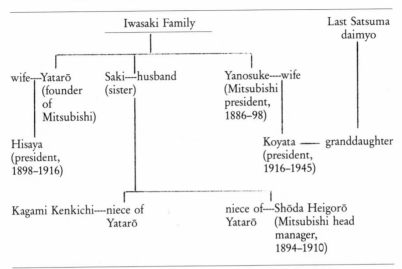

Source: Kagami Kōhei, fifth son of Shōda and temporarily adopted son of Kagami, Interview, 23 September 1975; drawn by Mrs. Kagami Kōhei. Cf. *Zaikai kakeizu* (Jinji kō-shinjo, 1962), p. 259.

that its shares were unsound. His reaction was unequivocal. By 1921, Tokio Marine had sold all its N.Y.K. shares.[27] But, in 1924, Kagami became an N.Y.K. director in the midst of the company's management crisis and served in that post until he took over the presidency on 24 May 1929, when Shirani resigned because of ill health.[28]

When Kagami became N.Y.K. president, he was clearly in the mainstream of Mitsubishi's financial policies. He was also considered a man for the times, a financier (rather than an entrepreneur) and a rationalist (*gōrishugisha*) whose forte was administering policies of consolidation (*seiri*) and restraint (*shōkyokusaku*).[29] Kagami's restorative mission to the N.Y.K. carried three goals: resumption of close capital ties between Mitsubishi and the N.Y.K.; renewal of the N.Y.K.'s financial health; and a reclamation of the N.Y.K.'s internal management.

KAGAMI'S MISSION: THE EARLY MOVES, 1929–1931

The first step toward Kagami's financial goals involved lowering the N.Y.K. dividend to prevent the flow of cash out of the company. Shirani had slowed this drain, but the dividend remained very high in terms of the profit rate. The interest of certain large N.Y.K. stockholders, however, threatened to clash with Kagami's policy. Between World War I and the later 1920s, Mitsubishi had been content with its 2-percent share of the N.Y.K. Circumstances changed after the N.Y.K.'s 1926 merger with the Yasuda-related Tōyō Kisen, for the combined holdings of this firm and the Yasuda Bank then reached 6.4 percent (10.4 percent in terms of par value).[30] This was a source of potential interference with Mitsubishi policy toward the N.Y.K. Just a week before Kagami became president, stockholders from Tōyō Kisen presented the N.Y.K. with an opinion paper concerning the need for reform in company operations, the lack of profitability of its new ships, the problem of cutting expenditures, and other such matters. Then, later in 1929, these stockholders began a movement to increase the dividend.[31]

The Imperial Household Ministry had long been the N.Y.K.'s largest stockholder. In the Meiji period it had acted in concert with government economic policy, investing in banks and new industries like railways and shipping as well as colonial companies like the South Manchurian Railway and the Oriental Development Company. In the interwar years, however, it did not invest in the emerging electrical, chemical, or heavy industries. Rather, it retained its early pattern of holdings, especially in banks, and acted like a conservative private investment institution intent on maximizing its own security. By 1940, its three largest holdings were the Bank of Japan, the Yokohama Specie Bank, and the N.Y.K., the last constituting 9.5 percent of the total market value of the Ministry's shares.[32] The conventional view is that the Imperial House did not interfere in the N.Y.K.'s business decisions despite its large share (see Table 5).[33] There is, however, certain indirect evidence that tends to modify this view. There were times when the company consulted the Imperial Household Ministry before finalizing its negotiating position for discussions with the government over subsidies. Also, a Ministry official usually served as an N.Y.K. auditor. Then, there were occasions in 1929 when N.Y.K. Vice President Ōtani Noboru went to the Ministry to

TABLE 5 Leading Stockholder Groups in the N.Y.K., 1924 and 1928

Year	Ranking	Name	Old Shares	New Shares	Total Shares	% of N.Y.K. Shares	Total Par Value (¥1,000)	% of Par Value of N.Y.K. Shares
1924	1.	Kunaishō*	161,100	201,375	362,475	18.1	10,572	18.2
	2.	Mitsubishi Shipbuilding	13,244	19,930	33,174	1.7	911	1.6
	12.	Meiji Life Insurance	2,900	3,625	6,525	0.3	190	0.3
		All N.Y.K. shares			2,000,000		58,000	
		Mitsubishi (#2 & 12)				2.0		1.9
1928	1.	Kunaishō*	161,000	201,375	362,475	17.1	10,572	16.4
	2.	Tōyō Kisen	125,000		125,000	5.9	6,250	9.7
	3.	Mitsubishi Shipbuilding	14,944	19,930	34,874	1.6	996	1.6
	6.	Yasuda Bank	7,380	4,165	11,545	0.5	421	0.7
	16.	Meiji Life Insurance	2,900	3,625	6,525	0.3	190	0.3
		All N.Y.K. shares			2,125,000		64,250	
		Tōyō Kisen & Yasuda (#2 & 6)				6.4		10.4
		Mitsubishi (#3 & 16)				1.9		1.9

(*) Imperial Household Ministry

Source: N.Y.K. Kabunishi seimeibo, 31 October of each year.

Note: Holders of new shares had the first right to pay in the outstanding portion of their shares (¥37.5 per share to be paid in 3 installments) whenever the company should call for a new installment. In this sense, new shares were as potentially valuable as old shares. Thus, the percentage of total shares is a more accurate index of influence within the company than the percentage of par value. The latter is simply a measure of the relative amount actually invested. See note 30.

discuss the company's financial reports and personnel.[34] Most important, in 1929, despite the need for retrenchment, the Ministry was reluctant to give its approval to a lowering of the dividend.[35]

Kagami acted with lightning speed to remove these potential sources of resistance to his policies. By 28 May, he had negotiated a deal for Mitsubishi to buy all of the Imperial Household Ministry's 201,375 new shares in N.Y.K. Mitsubishi Gōshi purchased 131,375 and Tokyo Marine 70,000. Mitsubishi is said to have paid about ¥4 million, equivalent to ¥19.9 per share, which was about market value. Together with the holdings of other Mitsubishi firms, this purchase increased Mitsubishi's overall share of the N.Y.K. to 11.49 percent, as shown in Table 6. For the first time since the nineteenth century Mitsubishi, as a group, had regained its position as the company's largest stockholder. Coming only four days after Kagami became N.Y.K. president, the deal created a sensation in the press, which declared that shipping had returned to the core of Mitsubishi's business and that the N.Y.K. was again a direct subsidiary of Mitsubishi.[36]

Once Kagami had secured Mitsubishi's control over the N.Y.K., the vertical dimension of his strategy, he set out in a horizontal direction to negotiate with the O.S.K. Terai Hisanobu, for one, believed that, from the time Kagami became N.Y.K. president, he had in mind a merger between the N.Y.K. and the O.S.K. Talks aimed at an agreement began in a semi-public fashion in October 1929 when Kagami visited the O.S.K.'s head office. They ebbed and flowed for a time before being virtually suspended; but rather specific press comment began on the advantages of cooperation or even merger.[37]

Whatever Kagami's original intentions, two large issues accelerated his planning. The first was the Great Depression following the stock market crash of October. This obviously increased pressure for cooperation to cut back on expenses. Second, the O.S.K. had implemented a daring strategy in June 1929 when it opened an express line to New York with new high-speed ships capable of 18.5 knots, about 50 percent faster than N.Y.K. vessels. The O.S.K.'s New York line was a gamble, considering the devastating effect the Depression was having on Japanese exports to the United States. But, strangely, the line succeeded partly because of the Depression. Prior to 1930, raw silk, Japan's principal export, was transshipped at west-coast ports (especially Seattle and Vancouver) to express trains for a run to New

TABLE 6 Leading Stockholder Groups in the N.Y.K., 1930

Year	Ranking	Name	Old Shares	New Shares	Total Shares	% of N.Y.K. Shares	Total Par Value (¥1,000)	% of Par Value of N.Y.K. Shares
1930	1.	Kunaishō*	161,000		161,000	7.6	8,055	12.5
	2.	Mitsubishi Gōshi		131,375	131,375	6.2	1,642	2.6
	3.	Tōyō Kisen	125,000		125,000	5.9	6,250	9.7
	4.	Tokio Marine Insurance	800	69,000	69,800	3.3	903	1.4
	6.	Mitsubishi Shipbuilding	14,944	19,930	34,874	1.6	996	1.6
	15.	Meiji Life Insurance	2,900	3,625	6,525	0.3	190	0.3
	19.	Yasuda Bank	1,070	4,165	5,235	0.3	106	0.2
	99.	Mitsubishi Trust Co.		1,500	1,500	0.1	19	0.0
		All N.Y.K. shares			2,125,000		64,250	
		Mitsubishi (#2, 4, 6, 15, & 99)				11.5		5.9
		Kunaishō (#1)				7.6		12.5
		Tōyō Kisen & Yasuda (#3 & 19)				6.2		9.9

Source: See Table 5.

(*) Imperial Household Ministry

York. The main deterrent to shipping raw silk through the Panama Canal had been the greater time required by that route. Time was of the essence because the shippers of the high-value raw silk had to borrow heavily, and they sought to reduce the interest on these loans which they had to pay while their cargo was in transit. Thus, the faster the route, the lower the interest charges. Although the direct sea route via Panama had lower freight rates, greater savings could be made in smaller interest payment on the faster rail service. However, the drastic fall in the price of raw silk during the Depression had the effect of reducing the interest charge. The difference in freight rates between the sea and rail routes was now greater than the extra interest incurred by shipping through the Canal. Therefore, even though the volume of raw silk shipped to New York fell during the Depression and never recovered to earlier levels, the O.S.K. gained because shipments, albeit smaller in total, were shifted to the Canal route.[38]

The O.S.K.'s New York line constituted a major challenge to the N.Y.K.'s own New York service as well as to the lines of both companies to the U.S. northwest coast. These lines had been in decline since the opening of the Panama Canal during World War I, but now they were also losing their raw-silk cargo. The O.S.K.'s new line, then, was a major impetus toward cooperation. The two firms resumed negotiations in December 1930 and finally reached agreement on 27 March 1931.[39] The terms were as follows:

(1) The N.Y.K. would withdraw from its South American east-coast line.
(2) The O.S.K. would relinquish its Puget Sound Line (Tacoma).
(3) The O.S.K. would entrust to the N.Y.K. the handling of business in Europe related to is eastbound line from the Continent.
(4) On the New York line, the O.S.K. would use 8 new ships and the N.Y.K. 6. However, "for the time being," the agreement allowed the O.S.K. to employ its 8 ships but it limited the N.Y.K. to 4. Both companies agreed to maintain existing conditions under the principle of joint management, until the N.Y.K. commissioned its new ships.
(5) On parallel lines the companies would mutually strive to avoid competition and as much as possible pool their earnings.
(6) In order to increase their common profits, the companies would cooperate concerning mutual utilization of land and sea equip-

ment, common acceptance of freight and passengers and common purchasing of supplies.

(7) The accord was to last for 10 years.

Nomura Jiichirō, an O.S.K. official who participated in earlier negotiations with the N.Y.K., believed that this March agreement was the opening wedge in a conspiracy led by Kagami, Murata, Sumitomo's Ogura Masatsune, and Yamashita Kamesaburō to merge the O.S.K. and the N.Y.K. and create a new company with Kagami as president and Murata as vice-president.[40] Though Kagami had initiated the talks late in the previous year, Nomura's view is hard to reconcile with the fact that Shimizu Yasuharu, an N.Y.K. director, handled most of the negotiations, and Vice-President Ōtani, not Kagami, worked out the final details with Murata on 26 March.[41] Furthermore, the accord itself was vague in certain respects. For the New York clause, Ōtani and Murata had been unable to agree on the circumstances and timing under which the N.Y.K. could increase its ships from 4 to 6. They thus had to compose an ambiguous statement. Also, the clause regarding an earnings pool was only an abstract commitment. The two firms thus established a joint working committee to implement the accord with Ōtani leading the N.Y.K. delegation, since Kagami went overseas on 14 April.[42] On Sunday, 19 April, officials of both firms gathered at the Hakone resort to create a "harmonious and cooperative spirit among executives in the aftermath of the accord." The meeting began shortly after 7:00 A.M. with Ōtani still in his bathtub, where he was joined by an O.S.K. negotiator (a Japanese posture conducive to openness and frankness). A round of golf followed in the afternoon, but, in the meantime, the executives discussed only general issues, leaving the details, that is, the difficult matters, to their special committee meetings.[43] The "harmony" they sought turned out to be somewhat superficial.

Though some successful cooperation was achieved among company branches, the joint committee could not overcome the competitive inclination of both firms. In the face of plummeting fortunes brought on by the Depression and by the boycott of Japanese goods after the Manchurian Incident in September, competition between the two firms resumed on their duplicate services. Meanwhile, with Kagami away in the West until October, no additional cooperative initiatives seem to have been attempted. While visiting Europe, however, Kagami was impressed by the large amalgamated groupings that had emerged in the shipping industries of Britain, Germany, and Italy. They provided a model for a more comprehensive, horizontal strategy than that envisaged in the March accord.[44]

N.Y.K.-O.S.K. MERGER: HORIZONTAL PRESSURES

The N.Y.K. and the O.S.K. had negotiated their accord at the end of a ten-year tradition of agitation favoring one large Japanese shipping combine (*senpaku gōdō*). The desire to retain Japan's international competitiveness after the war, amidst the proliferation of Japanese companies, had originally sparked this movement. It was blessed by Noda Utarō, Minister of Communications in the Seiyūkai Cabinet, who set up a committee in May 1920 to examine the shipping-combine issue. Since two N.Y.K. advisers, Gō Seinosuke (head of the Japan Economic Federation) and Wada Toyoji (of Fuji Gas Spinning), supported the combine movement, the matter soon became intertwined in N.Y.K. factionalism. Outside political agitation also exacerbated the dissension within the company. The most extreme proposals were advocated by Tachikawa Matahachirō, a large stockholder in both the N.Y.K. and O.S.K. and a speculator who was considered an eccentric within the shipping world. He favored nationalization, primarily on political grounds. Shipping, he said, could play the same supportive function for the Navy that the nationalized railways did for the Army. He compared shipping companies to daimyo and the Ministry of Communications to the Tokugawa shogun, arguing that the two should join in a nationalized combine that would be analogous to a "Restoration" enterprise. During the early 1920s, Tachikawa caused commotion in the General Meetings of both the N.Y.K. and the O.S.K. with these proposals.[45]

Tachikawa apparently had connections with the Kokuryūkai (Black Dragon Society), the right-wing patriotic society that was also supporting the combine movement for its own purposes of overseas expansion. In 1922, using the rationale that a combine would ensure continued high dividends, the Kokuryūkai began collecting proxy shares to argue its case in the N.Y.K.'s May General Meeting. Company executives, backed by the large shareholders, responded with a counter-movement. But, through some behind-the-scenes maneuver-

ing, Gō, Wada, and Noda persuaded N.Y.K. President Itō, an opponent of combines, to establish a committee to investigate the issue.
Journalists speculated that Gō and Wada were using the Kokuryūkai
for their own purposes.[46]

Nevertheless, this early phase of the movement was primarily
political. By forcing the N.Y.K. to consider the combine issue it probably did provide some impetus for the 1926 merger with Tōyō
Kisen. But, by the late 1920s, the principal forces working for merger
in the shipping industry were the businessmen themselves. The most
important of these leaders was Yamashita Kamesaburō, who was
close enough to Kagami to regard him as a man of action and not just
an advocate of financial restraint.[47] Yamashita saw that a rationalization of N.Y.K. and O.S.K. services would result in ships being
removed from lines. He hoped that they would be available at inexpensive charter rates. On 10 April 1931, just after the accord between
the two firms, a Yamashita executive approached Ōtani about having
his firm use those ships that the N.Y.K. would no longer need. One
problem this presented to the N.Y.K. was that Yamashita was primarily a bare-boat charterer, renting only the ship and not the crew of
the owner. A cutback in N.Y.K. ship use, however, threatened to lead
to extensive severance of crew, a matter Ōtani took up with the
Labor Investigative Committee of the Industrial Club. Chartering
out ships to Yamashita would thus not help the N.Y.K.'s labor problem. Ōtani did not want to lay off seamen, but it appears in the end
that the N.Y.K. followed a policy of mooring its ships, whereas the
O.S.K. was more positive in chartering out to Yamashita on a bare-
boat basis.[48]

By the later 1920s, the combine movement had been replaced by a
new sense of crisis resulting from the Depression and by a broader
program of industrial rationalization supported by both the Minseitō government in 1930–1931 and the Seiyūkai which replaced it in
December 1931. The rationalization movement meant technological
upgrading of plant facilities and improved management methods. In
some industries, it involved the creation of trade associations; in
others, like steel, automobiles, and paper, the government vigorously
promoted a merger policy.[49] Despite the increasing support for this
horizontal movement from the business world, the government was
not a prime mover in the N.Y.K.-O.S.K. "union" (the term used for
the accord). The initiative for the union came from the companies

with little or no government involvement.[50] Although officials from the Ministry of Communications expressed no disagreement when Ōtani explained the details of the accord to them on 30 March, press reports at the time speculated that the Ministry actually opposed it. The reasoning was as follows: (1) The withdrawal of the O.S.K. from the Puget Sound line and the N.Y.K. from the South American line meant an abandonment of market share built up through 20 years of subsidies. (2) There would be a weakening of Japanese competitive power on these lines against European and American companies now that each firm was operating alone. (3) The withdrawal of the N.Y.K. from South America would lead to a shortage of ships on that line and would necessitate additional subsidies if emigration increased.[51]

Rationalization was an issue addressed by N.Y.K. leaders as well. In 1932, Ōtani published an article on shipping in a volume of essays on rationalization. Whereas another contributor spoke glowingly of the benefits to be derived from joint purchases and an earnings pool under the O.S.K.-N.Y.K. accord, Ōtani employed a more general definition of rationalization. He called it a movement for the techno-logical upgrading of industry, improvement in organization, and eco-nomic efficiency through elimination of waste. As for benefits, he spoke of savings to the N.Y.K. from the introduction of diesel engines, which would lower fuel costs on the San Francisco line from about ¥120,000 to ¥70,000 per voyage.[52]

On other occasions, Ōtani spoke of the need for the N.Y.K. to build its own new ships for the New York line, and it was he who failed to reach agreement with Murata to clarify the New York clause in the accord. Furthermore, on 30 March, a newspaper article claimed that Ōtani himself opposed N.Y.K.-O.S.K. cooperation. He then had to explain at the next board meeting why the reporter had erred.[53] But had he? Indeed, rationalization to Ōtani and other N.Y.K. executives seems to have meant the application of technology for purposes of *expansion*, whereas to Kagami it meant *restraint*. An official of the British trading house Butterfield & Swire commented as follows in late 1932:

N.Y.K. have hitherto declined to take part in the race for the provision of fast ton-nage in the New York trade, but Mr. Shimizu has told me that the majority of his Directors have been in favor of modernizing their New York fleet only Mr. Kagami, President of N.Y.K. (who has never been under any illusions regarding the gravity of the world economic and financial disarrangements), has turned a deaf ear to all arguments of that nature which they have submitted for his consideration . . . He is a very strong minded man and is exceedingly strict in his control of the financial affairs of his Company.[54]

If Ōtani and his fellow executives were lukewarm in their support of the 1931 accord, there would be resistance within the company to the increasing horizontal pressure for merger. That would be a bad omen for Kagami even though he was gathering powerful backing for just that purpose in 1932.

N.Y.K.-O.S.K. MERGER: VERTICAL PRESSURE

The key to the pressure for merger lay in the intertwining of business and financial interests between Mitsubishi and Sumitomo in their dealings with both the N.Y.K. and the O.S.K. One view of the business relations within a zaibatsu is as follows: "One of the Mitsubishi mining companies might extract the minerals which one of the Mitsubishi manufacturing companies then fashioned into a product, which a Mitsubishi trading firm in turn marketed abroad, transporting it in ships of another Mitsubishi affiliate, and the whole process would be financed through the Mitsubishi banking interests." This interpretation, however, oversimplifies the structural relationship between the N.Y.K. and Mitsubishi, for the N.Y.K. and the O.S.K. did not develop close ties with the shippers within the Mitsubishi and Sumitomo zaibatsu to which they were connected.[55] The N.Y.K.'s primary importance to Mitsubishi was as a market for its ships. Shipbuilding became the core business from which Mitsubishi diversified, a process made possible by N.Y.K. purchases before World War I.[56] Table 7, however, shows that, between 1920 and 1932, the O.S.K. purchased more tonnage from Mitsubishi than did the N.Y.K. If the N.Y.K. functioned as a market for Mitsubishi, these figures suggest that Mitsubishi had become more dependent on the O.S.K. than on the N.Y.K.! Clearly, though, the financial health of both companies was essential to Mitsubishi's core industry.

Financially, both companies had transformed their capital structure, since they came to rely on bonds during the 1920s (see Tables 8 and 9). Again, this new financial structure reflected the growing mutual dependence between Mitsubishi and the O.S.K.. To finance

TABLE 7 Purchasers of Ships from Mitsubishi's Nagasaki Shipyard
(by % of gross tonnage)

Period	N.Y.K.	O.S.K.	Other
1896–1913	47.8	14.1	38.0
1914–1919	49.0	21.7	29.3
1920–1932	35.5	39.3	25.2

Source: Mishima Yasuo, *Mitsubishi zaibatsu shi: Taishō-Shōwa hen* (Kyōikusha, 1980), p. 85.

Note: According to figures supplied to me by Professor Shiba Takao, between 1920 and 1932 the O.S.K. purchased 32.7 percent and the N.Y.K. 30.5 percent of the output of all Mitsubishi yards.

its new ships for the New York line the O.S.K. issued bonds worth ¥25 million, of which the Mitsubishi Bank took ¥10 million. Later in the 1930s, after this first issue had been redeemed, Mitsubishi still held 25 percent of the O.S.K.'s bonds.[57] The timing of the first bond issue for the New York service is especially interesting for this study, for Kagami was the auditor of the Mitsubishi Bank. In that sense, he was indirectly involved in financing the N.Y.K.'s competitor. Furthermore the O.S.K. ordered two of its ships for the New York line from Mitsubishi's Nagasaki Shipyard in late February 1931, just shortly before it signed the accord with the N.Y.K.[58] The case of the N.Y.K. is similar. Both the Mitsubishi and Sumitomo banks purchased its bonds when they were issued in the later 1920s.[59] It is hardly surprising, therefore, that the banks put pressure on Kagami to improve conditions for the two shipping firms.[60]

This pressure was applied not simply for the sake of the banks' investment but for other industries like shipbuilding which were dependent upon a healthy shipping industry and to which the banks were also linked. In this interrelated mesh of business and financial interests the vertical pressure from the zaibatsu became fused with the problem of recovery for the shipping industry. The solution to that led in a horizontal direction toward merger. Both the O.S.K. and the N.Y.K. had to be rescued. If necessary, the rescue would be at the expense of the two firms' individual identity, for the health of the two zaibatsu depended on their recovery. In this sense, the fusion of vertical and horizontal pressure greatly eroded the individual autonomy of the two firms.

Mutual dependence in stockholding was not quite as dramatic as

TABLE 8 N.Y.K. Capital Structure, 1919–1934

Year	Paid-up Capital	%	Reserves & Profit	%	Bonds & Loans	%	Other	%
1919	58,000	25	150,705	65			23,428	10
1920	58,000	33	104,642	59			14,511	8
1921	58,000	35	96,734	58			11,714	7
1922	58,000	38	83,660	55			10,068	7
1923	58,000	41	79,291	55			5,866	4
1924	58,000	42	68,549	50			10,146	8
1925	58,000	41	66,268	47			15,939	12
1926	64,250	51	45,466	36			15,906	13
1927	64,250	46	45,608	33	15,000	11	14,777	10
1928	64,250	34	46,931	25	60,000	32	16,325	9
1929	64,250	34	46,411	25	60,000	32	17,197	9
1930	64,250	36	36,675	21	60,000	34	16,752	9
1931	64,250	37	37,866	22	60,000	35	11,411	6
1932	64,250	37	39,912	23	60,000	35	8,471	5
1933	64,250	36	43,597	25	60,000	34	10,024	5
1934	64,250	40	47,719	30	30,000	19	17,606	11

Source: NYK 70 nenshi, pp. 708–709.

TABLE 9 O.S.K. Capital Structure, 1919–1934

Year	Paid-up Capital	%	Reserves & Profit	%	Bonds & Loans	%	Other	%
1919	37,375	30	78,477	62	3,500	2	6,993	6
1920	62,500	47	64,706	49			4,419	4
1921	62,500	53	48,583	41			7,716	6
1922	62,500	58	40,263	37			5,512	5
1923	62,500	60	37,807	36			4,427	4
1924	62,500	56	36,528	32	8,917	8	4,671	4
1925	62,500	51	35,261	29	19,597	16	4,581	4
1926	62,500	50	35,850	29	21,896	18	4,778	3
1927	62,500	50	36,601	29	20,650	17	5,275	4
1928	62,500	47	37,417	28	29,641	22	4,425	3
1929	62,500	44	38,883	28	35,540	25	3,897	3
1930	62,500	50	24,147	19	34,860	28	4,053	3
1931	62,500	50	24,624	20	33,180	27	4,022	3
1932	62,500	50	26,990	22	31,500	25	4,322	3
1933	62,500	52	29,933	25	22,500	19	4,949	4
1934	62,500	54	33,392	29	12,404	11	6,782	6

Source: OSK 80 nenshi, pp. 812–813. I have subtracted from the O.S.K. figures the unpaid portion of the authorized capital stock. The O.S.K.'s authorized capital, like the N.Y.K.'s, was ¥100 million.

in the case of bonds, but the linkage is similar. Although Sumitomo was instrumental in founding the O.S.K. in 1884, it had never been a major stockholder. O.S.K. stockholding was quite diversified, but the major owners were Osaka businessmen and local ship operators like Hiromi Nisaburō. As shown in Table 10, Hiromi was the largest stockholder in 1923. Except for the Imperial House and O.S.K. President Hori Keijirō, I have not listed other large holders, since they do not figure in this study. Hori's appointment as a Sumitomo bank director in 1918 helped re-establish close ties between O.S.K. and Sumitomo. In the 1920s, Sumitomo began to send one of its officials to the O.S.K. as a director. Ogura Masatsune, the Sumitomo General Director, took up this post in 1931. New financial ties accompanied these interlocking directorships. Since the early 1920s, Sumitomo Gō-shi had held about 3,000 O.S.K. shares. Large purchases in 1933 made it, as shown in Table 10, the company's third largest stockholder.[61] Also noteworthy is the fact that Mitsubishi Gōshi and Mitsubishi Aircraft together owned 1.1 percent of the O.S.K. (as measured in par value Mitsubishi had 1.8 percent compared to Sumitomo's 0.6 percent). Mitsubishi purchased these shares during the negotiations over the N.Y.K.-O.S.K. accord, suggesting perhaps a strategy coordinated with the talks.[62] Through these financial ties, by 1932 cooperation had begun to take precedence over competition between the two zaibatsu.

MERGER NEGOTIATIONS AND THEIR COLLAPSE, 1932

Though the economics of mutual dependence provided a strong rationale for merger, the N.Y.K. and the O.S.K. had been competitors for almost fifty years. In the end, the autonomy that this long tradition had built for both firms proved to be a stronger force during the 1932 merger talks than either the vertical pressures from zaibatsu interests or the movement for horizontal cooperation. In the course of the year the issue went through three phases: (1) secret negotiations from February to October; (2) sensational exposés and public discussion from October to December; and (3) sudden collapse in anger and frustration in late December. The reactions of the key executives present a microcosm of zaibatsu-company relations and for that reason I have tried to determine precisely who did what and why.

Early in the year, Kagami began meeting secretly with Murata. By

TABLE 10 Some Leading O.S.K. Stockholders, 1923 and 1933

Year	Ranking	Name	Old Shares	New Shares	Total Shares	% of O.S.K. Total Shares*
1923	1.	Hiromi Shōji	14,500	13,250	27,750	1.4
	9.	Kunaishō	6,750	6,075	12,825	0.6
	10.	Hori Keijirō	5,000	4,500	9,500	0.5
1933	1.	Hiromi Nisaburō	21,600	19,650	41,250	2.1
	3.	Sumitomo Gōshi	2,254	20,278	22,532	1.1
	8.	Mitsubishi Gōshi	13,900		13,900	0.7
	9.	Kunaishō	6,750	6,075	12,825	0.6
	10.	Hori Keijirō	5,000	4,500	9,500	0.5
	12.	Mitsubishi Aircraft	8,700		8,700	0.4
	21.	Yasuda Bank	3,130	883	4,013	0.2

Source: OSK 50 nenshi (Dōshahen, 1934), pp. 481–489.

*Note: In both years, O.S.K. had 2 million shares issued.

fall they had reached wide-ranging agreements. As a first step toward unification of their firms, they would rationalize their business. As a second stage, to be implemented later, they would merge their capital.⁶³ The first stage alone, however, entailed a virtual merger of operations. The key plan envisaged building both overseas and domestic lines into systematic structures by eliminating duplicate services in each area. This involved entrusting a line which both presently offered to the firm with the superior service. The other would withdraw, thereby eliminating a "duplicate investment" and wasteful expenses for both. Arrangements between the giant German firms, the Hamburg-American Line and the North German Lloyd, where executives worked together in a cooperative business division, provided a model for the plan. Cooperation in this first stage would involve an interchange of directors, joint purchasing of supplies, joint management of a research agency, a consultative system for new ship orders, and abolition or merger of branches. Besides these managerial details, the plan put heavy emphasis on "serving the national mission as a regular liner company on government subsidized services in overseas and domestic routes." With the elimination of duplicate services, this mission would be accomplished through "controlled monopolistic lines that would greatly expand the power of both firms in competition with foreign shipping companies."

Much to the chagrin of Kagami and Murata, in October newspaper articles began discussing the possible merger. Until December, comment was basically speculative, but also increasingly concrete. Then, on Sunday 11 December, an exposé in the *Osaka Mainichi* and *Tokyo Nichinichi*, which were affiliated papers, described the plan outlined above.⁶⁴ This set off widespread discussion in which key participants made public statements.

Coming to the support of the merger plan were Iwasaki Koyata and Kimura Kusuyata, Mitsubishi's general director, who had also served on the N.Y.K.'s Board since 1924. Kimura had had wide experience in Mitsubishi's banking, mining, shipbuilding, and trading enterprises and had also been responsible for Mitsubishi's own shipping for a time during his rise to the head office.⁶⁵ He thus represented vertical pressure in support of Kagami. In response to the negotiated plan, Kimura argued that a combine would make more effective use of state subsidies, thereby easing the burden on the treasury, and that it could select its ships and lines more appropriately to meet foreign competition. He also felt that the first stage of the plan involving elimination of duplicate services could be achieved, but he warned that the long histories of the two firms would make a full union difficult. Sumitomo's Ogura also took a nationalist approach. Discarding duplicate investment, he said, would be good state policy. He expressed concern over the large severance pay the companies would have to provide dismissed personnel, but speculated that the newspaper article might spark movement from the public in support of the combine.

The statements of the two zaibatsu leaders had focused on the value to the state of eliminating duplicate investments. On the other hand, the two company presidents spoke more explicitly about the effect of the union on their companies, but in so doing they publicly revealed their great differences. "We have been negotiating with the O.S.K.," said Kagami, "over methods of turning the management of our two companies into a single unit and over ways to control (*tōsei*) this." Though there had been numerous difficulties in the talks, he believed that "achieving such a union (*gōdō*) would not be difficult . . . Also, from the viewpoint of national ideals, I think that it is essential for both companies to come together." O.S.K. President Hori, an opponent of the plan, claimed that, in the event of a merger, "the O.S.K. would be swallowed up by the N.Y.K. That situation might make the stockholders happy, but the employees would not give their consent. The N.Y.K. and the O.S.K. each have histories of nearly fifty years . . . If a union were instituted, afterwards it would be extremely difficult to achieve harmony (*yūwa*) between company staffs." In reference to Kagami's views, Hori mentioned "that there has been talk of managing the business departments of both companies through a single control agency (*tōsei kikan*)," but he questioned whether the results of the German experiment justified imitation.[66]

Everyone favored cooperation, including Hori, who seemed satisfied with the previous year's accord. Kagami, however, reportedly opposed "intensified cooperation" for fear that it would be too quickly institutionalized, acting as a disincentive to a larger amalgamation. He thus wanted to take immediate steps toward merger. If there was a difference between Murata and Kagami, it was Murata's concern about the potentially negative reaction to Kagami's approach. Murata seems to have favored the creation of a holding company under which the two firms would initially cooperate, and then, after two or three years, they would merge. Also, Murata, being younger than Kagami, is said to have acted more out of personal motive. Anticipating that he would be the vice-president of the new company under Kagami, Murata assumed that Kagami would retire after a few years, leaving to him the leadership of the new shipping empire.[67]

The two views offered most frequently in favor of merger were the possible gains in international competitiveness and the hope that it would restore the dividend, suspended by both companies since 1930. The many counter-arguments reflect Hori's views. The head of the seamen's union had already made demands for a guarantee against termination of seamen, for it was assumed that the laying-up of ships would result in an excess of crew. The severance pay to terminated staff might have exceeded the value of the assets to be disposed of in the program of consolidation. Perhaps the most fundamental criticism was that all the arguments for merger simply assumed the necessity of retrenchment. In the event of future business expansion, a merger of that nature might have limited earning capacity and required heavy start-up costs. However, the government of Saitō Makoto appears to have been more receptive to the plan than the Minseitō Cabinet had been to the accord of the previous year. This response was consistent with the emerging ideology of economic control.[68]

Immediately after the major leak of 11 December, opposition formed within the O.S.K. ranks. Its main concern focused on Mitsubishi's capital assets. A merger would result in the O.S.K.'s being absorbed in the N.Y.K. or, in effect, sold to Mitsubishi. The head office would probably move to Tokyo, a matter of some humiliation, because the O.S.K. was thought of as part of the consciousness of Osaka citizenry.[69] It is not known whether a name for a future merged company was discussed, but, if the 1964 merger of the O.S.K. and Mitsui Senpaku (Mitsui Senpaku-Osaka Shōsen) is any indication, it would have resulted in an awkward mouthful.[70] The opposition within the O.S.K. led to a breakdown in the talks within ten days of the 11 December exposé. There were plans to resume negotiations with Sumitomi's Ogura in mid-January, but, on 25 December, Kagami wrote a long letter to Murata suggesting that they suspend the present talks and wait until later in the next year to see if the opposition from within the O.S.K. might abate.[71] It didn't.

Most commentators had focused on O.S.K. opposition to the merger, yet Terai stated that "there was considerable discontent within the ranks of both companies, but it was especially severe among N.Y.K. staff."[72] Many felt that the N.Y.K. had received a "bad bargain" in the previous year's accord. This raises another question that has been a tantalizing mystery for fifty years. Who was the source of the famous leak that led to the exposé?

An attempt to answer this question must begin with a summary of the people involved. First, Kagami had excluded Ōtani from his secret negotiations with Murata and had failed to inform either Ōtani or other N.Y.K. executives about them. Murata, however, had briefed Hori. Why was Ōtani excluded? Superficially it was because he was ill throughout most of 1932 (he did not resume his diary until 8 November), but, as told to Murata, it was because the previous year some N.Y.K. managers had not sympathized with Kagami's objectives. Ōtani was conspicuously silent during the public controversy in December, but he either was personally against the merger or was willing to act on behalf of large N.Y.K. stockholders who were themselves opposed.[73] Ōtani was not brought into the negotiations until 13 October, when all four leaders named in Chart 4 met together for the first time. Disagreement then ensued. Prior to that time, with the exception of a few meetings Hori attended, Kagami had avoided his office and conducted negotiations with Murata at his winter residence in Hayama, his summer house in Ikaho (a hotsprings area in Gumma prefecture), and at a Nihonbashi restaurant (*ryōtei*) called the Kasuga. Newspaper reporters had begun tracking Kagami like detectives because it seemed reasonable to follow "the daily activities of Mr. Kagami, who was said to be the No. 1 man in the business world."[74] By observing the comings and goings at Kagami's houses, reporters were able to assume what subject was under discussion. But knowing the time and place of the meeting as well as the participants was not enough to divulge the content of the negotiations.

Indirect comment on the source of the leak has been given by Murata, who later talked with the reporter but failed to name him; by Yoneda Fujio (of the Ministry of Communications), who was told that the reporter was a man named Obama Ritoku but was unsure whether this information was true; and by Nomura Jiichirō of the O.S.K., who wrote that "some of the directors who opposed the

CHART 4 Contending Forces in the Merger Negotiations

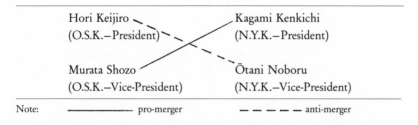

Hori Keijiro		Kagami Kenkichi	
(O.S.K.–President)		(N.Y.K.–President)	
Murata Shozo		Ōtani Noboru	
(O.S.K.–Vice-President)		(N.Y.K.–Vice-President)	

Note: ——————— pro-merger   — — — — — anti-merger

merger might have intentionally leaked the information to a news-paper."[75] None of these speculations was able to link a specific reporter with a specific director. However, on 8 November and 14 December, a reporter for the *Tokyo Nichinichi* named Hidaka had long interviews with Hori. Then, in the evening of both days, Hidaka visited Ōtani's home and described to Ōtani at considerable length his conversation with Hori.[76] Was Hidaka acting as a messenger between the two merger opponents? Did either Hori or Ōtani leak the sub-stance of the negotiations to Hidaka? Ōtani provides no conclusive answers, but the evidence at least shows that there was extensive con-tact between reporters and the highest executives. It further buttresses the suspicion at the time that "the attempt to combine the N.Y.K. and the O.S.K. failed because of the opposition of O.S.K. President Hori Keijirō and N.Y.K. Vice-President Ōtani Noboru."[77]

The failure to win Ōtani's support was fatal, for, if Kagami sym-bolized Mitsubishi, Ōtani symbolized the N.Y.K. He had spent his whole career with the company, serving it in virtually all parts of the globe—Hong Kong, Singapore, the Philippines, the Dutch East Indies, London, and New York. Like Murata, who had established the O.S.K.'s Panama line in 1919, Ōtani had been the key young executive in the N.Y.K. who planned the company's round-the-world service dur-ing World War I.[78] Furthermore, he was the only managing director left over from the factionalism of the 1920s. In short, he represented the company's mainstream and embodied its autonomy.

Opposition would certainly have thwarted the merger even with-out the leak. While not decisive, the leak was still a highly dramatic event that shed light on the actors behind the scenes and in a broader sense brought into focus the clash of more general forces: the conflict between zaibatsu control and company autonomy and the resolve of companies to retain their identity against horizontal movements.

ECONOMIC CONTEXT OF THE ABORTIVE MERGER

The underlying flaw in the pro-merger argument, the failure of Kagami's plan to make accommodation for business expansion, also helped seal its fate. In 1932, Japan's economy was already undergoing recovery, the result of what Hugh Patrick has called "one of the most successful combinations of fiscal, monetary, and foreign exchange rate policies, in an adverse international environment, that the world has ever seen."[79] When Takahashi Korekiyo took office as Finance Minister in December 1931, he took Japan off the gold standard and allowed the value of the yen to plummet from 49 cents to just over 20 cents, though it later rose to about 28 cents after the dollar devaluation of 1933. This greatly accelerated an emerging transformation in Japan's industrial structure. It created a boom in Japanese exports (as well as in imports with which to manufacture them) that increased cargo for Japanese shipping firms. The fall in the yen benefited Japanese shipping firms financially and made them more competitive. Since about three-quarters of N.Y.K. and O.S.K. income was derived from freight charges denominated in foreign currency, mostly sterling and dollars, receipts as measured in yen book value increased by about a third.[80] This reversed the situation that had briefly prevailed after Britain went off the gold standard in September 1931, causing a fall in the value of the pound.

The competitive edge given to the Japanese firms by the fall of the yen took a year or more to be realized. N.Y.K. old shares, which had been trading at about ¥38 in late 1931, rallied into the mid-¥40 range in early 1932 but fell again to around ¥30 by mid-year. This fall was caused primarily by boycotts of Japanese goods and services that spread after the Shanghai Incident in January 1932. These boycotts, plus the losses in sterling income incurred in late 1931 after Britain's withdrawal from the gold standard, are said to have cost Japanese shipping ¥100 million. It was not until late 1933 that the N.Y.K. share price rose back above par (¥50).[81] Thus, short-term problems continued to cause difficulties for the industry, but the long-term recovery that began in 1932 made merger seem less urgent than it might have been a year earlier.

A second change in the economic circumstances of shipping firms occurred in late 1932 when the government introduced a new subsidy law, commonly known as the scrap-and-build recovery program.

This paid subsidies to firms according to minimum standard criteria such as ships size (4,000 gross tons) and speed (13.5 knots). Companies, however were eligible for subsidies only when they had scrapped twice the tonnage of the new vessels.[82] Later in the decade, the government introduced more generous measures under this law, which helped the country to rebuild its fleet. Also, since excess capacity had been perhaps the source of the greatest structural pressure within the industry for horizontal combination or merger, the scrapping provisions of this law undercut Kagami's arguments in December 1932. By enabling companies to overcome structural problems left over from World War I, the program enhanced the capacity of companies like the N.Y.K. and the O.S.K. to maintain their autonomy and still operate profitably. The 1932 recovery and the new subsidies help explain why the merger talks collapsed just at a time when competitive rivalry among Japanese companies on the strategic New York line was heating up. The strength of firms such as Mitsui Bussan, Kokusai, and Kawasaki had cut O.S.K. profits on this line below earlier expectations. To remain competitive the O.S.K. kept building. Indeed, the late 1932 negotiations with the N.Y.K. were in a sense a race against the clock, for two new O.S.K. vessels for the New York line were due in February 1933. This competitive building undermined trust among companies. In March 1933, a Butterfield & Swire official, H. W. Kent, commented on the O.S.K.'s attitude toward the N.Y.K. and Kokusai as follows: "Having withdrawn from the North Pacific they apparently feel that they are entitled to enjoy predominance in the New York trade, and their confreres are naturally unwilling to concede that. Obviously they don't trust one another."[83] Finally, in February 1933, the N.Y.K. itself decided to build new vessels for the New York line, a move Kent interpreted as signifying that "[N.Y.K.] negotiations for a merger with O.S.K. had evaporated for the time being."[84]

In the other area of government aid—subsidies for specific lines— amounts had been fixed at an earlier date based on standards applicable to the older and smaller ships that were then in operation. In 1932, a campaign began to increase aid by making standards more appropriate to the newer ships. In the two months prior to the newspaper article of 11 December, while Kagami was preoccupied with merger negotiations, Ōtani, Shimizu, and other N.Y.K. executives, who had negotiated the accord with the O.S.K. in 1931, met frequently with Ministry of Communications officials. It would appear that they spoke almost exclusively about subsidies. It was only after the exposé of 11 December that these aid talks were interrupted, for N.Y.K. leaders then had to spend much of the next three days giving explanations to the Ministry of the merger negotiations.[85] The merger issue, however, cannot be separated from the subsidies. Mitsubishi's Kimura, for example, supported the merger because he feared that, owing to the Depression, the government would not be able to afford adequate subsidies for both firms in the future.[86] In contrast to Kimura's pessimism, however, it seems clear that N.Y.K. executives focused more optimistically on the use of subsidies in the recovery. When the merger fell through, Kagami himself seems to have become more involved in the lobbying effort.[87] In this sense, government aid became the ally of company autonomy and the counterweight to zaibatsu control over its affiliates.

N.Y.K. MANAGEMENT AND THE ABORTIVE MERGER

In Kagami's restorative mission to the N.Y.K., mentioned above, he had succeeded in strengthening Mitsubishi's financial ties to the N.Y.K. His strategy for improving its financial health, that of horizontal combination, had fallen apart, government policy being an effective substitute. On the other hand, he succeeded admirably in this third goal, that of renewing N.Y.K.'s internal management after the shambles of the early 1920s. In fact, one can argue that his accomplishments in this area undermined his strategy of merger.

There had been times before Kagami became N.Y.K. president, particularly between 1911 and the middle of World War I, when the N.Y.K. Board consisted primarily of internally promoted managers. This system had not yet, however, become a routinized principle, in part because of internal dissension between 1915 and 1924. When Shirani came to the N.Y.K. as president in 1924 he brought with him several businessmen from outside the N.Y.K. to sit on the company's board. The most important of these were Kagami, Kimura, Ōhashi Shintarō (from Mitsui), Hara Tomitarō (representing Yokohama business), and Kikuchi Kyōzō (from the Osaka textile industry).[88] Ōtani was the only managing director (*senmu torishimariyaku*) in 1924, others who occupied that rank with him having all resigned. Still young, Ōtani was thus the senior ranking officer among N.Y.K.

career personnel. Shirani appointed another N.Y.K. man, Takeda Ryōtarō, as managing director, but Kagami later relieved him of this post in 1929, though he remained a board member until 1932. Apart from Ōtani, then, the leadership had a non-N.Y.K. cast.

Kagami brought reform to both the board and the executive level. When Shirani and Hara resigned from the board in 1929, this left only Kagami, Kimura, Ōhashi, and Kikuchi from among the 1924 appointees. The latter two remained because they represented the N.Y.K.'s major shippers. Outside directors now represented Mitsubishi, Mitsui, and the textile industry, the same combination that led the board during the expansionary period of 1893 to 1911.

Next, Kagami appointed Ōtani as vice-president (the position had been vacant from 1924 to 1929). He then promoted three executives, Shimizu Yasuharu (head of the Business Department), Komatsubara Sadakichi (head of the Ship Department), and Watanabe Mizutarō (head of the Supplies Department) to the rank of managing director, and, of course, to the board. The purpose of these promotions was primarily to upgrade the ranks of N.Y.K. career executives. They did not result in any change in the executive function of the men being promoted. Instead, the departments they formerly headed were abolished and they retained, as managing directors, the same functional responsibilities they exercised as department heads.[89] But they changed the cast of the board, for half of it now consisted of N.Y.K. mainstreamers. Finally, in 1935, Kagami himself became chairman (the first occupant of that post), leaving the presidency to Ōtani, who promoted more career managers to the board and to top executive posts.

The point here is that officials newly promoted to positions of responsibility were reluctant to risk the possible abolition of those positions in the case of a merger. Furthermore, the new leaders built up a strong sense of loyalty to the firm. Though it is outside the scope of this study, it is relevant to note that several of them, like Shimizu and Terai Hisanobu, Ōtani's successor as president, were bitterly resentful when they were forced to leave the firm later in the 1930s to join national-policy companies under government sponsorship. They tried hard to return to the N.Y.K., and Terai at least succeeded.[90]

To these newly risen executives, intent on restoring the N.Y.K.'s integrity, Kagami was in several respects an outsider. First, he did not have much executive experience in shipping, despite his service on the N.Y.K. Board since 1924 and his long years in the related insurance field. Murata suggested that, because of that, he did not develop a strong feeling of affection for the company.[91] Second, he was really only a part-time N.Y.K. president. Usually he would spend half his day at Tokio Marine, where he was still chairman (an executive post, since there was no president) and half at the N.Y.K. Ōtani often had to go to the Tokio Marine building to discuss N.Y.K. business with him (though this was not as inconvenient as it might seem, since Tokio Marine was right across the street).[92] Third, according to Terai, Kagami ruled the N.Y.K. like a dictator, not permitting criticism and making it difficult for others to express contrary opinions.[93] Insofar as the new N.Y.K. top managers owed their promotion to Kagami and insofar as they may have resisted Kagami's merger strategy, this chapter can be regarded as a dual study of treachery (to Kagami) and loyalty (to the company). Out of the tension engendered by this choice and by the reaction against Kagami's strategy emerged a stronger commitment to company autonomy.

CONCLUSION

To date, a high proportion of research in Japanese business history has focused on specific or single categories, such as a zaibatsu, a company, or an industry. If we take a more integrated approach, however, studying a company and its relations with the other categories—its zaibatsu or its industry—it becomes possible to trace the tensions that are the motor of historical change and that lead to new institutional forms. In the case of the N.Y.K., Mitsubishi's business and financial needs prompted it to increase vertical pressure on the N.Y.K. to follow a strategy of horizontal combination. For a number of reasons, this strategy proved abortive. Government policy in the form of new subsidies and the economic recovery that began in 1932 rescued the industry, and career managers sought to maintain the autonomy of their firms. But, while Kagami's strategy was abortive, the reaction against it, together with Kagami's other restorative measures (Mitsubishi's purchase of N.Y.K. stock and the elevation of internal career managers), led to a more stable institutional structure.

Certain general comparisons can be made regarding Kagami's merger attempt and its aftermath. Leaders of the shipping companies themselves planned the accords and horizontal combinations of the early 1930s. They were thus different from the mergers that did occur at that time, such as Japan Steel, which the government itself encouraged; even in this case, the economic recovery of the early 1930s enabled several firms, the largest being Nippon Kōkan, to maintain their independence and stay out of the merger.[94] I have also argued that government aid, by rescuing the shipping industry, buttressed company autonomy by freeing it from additional dependence on horizontal combination. This, however, has not always been the effect of government aid on the shipping industry. The opposite was the case in 1964 when companies themselves sought merger partners under the stimulus of promised government aid that was contingent upon formation of horizontal groupings. Nevertheless, the 1932 abortive merger provides the closest historical parallel to the 1964 mergers, especially that between the O.S.K. and Mitsui Senpaku. In that year, too, the N.Y.K. preserved its identity by merging with Mitsubishi Kaiun (Mitsubishi Shipping Co.), the shipping firm that grew out of Mitsubishi's trading company. Finding a partner within its own "vertical" group forced less change in its traditional autonomy than would have resulted from a more "horizontal" merger.[95]

The negotiations of late 1932 reflected sentiment among zaibatsu leaders for a lessening of competition. Kagami's moves received support not only from Mitsubishi and Sumitomo but also from Mitsui, especially from Mitsui Bussan's Yasukawa Yūnosuke.[96] Kagami had used the word *control* (*tōsei*) to suggest private management over a horizontal grouping, a concept that became popular in the mid-to-late 1930s before the onrush of mobilization and government controls. Yet, in the case of the N.Y.K. and the O.S.K., not only were the negotiations initiated by the private sector but its continued "control" after a merger was assumed. In this sense, Kagami would have distinguished his projected company from the national policy companies established under government promotion or legislation in the 1930s.[97] The most important of these in the shipping industry was the Tōa Kaiun Kaisha (East Asian Shipping Co.), privately owned but established in 1939 primarily to replace Nisshin Kisen and to give the military broader controls over shipping in China.

The failure to merge the N.Y.K. and the O.S.K. reflected not only the distinct history of the two firms and the relative independence of their freight from the business of the two zaibatsu but also internal trends within companies. Zaibatsu-related firms are usually regarded as examples of financial capitalism because representatives of the zaibatsu sat on their Boards and influenced policy. Alfred Chandler made the distinction between this form of financial capitalism on the one hand and managerial capitalism on the other, in which managers, rather than owners or outside representatives, made the key strategic decisions.[98] The two key figures in this study, Kagami and Ōtani, represent a shift within the N.Y.K. during the interwar years from financial to managerial leadership.[99] Kagami, of course, performed the role of specialized manager within the context of his own insurance business. On the other hand, within the N.Y.K., at least between 1929 and 1932, he functioned as a financial capitalist, a representative of his insurance business and of Mitsubishi financial policy. In the end, however, the successful resistance to his merger policy by N.Y.K. mainstreamers led by Ōtani preserved the identity of the firm and ensured that these managers would occupy the key positions for making strategic decisions. Furthermore, after 1932 Kagami's role itself seems to have shifted from that of a financial capitalist imposing "outside" policies to that of an outsider nurturing internal management. Though Kagami did continue to exercise strategic authority in the firm from the time he became N.Y.K. chairman in 1935 to his death in 1939, he did promote Ōtani to the presidency and he succeeded in bringing Terai back to the N.Y.K., not simply as a presidential prospect but as someone who was regarded as the "hope of the N.Y.K."[100] Despite his brief service in the Nan'yō Kaiun Kaisha (South Seas Shipping Co.), which was prompted by government intervention, Terai was also an N.Y.K. career-manager. Finally, although a Mitsubishi representative continued to sit on the N.Y.K. Board during the war, no outsider ever again occupied the key positions within the company the way Kagami did. The fact that Ōtani and Terai had begun to make strategic decisions in the 1930s made it all the more possible for managers like them—managers promoted from within the N.Y.K.—to resume the tradition of autonomous management after the war and Occupation.[101]

Though there have been many mergers in modern Japan, the stress on corporate autonomy points to a distinction between Japanese and American capitalism. Chandler's account of managerial capitalism allows for considerable mobility of managers between firms. The leaders are thus like a managerial class. In Japan, however, such movement has been unusual, at least in firms with a history long enough to enable them to promote managers internally. It is not enough, then, to argue that specialized managers came to lead Japan's corporations in the interwar years. One must add that they were managers risen within their own firms. This career experience naturally reinforced the emphasis on corporate autonomy.

CHAPTER SEVEN

Noguchi Jun and Nitchitsu: Investment Strategy of a High-Technology Enterprise

BARBARA MOLONY

In 1868, as the Meiji period (1868–1912) began, Japan's countryside was largely untouched by the technologies then rapidly developing in the West. In little more than a century, Japan has become an archetypal high-technology society and economy. The course of Japan's technological development was, of course, radically affected by World War II and its aftermath, but its basic contours were already evident before the war. By then, the defining characteristics of a technologically advanced society and economy were underway. These included the creation of a sophisticated consumer population, the recognition of the need to import and innovate technology to remain competitive, and the establishment of research organizations and a school system to create a pool of scientists and engineers able to commercialize new ideas.

Perhaps most important, there were entrepreneurs willing and able to build Japan's high-technology industrial structure. As in the West, the innovators who created the technologically sophisticated products and molded the character of the businesses producing these products were scientist-entrepreneurs. Also as in the West, the most representative high-technology industry of the late nineteenth and early twentieth centuries was the chemical industry. The chemical industry required—and engendered—sophistication among consumers; it encouraged innovation and imitation of technology; it benefited from well-trained employees; and its companies were some of the first modern multi-unit firms in Japan and the West. Among such modern enterprises in Japan, none is more significant that Nippon Chisso Hiryō (Japan Nitrogenous Fertilizers, hereafter called Nitchitsu), founded in 1908 by scientist-entrepreneur Noguchi Jun (1873–1944).

Nitchitsu and other companies like it pioneered the most advanced technologies in fields like electrochemicals (chemicals produced through the use of electricity). Virtually none of the developments in these fields came from the larger and wealthier zaibatsu. To be sure, tiny chemical companies like Nitchitsu prospered and became immense corporations themselves within three decades—and were therefore called "new zaibatsu" (shinkō zaibatsu)—but their origins as innovative firms dedicated to commercializing technology determined the manner in which they later grew and diversified. Companies like Nitchitsu, and not the zaibatsu, were, both in character and structure, the predecessors of the innovative new corporations of postwar Japan. It is often asserted that "the zaibatsu pioneered the commercialization of modern technologies in Japan" at the urging of the government and that government ministries collaborated closely with the zaibatsu because they believed them to be the firms best equipped for rapid adoption of technology.[1] But this is only part of the story. The zaibatsu were not themselves innovators in all key areas. However, they often did have relationships with companies that were innovators. In the case of Nitchitsu, Mitsubishi Bank lent large sums at critical times, and top managers in Mitsubishi had significant personal investments in the chemical company. It would be no exaggeration to say there were times when Nitchitsu owed its continued solvency to Mitsubishi and other lenders. But Nitchitsu was an independent company, and Noguchi Jun and his managers did not feel bound to solicit their benefactors' opinions when making company decisions.

Indeed, investment decisions—that is, decisions concerning how resources could best be allocated to promote the company's well-being—were made in conformity with its business strategy. When determining whether to use a new technology, Noguchi and his managers assessed their access to resources, labor, capital, and specialists skilled in application of technology. Established technologies often spawned new ones, and managers of companies like Nitchitsu had to decide whether to diversify by investing in spun-off technologies. Failure to invest when the company had adequate resources to do so could produce a lag in innovation and ultimately in competitiveness. Thus, investment in innovation was often driven by the availability of a particular technology. Choice of technologies had other effects. Some technologies required resources obtainable only from public officials, so their selection also helped define the company's relationship with government officials and determined, in the case of a colonial country like Japan, the connection between business strategy and imperialism. In particular, the type of technology Nitchitsu developed required close ties with government and encouraged investment in Korea and other Japanese-held territory.

This chapter will examine the investment strategy of one of Japan's most important technology-intensive companies. It will indicate the important role played by this non-zaibatsu firm in high-technology innovation. It will also suggest some of the reasons for the interaction of government and business, and tell how one Japanese entrepreneur became involved in colonial expansion.

NOGUCHI JUN AS INNOVATIVE ENTREPRENEUR

A quarter of a century separated the founding of Noguchi Jun's chemical company from the beginning of its cooperation with colonial authorities in the development of Korea. Noguchi was an independent scientist-entrepreneur, but ties to influential men in politics and business aided his company throughout the period. Whether businessmen or politicians were more important to him at any given time depended on strategic needs of his developing company. During its early years, Nitchitsu raised most of its funds by selling shares to investors, but loans were vital at certain crucial times when the company's solvency was threatened. It was then that Noguchi approached businessmen. During the 1930s, alternate sources of capital, in particular loans from semi-governmental banks, substituted for Nitchitsu's previous reliance on private-sector banks, especially Mitsubishi Bank. Thus, Noguchi's ties to influential businessmen decreased in importance. His ties to government officials followed a different pattern. When his company needed more reliable sources of electricity to expand production, Noguchi sought the approval of government officials to develop hydroelectric power. Unlike his need to cooperate with private financiers, Noguchi's need to work with government officials to obtain water rights increased as Nitchitsu's technology demanded ever-increasing supplies of electricity.

Noguchi Jun was not a chemist by training. Like several other important entrepreneurs in high-technology industries in Japan, he had graduated from the Faculty of Engineering of Tokyo Imperial University (Class of 1896).[2] After college he worked for an electric company in Sankyozawa in the Tōhoku, where he was joined by another Tokyo graduate (Class of 1898), Fujiyama Tsuneichi, in experimenting with the manufacture of calcium carbide, a product used in lighting.[3] Indeed, Fujiyama produced Japan's first calcium carbide at Sankyozawa in 1901. Noguchi had left the electric company in 1898 to join an American trading firm in Tokyo, and then settled down for a couple of years to work with the Japanese branch of the German Siemens-Schuckert company. After several more short-term jobs and a trip to the United States during the Russo-Japanese War, Noguchi decided to return to Japan to begin his own enterprise. Two friends working in the gold mines of Kyushu urged him to develop hydroelectricity for ventures like their own. Hydroelectricity was a new industry at the turn of the century. Coal had supplied the energy to produce most of Japan's electricity until the 1890s, and conversion to water power was seen as imperative to increase generation and lower the cost of energy.[4] Noguchi found his Kyushu friends' suggestion attractive, and appealed to other friends for capital to start his own hydroelectric plant. He succeeded in persuading a friend who was a Tokyo banker to advance him ¥100,000.[5] This loan permitted Noguchi to found his first company, Sogi Electric (capitalization ¥200,000, with ¥50,000 paid up), in January 1906.

Sogi Electric surprised Noguchi by producing more electricity than the goldminers and other local customers could use. This offered Noguchi the opportunity to return to his earlier interest in producing calcium carbide, a process that required a large amount of electricity. Noguchi invited his old friend Fujiyama, who was still in the north, to join him in using Sogi Electric's surplus electricity to produce the chemical at his new plant, called Nippon Carbide Company, established at Minamata in March 1907. Demand for electricity soon outpaced its supply, but the potential profitability of carbide production was sufficient to persuade Noguchi to expand generating capacity to facilitate it. When the expansion placed the firm on the verge of bankruptcy, he solicited a small but timely loan from a Kagoshima businessman to save his company.[6] Although the decision to expand appeared ill-advised to some at the time, this bold strategic decision resulted in the firm's becoming Japan's largest producer of calcium carbide by the end of 1907. Surmounting their solvency problems, Noguchi and Fujiyama embarked on a program of technology acquisition.

The two scientists were most interested in a new German process, commercially exploited for the first time in Italy in 1906, for using calcium carbide in the manufacture of calcium cyanamide, a nitrogenous fertilizer.[7] This was significant for two reasons. First, the young engineers' understanding of a process only recently developed in Europe was an index of the rapid advances of scientific education in Japan; adoption of new technology is not possible with inadequate training. Second, they chose a product that linked a traditional industry—farming—with the most advanced form of industrial technology. Noguchi and Fujiyama calculated that the market for a synthetic nitrogenous fertilizer was limitless in a predominantly agrarian country like Japan which relied on such natural imported nitrogenous fertilizers as soy cakes and dried fish. They lost no time traveling to Berlin and Italy to negotiate for the rights to the fertilizer license. When they arrived in Europe, however, they encountered powerful competition from negotiators from Mitsui (Masuda Takashi) and Furukawa (Hara Kei).[8] While the European license holders were impressed by the young scientists' knowledge and their previous success with calcium carbide, they were naturally concerned about their lack of capital. Fortunately for Noguchi and Fujiyama, they had some powerful supporters in Europe. One of Noguchi's mentors from his days with Siemens, Hermann Kessler, former head of the Japanese branch, had returned home and was by 1908 an influential man within the German company. The German firm happened to be the Italian manufacturing company's principal stockholder. Kessler not only praised Noguchi, but may also have persuaded the Italians that Noguchi planned to develop the license with the safe financial help of Mitsui.[9] In the end, the Europeans chose to award the license to the two unknown young men rather than to the wealthy zaibatsu.

Noguchi and Fujiyama now had the right to the license, but they could not afford to pay for it. The license was extraordinarily expensive, costing more than the total worth of Noguchi's investments in Kyushu. Noguchi entered negotiations with Mitsui, as Kessler may have suggested, in search of aid. But Mitsui's offer to pay for start-up expenses in return for 50 percent of the first shares issued doomed the negotiations.[10] Noguchi refused to give up so much of his company. He therefore turned to friends and relations in the financial communities of both Osaka and Tokyo for help.

Noguchi first appealed to a relative, Hori Tatsu, a member of the Board of Directors of the Tokyo-based Japan Mail Steamship Company (Nippon Yūsen Kaisha, N.Y.K.). Hori asked Kondō Renpei, President of N.Y.K., how he might help Noguchi. Kondō then solicited the advice of Toyokawa Ryōhei, head of the banking division (later Mitsubishi Bank) of Mitsubishi Gōshi Kaisha. Sufficiently impressed with Noguchi to support his venture, Toyokawa made a large personal investment in the new company, Nippon Chisso Hiryō, created by the merger of Sogi Electric and Nippon Carbide in 1908. Toyokawa's terms were far more flexible than Mitsui's. He agreed that "Noguchi and Fujiyama should keep as many shares as they can. Mitsubishi will take care of the rest. We will give them sufficient financing also."[11]

Toyokawa not only promised to help Noguchi, but also introduced him to Iwasaki Hisaya, President of Mitsubishi Gōshi Kaisha, and Nakahashi Tokugorō, President of Osaka Merchant Steamship Company (Ōsaka Shōsen Kaisha, O.S.K.). All these influential men helped develop Noguchi's enterprise. All were investors; it is significant that Iwasaki and Toyokawa invested as private venture capitalists rather than as representatives of Mitsubishi. A later Mitsubishi Bank president, Katō Takeo, remarked that Iwasaki often lent his support, independent of Mitsubishi Gōshi, to promising entrepreneurs.[12]

These introductions helped Noguchi in less tangible but equally important ways as well. Noguchi became a protégé of Nakahashi

Tokugorō, one of the most influential men of affairs in Osaka. Born in Noguchi's birthplace, Ishikawa prefecture, Nakahashi had graduated from Tokyo University ten years before his young friend. Nakahashi was as conversant with the world of politics as with commercial circles. He later became a potent force in the Seiyūkai, one of the two major political parties before World War II, and held various Cabinet portfolios. Both his political and financial ties were of help to Noguchi.[13]

The Mitsubishi investors wished to protect their investment and therefore placed three Mitsubishi managers on the first Board of Directors. O.S.K.'s Nakahashi became President of Nitchitsu in 1909.[14] Nevertheless, Noguchi and Fujiyama, together with Ichikawa Seiji, Noguchi's long-time friend, classmate, and a research partner in Sankyozawa, retained control of daily operations and decision making for Nitchitsu. It was Noguchi who decided what types of technology would be used and what kinds of plants would be built.[15] Noguchi used several sources of funds rather than relying entirely on Mitsubishi. He invited other individuals and banks—in particular, his classmate at the First Higher School, Watanabe Yoshirō, President of Aichi Bank—to invest in Nitchitsu. He also received aid in 1910 from a government lending institution, Nihon Kangyō Ginkō (Japan Hypothec Bank), whose vice-president, Shimura Gentarō, was a brother of Watanabe Yoshirō.[16] Thus, although men from Mitsubishi were clearly important in Noguchi's company, Noguchi maintained independence in decision making by diversifying his sources of managers and of capital. Since Nitchitsu continued to prove it was a viable venture during the next decade, Mitsubishi managers remained relatively disinterested investors.

Between 1908 and 1912, Noguchi made some crucial decisions. Most important was the 1909 plan to use calcium cyanamide as a raw material in the manufacture of ammonium sulfate. Ammonium sulfate was a more marketable fertilizer than calcium cyanamide; farmers had had several years of experience with the product and preferred it to calcium cyanamide. A simple method of making ammonium sulfate involved breaking calcium cyanamide into limestone and ammonia, then combining the ammonia with sulfuric acid. To apply this method, Noguchi constructed a pilot plant near Nitchitsu's Osaka headquarters in 1910 and invited an Italian specialist to help Fujiyama solve problems of production. Noguchi and

Fujiyama had already begun to express different opinions about how to market Nitchitsu's products; calling in an outside specialist exacerbated tensions in their relationship. Fujiyama then left to establish his own electrochemical firm in Hokkaido (Denki Kagaku Kōgyō).[17] At the same time, a freak flood destroyed a plant under construction in Niigata, leaving Noguchi with large capital losses.[18] At the end of the Meiji period, therefore, Noguchi had to make some crucial decisions about what types of investment to pursue to save his company.

Noguchi recognized as early as 1909 that progressing to the next higher stage of technological development, manufacture of ammonium sulfate, was far more profitable than producing calcium cyanamide. His funds remained insufficient to carry out his plans as late as 1912; government decisions during that year, however, solved his financial problems. The Railroad Board of the Ministry of Communications, interested in obtaining already-developed sources of electricity to use in the electrification of railroads in Kyūshū, acquired ownership of Noguchi's Sogi generating plant and parts of his manufacturing plant at nearby Minamata. Nitchitsu made the best of the negotiations with the Railroad Board. The company netted ¥1.57 million for the facilities, but, because the Railroad Board was not yet ready to use Nitchitsu's plant, the company continued to function as usual, paying only a small fee to the Board for use of the electricity. Nitchitsu's supply of electricity was further augmented in October 1912, when the government approved Noguchi's earlier request for the right to develop hydroelectric power at yet another site in Kyushu.[19] Relations between Nitchitsu and the Railroad Board remained cordial; personal connections smoothed any possible friction. Nitchitsu President Nakahashi was a former head of the Railroad Board; the Railroad Board's head during the negotiations with Nitchitsu later left to become a member of Nitchitsu's Board of Directors;[20] and Noguchi and his colleague Ichikawa claimed to welcome the chance to work "for an enterprise benefiting the nation."[21]

Sustained by government aid in 1912, Noguchi was ready to implement his plan to manufacture ammonium sulfate. He lost no time in setting up the necessary generating plant. By 1914, his second major chemical plant came on stream at Kagami, producing Japan's first commercial ammonium sulfate by the electrochemical method. The technology at the new Kagami plant surpassed that at the old Minamata plant, inducing Noguchi to upgrade Minamata to Kagami's level. Noguchi's timing was fortunate. Just as the output from the two plants was expanded, fertilizer shortages became acute in Japan because European imports were cut off by World War I. In 1915, when Noguchi could better afford it, ownership of Nitchitsu's original facilities reverted to the private company from the Railroad Board. Compounding the company's success during World War I, Nakahashi persuaded his sometime colleagues in the government to lift export controls on fertilizer to permit Japanese manufacturers to claim the lucrative Southeast Asian market temporarily abandoned by the warring Europeans. This combination of events allowed extraordinarily high profit rates for the company, profits used not only for higher dividend payments to shareholders but also for later technology acquisition[22] (see Appendix A).

Expansion of the company brought new concerns to Nitchitsu's management. Labor was one such concern. The greatly expanded work force and the demanding amount of work required of each worker worsened labor relations.[23] Noguchi's relations with his middle managers proved more successful than those with his blue-collar employees. White-collar workers' sense of identification with the company was encouraged by the structure of the plants. Each of his two plants, Kagami and Minamata, was divided into sections corresponding to the technological processes involved in manufacture of ammonium sulfate by the "three-product cycle" used at Nitchitsu (see Appendix B). The three-product cycle was the process linking calcium carbide to calcium cyanamide to ammonium sulfate. Each of the first two was a raw material for the next stage of production; all were marketable products in their own right. The head of each production section held concurrent posts at both plants, which were essentially replicas of each other.[24] Thus, Minamata's manager in charge of generation of electricity served in the same capacity at Kagami.

Commuting by managers between facilities had two major effects on the training of management. First, it created a sense of company integration, even as Noguchi's enterprise expanded in Japan and Korea. Second, commuting by top managers produced devolution of daily operations to lower levels of management. This permitted a large number of technically trained employees to acquire managerial skills in subdivisions structured along lines of production. In time, these manager-technicians rose to higher positions in the company.

Furthermore, their skills were in demand; technically trained men could move to other companies or government positions. Even members of the Board moved to establish their own firms or take positions in the government. Because not all employees felt obliged to stay with the company, rewards were offered for technical expertise and perseverance in management. Noguchi's responsive creation of pleasant working conditions is frequently mentioned in white-collar employees' accounts of their years at Nitchitsu.[25]

A second problem Noguchi faced during the 1910s was financial. As demand for fertilizer grew during the World War I cutoff, Noguchi returned to his stockholders every year for authorization to increase capitalization or to borrow for current expenses.[26] It should have been apparent that European recovery after the war would eventually lead to massive importation of cheaper fertilizer, thereby making it difficult for Nitchitsu to pay off its loans with (predictably) lower profits. Nevertheless, Noguchi kept borrowing. Wartime profits were so high and start-up time for expanded capacity in plants run on the three-product cycle relatively so short, that Noguchi could project sufficient return on his investment even if the Europeans recovered quickly. What appeared to be short-sighted borrowing during the war, then, paid off; Noguchi's firm remained in the black even during the years of reinstated imports. Through these decisions, Mitsubishi bankers supported Noguchi; for the next two decades, Mitsubishi remained at the center of a consortium of banks—also usually including the Aichi and Yamaguchi Banks—underwriting Noguchi's requests for bonds and loans.

EXPANSION AND DIVERSIFICATION AFTER WORLD WAR I

Noguchi Jun began to contemplate upgrading his technology after World War I. During the war, high demand for fertilizer obviated the need for a production method more efficient than the three-product cycle. To remain competitive after the war, however, Noguchi had to develop more profitable methods of production. Most governments involved in the war had spent large sums of money on research in electrochemicals, especially in ammonia, the main component in both fertilizers and explosives. Ammonia was viewed as strategically necessary to a war economy. Noguchi was aware of the advanced research by which ammonia could be produced directly from nitrogen and hydrogen, using a catalyst and enormous quantities of electricity, bypassing the calcium cyanamide stage. He wrote articles on that procedure as early as 1914.[27] Methods developed by government-sponsored and private researchers in the United States, the United Kingdom, France, and Italy were all modifications of an elegantly simple method created by Germans Fritz Haber and Karl Bosch, requiring sophisticated machinery capable of withstanding high temperatures and pressures.[28]

Though Noguchi may have wished to obtain the Haber-Bosch license to upgrade his technology, another group of potential investors began earlier negotiations for the license. This group—called after their formal organization in 1923 the Eastern Nitrogen Association (Tōyō Chisso Kumiai)—had originally coalesced during the war as an informal association interested in purchasing the license for ammonia from America's General Chemical Corporation.[29] One important member company was Mitsubishi Gōshi Kaisha, the parent company of Mitsubishi Bank. The men at Mitsubishi Gōshi were either unaware or unconcerned that their involvement in the Association might adversely affect a company dependent on Mitsubishi Bank loans. Conclusion of the war shifted the interest of the members of the Eastern Nitrogen Association to the original German method, the Haber-Bosch, recently made available to Germany's former adversaries. The German possessors of the rights, Badische Anilin und Soda Fabrik (BASF), began negotiating a license with the Japanese group.

Just as the group was considering the extraordinarily expensive license, the Japanese government obtained the license as spoils of war and made it available for private development. Although Japanese developers would be required to pay only a nominal fee to the government for transfer of the license, they would continue to owe prohibitively large royalties to the German firm. None of the members of the Eastern Nitrogen Association believed it could afford the high payments. As a result, they were slow to exploit the license, and, by 1923, a price war between English and German producers attempting to capture the Japanese market prevented its profitable use. Members subsequently negotiated a deal with the German nitrogen producers' syndicate whereby Association members would receive an ad valorem royalty of 2 to 3 percent on imported ammonia, and

Mitsui, Mitsubishi, and Suzuki Shōten would replace H. Ahrens of Kobe as the importer of German fertilizer in return for members' not using the license.[30] Because Mitsubishi Gōshi earned money for not producing, it had little incentive to produce ammonia until market and investment conditions improved during the following decade. But the interests of Nitchitsu suffered, though not for the first time. Three years earlier, Nitchitsu's fertilizer distributors—most of them related to Mitsubishi Trading Company—had already hurt Nitchitsu when they failed to pay the company the contracted price per ton because they said the market would not support high fertilizer prices. Bearing the cost of overproduction themselves, Nitchitsu leaders realized they had to lower costs.[31]

Noguchi formulated his response to competition from inexpensive imports marketed by some of the members of the Eastern Nitrogen Association during a trip to Europe in 1921. Traveling to Italy to consider renewing Nitchitsu's nearly expired license for calcium cyanamide, Noguchi detoured to visit the laboratory of Luigi Casale, a scientist struggling with new commercially viable ways of making ammonia.[32] Impressed, Noguchi negotiated for the license to use Casale's methods. Casale was still experimenting with ammonia and had not yet produced on any large scale, but discussions with Noguchi persuaded him that the Japanese engineer had the expertise to start commercial production. Casale demanded a steep price for the privilege, about ¥1 million, which Noguchi, though the top managing officer in Nitchitsu, was unwilling to authorize alone. Requesting additional time to consult with his colleagues in Japan, Noguchi paid a deposit of 10 percent for a two-week extension of the decision period.

He immediately telegraphed his colleagues at company headquarters in Osaka. They were taken by surprise by Noguchi's precipitous actions, and called a meeting of the entire Board of Directors. Most thought Noguchi's action deserved further study and began to consider some of the requirements of the new technology. Finding an appropriate site for a plant for synthesizing ammonia under the new license was essential. The Casale method required even greater quantities of electricity than the less sophisticated three-product cycle already in use at Nitchitsu. Good sources of electricity were secured through Noguchi's contacts with Kenseikai politicians in Miyazaki prefecture, who persuaded the Seiyūkai Cabinet to change the rules for transmission of electricity to help Noguchi.[33] For an unexplained reason, Casale waited until Noguchi's return to Italy in December 1921, far more than the two weeks agreed upon, and transferred the license to Noguchi on receipt of 10 million lira (about ¥1 million). Construction began in April 1922, and the new plant at Nobeoka came on stream in September 1923. So successful was Nobeoka that the Minamata plant was refitted with Nobeoka's modern technology. Since the Kagami plant was poorly situated to permit conversion to the Casale method of production, its machinery was transferred to other branches of Nitchitsu and its building sold to another chemical firm.[34] By 1927, the output at Minamata had reached three times that at Nobeoka, but Noguchi was ready for further growth, both through product diversification and through expansion to colonial soil.

During the 1920s, Noguchi developed policies in two new areas. First, he ventured into Korean production. The ways in which this policy was implemented eventually alienated Noguchi from his benefactors at Mitsubishi Bank. He could afford to lose the zaibatsu bank's support because the technology of his main product, ammonia, lent itself to strategic uses of interest to other potential benefactors in the colonial government. Ammonia production was an important part of munitions production, and the high-pressure processing technology for ammonia could be used in manufacture of synthetic oil and other strategic products. Moreover, his need to develop hydroelectricity in Korea was shared by the Japanese authorities wishing to industrialize the peninsula; this strengthened Noguchi's cooperation with government authorities.

A second radical change, in the late 1920s, was structural. Nitchitsu had until then been a company making principally ammonia and ammonium sulfate. Expansion had been accomplished through replicating technology and creating similar plants subdivided into sections by productive function. Though perhaps a successful way for a young firm to grow, this was hardly conducive to rapid generation of new technology. During the late 1920s and into the 1930s, Noguchi abandoned this method of expansion. As he diversified, he established separate facilities for different types of products. But each of the new products was chemically related to the others; each was a derivative of some other Nitchitsu product. Until 1937, Noguchi minimized involvement in products that did not have similar production methods; even his non-chemical investment was in support of already produced chemicals. For example, he expanded vertically by investing in transportation—a railroad—for his chemical products, as no railroad was available to his Hungnam plant in Korea. Shared interests were also fostered by regularly scheduled conferences which brought together scientists from various Nitchitsu subsidiaries.[35] Because all worked on technology similar to their colleagues' in other subsidiaries, all understood the goals and problems of others. The resulting highly efficient cross-fertilization of ideas produced far more successful innovation than had been possible under the old company structure. Just as a changing structure fostered innovation, conversely, technological developments accelerated Nitchitsu's structural conversion to a conglomerate—called a "new zaibatsu" by contemporaries—consisting of a parent company surrounded by numerous subsidiaries in Japan and Korea.

Noguchi encouraged diversification in products technologically close to already-manufactured products because it made sense from a scientist's perspective. But it also made sense from a manager's perspective. Studies done decades after Noguchi's diversification indicate that diversification increases profitability, but only if the relationship among diversified fields is close. Wide-ranging diversification diminishes performance.[36]

The first type of related diversification was in rayon. Against the advice of the rest of the Nitchitsu Board of Directors, Noguchi acquired the license for a German method of rayon manufacture. More than half a decade later, Noguchi's decision bore fruit, but low product quality initially kept the rayon operation in the red.[37] His decision to develop explosives also encountered snags; these were legal problems in obtaining government permission to manufacture explosives, eventually overcome through the help of friends in the government. Ability to make munitions later recommended him to necessary supporters like Ugaki Kazushige, Governor General of Korea. Another technology developed at Minamata during the late 1920s was for acetic acid, a basis for plastics, using mercury as a catalyst. In this case, success preceded tragedy. Though the new method appeared efficient and advanced—and together with explosives, rayon, and nitrogenous fertilizers recommended his enterprise to Ugaki—it also polluted the land and water around the village of Minamata, poisoning its population by the 1960s.[38] The ultimate evil of mercury poisoning was not foreseen when the process was developed, and so acetic acid joined the group of technologically related but non-fertilizer products whose combined sales (but not profits) surpassed those of fertilizers by 1935.[39]

Accelerated growth accompanying innovation and diversification demanded new sources of electricity. Most Japanese rivers were already developed for hydroelectricity by the late 1920s, and talk of nationalization of electrical generation and transmission had entered political discussions. Furthermore, dumping by European fertilizer makers had resumed with increased vigor and with some degree of cooperation by Japanese trading companies which benefited from expanded transactions in fertilizers. To respond to this last challenge, the manufacturers had to find ways to cut costs. Noguchi's solution to both problems was to develop the potentially rich hydroelectric sources in Korea; Korean electricity would replace the soon-to-be exhausted sources of new supply in Japan, and on-site manufacture in the colony would shave several yen off the cost of labor and electricity per ton of fertilizer.[40] Thus, continued use of electrochemical technology increasingly required colonial expansion and was closely tied to economic imperialism. But colonial investment meant seeking to develop rivers for which Mitsubishi held the operational rights, a potentially risky decision for Nitchitsu. In the end, Noguchi was able to retain fertilizer markets in Japan, to diversify sufficiently to compensate for possible losses in fertilizer profits, and to ally himself closely with colonial authorities.

MAINTAINING A MARKET WITH CARTELS AND COOPERATIVES

Noguchi was also successful in retaining Nitchitsu's share of the market in Japan. European dumping had been increasing in the 1920s against the backdrop of political discussion of the merits of controlling prices and distribution of fertilizer. Farmers' organizations had been lobbying with political parties for price controls and marketing reforms. At the low, controlled prices that would help the farmers, only the cheaper European products could earn profits for their manufacturers. The political parties and the bureaucrats were torn, therefore, between aiding the farmers and destroying the domestic fertilizer industry. The problem was complicated by the presence of middlemen; the large importers of European fertilizer were, at the same time, also the main distributors of fertilizers in Japan and, in several cases, struggling new fertilizer manufacturers themselves. Most Japanese manufacturers were, as a result, dependent on these companies for distribution. In 1930, the European manufacturers, exhausted from having to compete with each other, formed two international cartels for fertilizer, one for ammonium sulfate and one for calcium cyanamide. Of the fertilizer-producing nations, only Japan and the United States were excluded from the cartels, the United States for legal reasons and Japan because it was the main target of the European exporters.[41] The import problem worsened. Noguchi and other producers argued before cabinet members that, since it was in the farmers' interest that Japan have a viable fertilizer industry, imports must be restricted.[42]

But restrictive measures would fail if they were directed only at the European producers competing for the Japanese market. Indeed, actions taken by the Japanese importers and distributors of fertilizer were even more responsible for the serious import problem than those of the European manufacturers. It was the Japanese importers and distributors who controlled price and quantity of imports. In fact, Japanese farmers could have purchased fertilizer even more cheaply without the distribution middlemen. The experience of American exporters is informative in this regard. At the end of the 1920s and into the 1930s, American-made ammonium sulfate was generally cheaper than the German or British product. Yet, the Americans' market share in Japan dropped from 59 percent in 1923 to 20 percent in 1924, and to 10 percent in 1928.[43] Japanese importers apparently favored certain foreign firms. Thus, restrictions directed against foreign exporters alone would not solve manufacturers' problems. Stronger measures, including sales through marketing cartels, the use of farmers' cooperatives, and agreements with foreign companies, were necessary to undersell foreign products and control marketing.

Cooperatives were established in 1923, but played only a small role in fertilizer distribution until the Ministry of Agriculture and Forestry announced the Fertilizer Distribution Improvement Regulations in August 1930. These regulations were decided by the Cabinet and implemented by the bureaucracy; the Diet was not involved, which prevented political fights and expedited implementation. The regulations provided government subsidies for private cooperatives amounting to ¥4,083,065 over a ten-year period. The funds were to be used by cooperatives to buy fertilizers directly from manufacturers. As fertilizer prices continued to erode between 1930 and 1932, manufacturers turned to direct negotiations with the cooperatives. Close ties with farmers aided manufacturers in two ways. Good relations meant domestic manufacturers had a way of avoiding some of the ill effects of dumping without having to sell through Mitsui or Mitsubishi dealerships. Another benefit for manufacturers was the growth in fertilizer use as direct marketing lowered prices by eliminating the middleman's profits (see Appendix C).

Before benefiting from government programs allowing them to circumvent dealers and importers, the manufacturers had to confront the power of the importers to influence the rules for distribution. This confrontation is evident in the differing approaches of Noguchi Jun, on the one hand, and representatives of other manufacturers and importers, on the other, to the formation of the International Nitrogen Cartel (the Convention de l'Industrie de l'Azote, hereafter I.N.C.) and to the Fujiwara-Bosch Agreement of 1930.

Three of Japan's largest producers of ammonium sulfate reacted to the threat of a European cartel without hesitation, forming the Nitrogen Deliberative Association (Chisso Kyōgikai) in March 1930.[44] The three—Nitchitsu, Denki Kagaku (Denka), and Dai Nippon—were joined by four other non-members in petitioning the Finance Ministry to apply the Unfair Dumping Law (*Futō renbai hō*) of 1910 against the members of the international cartel. Fujiwara Ginjirō, president of Denki Kagaku, was spokesman for the producers' group, and other manufacturers aired their views as well. Noguchi stated that the government had only once helped the fertilizer industry, when it relaxed restrictions on exports of fertilizers during World War I. By not regulating imports now, Noguchi added, the government was losing a valuable source of customs revenue by failing to tax imported fertilizer adequately.[45]

In addition to negotiating with the government, the members of the Nitrogen Deliberative Association also had to compromise with each other because their solutions to import problems varied. Fujiwara Ginjirō and Noguchi Jun began secret negotiations with Hermann Bosch, president of the Japan office of H. Ahrens, importers of German ammonium sulfate, in November 1930. They negotiated reductions of German imports from 380,000 tons in 1929 to 200,000 tons in 1930. Moreover, the proposal provided:[46]

(1) That the Japanese ammonium sulfate producers be absolutely prohibited from exporting;
(2) That the Japanese producers form an importing cartel, and agree to take 200,000 tons of imports during the first year of the agreement, followed by scheduled reductions of 50,000 tons each year for the next four years until imports were phased out;
(3) That the import price be set at ¥85;
(4) That the Japanese producers be prohibited from building new plants or expanding capacity;
(5) That all imported ammonium sulfate be sold through Mitsui or Mitsubishi;
(6) And that the agreement be in effect for five years.

Noguchi was not pleased with these terms, however, and withdrew his support. The agreement was, therefore, considered to be Fujiwara's. It has been argued that Fujiwara Ginjirō's terms unnecessarily harmed Japanese makers of fertilizer by stipulating a low import price and by restricting expansion of firms in the process of construction.[47] These included Nitchitsu's plant at Hungnam, Korea. (Because of Korea's colonial status, Hungnam products were considered domestic rather than imported.) Furthermore, Fujiwara was president of two Mitsui-related companies—Ōji Paper and Denki Kagaku—and Mitsui and Mitsubishi Trading Companies appeared to be the major beneficiaries of the Fujiwara-Bosch agreement, as these negotiations were called. This has raised the question of whether Fujiwara took a relatively weak position on import controls because of his relationship to Mitsui.

A closer examination reveals the restrictions to be less damaging than they appear. In 1929, Japanese exports of fertilizer were minuscule—just 0.79 percent of production—and, by 1930, had risen to 5.6 percent.[48] To be sure, exports had grown quickly, but they still accounted for just a small percentage of production. Moreover, imports remained above 300,000 tons in 1930; this left plenty of opportunity to expand sales in the domestic market even if Japanese exports were eliminated, as stipulated in the first provision of the agreement. Similarly, the impact of the third provision was not completely damaging; the low import price of ¥85 cut profits, but most firms, including Nitchitsu, did make some profit at that price.

The clause restricting plant expansion was the only injurious one, even for companies related to Mitsui, Sumitomo, and Mitsubishi, which were continuing negotiations to acquire licenses for ammonia at that time.[49] The fifth clause would principally affect the European fertilizer importers by requiring domestic marketing.

Even this relatively benign proposal was rejected by Noguchi, however, who reopened negotiations with Bosch. The resulting Noguchi-Bosch proposal differed from Fujiwara's draft in the following ways: Noguchi would lift restrictions on Japanese exports; Noguchi would eliminate sales of American fertilizer in Japan; and Noguchi would prohibit direct sales by foreign firms to Japanese consumers.[50] Noguchi rejected the suggestion that plants under construction be eliminated.

The Fujiwara-Bosch agreement was therefore revised in April 1931, after consideration of Noguchi's proposals. It provided:

(1) That English and German manufacturers be required to cease direct marketing, and all imports be handled by Mitsui and Mitsubishi, including imports from the United States which had formerly been contracted only to Mitsubishi;
(2) That the agreement be in effect for three years from 1 July 1931;
(3) That British and German imports could total 100,000 tons during the first year, 80,000 tons the second year, and 50,000 tons the third year, unless Japanese-made supply failed to keep pace with demand;
(4) That, although exports of Japanese-made ammonia were not recognized by this agreement, future exports could be negotiated in good faith with the Germans and the British.

These revised proposals were more favorable to manufacturers than Fujiwara's original suggestions. In the end, these negotiations were superseded by environmental changes. The manufacturers' problems were finally solved in 1932, when the devaluation of the yen made imports uncompetitive with domestic fertilizers. By then, the farmers' cooperatives were also running smoothly. Nevertheless, Japanese fertilizer manufacturers decided that they should improve fertilizer distribution. So they formed a distribution cartel, the Ammonium Sulfate Distribution Association (Ryūan Haikyū Kumiai), whose leading member was Noguchi Jun.[51]

As Noguchi developed effective techniques to counter adverse market conditions, however, he discovered the benefits of greater independence from his distributors. Gradually separating himself from Mitsubishi, Noguchi sought to establish a base in Korea.

NOGUCHI IN KOREA

Disagreements with Mitsubishi emerged over Korean investment. Noguchi was the major private investor and developer of industry in Korea and became known as the "Entrepreneurial King of the Peninsula." Nitchitsu capital accounted for over one-quarter of all investment there as late as 1942,[52] and one of his wartime admirers compared his role in Korea to that of Columbus in America.[53]

Noguchi's interest in Korea had been kindled before World War I when a boyhood friend told him of his plans to generate electricity there.[54] But the Korean Corporation Law of 1911 limited investment opportunities in Korea just as opportunities were expanding at home. There was little reason for Noguchi to think of Korean investment till the mid-1920s. Colonial policy had changed in 1920. Korean agricultural production for export to Japan was encouraged after the Japanese Rice Riots of 1918 indicated the need for greater supplies of rice at home. Increasing output in Korea would require fertilizers. The Corporation Law was abolished in 1920, permitting Japanese investment in the colony.[55] Within the decade, official policy called for Korean industrialization, including electrification of rivers. These policy changes coincided with the needs of Nitchitsu to find new rivers to harness, to develop factory sites near electricity and labor, and to receive encouragement for technological advancement and diversification.

The Government General in Korea had begun studying rivers as early as 1911, and announced that developing hydroelectricity would be profitable.[56] But some potential developers of this electricity failed to act quickly to take advantage of the opportunities. Mitsubishi Gōshi Kaisha, for one, had begun investigating the Yalu and the Changjin, two of Korea's largest and most promising rivers, but made no move to harness them.[57] As with other new industrial ventures, the task was left to smaller, less risk-averse entrepreneurs.

Two such entrepreneurs were Morita Kazuo and Kubota Yutaka. Morita, a university classmate of Noguchi's, became interested in Korean electricity development while visiting a journalist friend in Seoul in 1923. On his return to Japan, he called on Kubota, a younger engineer, who had just returned to Japan from Seoul with topographical maps of the Pujon and the Changjin Rivers.[58] Morita's enthusiasm was infectious, and the two became excited by the challenge of developing those rivers. They next applied to Governor General Saitō Makoto for permission to begin their investigation and possible development. But, despite the Government General's avowed desire to produce electricity in Korea, Saitō demanded that Morita and Kubota find industrial customers to make the project economically feasible.[59] Saitō had reasons for this demand. There was another applicant for the project; this was Saitō's way of determining which applicant was better. Morita and Kubota recalled Morita's classmate Noguchi and Noguchi's former partner Fujiyama Tsuneichi. Both were good at their craft, but Noguchi had additional talents—his useful political skills. Noguchi had contributed generously to a Kenseikai politician in a campaign in which Kubota had worked. Kubota felt that Noguchi's ease with politicians would speed project development. Morita and Kubota therefore invited Noguchi to join the project.

Noguchi responded without hesitation. He could finally go to the colony. He joined the project initiated by Kubota and Morita and petitioned Shimooka Chūji, Political Affairs Officer for the Government General, for the water-development rights originally requested of Governor General Saitō.[60]

Noguchi was a successful industrial user of electricity—which Saitō had demanded in granting development rights—and Shimooka liked Noguchi. But there was the matter of the other applicant—Mitsubishi Gōshi Kaisha, Mitsubishi Bank's parent company—a formidable challenger. It had a proven interest in the rivers, having already studied them for generative capacity. Most formidable to Nitchitsu was, of course, the relationship between the two firms. Mitsubishi Bank was Nitchitsu's creditor. Although Shimooka admitted that he did not like large zaibatsu,[61] he permitted Mitsubishi to develop the larger of the two rivers, the Changjin, while granting the Pujon to Noguchi. Although Mitsubishi would vigorously object to some of Noguchi's later attempts to expand in Korea, Shimooka's June 1925 decision to grant Noguchi the Pujon was quite acceptable to them. First, they were convinced that developing the Pujon was a good investment for Nitchitsu, and, as Nitchitsu's creditors, Mitsubishi bankers were pleased. And, second, some Mitsubishi leaders were personally pleased, especially the Iwasaki family, who had significant shareholdings in Nitchitsu.[62]

Noguchi wasted no time developing the Pujon project. Within two months he had traveled on horseback through rough, roadless terrain, investigating the source of the Pujon.[63] By 27 January 1926, he was ready to incorporate Chōsen Hydroelectric (Chōsen Suiden) with himself as president. The founding of Chōsen Hydroelectric was a monumental step forward in Japan's electrical generating industry. Although generation fell short of the 200,000 kw. anticipated, the scale of the project—more than 80,000 kw.—far surpassed other Japanese electrical works. The project was also an important stimulus to Japan's machinery industry, since it was one of the first major projects in Japan or its colonies to use Japanese-made machinery.[64]

Even before the hydroelectric plant was operating, Noguchi began construction in May 1927 of its sister chemical plant at Hungnam; this was completed within two and a half years. Chōsen Chisso Hiryō came on line in January 1930, just as world prices for fertilizer were dropping. Interestingly, Nitchitsu profited from the increased production at Chōsen Chisso, despite the world glut of cheap fertilizer, because Chōsen's production costs were low enough to remain competitive. The Chōsen product lowered Nitchitsu's overall average cost to a profitable level. Korean-made fertilizer was much cheaper than the fertilizer Nitchitsu made in Japan. Taxes, wages, and costs of energy were all lower, and Noguchi had eager customers in Korea.

While Noguchi's production soared in Korea, it declined in Japan, and, by 1935, had fallen to just 15 percent of Nitchitsu's total ammonium sulfate output.[65] But Hungnam was not one big fertilizer plant, for it was there that Noguchi was able to diversify. The low costs of electricity, wages, and taxes at Hungnam permitted higher profitability and lessened the risk of investment in applications of spin-off technology. Indeed, as the risk of investment declined, the cost of *not* investing loomed larger. The company maintained its competitiveness by innovating in new areas. Innovative investment was fostered by the profitability of business expansion in Korea. Thus, Korean investment fostered Nitchitsu's competitiveness. Experienced staff, another requirement for expansion, were increasingly available as technically trained employees worked their way up through manufacturing subsections of the company. By the time the Hungnam fertilizer plant came on line, another new Korean subsidiary of Nitchitsu was producing glycerine from Korean sardines to be used in the manufacture of explosives at Nobeoka in Kyushu. (By law, Noguchi was not yet permitted to manufacture explosives in Korea.) In time, numerous such ties would be established among Nitchitsu subsidiaries. Futhermore, twelve major intra-company scientific conferences between 1931 and 1943 brought Nitchitsu scientists together for regular exchanges on ways of using different subsidiaries' products.[66]

Noguchi's plans sounded ambitious and appeared to be successful. But the initial optimism expressed by Mitsubishi bankers for Noguchi's Korean advances began to fade. They were concerned about his ability to repay the large loans needed for his massive construction projects. More risk-averse bankers had replaced the earlier more enthusiastic bankers. Kushida Manzō, with whom Noguchi dealt at Mitsubishi Bank, took a cautious approach to investment during the Depression.[67] This caution was shared by others with Mitsubishi connections. At Nitchitsu Board meetings, they began to object to Noguchi's plans for expansion, while Noguchi's own appointees generally approved his ideas.

Although Noguchi's bold actions would ultimately benefit his company, the more cautious Mitsubishi men appeared, in the early 1930s, far more rational. A drought in the summer of 1930 lowered the water level in the Pujon reservoir, destroying hopes that the project could quickly recoup the enormous investment already made.[68] Although Mitsubishi Bank permitted additional borrowing in 1931, in 1933 the bank decided to terminate its formal relationship with Noguchi, and required him to repay ¥25 million in loans. After a quarter of a century of support, Mitsubishi withdrew a large part of its aid to Nitchitsu. But Nitchitsu remained in operation and even prospered. The company's technological requirements for certain resources and the strategic value of its products led to its increasingly intimate relationship with government officials and permitted its survival.

NOGUCHI AND UGAKI

Nitchitsu could survive the loss of support from Mitsubishi because of the growing cooperation between Noguchi and Ugaki Kazushige, Governor General of Korea from 1931 to 1936. This cooperation depended on the type of technology Nitchitsu employed for ammonia manufacture—electrochemistry. After 1932, electrochemistry generally became uncompetitive with a new method of ammonia manufacture, the gas method. A decline in access to new sources of hydroelectric power due to restraint of competition through organization of the electrical industry meant that Noguchi's form of technology would become increasingly rare in Japan.[69] The gas method used large quantities of coal rather than electricity and was the method employed by companies like Mitsui and Mitsubishi, which had their own coal supplies when they entered the chemical field in the early 1930s. By contrast, the energy requirements of the electrochemical method demanded a good working relationship with government officials, such as Noguchi had with Ugaki Kazushige, to guarantee access to electricity. Close ties between Ugaki and Noguchi were possible because the Governor General saw an electrical industry necessary for industrialization. Ugaki was also pleased to find an entrepreneur able to cooperate on projects like construction of harbor facilities and to fill government and military contracts.[70] The resulting government encouragement permitted the chemical industry to grow far larger than would be expected under more normal circumstances of industrialization in a developing country like Korea.[71]

By the time Ugaki arrived in Korea in 1931, Noguchi was practically a resident there. Concerned about starting production at Hungnam and fighting the drought of 1930, Noguchi rarely left Korea even to visit his family. He was extremely energetic in acquiring the right to develop the Changjin River, then held by Mitsubishi Gōshi Kaisha, to compensate for his losses on the Pujon.

Acquiring the rights to the Changjin took some time, but Ugaki, who advocated rapid industrialization, did attempt to expedite electrification of the river. This ultimately speeded the transfer of rights from Mitsubishi to Chōsen Chisso. On his appointment as Governor General, Ugaki interviewed the major Japanese investors in Korea. He asked them about their continuing interest in investment.

In particular, he asked Kimura Kusuyata of Mitsubishi Gōshi Kaisha what his company planned to do with the Changjin.[72] Kimura replied that, as Mitsubishi had already made a significant investment in the project, he wished to have a year to review their accomplishments and projections and to prepare an explanatory report. Ugaki granted the year. Shortly thereafter, in February 1932, Ugaki issued tough new regulations for electrical companies in Korea. These included the government's right to establish national-policy companies to transmit privately generated electricity within the four districts into which Korea would be divided, to approve all construction plans for plants, and to veto selection of upper-level managers in electrical companies.[73] These regulations permitted Ugaki to transfer Mitsubishi's water-development rights in 1932 when company officials decided they had no immediate plans to develop the river.

Noguchi requested the rights to the Changjin immediately after Mitsubishi announced its hesitancy to develop it. Ugaki demurred in granting Noguchi's request because of his concern that Mitsubishi might discontinue financial support for the venture; he was right.[74] But Noguchi decided to risk Mitsubishi's objections. Technological considerations made Chōsen Chisso far more dependent on electricity than Mitsubishi was. Chōsen Chisso was already manufacturing products needing electricity; and therefore any reduction in its supply would lead to a cutback in production and sales. On the other hand, Mitsubishi had not yet begun electrochemical manufacture, so inability to increase electricity supplies could not affect current output of fertilizer and other manufactured goods. Mitsubishi continued to have a less pressing need for electricity, even when it did begin production of electrochemicals, because it used the gas method, which required materials Mitsubishi itself possessed. Noguchi was dependent on the government in ways the more self-sufficient zaibatsu never was. Thus, although Mitsubishi Bank threatened to withdraw funding because of their objection to Chōsen Chisso's fertilizer production during the Depression[75]—and perhaps because Mitsubishi was considering eventual production of ammonia as well—Noguchi's choice of technology demanded that he invest in increasing his generative capacity.

Noguchi went ahead with his application for the development rights. His cause was aided by his employee Kubota Yutaka, who persuaded Government General officials that Mitsubishi's cost projections were too high and that Chōsen Chisso could complete the project more efficiently. But, even if costs were as low as Kubota estimated, Chōsen Chisso's debt would be enormous. In the end, Noguchi's decision was aided by several considerations. First, he found alternate sources of financing from other banks.[76] Second, Ugaki permitted Noguchi to acquire the rights for the small sum of ¥400,000; Mitsubishi had already invested ¥1.2 million in the project.[77] Third, Chōsen Chisso was able to use flexible accounting procedures to minimize taxable income even while expanding output.[78] That is, Chōsen Chisso and other subsidiaries of Nitchitsu were legally separate corporations, but were usually wholly owned by Nitchitsu. Nitchitsu was paid fees by its subsidiaries for marketing their products and supplying their resources, thereby lowering the subsidiaries' profits according to the accounting methods the company used. Lower profits meant lower taxable income for Chōsen Chisso. Nitchitsu did not collect dividends for its shares of Chōsen Chisso after 1933; these fees for service were collected instead. Income could, by such accounting methods, be shifted among subsidiaries and the parent company to permit tax savings. Fourth, some of the electricity generated at the Changjin was sold to a National Policy Company, a requirement of Ugaki's regulations, which increased the cash income Chōsen Chisso could expect from its investment in the Changjin.[79]

Noguchi's first consideration—funding—was handled by the government-managed Bank of Chōsen, the Industrial Bank (Kōgyō Ginkō), and the Industrial Bank of Korea (Shokusan Ginkō). The banks underwrote long-term bonds and made regular commercial loans, some of which were repeatedly rolled over. Chōsen Chisso, the main fertilizer company, received most of these loans before 1937, but, thereafter, larger loans were granted to strategically important subsidiaries like Chōsen Oil.[80] The parent company—Nitchitsu—also received separate Bank of Chōsen loans through the bank's Tokyo office. When Chōsen Chisso was merged with the parent company in 1941 under government orders, the amount loaned to Nitchitsu represented the combined total of loans to several of Nitchitsu's operations in Korea and Japan, and thus appeared to make a large leap in 1941, as did all loans from official and semi-governmental banks to other companies involved in high-technology munitions production.

Katō Keisaburō, president of the Bank of Chōsen and an enthusiastic advocate of industrialization in Korea, was Noguchi's most important financial contact. There are several reasons why Noguchi and Katō found it mutually profitable to cooperate. Katō may have been impelled by ideological reasons. Katō took it as his "special mission" to lend to prospective developers, especially one recommended by Ugaki.[81] A commercial bank might have spent more time investigating the potential profitability of each loan. Fortunately for Noguchi, Katō believed nitrogenous fertilizers, related to munitions production, to be strategically necessary.

Katō Keisaburō may also have cooperated with Noguchi because he viewed assistance to Noguchi Jun as an important investment in strengthening the independence of his Bank of Chōsen vis-à-vis Tokyo. The bank faced serious financial problems during the late 1920s. In the wake of the liquidity crisis which forced the bankruptcy of the similarly government-managed Bank of Taiwan, both colonial banks were placed under close scrutiny by the Ministry of Finance in Tokyo.[82] The presidents of both banks had to divide their working time between Tokyo and their colonial headquarters. Katō Keisaburō wished to avoid the stifling effects of intense scrutiny in Tokyo, and felt that a major success in lending in Korea would underscore the effectiveness of the Seoul office as well as provide an indisputable justification for his remaining in Seoul. Katō therefore used the Seoul office to lend large amounts of money to Noguchi. Although later loans to subsidiaries of Nitchitsu were delivered through different branches of the Bank of Chōsen, it was initially important that Katō establish the centrality of the Seoul headquarters.

Noguchi seemed a good risk, and the Bank's president authorized loans to the chemical firm's president. As collateral, Noguchi offered 37,000 of his own shares in Nitchitsu as well as a portion of the fertilizer output of Chōsen Chisso. Other short-term loans to Noguchi came from the Industrial Bank of Korea, but the Bank of Chōsen remained the most important source of funds.[83] Both Korea-based banks also served as agents for other Japanese banks, which could be assured that these agents would offer Noguchi such services as loan transfers and payments of taxes and fees.

Nitchitsu sustained the loss of Mitsubishi's aid because it received government assistance as a company able to cooperate with Ugaki in the industrial development of Korea. So successful was this industrialization that it produced unforseen demographic and sociological changes in the colony. The chemical industry grew by a factor of 100 from 1924 to 1940, while consumer industries such as textiles and food increased only 10 times during that same period. The chemical industry was centered around Hungnam and the Pujon and Chang-jin Rivers' generating facilities in northern Korea. Consequently, industrial output per capita jumped in the north and stagnated in the south. Population growth was similarly more rapid in the north. Though their productivity increased during the 1930s, most workers in Chōsen Chisso produced little except fertilizer that was of use within Korea.[84] Most of Noguchi's new products were developed with Japan's strategic needs in mind.

STRATEGIC DIVERSIFICATION

Diversification at Noguchi's enterprise occurred in two different phases. The first, from 1932 to 1937, was one of informal cooperation between the military and civilian leaders and the industry. Decisions affecting the company were usually initiated internally by Noguchi, the Board of Directors, and managers involved in daily operations. Company priorities coincident with the ideology of men in the military or administration could be easily implemented, however. Without government-supported loans and official permission to build plants, for example, Noguchi would have had to modify or even suspend his plans for development in Korea. Outsiders like Ugaki, therefore, played an important role in company decisions. Ugaki could suggest certain types of development—such as helping Noguchi locate his Hungnam complex so that it could double as "Japan's first line of defense" against the neighboring Russians[85]—and the Governor General could create the conditions conducive to Noguchi's decision to risk investment.

Cooperation was fostered more by a confluence of goals than by overt coercion by the Japanese government in Korea, though there are examples of government persuasion. When the Japanese and Korean economies were mobilized for war during the late 1930s, however, the government's role in making investment policy became more active. It was during the mid-1930s that the groundwork for later cooperation between the government and the chemical industry was laid; companies like Noguchi's could produce the products demanded by the military in the second phase of cooperation after 1937 because they had diversified, with government assistance, during the first.

Diversification occurred throughout Noguchi's enterprise in Japan and Korea, but the most interesting developments were in Korea around Hungnam. In a little more than a decade, Nitchitsu grew from a fertilizer company to a ¥500-million multifaceted chemical company with 26 subsidiaries (1937). Of the two major types of diversification undertaken during the 1920s in Kyushu—rayon and explosives—the latter became an important part of Nitchitsu's growth in Korea in the 1930s. Other areas of expansion included fats and oils, carbide, metal refining, coal-tar derivatives and synthetic fuel, soybean derivatives, and bleach and soda.

Not all were successful ventures. Some of Noguchi's investments in the areas encouraged by officials had less initial success than those in areas selected by company men on the basis of production priorities. Indeed, Noguchi occasionally encountered resistance from his managers when he wished to follow government plans his managers felt were antithetical to company interests. Some of the company's less profitable products were unsuccessful because they failed to have a real market until the late 1930s, others because the company's technological capabilities, the highest in Japan and the colonies and essentially at international levels, still fell short of Noguchi's aspirations.

The first two areas of diversification of product were in the manufacture of glycerine from sardine oil and the carbonization of coal. The waters around Korea were the world's richest sardine fishing grounds.[86] Noguchi found ready use for Korean sardines; he could pulverize sardines as fertilizer and use the fish oil as glycerine for explosives made at Nobeoka. Production of glycerine began in 1932, and Noguchi sent most of this Korean product to Nobeoka. In 1934, however, management in Korea decided that production of explosives on the spot was more practical. But Japanese policy in Korea forbade production of explosives for civilian use; Noguchi would have to obtain a waiver of this restriction. This was easily done. Governor General Ugaki encouraged industrialization, mining, and construction, which all needed explosives. Permission was granted in 1934.

Explosive manufacture combined contributions from several subsidiaries of Nitchitsu. In addition to the Changjin project's contribution of electricity, nearby Hungnam supplied ammonia, oxygen, glycerine, and nitric acid. The Pon'gung plant, opened a few years later, sent glycol. Nobeoka continued to send trained scientists and technicians.[87] The finished product was marketed by Chōsen 'Mite Inc. (Chōsen Maito KK—"Maito" was an abbreviation for dynamite). Nitchitsu's operations in Korea were fast taking on the character of a modern multi-unit, vertically integrated firm.

Military scientists were actively involved in research, especially in detonators appropriate to Hungnam's conditions. The Korean plant made numerous types of explosives including carlite, black powder, ammonium nitrate, and dynamite. Within two years of first production, Chōsen Explosives at Hungnam was among a group of companies designated by the military as contributing to the national security and therefore amenable to military direction.[88] By the early 1940s, Nitchitsu was Japan's largest civilian producer of arms and munitions.

Carbonization for production of coal-based products was the other of Noguchi's early attempts at diversification in Korea. Plans for a distillation plant at Yong'an in north Korea were begun in 1931. In the next few years, a variety of derivative products were made from the coal tar produced at Yong'an. Methanol, formalin, and other oil products were of great interest to military procurers. In the early 1930s, however, creating the ability to produce synthetic oil products in Japan appeared ridiculous to many observers. The technology for synthetic fuel was extraordinarily sophisticated; indeed, it was far more sophisticated than the complicated technology for production of ammonium sulfate which it in some ways resembled. Japanese industry enjoyed a plentiful supply of the cheap imported petroleum internationally available in the 1930s from the United States. Noguchi's decision to invest in upgrading his technological level from its primitive ability to carbonize coal to being able to liquify it was, therefore, a major one and one that required substantial government assistance.

Certain preliminary stages toward the advancement of fuel technology in Japan had been achieved by the middle of the 1930s, due in no small part to advances in ammonia technology. As in Germany, the world leader in synthetic fuels at that time, Japanese scientists involved in synthesis of ammonia were best equipped to make synthetic fuel.[89] The Japanese Navy was particularly interested in a fuel independent of foreign sources and had conducted experiments in synthesis for years.[90] Noguchi's coal-tar operations, therefore, caught the eye of Navy men, who urged him to produce fuel using the Navy's methods. But there was no profit to be made from synthetic oil until several years later, at the height of World War II.[91] The only justification for making it was Noguchi's patriotism and large loans from the Bank of Chōsen. Combining research results obtained by Navy and Nitchitsu scientists, Noguchi founded Chōsen Coal Industries (Chōsen Sekitan Kōgyō KK, later renamed Chōsen Artificial Oil [Chōsen Jinzō Sekiyu]) in 1935.

Areas of diversification were metals, acetone, methanol, soybean products, and more than two dozen others. Not all diversification decisions were as dramatic as the decision to invest in synthetic oil, and some were more profitable to the company. The areas of explosives and synthetic oil are, however, typical of the kinds of diversification undertaken by Noguchi on behalf of the Government General in the 1930s.

Technologically, diversification generally followed productive lines. The new chemicals usually modified the technology of products already made by Nitchitsu or its subsidiaries (see Appendix D). Almost all, therefore, used processes dependent on large amounts of electricity. Such great amounts were available to the company because of Noguchi's close interaction with officials able to offer him rights to hydroelectric sources, even after the institution of controls on electricity. Political considerations and personal relationships, then, helped determine the form of diversification. And, conversely, technological requirements drove Noguchi closer to the authorities. But, until controls were imposed on the products themselves during the China War, Noguchi generally determined the specific areas for investment within official guidelines.

CONCLUSION

Noguchi Jun, with his Nitchitsu empire in Japan and Korea—and later throughout China and Southeast Asia as well—was Japan's archetypal scientist-entrepreneur. Starting his career as an aggressive and well trained but cash-poor young industrial visionary, he pioneered in Japan the most sophisticated technology of the prewar era, electrochemicals. He made use of financing from a variety of sources, including loans from banks like Mitsubishi and, most important, payments from shareholders, some of the largest of whom were Mitsubishi's owners and top managers. Nitchitsu's Board of Directors reflected the company's debt to Mitsubishi; several Mitsubishi managers also served on Nitchitsu's Board, overseeing their company's investment. Yet Nitchitsu was clearly an independent company, making its own decisions about investment in innovation to further the company's interests. Business strategy was planned independent of Mitsubishi. When Mitsubishi Bank's managers differed with Noguchi on the further expansion of Nitchitsu in Korea, Noguchi did not hesitate to risk loss of Mitsubishi Bank loans in steadfastly promoting the strategic interests of his company.

We should recall that this estrangement was not actually a full-blown divorce, complete with custody battles. There was no struggle over the right to the Changjin River, for example, as is usually asserted. Moreover, Noguchi was allowed to repay the ¥25 million in loans from Mitsubishi Bank in installments over several years rather than being required to pay the entire amount at once. Furthermore, members of Mitsubishi's Iwasaki family, who personally owned shares, did not divest. Nevertheless, the loss of even the borrowed funds required belt-tightening. Why did Noguchi risk the estrangement?

There are several ways to interpret the estrangement between Mitsubishi Bank and Nitchitsu. First, successful innovative companies invest in new technology or in expansion of existing technology because the technology is available; not to invest would mean stagnation and loss of competitiveness. Other conditions for investment must also exist: sufficient capital, adequate resources, skilled workers and managers, a lively market for the product, and an encouraging investment environment, including supportive government officials. As we have seen, these conditions were met in Korea, and Nitchitsu's expansive business strategy demanded investment despite some drawbacks. The imperative to continue investment in technological innovation represented by this scenario parallels the experience of post-World War II technology-intensive companies as well.

Second, the estrangement of Nitchitsu from Mitsubishi may be interpreted in light of Nitchitsu's increasingly intimate relations with government officials who, in some sense, may be said to have taken the place of Mitsubishi as supporters outside the company. The existence of government-sponsored support not only passively eased the removal of Mitsubishi aid; in time, it also actively encouraged even more diverse technological innovations as Nitchitsu began manufacturing products for civilian or military officials in the colony. Thus, colonial expansion was necessary for Nitchitsu's survival and was an important result of its business strategy. Subsequently, particularly after 1937, business strategy was itself affected by the company's presence in the colony and its relationship to colonial officials.

Much seemed to change with the end of the war. Japan in defeat lost its colonies, and Nitchitsu, renamed Chisso after the war, came to epitomize at Minamata all that was wrong with rapid development of high technology. Whether to fill government contracts or to follow the technological imperative of expansion and diversification, Minamata's managers planned investment with little concern for the health of the surrounding community. Despite obvious changes in the business environment since the prewar period, Japan's postwar high-technology companies share some interesting characteristics with their prewar predecessors. As Nitchitsu was relatively independent of Mitsubishi, many—though not all—are independent of "groups." Electronics makers Sony, Matsushita, and Sharp, automakers Toyota and Honda, and camera, copier, and watchmakers Canon, Ricoh, and Seiko exemplify this independence.[92] Another characteristic of companies either founded or newly expanded from virtual workshops after the war—the presence of strong founder-executives[93]—replicates Nitchitsu's experience under scientist-entrepreneur Noguchi Jun.

More general but equally instructive comparisons are also evident in pre- and postwar government-business relations. Other scholars, most notably Chalmers Johnson, have made a convincing case that the World War II years bridged the era of weak government involvement in the affairs of businesses and the postwar era of rational planning.[94] Johnson notes that the basis for later cooperation was laid in the decades before World War II, when policy subtly fostered a climate within which private businesses were able to weather the storms of relatively unfettered capitalism. These storms were milder for firms favored by the government. But non-zaibatsu firms like Nitchitsu, rather than the zaibatsu firms cited by Johnson and most other authors, were more likely to take advantage of this benign climate for investment. The tightening of wartime regulations altered these conditions and ushered in the postwar types of government-business relations.

The broad strokes of Johnson's scenario are well designed. Yet, it is the subtler strokes that add contour and interest to the picture. The types of policies created by the government (the subtle strokes) are as interesting as the degree of rationality of planning (the broad strokes). These types may be categorized as "supply side" and "demand side." Wartime industrial policy typically emphasized the demand side. The government, through its purchase of military supplies from companies like Nitchitsu, permitted and even encouraged private investment in high-technology research and production. After 1937, the government increasingly became Nitchitsu's major market for its otherwise unprofitable non-fertilizer products. Postwar policy was quite different, generally supporting the supply side. The government tended to facilitate investment and production in areas seen as important. The market, whether domestic or international, was supposed to contribute to this effort by absorbing the products of the investment. The government itself created demand only in a few areas, albeit significant ones. For example, the government encouraged research to improve Japan's transistor technology after 1948, starting with research sponsored by universities, by Nippon Telegraph and Telephone, and by the Ministry of International Trade and Industry. MITI also encouraged importation of transistor technology.[95] A few years later, it established research projects, donated subsidies, regulated manufacture, and limited imports to aid the related computer industry. These efforts helped diffuse advanced technology and increased the supply of Japanese computers. This typical supply-side assistance was joined by less common demand-side assistance in 1961 when MITI encouraged the Japanese computer manufacturers to create the Japan Electronics Computer Corporation (JECC) to buy Japanese computers for lease to users. The more usual form of postwar government assistance, the improvement of supply, recalls the prewar government's creation of a benign investment climate, although it differs in its greater degree of rationality and regulation.

Government policies toward high technology businesses in the prewar and postwar eras have one final significant but usually overlooked difference. The postwar policies assumed that supply-side aid was usually sufficient, that the growing domestic market would absorb the products of assisted high-technology companies, and that, whatever the domestic market failed to absorb, the foreign market would. This produced unanticipated but now well-known tensions from the resulting export drive. In the prewar period, there were few high-technology exports from Japan to advanced industrial countries, but, as Nitchitsu's case indicates, the most sophisticated Japanese companies were dependent on their manufactures in, and sales to, the colonies. Colonial expansion was integral to the growth of prewar technology-intensive companies like Nitchitsu. Thus, just as the prewar and postwar eras manifest parallels (and some differences) in the diffusion and development of technology, so too do they show technology's evolving challenges to Japan's society, economy, and international position.

APPENDIX A. Nitchitsu Capital and Profits, 1908–1923

Semiannum	Capital[a] (¥1,000,000)	Paid-up[a] Capital (¥1,000,000)	Internal[b] Capital (¥1,000)	Bonds[c] (¥1,000,000)	Profits[d] (¥1,000)	Profit[e] Rate %	Dividend[f] Rate %	Dividends/Profits[g]
1908.1	1.0	0.64						
1908.2	1.0	0.64			25	7.8	10	
1909.1	1.0	0.82			42	10.2	10	
1909.2	1.0	1.0			53	10.4	10	
1910.1	1.0	1.0			74	14.9	10	
1910.2	2.0	1.25			68	10.9	10	
1911.1	2.0	1.5			67	8.9	10	
1911.2	2.0	1.75			79	9.0	8	
1912.1	4.0	2.0			123	12.3	10	
1912.2	4.0	2.0			163	16.4	10	
1913.1	4.0	2.5	65		198	11.7	10	81.3
1913.1	4.0	2.5	49		186	12.5	10	80.2
1914.1	4.0	3.0	-64		94	6.3	8	123.4
1914.2	4.0	3.2	199		370	13.7	10	69.6
1915.1	4.0	3.4	482		704	14.9	12	77.5
1915.2	4.0	3.8	601	1.0	354	18.7	15	75.7
1916.1	4.0	4.0	758		447	22.4	15	65.8
1916.2	10.0	5.5	772		654	23.8	20	79.0
1917.1	10.0	6.4	600	1.0	930	29.1	25	79.3

APPENDIX A *(Continued)*

1917.2	10.0	7.0	977	1.0	1,150	32.9	25	74.6
1918.1	10.0	7.6	1,116		1,345	35.4	30	81.4
1918.2	10.0	7.6	1,376		1,684	44.3	30	67.7
1919.1	10.0	7.6	1,462		1,758	46.3	30	64.9
1919.2	10.0	7.6	1,707		1,830	48.2	30	62.3
1920.1	10.0	10.0			5,179	103.6	104	73.6
1920.2	22.0	13.0			1,519	23.4	20	82.3
1921.1	22.0	13.0			1,204	18.5	15	81.0
1921.2	22.0	13.0			1,186	18.2	15	82.2
1922.1	22.0	13.0			1,196	18.4	15	81.5
1922.2	22.0	13.0			1,199	18.4	15	81.3
1923.1	22.0	13.0			1,210	18.6	15	80.6
1923.2	22.0	13.0			1,196	18.4	15	81.6

a. Ōshio Takeshi, "Nitchitsu kontsuerun no seiritsu to kigyō kin'yū," *Keizai Kenkyū* 27:61–127 (March 1977), pp. 116–117.

b. Internal capital includes: reserves, balances forwarded, debt amortization; Suzuki Tsuneo, "Daiichiji taisenki Nitchitsu, Denka no tōshi to shikin chōtatsu," *Kurume Daigaku Shōgakubu seiritsu 30 shūnen kinen ronbunshū.* August 1980, p. 147. Data for 1913–1919 only.

c. Ōshio Takeshi, "Nitchitsu kontsuerun," p. 109. These bonds were underwritten by Mitsubishi, Aichi, and Yamaguchi Banks. Interest rates were low: 7% for the first issue, thereafter 6% or lower. Most bonds were issued after 1926.

d. 1908–1913: Shimotani Masahiro, "Nitchitsu kontsuerun," p. 69; 1913–1923: Suzuki Tsuneo, "Daiichiji taisen," p. 142.

e. Profit rates were calculated as a percentage of paid-up capital, adjusted to annual rates, a frequently used method in prewar Japan. Suzuki Tsuneo, p. 142.

f. Percentage of par value paid out as dividends; Suzuki Tsuneo, p. 142.

g. Dividends as percentage of profits; Suzuki Tsuneo, p. 142.

APPENDIX B. Three-Product Cycle

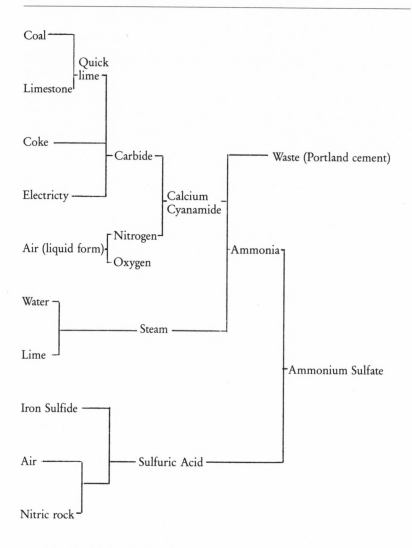

Source: Yamamoto Tomio, *Nippon Chisso Hiryō jigyō taikan* (Osaka, Nippon Chisso Hiryō, 1937).

Appendix C. Role of Cooperatives in Fertilizer Distribution
(in tons; 1,000 yen)

Year	All Types of Fertilizer		Ammonium Sulfate	
	Amount	Value	Amount	Value
1923	15,568	1,463	1,497	245
1924	26,610	2,590	3,757	614
1925	31,659	3,166	5,290	794
1926	36,343	3,122	6,234	898
1927	46,399	3,638	6,767	911
1928	64,912	5,358	7,614	924
1929	116,769	8,418	7,423	758
1930	214,432	10,365	24,512	1,667

Source: Hashimoto Jūrō, "1920 nendai no ryūan shijo," *Shakai keizai shigaku* 43.4:62 (1978).

APPENDIX D

PRODUCTIVE RELATIONSHIPS IN CHŌSEN CHISSO - 1935

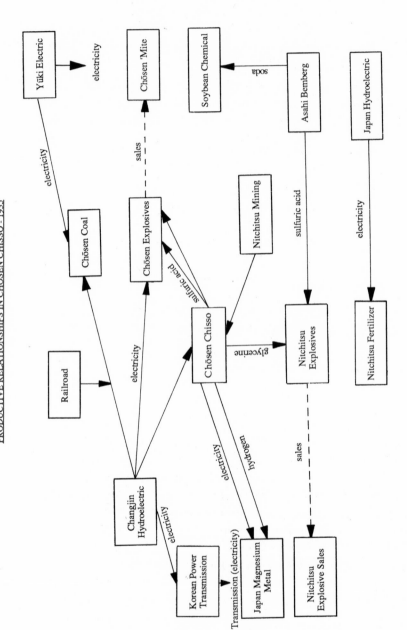

Source: Shimotani Masahiro, "Nitchitsu kontsuerun to gōsei ryūan kōgyō," <u>Osaka Keidai ronshu</u> 114 (November 1976), p. 61

"Scientific Industry": Strategy, Technology,
and Entrepreneurship in Prewar Japan

MICHAEL A. CUSUMANO

Between the mid-1930s and the end of World War II, Japan's economy shifted from a structural bias toward agriculture and light manufacturing to heavy-manufacturing fields requiring the importation
or development of new technologies. Domestic investment in metals,
machinery, and chemicals alone rose from merely 20 percent of the
total paid-up capital in Japanese companies during 1937 to 45 percent
by 1945.[1] Private investment mergers during the late 1930s and war
years also created numerous large firms that provided armaments to
the Japanese military while gaining invaluable experience in production management and product engineering. Even excluding plant
and equipment damaged in air raids or through neglect during World
War II, once the recovery of the Japanese economy was underway by
the early 1950s, Japan was well prepared to resume and then expand

its output of steel, ships, automobiles, electrical and industrial machinery, and a host of other products that had military as well as civilian applications.

This chapter examines a series of technological innovations and entrepreneurial activities centered around Japan's largest prewar facility for theoretical and applied scientific research, the Institute of Physical and Chemical Research (Rikagaku Kenkyūjo), abbreviated in Japanese as "Riken." By 1940, the Institute had accumulated a staff of 1,800 and either established or invested in approximately 60 companies employing as many as 40,000 workers making machine parts, machine tools, synthetic liquor, industrial chemicals, metals, pharmaceuticals, photographic or optical equipment, and other related products. The head of the Riken industrial group and founder of most of these firms, Ōkōchi Masatoshi (1878–1952), helped establish the Institute in 1917 and served as its director from 1921 to 1946. Although the American authorities severed the ties between the Institute and operating subsidiaries during the postwar Occupation, the facility diversified its research areas after World War II, while several firms formerly from the Riken group became independent companies. The largest of these, Ricoh, developed into Japan's top producer of copiers and a manufacturer of cameras, sensitized paper, and data-processing equipment. The Riken Corporation (formerly Riken Piston Ring), the second largest firm from the group, produced piston rings for automobile engines and other metal components. During the early 1980s, several other companies originally affiliated with the Institute continued to rely on technology first commercialized prior to World War II to manufacture products such as synthetic resins, electrical wires, precision measuring instruments, synthetic vitamins and other health products, construction materials, polishing materials made from corundum, and various rubber goods.

As seen in Table 1, measured by paid-up capital in subsidiaries or affiliates of the Institute or other group holding companies, Riken was the smallest of more than a dozen combines or zaibatsu that dominated Japanese industry prior to their dissolution after World War II. Yet, the Riken group is significant less for its size than for its unique combination of a research institute and operating companies that, prior to 1945, commercialized patents in several "high-technology" fields. Ōkōchi Masatoshi also had an extraordinary career as an academic scientist, entrepreneur, and government

TABLE 1 Major Combines, 1937 and War's End
(units: million yen paid-up capital, percentage of
national paid-up capital totals)

Combine	1937	%	Rank	1946	%	Rank
Mitsui	913	5.2	1	3,461	10.7	1
Mitsubishi	694	3.9	2	2,944	9.1	2
Nissan-Aikawa	592	3.4	3	2,083	6.4	3
Sumitomo	537	3.0	4	1,892	5.8	4
Chisso	162	0.9	7	469	1.4	8
Furukawa	99	0.6	9	540	1.7	7
Asano	251	1.4	6	599	1.8	5
Yasuda	285	1.6	5	540	1.7	6
Ōkura	156	0.9	8	364	1.1	9
Nakajima	40	0.2	13	263	0.8	10
Shōwa Denkō	70	0.4	12	254	0.8	11
Nomura	78	0.4	11	185	0.6	12
Nippon Soda	87	0.5	10	143	0.4	13
Riken	25	0.1	14	99	0.3	14
Above 14	3,987	22.5		13,829	42.6	
National Total	17,655	100.0		32,380	100.0	

Source: Yamazaki Hiroaki, "Senji shita no sangyō kōzō to dokusen soshiki," in Tōkyō Daigaku Shakai Kagaku Kenkyūsho, ed., *Senji Nihon keizai* (1979), II, 236–237, Table 11, with minor revisions. Data primarily taken from the Holding Company Liquidation Commission. See Mochikabu Kaisha Seiri Iin-kai, ed., *Nihon zaibatsu to sono kaitai* (1951), Vols. I and II.

Note: Includes domestic investments only, in both holding companies and their subsidiaries or affiliates, in which at least 10% of outstanding shares were controlled within the respective combine.

official. Born in 1878 as the son of a former lord of a domain in the present Chiba prefecture, Ōkōchi graduated in 1903 from the Engineering Department of Tokyo Imperial University (hereafter the University of Tokyo), majoring in ordnance and mechanical engineering. He remained at the university to attend graduate school and to teach, and then studied in Germany and Austria during 1908–1911. Ōkōchi returned to the University of Tokyo as a full professor and received an engineering doctorate in 1914. Although he retained his university post until 1925, he began working for the Institute in 1917 and became known in Japan for promoting close relations between the Institute and the University of Tokyo. Between 1915 and 1945, Ōkōchi also served in the upper house of the Diet and on numerous government committees to promote industry, science, and technical education. In addition, he headed the Industrial Machinery Control Association during 1942–1944 and advised the Japanese Cabinet on armaments production during World War II.[2]

While Ōkōchi experimented in business by commercializing patents that Institute researchers produced, he based most of his investments on a set of managerial principles that he called "scientific industry" (kagaku-shugi kōgyō). His basic premise, and the publicly stated reason for establishing the Institute at the end of World War I, was that Japan had to make a special effort to apply the latest technology available so as to catch up with the West and to offset a lack of natural resources. This conviction also led Ōkōchi to criticize managers in Mitsui, Mitsubishi, Sumitomo, and other "old-zaibatsu" combines founded in the nineteenth century, for valuing short-term profits and "capital preservation" over technological innovation and investment to insure the continued modernization of Japanese industry. Not only did he stress the need for more applied research; he also encouraged firms to commercialize innovative technologies developed in Japan or abroad and to apply "scientific management" and mass-production concepts more widely. Ōkōchi also advocated the placement of factories in agricultural villages to utilize unskilled surplus labor, although he insisted that companies focus on producing "low-price, high-quality goods" rather than merely on lowering costs, and maintained that, as Ford demonstrated in the United States, raising wages would lead to higher productivity.

Ōkōchi's conception of "scientific industry" evolved from his study of economic history and managerial thought in the United States and Western Europe. Similar to other Japanese born during the middle or late nineteenth century, he saw himself as a synthesizer, interpreter, and popularizer of Western or "modern" ideas, and concentrated on industrial development and the management of science and technology. To aid in this effort, Ōkōchi established a publishing company and a journal and wrote dozens of essays and books, some of which ranked as "bestsellers" in prewar Japan. Founders of other industrial groups that expanded rapidly in the decade prior to World War II such as Nitchitsu's Noguchi Jun (1873–1944) and Nissan's Aikawa Yoshisuke (1880–1967), a classmate of Ōkōchi's at the University of Tokyo, also focused on new engineering industries that older Japanese combines were slow to enter. Ōkōchi's prolific output as a writer, however, and his status as an academic, gained him the reputation among prewar journalists and scholars of Japanese business history as the chief ideological spokesman for these "new zaibatsu" of the 1930s.[3] More important, Ōkōchi's concept of scientific industry, and conviction that Japan had to exploit the skills of its people to compensate for its few mineral resources and late development, not only showed remarkable foresight but reflected a mentality that played a fundamental role in the strategies of company managers and economic planners after World War II.

This chapter first examines the foundation of the Institute and Ōkōchi's decision to invest in commercial manufacturing ventures. The second section analyzes Ōkōchi's major ideas and managerial strategies, which revolved around a contrast between "capitalistic industry" and "scientific industry." The third looks at how Ōkōchi tested his ideas in forming three of the Institute's main subsidiaries: Riken Piston Ring, Riken Metals, and Ricoh. The fourth section discusses problems in financial management and control over subsidiaries and in product quality that occurred as operations expanded during the 1930s, resulting in the partial disintegration of the Riken industrial group before the end of World War II.

THE INSTITUTE OF PHYSICAL AND CHEMICAL RESEARCH

The movement to found a domestic institute for applied research in physics and chemistry began prior to the start of World War I. Takamine Jōkichi (1854–1922), a chemical engineer educated in Japan and Scotland (Glasgow) who had established the Takamine Chemical Laboratories in New York and Chicago during the 1890s and then isolated adrenalin in 1900, returned to Japan in 1913, convinced that his country needed a facility similar to Germany's Imperial Institute for Physics, founded in 1887. He enlisted the support of Shibusawa Eiichi (1840–1931), one of Japan's most prominent businessmen, and Kikuchi Dairoku (1855–1917), a graduate of Cambridge University who had founded the Mathematics Department at the University of Tokyo and served as president of the same institution. While it took several years to acquire sufficient funds to establish the Institute of

Physical and Chemical Research, businessmen, academics, and government officials during World War I recognized the need for a large scientific facility after Japan experienced difficulties importing critical machinery, chemical, and pharmaceutical products from the West.[4]

Kikuchi agreed to serve as the first director of the facility. Shibusawa became the chairman of the founding committee and helped persuade 180 Japanese businessmen to become financial guarantors. The committee then received permission from the Ministry of Agriculture and Commerce to set up the Institute as a private foundation in March 1917. Four professors at the University of Tokyo took charge of designing and constructing the facilities: Ōkōchi and Nagaoka Hantarō were responsible for the physics division, and Ikeda Kikunae and Inoue Jinkichi set up the chemistry division. They built 20 laboratories in Tokyo's Bunkyō-ku ward with funds received from the Imperial Family, the national government, private individuals, and domestic companies. Buildings and equipment consumed ¥3 million ($1.5 million), while the endowment required another ¥2.5 million ($1.25 million).[5] The Institute's charter stressed the necessity of scientific research for industrial development and, rather presciently, pointed out that Japan, as a nation poor in natural resources, had to create a domestic foundation in science to insure the country's future prosperity and national strength:

> To promote the development of industry, the Institute of Physical and Chemical Research shall perform pure research in the fields of physics and chemistry as well as research relating to its various possible applications. No industry, whether engaged in manufacturing or agriculture, can develop properly if it lacks a sound basis in physics and chemistry. In our country especially, given its dense population and paucity of industrial raw materials, science is really the only means by which industrial development and national power can be made to grow. The Institute has thus set forth this important mission as its basic objective.[6]

While the facility showed a surplus of income over expenditures for the first five years of its operations (Table 2), two main problems had developed by the time Ōkōchi became director in 1921. One was a rivalry between the physics and chemistry divisions for funds and personnel. Ōkōchi solved this by making each division independent in finances, staff recruitment, and the selection of research topics—a move that gave the entire Institute a reputation for a liberal atmos-

TABLE 2 Institute Income and Expenditures, 1917–1929
(1,000 yen)

	1917	1918	1919	1920	1921	1922	1923	1924	1925	1926	1927	1928	1929
Income	53	136	211	276	306	271	943	885	987	1181	660	855	817
Expenditures	22	63	110	162	248	319	091	886	987	1046	621	690	720
Surplus	31	73	101	114	58	-48	42	-1	0	135	39	165	97

Source: Miyake Haruteru, *Shinkō kontsuerun tokuhon* (1937), pp. 323–324.

phere highly conducive to scientific creativity.[7] A more pressing dilemma, however, was the budget. The only source of revenue for the Institute was a 6-percent annual return on the ¥2.5 million endowment, a sum that was becoming increasingly inadequate to meet the rising costs of equipment, supplies, and personnel. Without severe retrenchment or additional income, the Institute would be bankrupt by 1925.[8]

One idea that Ōkōchi had to relieve the Institute's financial plight was to sell technology that his researchers developed to Japanese companies. He encouraged the staff to conduct more reseach with commercial applications and began contacting local businessmen, only to find that most preferred to acquire perfected patents from the United States or Europe. Ōkōchi believed that this was because most Japanese managers lacked faith in Japanese science and had inadequate technical knowledge; therefore they gave little priority to investing in research or new products and production technologies.[9] He nonetheless carried out his plan to commercialize Institute patents by having the foundation incorporate two companies during 1923–1925 to manufacture synthetically fermented liquor and establish another plant to make vitamin A, which the Institute marketed as a nutritive supplement to aid against tuberculosis. Sales of vitamin A alone brought in nearly ¥500,000 ($250,000) for the Institute in 1923 and subsequent years, tripling its revenues and resulting in a small surplus despite much higher expenditures[10] (see Table 2).

The strength of the Institute was its research team, consisting mainly of professors at the University of Tokyo and other leading institutions in Japan. The expert in synthetic liquor and vitamins was Suzuki Umetarō (1874–1943), a chemistry professor at the University of Tokyo who had succeeded in extracting vitamin B during 1910.[11] Nagaoka Hantarō (1865–1950), who headed the physics divi-

TABLE 3 Institute Staff, Laboratories, and Patents, 1917–1940

	Staff	Laboratories	Domestic Patents	Foreign Patents	Utility Models
1917	?	20	–	–	–
1920	?	20	10	–	–
1925	340	23	90	20	10
1930	610	22	275	96	17
1935	750	27	431	118	57
1940	1800	33	620	150	180

Source: "Tokushū: Rikagaku Kenkyūsho 60 nen no ayumi," *Shizen*, December 1978, p. 171, adapted from Tables 1 and 2.

sion and then replaced Ōkōchi as director of the Institute after World War II, was also a professor at the University of Tokyo and a leading Japanese specialist in elementary particles, atomic structure, and magnetism. Nishina Yoshio (1890–1951), another graduate of the University of Tokyo who studied abroad with physicists such as Niels Bohr and Ernest Rutherford, directed the Institute's research on mesotron particles and built Japan's first cyclotron at the Institute during 1937. Honda Kōtarō (1870–1954), a former student of Nagaoka who specialized in magnetic phenomena and ferro-alloys, later headed a metals institute at Tōhoku University and became president of the university in 1931.[12] A researcher from Kyoto University, Tomonaga Shinichirō (b. 1906), joined Nishina's laboratory in 1932 and went on to receive the Nobel Prize for physics in 1965. Yukawa Hideki (b. 1907), also from Kyoto University, worked at the Institute as well before receiving Japan's first Nobel Prize for physics in 1949.[13]

Ōkōchi increased the Institute's staff from 350 in 1925 to 750 by 1935 and to 1800 by 1940 (Table 3). During the 1930s, he assigned approximately one-fourth of all personnel to experimental manufacturing rather than research. Annual research outlays rose from merely ¥629,000 (US$308,000) in 1930 to over ¥2.3 million in 1939, totaling ¥11 million between 1930–1939.[14] As Table 4 indicates, these outlays accounted for more than 93 percent of expenditures and nearly 70 percent of revenues. The number of patents the Institute produced also increased in proportion to expenditures and staff. As of 1936, the Institute or affiliated companies manufactured 167 products: basic chemicals or electrochemicals (39 items); electrical machin-

TABLE 4 Institute Income and Expenditures, 1930–1939
(units: 1,000 yen, %)

	1930	1931	1932	1933	1934	1935	1936	1937	1938	1939
A. Income	597	652	669	843	840	937	2150	2387	3074	3705
B. Provided by Group	–	–	–	–	(162)	(219)	(1142)	(1531)	(2599)	(3033)
B+A (%)	–	–	–	–	19.3	23.4	53.1	64.1	84.5	81.9
C. Expenditures	674	647	684	829	823	915	1240	1520	1889	2421
D. Research Expenses	(629)	(604)	(637)	(775)	(744)	(835)	(1158)	(1439)	(1786)	(2311)
D+A (%)	105.4	92.6	95.2	91.9	88.6	89.1	53.9	60.3	58.1	62.4
Surplus	-77	5	-15	14	17	22	910	867	1185	1284
D÷C (%)	93.3	93.4	93.1	93.5	90.4	91.3	93.4	94.7	94.5	95.5

Source: Saitō Ken, "Riken Sangyō-dan no keisei," *Keiei Shigaku* 17.2:70 (July 1982), adapted from
Tables 12 and 13. Percentages added.

ery and apparatus (27); optical equipment (27); pharmaceuticals, nutrients, and related health items (21); measuring instruments (20); metal components and mechanical apparatus (17); and precision machine tools (16). In addition, between 1925 and 1930, 20 companies outside the Riken group bought patent rights from the Institute ranging from pharmaceuticals to aluminum processing.[15]

Ōkōchi thus succeeded in creating a sound financial base for the Institute, as the number of companies under his control rose from 1 in 1927, with a paid-up capitalization of ¥900,000 ($426,000), to 60 by 1939–1940. As shown in Table 5, this represented investments totaling nearly ¥136 million. The Institute's revenues more than doubled between 1935 and 1936, and then almost doubled again by 1939. Most of the new income came from affiliated firms as compensation for using patents or other Institute inventions.[16] Revenue received from within the Riken group rose to more than 80 percent of the Institute's total income by the late 1930s, fully covering annual expenditures and leaving substantial surpluses. While synthetic liquor and vitamins were the group's main products until the early 1930s, the commercialization of a patent for piston rings suitable for engines in naval aircraft provided the impetus for expansion during the middle and late 1930s as Ōkōchi established or acquired firms to make metals, machine tools, and other equipment used in piston-ring manufacturing. As demand for air-craft and other armaments rose after the Manchurian Incident in 1931, the Riken group developed into a

TABLE 5 The Riken Industrial Group, 1927–1945
(1,000 yen)

	Number of Firms	Paid-Up Capital
1927	1	900
1930	1	1,500
1935	8	6,790
1936	15	14,380
1937	32	37,290
1938	48	76,180
1939	63	118,150
1940	58	135,710
1945	19	88,795

Source: Saitō, p. 48, Table 1, plus 1945 figures from Mochikabu Kaisha Seri Iin-Kai, ed., *Nihon zaibatsu to sono kaitai*, I, 503, Table 7 (1951). Excludes the Institute and, for 1945, companies with less than 10% of their shares held within the Riken group.

major supplier for the Navy and Army, while the Institute, though it remained a private foundation, devoted an increasing share of its budget to research with military applications.[17]

CAPITALISTIC VERSUS SCIENTIFIC INDUSTRY

Ōkōchi popularized his ideas on management and technology through speeches, in-house publications, newspapers, magazines, journals, and books. One of his earliest essays, titled "Nōson no kōson-ka" (The industrialization of rural villages), was originally a speech he gave at the Institute in 1925. A more detailed exposition on the same theme, "Nōson no kōgyō" (Industry in rural villages), appeared as a series of articles in the daily *Asahi* newspaper during January 1934, before Ōkōchi published this as a book in April of the same year.[18] *Kōgyō keiei sōron* (General theory of industrial management), published in November 1936 and reprinted 20 times during the next five years, was Ōkōchi's most scholarly treatment of the themes that appeared throughout his writings—the problems of capitalism in Japan and the West, the benefits of scientific research and new technology to industrial development, basic principals of scientific management applicable to industries such as machinery, metals, chemicals, and electrical equipment, and the advantages of employing agricultural workers in manufacturing.

A summary of Ōkōchi's main conclusions and observations appeared as a series of articles between December 1937 and February 1938 under the title "Shihon-shugi kōgyō to kagaku-shugi kōgyō" (Capitalistic industry and scientific industry) in a journal that he founded, *Kagaku-shugi kōgyō* (Scientific industry). Ōkōchi's publishing company, Kagaku-shugi Kōgyōsha, established in 1937, published these articles as a book in May 1938.[19] Another major book, *Moteru kuni Nihon* (Japan, the have nation), which appeared in January 1939 and went through 15 printings in one year, focused on the same theme suggested in the Institute's charter: that, while Japan seemed to be a "have-not" nation since it lacked raw materials, it was actually a "have nation" in terms of human resources for science and industry.[20] In light of Japan's postwar development, this observation proved to be surprisingly accurate. In 1939, however, Ōkōchi was mainly interested in convincing the Japanese public that Japan could apply its human skills in science and technology to stretch limited amounts of raw materials and increase industrial output to achieve the self-sufficiency necessary for "national defense." Other publications included *Kōgyō keiei no kagaku-ka* (Industrial management as science, 1935); *Shinkō Nihon no kōgyō to hatsumei* (Industry and inventions of the new Japan, 1937); *Nōson no kōgyō to fukugyō* (Industry and side-businesses in rural villages, 1937); *Nōson no kikai kōgyō* (Machinery industries in rural villages, 1938); *Tōsei keizai to keizai-sen* (The controlled economy and economic war, 1940); *Seisan dai-ichi-shugi* (Production as primary, 1941); "Nikkeru-kō no jikyū taisaku to sono gijutsu" (Countermeasures and technology for self-sufficiency in nickel steel), *Tōyō keizai* (The Oriental economist), 25 January 1941; *Kokubō keizai to kagaku* (The national defense economy and science, 1942); *Hisshō no zōsan* (The ultimate success of increasing production, 1942); *Kōkūki zōsan no hōto* (Ways to increase aircraft production, 1944); *Nōkō ittai no nōson kōgyō* (Rural industries combining agriculture and manufacturing, 1947).[21]

A theme that continued to link all of Ōkōchi's writings, and that reflected his broader concern for balanced economic development in Japan, was a critique of capitalistic industry. He defined this as industry that gave priority to capital preservation and short-term profits rather than to investment in risky ventures or technological research.

Ōkōchi insisted that this mentality had caused the economic decline of Britain beginning in the late nineteenth century and enabled Germany, the United States, and even Japan to challenge Britain in world markets. He worried that all Western countries, with the possible exception of Germany, faced a decline similar to Britain's if managers and bankers did not change their attitudes.[22] Protective tariffs and monopolies or cartels, common in Japan and Western countries during the late nineteenth and early twentieth centuries, tended to depress innovation or risk-taking and resulted in a general stagnation of industry that Ōkōchi decried as "passive capitalism" (*shōkyokuteki shihon-shugi*). In this type of system, managers expended their energies on increasing or maintaining current profits, but stopped short of investing in the capital improvement necessary to reduce the reliance of their factories on worker skills.[23] Technological development came under the control of managers and bankers who failed to understand that the most efficient long-term method of reducing costs and raising profits was to utilize scientists and engineers to modernize production technology:

> The defect found naturally in capitalistic industry, apparent already in its history, is that capital controls industrial management and authority. Not only does science come under this control as well, but managers do not recognize its value nor do they succeed in understanding it because they lack the knowledge. Large industrial enterprises utilizing mass-production techniques have merely electrified, mechanized, or applied other scientific principles to old production methods. Ignorant men still control management, and development stays only at the level to which they bring it. Most engineers, of course, combine science with jobs in industry, so one would expect them to have constant contact with the latest scientific developments. Yet they are no more than employees, and, however often they suggest innovations, managers who do not understand them cannot judge the merits of these proposals. Or, even if managers more or less understand a proposal, their first concern is how much money it will cost. Then they usually try to postpone a decision until they have accumulated more profits. The primary defect of capitalistic industry is that businessmen lack this understanding but still control managerial authority in industry.[24]

Ōkōchi admitted that there were differences between "passive capitalism" in Britain and the "positive capitalism" (*sekkyokuteki shihon-shugi*) of the United States. British factories suffered from an over-reliance on worker skills, because managers avoided investing in modern equipment and tried to reduce costs by lowering wages once they reached the limits of economies of scale based on existing manufacturing technology. This cycle was self-defeating, Ōkōchi insisted, in that skilled workers became increasingly difficult to hire as firms cut wage levels. American businessmen appeared more willing to invest in research and new technologies, although firms in the United States still exhibited "passive" tendencies whenever production exceeded demand. Their response to surplus capacity was usually to reduce output, raising unit costs and encouraging the formation of cartels to maintain high prices by setting production limits for entire industries. In the United States as well as in Britain, therefore, Ōkōchi concluded that managers ultimately chose to emphasize short-term performance and to restrict technological progress, resulting in high commodity prices and low wages for the average citizen.[25]

In Ōkōchi's opinion, Japan had also begun to exhibit characteristics of passive capitalism during the 1920s and 1930s. Managers with little or no technical training neglected investment in research and development and the commercializing of advanced technologies; old zaibatsu combines formed cartels and hindered entrepreneurship while perpetuating high production costs; companies concentrated in light manufacturing where profitability relied on low wages, creating little incentive to invest in expensive, innovative equipment that would raise productivity. Japanese capitalism was "irrational," Ōkōchi concluded, because managers restricted technical advances while high commodity prices and low wages depressed consumer demand. At the same time, while exports were necessary to maintain economic growth, foreign countries had become increasingly critical of Japan for "social dumping"—flooding export markets with cheap manufactures that took advantage of low Japanese wages.[26]

Another danger that concerned Ōkōchi was Japan's continued reliance on imported technology and Western assistance in science and engineering. While Japan had industrialized by transferring technology from the West, and much foreign technology was still superior to techniques or equipment used in Japan, he worried that too much dependence on foreign companies or experts would perpetuate the backwardness of Japanese science and frustrate national efforts to build a strong, independent state. Ōkōchi wanted Japan to develop more technology on its own, even though he realized how difficult this was going to be after he tried to sell Institute patents to Japanese firms during the early 1920s. He understood why managers lacked confidence in Japanese scientists, yet it bothered Ōkōchi that old zaibatsu companies often failed to take advantage of the technology available to them, whether its origin was domestic or foreign. To demonstrate this point, in Diet debates after World War I he often referred to the case of a German technique for producing ammonia through the fixation of atmospheric nitrogen. Ōkōchi also used the example of this patent to demonstrate the conservatism of old zaibatsu firms in his 1936 book, *Kōgyō keiei sōron* (General theory of industrial management):

Japanese capitalists and businessmen lack the ability to commercialize inventions. Even when looking at a list of patents, they are unable to judge if an invention is promising. For this reason they spend large sums of money to buy inventions perfected in foreign countries. What is more, in proportion to the level of production, often these patent rights are very expensive. What lack of initiative! A most appropriate example involved the Haber nitrogen fixation process. After the world war, the Japanese government confiscated the patent rights from the Germans and sold them for ten or twenty thousand yen to a group of companies composed of Japan's leading zaibatsu, fertilizer, and industrial chemical firms. A condition in the sales contract was that the patent had to be used commercially yet, two decades later, there is not a sign of it. Although the patent expired five years ago, the cartel applied for and received an extension, and still owns the Haber patent.[27]

The incident referred to involved the Tōyō Nitrogen cartel that Sumitomo, Mitsui, Mitsubishi, and several other companies formed in 1917 to acquire the technique developed by L. Fritz Haber and Karl Bosch, chemists at leading German chemical company, Badische Aniline und Soda Fabrik (BASF). The process enabled Germany to manufacture a nearly unlimited supply of explosives during World War I and possessed enormous commercial value because of the many industrial uses of ammonia, including the production of ammonium sulfate and ammonium nitrate fertilizers, nitric acid, sodium carbonate, synthetic dyes and fibers, and cleansers. The patent remained in virtual limbo until a Mitsubishi company used it in 1937—nearly twenty years after the cartel acquired the technology. While there were numerous reasons for the delay, a major cause was the large investment in royalties and in plant and equipment that commercializing the technology required.[28]

Although Ōkōchi complained that the failure of the zaibatsu cartel to use the Haber patent inhibited the growth of Japan's entire electrochemical industry, growing demand for ammonia during the 1920s prompted several chemical firms unaffiliated with Mitsui, Mitsubishi, or Sumitomo to introduce alternative but largely untested ammonia synthesis techniques that used different catalysts or combinations of pressure and temperature. Nitchitsu (Japan Nitrogen), for example, began its expansion into a huge electrochemical combine when its founder, Noguchi Jun, purchased patent rights to a still experimental Italian process (Casale) in 1921. Suzuki Trading introduced a French patent (Claude) in 1922, before Mitsui Mining took over Suzuki's chemical subsidiary after the trading company went bankrupt a few years later. The predecessor to Nissan Chemical, Dai-Nippon Man-Made Fertilizer, began manufacturing ammonia with another European technique (Fauser) in 1928, while Shōwa Denkō grew out of the Shōwa Fertilizer Company after Mori Nobuteru (1884–1941) acquired a Japanese patent, free of charge, from the Tokyo Industrial Research Laboratory in 1930. Even Sumitomo Chemical decided to abandon the cartel and import an American technique from the Nitrogen Engineering Corporation (NEC) in 1928.[29]

While Mitsui, Mitsubishi, Sumitomo, and the other older zaibatsu had pioneered heavy industries in Japan, such as shipbuilding and the manufacturing of industrial chemicals and various machinery products, they kept a majority of their investments in finance, trading, mining, and light manufacturing. Family control over holding companies, and the large size and bureaucratic structures of these combines, contributed to the conservatism of old zaibatsu managers and made it possible for smaller companies to gain a head start in electrochemicals and other promising fields, such as automobiles and synthetic fibers. During the 1930s, some of these non-zaibatsu firms developed into large concerns, or what Japanese business historians have called the "new zaibatsu"–Nissan, Nitchitsu, Shōwa Denkō, Nippon Soda, and Riken.

Ōkōchi was aware of the difference between old-zaibatsu managers, whom he likened to British financiers and capitalists, and the founders of the new zaibatsu, nearly all of whom had university degrees in engineering. But his primary concern was to alert all Japanese businessmen of the need to invest more in applied research and to incorporate new developments in product and production technologies to improve the competitiveness and long-term prosperity of Japanese industry. Ōkōchi did not oppose the right of companies to seek high profits, but he insisted that managers strive to make capital more efficient—that profits come from mass production and mass distribution, rather than from cartelization or the exploitation of low wages and obsolete plant and equipment. He also believed that the institution of higher wages and reductions in commodity prices would create enough new demand to maintain adequate profit margins once managers became committed to upgrading their technological standards:

Without progress in industrial innovation, production costs will not become lower, nor will the quality of goods improve. We need new production methods and equipment to produce better quality goods at lower prices, even if wages rise. With old methods and machinery, production costs will remain high, despite the maintenance of average wage levels. With new methods and machinery production, costs will drop. Compared to the past, high wages and low costs, possible only with new production methods, will create new conditions. Applying the most advanced science to industry will guarantee constant progress through innovation and invention. We should call this type of industry 'scientific industry.'[30]

"Scientific industry," in Ōkōchi's interpretation, meant the continuous development of new products and production methods or equipment, and the raising of wages while lowering commodity prices to stimulate new demand. On the one hand, he encouraged Japanese managers to study the operations management techniques developed in the United States and to improve factory conditions to help raise productivity. But his experiences with Riken factories in several agricultural areas in Japan, and a visit to Manchuria in 1936, reinforced Ōkōchi's conviction that high wages were necessary both to increase the purchasing power of consumers and to motivate workers, and that an economy could not maintain low prices if meager wages continued to depress consumer demand. In addition, Ōkōchi maintained that raising wage levels would not only pay off in greater productivity and quality, but that improvements in production technology would eventually allow firms to cut prices to meet the ultimate objective of scientific industry, which he defined as "low-price, high-quality goods."[31]

While the Riken group produced general-purpose machinery, metals, and chemical products, it must also be pointed out that much of its expansion depended on orders from the Japanese Army and Navy, either directly or from companies manufacturing aircraft and trucks. This situation was not unusual, since all the industrial groups that grew into new zaibatsu prior to World War II were large military suppliers. Compared to Nissan and Nitchitsu, the scale of Riken's investments was small, although one reason Riken grew rapidly was that Ōkōchi was a leading Japanese expert on weapons production. He not only majored in ordnance engineering in college but pursued the subject to a doctorate and taught it at the University of Tokyo. In the Diet, he closely followed the progress of Japan's armaments producers and, as head of the Institute, he directed research with military applications. Not until after the outbreak of war with China in 1937 did Ōkōchi publicly advocate the application of his ideas on "scientific industry" to problems stemming from the need to increase military production relying exclusively on domestically available technology. During the late 1930s, however, he began to argue that the best means of national defense was to use technology to achieve self-sufficiency: "Only scientific industry, based on scientific research, inquiry, and invention, can encourage new industries not previously existing in Japan and accomplish this without subsidies or protection. . . . Science has produced our flourishing military capability. The strong attraction of industry with a foundation based in science lies here."[32]

During 1937–1938, even though Ōkōchi proposed new tax measures to stimulate "strategic" defense industries, he consistently opposed measures associated with passive capitalism, such as government subsidies, protectionism, or economic controls.[33] In one sense, this opposition demonstrated his continued preoccupation with creating a free market economy conducive to entrepreneurship. As a businessman, he also feared too many government restrictions—on profits, credit, materials, and management. Thus, Ōkōchi criticized the policy of reducing public consumption and shifting resources to war production to alleviate shortages of raw materials, since this would skew industrial development too heavily in favor of armaments industries. As late as 1942, he still maintained that the principles of scientific industry, faithfully applied with managerial "rationalizations," would be enough to fill the needs of national defense without total government control over the economy. He also continued to link production expansion with reductions in costs and market prices and opposed extreme ideas of economic autarky that would have eliminated Japan's foreign trade.[34]

Since he began discussing "rural industry" during the mid-1920s and the concept of scientific industry prior to 1937, it appears that Ōkōchi did not intend his ideas to be mere tools to assist the Japanese military in procuring an adequate supply of weapons and other equipment. But there were contradictions between his writings and his actions as a manager: Ōkōchi was more than willing to accept large military contracts from the Navy and the South Manchurian Railway, for instance. His companies also tended to pay low wages and have problems with product quality. In addition, while *Moteru kuni Nihon* (Japan, the have nation, 1939) displayed a strong faith in Japan's future, despite the paucity of raw materials in the country, the main purpose of the book was to suggest that the intelligent management of technology, combined with Japan's "human resources," would solve any problems that arose due to the war. In particular, Ōkōchi believed that introducing more single-function machine tools and integrating production operations precisely with national needs and the wartime mobilization program would alleviate labor shortages in machinery industries.[35]

An essay of 1940, "Shitauke seido no gōrika" (Rationalization of the subcontracting system), proposed to increase productivity by revising supplier networks along the principle of "one factory, one product" to take greater advantage of specialization and economies of scale. Ōkōchi again stressed the need for firms to adopt methods utilizing "specialized or compartmentalized production operations, with raw materials supplied from a main factory," and to follow the technique of exploiting by-products in manufacturing to reduce total costs.[36] Ōkōchi also wrote *Kokubō keizai to kagaku* (The national-defense economy and science) in 1942 to explain how scientists could contribute to materials conservation and, therefore, to Japan's long-term defense and prosperity:

The first requirement to construct a fully armed state is self-sufficiency in national defense materials. With increased numbers of people under mobilization, through mechanization and rationalization, not only will the quantity of defense materials increase but their variety will also grow rapidly. Yet, it could prove disastrous if Japan does not exercise extreme caution in the use of rare metals and ores. Severe difficulties could arise in supplying industry with this huge increment in necessary materials in their proper variety, which has become extremely complex. The establishment of a fully armed state depends completely on scientists, whose responsibility has been no greater than it is today. Even for those scientists who previously exhibited an international character, national defense is now their top priority. Since the ban on publications has made it difficult to visit research institutes abroad and consult Western research, it is all the more essential to eliminate our dependence on the West. The time to rouse our scientists to action is today.[37]

Ōkōchi's wartime publications reflected Japan's increasingly desperate attempts to maintain output levels and to compensate for the drop in imports from the United States and Europe and the cutoff of ties between Japan and countries allied with the United States during the late 1930s and early 1940s. In *Kokubō keizai to kagaku*, he even abandoned the principle of striving for low prices; later essays stressed production volume and self-sufficiency more than unit costs.[38] But, while earlier goals such as "low priced quality goods" or "high wages and low costs" became all but irrelevant as the war progressed, military contracts and isolation from Western technology provided opportunities for Ōkōchi to expand the Institute. He was also able to establish dozens of companies that required Japanese engineers, scientists, and managers to innovate in product development and manufacturing.

SCIENTIFIC INDUSTRY APPLIED: THE RIKEN INDUSTRIAL GROUP

Ōkōchi saw scientific industry as a solution for two problems: technological backwardness in nearly all industries in Japan; and economic depression in rural areas, where "surplus" agricultural workers had yet to become a modern labor force. His study of management in the West, and Britain in particular, had convinced him that overreliance on worker skills was a major hindrance to technological progress. It also appeared to him that Japan did not have enough trained workers to accommodate industrial development on the scale that existed in the United States or Western Europe. Ōkōchi thus encouraged Japanese managers to devote themselves to learning and applying the principles of "scientific management" that had become so popular in American and European factories during the early twentieth century, especially the techniques to break down manufacturing operations into simplified routines and to devise single-function or specialized machine tools that required little skill to use.[39]

Ōkōchi insisted that scientific industry could bring about a virtual revolution in the Japanese countryside, where the commercialization of rayon during the mid-1920s, exacerbated by the worldwide economic depression, threatened to ruin the silk industry. He encouraged farm families to stay in rural villages and to establish new sideline businesses, such as precision instruments or machine-parts manufacturing, to supplement their incomes from agriculture. The successful cases of Switzerland's rural clock industry and Ford's diffusion of automobile-parts manufacturing among small shops in middle America had already convinced him that Japan could establish similar industries.[40]

There was, in fact, great potential for industrialization in rural areas. The Toyota concern demonstrated this prior to World War II by diversifying from the manufacturing of thread to loom machinery and then to automobiles, all from a base in the countryside of Aichi prefecture. Many of the rural shops and factories that used the Institute's patents also reported high levels of productivity and profits during the 1930s, even though wartime controls and shortages of materials and skilled managers made it difficult to train workers, maintain standards of quality and precision, and transport supplies as well as finished goods.[41] For this reason, by the late 1930s the Riken industrial group had become better known for "low-price goods" than for "low-price quality goods." Nevertheless, the group's rapid expansion during the 1930s demonstrated the effectiveness of Ōkōchi's concepts of scientific industry and rural industrialization as strategies for establishing and managing new manufacturing enterprises.

Before evolving into a machinery concern focused on the manufacture of piston rings, the Institute invested in foodstuffs, mainly the synthetic liquor produced at Yamato Brewing beginning in 1923 and then at other subsidiaries, and health products, primarily synthetic vitamins. Ōkōchi then established Rikagaku Industries in 1927, capitalized initially at ¥900,000 (US $450,000), to manage the Institute's liquor-manufacturing operations (consolidated during 1938 into one firm, Riken Liquor), and to oversee commercial applications in the Institute's other areas of research, such as photographic or optical equipment and supplies, precision machine parts, machine tools, and metallurgy. The Institute served as the largest stockholder and owned 16.7 percent of its outstanding shares, although Rikagaku Industries was sufficiently attractive as an investment for each of the holding companies in the Mitsui, Mitsubishi, Sumitomo, Yasuda, and Ōkura zaibatsu to purchase 3.3 percent of the company's stock.[42]

Ōkōchi took the post of chairman at Rikagaku Industries, as he did at 19 other group subsidiaries during the 1920s and 1930s, and hired Ōhashi Shintarō (1863–1944), an entrepreneur with experience in the publishing, milling, textile, and brewing industries, as a company director in charge of daily operations.[43] Ōhashi, a native of rural Niigata prefecture, helped Rikagaku Industries set up several factories in this area of Japan. By the time Rikagaku Industries merged with the main operating firm in the group in 1941, Riken Heavy Industries, it had become primarily a machinery producer, operating plants in Tokyo (Arakawa) as well as in Niigata (Miyauchi).[44] Despite the production of several product lines and Ōkōchi's decision to detach some of its most profitable departments as separate companies, as indicated in Table 6, Rikagaku Industries averaged a return on paid-up capital of nearly 21 percent between 1935 and 1940.

Table 7 details the expansion of the Riken group between 1927 and 1941, beginning with the incorporation of Rikagaku Industries and ending with the merger of several machinery and metals subsidiaries to form Riken Industries. Of the 70 firms affiliated with the Riken group during this period, 28 (40 percent) relied on patents developed at the Institute. Ōkōchi established 7 of the first 8 firms added to the group by 1935 specifically to commercialize Institute patents for synthetic liquor (alcohol), metallic magnesium, piston rings, special steel, electrical-wire insulation, sensitized photographic paper, and optical equipment. Basing each new company on one product line took advantage of specialization and economies of scale and worked especially well as a strategy for expansion when Ōkōchi detached already profitable departments from the Institute or large subsidiaries such as Rikagaku Industries and Riken Piston Ring. After 1935, however, only about one-third of the firms newly added to the Riken group relied on Institute patents.[45] They represented a departure from Ōkōchi's original intention to limit his investments to commercializing technology produced at the Institute, although nearly all the firms he acquired during the late 1930s complemented existing Riken companies, as indicated in Table 8.

The Institute, Rikagaku Industries, and Fukoku Industries served as holding companies. The Institute's main functions, however, continued to be research and development, and experimental manufacturing. Rikagaku Industries managed several commercial factories, while Fukoku Industries, established in 1936, supervised subsidiaries, marketed group products, and arranged loans and insurance.[46] Most affiliated companies provided or processed metal materials, produced machine tools and other equipment, and made finished machinery or parts such as piston rings. A small group of Riken firms manufactured industrial chemicals, rubber goods, testing instruments, gauges, binding strips for rolled steel, grinding and polishing cloths, and even wooden boxes for shipping, but Ōkōchi gradually concentrated most of his investments in the machinery industry. In 1937, as indicated in Table 9, the group has just over one-third of its paid-up capital in metals and only one-fifth in machinery (including machine tools and machine parts), whereas chemicals, foodstuffs, and other fields accounted for about half of this investment. By the end of World War II, however, 84 percent of the Riken group's capital was in machinery, while investments in other fields declined from ¥14.6 million in 1937 to ¥9.3 million by 1945.

The cases of Riken Piston Ring, Riken Metals, and Ricoh illustrate how Ōkōchi founded and managed the group's largest machinery, metal and photographic/optical equipment subsidiaries. Riken Piston Ring grew out of a small gasoline refinery, located in the town of Kashiwazaki, Niigata prefecture, that the Institute had constructed in 1929. After there turned out to be less oil in the region than Ōkōchi expected, he began looking for another use for the facility. In 1932, he decided to convert the existing building into a small factory to commercialize a process for manufacturing piston rings for automobile engines that he and another Institute researcher had patented in 1926. Ōkōchi employed only about 20 workers, mostly women, until Yamamoto Isoroku (1884–1943), a native of Niigata prefecture and a top officer in the Navy's aircraft division, suggested that Ōkōchi expand the factory to supply the Navy with piston rings for aircraft engines. Ōkōchi enlarged the plant to accommodate several hundred workers and in 1934 incorporated it as Riken Piston Ring. By 1940, the factory had 5,000 workers; by the end of World War II, 11,000.[47]

As indicated in Table 10, the piston-ring subsidiary averaged

TABLE 6 Rikagaku Industries, 1935–1940
(1,000 yen, %)

Period	Paid-Up Capital	Profits	Profit Rate*	Dividend
1935.1	1,650	170	20.7%	8.0%
.2	1,875	274	29.2	"
1936.1	2,325	368	31.7	"
.2	3,875	393	20.5	"
1937.1	4,750	474	20.0	"
.2	6,792	660	19.4	"
1938.1	9,125	935	20.5	"
.2	10,833	905	16.7	"
1939.1	12,917	1,075	16.6	"
.2	15,000	1,245	16.6	10.0
1940.1	15,302	1,322	17.3	"

Source: Tōyō Keizai, *Kabushiki kaisha nenkan*, 1938–1940.
   Note: *as a percentage of sales.

annual pre-tax profit rates on paid-up capital of over 23 percent during 1934–1937, and paid a stock dividend beginning in the second half-year of operations. Simplified production methods and special machine tools made it possible to hire unskilled female workers. Ōkōchi paid them one-eighth the wages of male machine-shop workers in Tokyo, even though the Kashiwazaki employees were roughly 2.5 times more productive than comparable factory workers elsewhere in Japan.[48] Not only did low labor costs make Riken piston rings competitive in price with imports, but the company provided the Navy and private firms making aircraft and motor vehicles with a domestic source for this critical engine component. As Riken Piston Rings became the largest subsidiary in the group, Ōkōchi used profits earned from the sale of piston rings, and from selling shares in the company that the Institute and Rikagaku Industries owned, to establish or acquire firms to make metals, machine tools, machine parts, and other supplies.

In Kakizaki, Niigata prefecture, Ōkōchi set up a factory in 1935 to manufacture drills, screw drivers, and milling cutters. From just 300 workers it grew to 6,000 by 1942, of whom half were unskilled women laborers. Between 1935 and 1937, he opened several other plants in the nearby town of Miyauchi, including a precision-

TABLE 7 The Riken Industrial Group, 1927–1941

Note: Capital letters indicate a company founded to commercialize an Institute patent. A single asterisk(*) indicates a firm for which Ōkōchi served as chairman; a double asterisk indicates that he served as a consultant. Under capital, the first figure listed is paid-up capital (in ¥ 1,000 units) at the time of incorporation, and the second figure is paid-up capitalization at year's end, 1941.

Year	Company Name	Capital (¥ 1,000)	Comments
1927	RIKAGAKU INDUSTRIES*	900–20,000	Founded to oversee commercialization of Institute patents. Merged into Riken Industries in 1941.
1932	RIKEN MAGNESIUM*	600	Absorbed into Nichi-Man Magnesium in 1933, then into Riken Metals in 1938.
1934	RIKEN PISTON RING*	1,600–9,000	Formerly the piston-ring department of Rikagaku Industries. Merged into Riken Heavy Industries in 1938.
	RIKEN FLASHPLATES	30–110	An acquired firm that commercialized an Institute patent.
1935	RIKEN SPECIAL STEEL	1,000–6,000	Provided materials to Riken Piston Ring, using an Institute process patented in 1934. Merged into Riken Heavy Industries.
	RIKEN CABLE**	150–1,650	Commercialized an Institute process for coating electric wires with enamel insulation.
	RIKEN OPTICAL INSTRUMENTS	70–300	Manufactured sunglasses, protective glasses for welding, electrical work, and skiing, as well as photographic filters and darkroom lamps.
	Riken Spinning	40–500	Manufactured rayon and knit goods.
	RIKEN CORUNDUM*	700–2,000	Manufactured polishing cloth and paper using pulverized corundum.
1936	RICOH*	350–3,000	Separated from Rikagaku Industries to specialize in manufacturing sensitized paper for positive photographic prints. The company name was Riken Sensitized Paper until 1938.

TABLE 7 (Continued)

Year	Company Name	Capital (¥ 1,000)	Comments
1936	RIKEN LIGHT ALLOYS	140–800	Absorbed Nitto Light Alloys. Manufactured copper alloys and other cast products.
	Riken Liquor Sales	137.5	A marketing organ for the Institute's synthetic alcohol.
	RIKEN STEEL MATERIALS*	200–6,000	Manufactured steel products through rolling and forging. Merged into Riken Industries.
	RIKEN ROLLING*	1,000–5,000	Formerly Nihon Rolling Industries added to the Riken group. Merged into Riken Industries.
	Fukoku Industries	250–1,000	Founded as an organ to oversee group investment, marketing, real estate, insurance, etc.
	Sanko Trading	185– 500	Acquired to manufacture electric wires. Merged into Riken Cable in 1940.
1937	Hikaku Bicycles	25–100	Manufactured bicycles from scrap iron. Later made machine tools as a subcontractor.
	RIKEN STEEL-AMAGASAKI	500	Merged into Riken Steel Materials in 1938.
	Riken Chuck-Miyauchi	200–2,000	A chuck specialty factory separated from Riken Piston Ring. Merged into Riken Casting in 1940, then Riken Industries.
	Riken Lathes-Miyauchi	200–450	A lathe specialty factory separated from Riken Piston Ring. Merged into Riken Casting in 1940, then Riken Industries.
	Tōyō Binding Strips	100–150	Affiliated belt lacing producer which provided binding strips for rolled steel.
	RIKEN RUBBER*	2,000–3,600	Utilized a tetraline process to reclaim rubber then made hoses and other rubber products.
	Kagaku-shugi Kōgyō-sha** (Scientific Industry, Inc.)	50–200	Founded by Ōkōchi to publish the *Kagaku-shugi Kōgyō* journal as well as books on industry and technology.

TABLE 7 (Continued)

Year	Company Name	Capital (¥ 1,000)	Comments
1937	RIKEN ELECTRICAL EQUIPMENT*	375–1,035	Manufactured resistors with an Institute patent.
	Riken Automobile Rebuilding	375–750	Rebuilt engines and made charcoal-gas generation equipment. Merged into Riken Heavy Industries.
	Riken Electromagnetic	300–1,500	A specialty factory for magnetic chucks separated from Riken Piston Ring. Merged into Riken Electric Machinery in 1940.
	Riken Miyauchi Casting	150–2,000	Supplied casting materials for machine tools to Riken factories. Merged into Riken Casting in 1940.
	Riken Seiki	70–3,900	Formerly a jacks manufacturer added to the Riken group.
	Naniwa Machine Works	50–200	Founded to aid Riken factories in sales and materials procurement.
	Kashiwazaki Industries	50–200	Founded to provide raw materials (sweet potatoes, starch) for Riken Liquor. Also utilized agricultural workers for piston ring subcontracting.
	Jōetsu Industries	50	Made wooden boxes for packing Riken machine products. Also produced wooden toys for export.
	Asahi Optical	450	Acquired as a Ricoh subsidiary to manufacture cameras. Absorbed by Ricoh in 1953.
	RIKEN SYNTHETIC RESINS*	150–600	Company name was Riken Amber until 1939.
1938	Aircraft Specialty Parts	300–725	Made fuselage and engine parts, as well as jigs.
	Riken Springs	112.5–1,000	An automobile springs maker added to the group.
	Riken Headstocks-Ojiya	230	A lathe headstock specialty factory separated from Riken Piston Ring. Merged into Riken Heavy Industries.
	RIKEN METALS*	3,500–10,500	Formerly Riken Magnesium, later Nichi-Man Magnesium, a subsidiary of the South Manchurian Railway. Made magnesium as well as potassium chlorate, bromine, and other products.

TABLE 7 (Continued)

Year	Company Name	Capital (¥ 1,000)	Comments
1938	Riken Export Toys	62.5–211.5	Replaced Jōetsu Industries. Besides wooden boxes, it made wooden toys for export, artificial hands and legs.
	Riken Forging*	1,250–5,000	Based on an acquired forging company. Merged into Riken Industries.
	Riken Machine Tools*	2,000–4,000	Made machine tools as well as armaments products. Merged into Riken Industries.
	Riken Science Films*	225–337.5	Produced "talking" movies.
	RIKEN LIQUOR*	480	Formerly the liquor-manufacturing department of Rikagaku Industries.
	NIHON OPTICAL	450	Made glass filters and optical lenses.
	Riken Hydraulic Machinery	450–1,500	Based on an acquired aircraft-fuel-pump manufacturer. Merged into Riken Electric Machinery in 1940.
	RIKEN INDUSTRIAL CHEMICALS*	240–480	Formerly the organic-acid division of the Institute.
	RIKEN NUTRITIVE DRUGS*	480	Made vitamins A and D.
	RIKEN ELECTRIC MOTORS	450	Formerly the electric-machinery division of the Institute. Produced motors for machine tools.
	CHŌSEN RIKEN METALS	3,750–11,250	Made steel, aluminum, and magnesium in Korea.
	Riken Pneumatic Machinery	150–1,350	Formerly Nihon Pneumatic Machinery, added to the Riken group.
	Riken Heavy Industries*	15,000–31,350	October 1938 merger of Riken Piston Ring and Riken Special Steel. Also absorbed other firms.
	RIKEN KEIKI**	100–450	Made mining and optical equipment developed by the Institute.
1939	Mukōjima Works	150	A subsidiary of Riken Cable, which made noncombustible wires. Absorbed by Riken Cable in 1940.
	Naniwa Machine Works-Sankōtō	150	A sales affiliate of Naniwa Machine Works for the Chinese market.

TABLE 7 (Continued)

Year	Company Name	Capital (¥ 1,000)	Comments
1939	Chosen Steel Works	407–875	An affiliated steel and iron-casting firm in Korea.
	Tōyō Binding Strips-Sankoku	150	Subsidiary of Tōyō Binding Strips.
	Yamaga Works	150	Added to the group to supply electrical components to Riken Electromagnetic Instruments.
	Naniwa Machine Works-Kyōjō	150	A sales affiliate of Naniwa Machine Works for the Korean market.
	RIKEN FISHERIES PROCESSING	150	Founded to supply vitamins and oils to Riken Nutritive Drugs.
	Kuzuu Ceramic Industries	120	An affiliated supplier of high-quality coke to Riken Heavy Industries.
	Tokoshi Precision Machinery	180	An affiliated manufacturer of hardness testers and dial indicators.
	Iida Machine Works	170	An affiliated printing-machinery manufacturer.
	Takasaki Automobile Parts	150	Separated from Riken Heavy Industries to make valves.
	Special Rubber Manufacturing	180	An acquired rubber-lining manufacturer.
	CHŌSEN RIKEN MINING	750–3,000	Used Institute techniques to mine gold dust, lignite, and magnetite in Korea.
	Tōyō Steel Works	1,000	An acquired thin-sheet-metal manufacturer.
	CHŌSEN RIKEN RUBBER	500–1,000	Reclaimed rubber in Korea.
	Watanabe Iron Works	150	An affiliated manufacturer of chemical machinery and agricultural tools.
1940	RIKEN NUTRITIVE FODDER	30–375	Made an animal feed called "Riken Food."
	RIKEN ELECTROCHEMICAL**	800	Formerly the Shizuoka factory of the Institute, which made alumite products and other aircraft parts.
	Riken Casting*	4,450	October 1940 merger of Riken Chuck-Miyauchi, Riken Lathes-Miyauchi, and Riken Miyauchi Casting. Merged into Riken Industries.

TABLE 7 *(Continued)*

Year	Company Name	Capital (¥ 1,000)	Comments
1940	Riken Electric Machinery	3,000	October 1940 merger of Riken Electromagnetic Instruments and Riken Hydraulic Machinery. Made mining equipment, hydraulic machinery, and aircraft parts.
	Riken Mining	400	Separation of the Japan holdings of Chosen Riken Mining.
1941	Riken Industries*	67,000	July 1941 merger of Rikagaku Industries, Riken Heavy Industries, Riken Rolling, Riken Forging, Riken Casting, Riken Machine Tools, and Riken Steel Materials.

Sources: Adapted from Saitō, pp. 62–66, Table 9. Indications of Ōkōchi's positions (chairman, consultant) taken from Ōkōchi Kinen-kai, ed., *Ōkōchi Masatoshi: Hito to sono jigyō* (1954), pp. 371–379.

TABLE 8   The Riken Industrial Group, 1917–1940
(Functional Analysis)

I. Group Holding Companies (Shareholding, R&D, Experimental Manufacturing)
Institute (1917); Rikagaku Industries (1927); Fukoku Industries (1936)

II. Machine Parts Industry

   1. *Metals Mining and Manufacturing*
Riken Magnesium (1932); Riken Special Steel (1935); Riken Light Alloys (1936);
Riken Steel Materials (1936); Riken Steel-Amagasaki (1937); Riken Metals (1938);
Chōsen Riken Metals (1938); Chōsen Steel Works (1939); Tōyō Steel Works
(1939); Chōsen Riken Mining (1939); Riken Mining (1940)

   2. *Metals Processing*
Riken Cable (1935); Sankō Trading (1936); Riken Rolling (1936); Riken Miyauchi
Casting (1937); Riken Forging (1938); Mukōjima Works (1939); Riken Casting
(1940)

   3. *Machine Tools and Components*
Riken Chuck (1937); Riken Lathes (1937); Riken Electromagnetic Instruments
(1937); Riken Seiki (1937); Riken Headstocks-Ojiya (1938); Riken Machine Tools
(1938); Riken Electric Motors (1938); Riken Pneumatic Machinery (1938)

   4. *Machine Parts and Machinery*
Rikagaku Industries (1927); Riken Piston Ring (1934); Riken Automobile
Rebuilding (1937); Hikaku Bicycle (1937); Aircraft Specialty Parts (1938); Riken
Springs (1938); Riken Hydraulic Machinery (1938); Takasaki Automobile Parts
(1939); Watanabe Iron Works (1939); Riken Electric Machinery (1940)

   5. *Industrial Chemicals and Rubber*
Riken Synthetic Resins (1937); Riken Rubber (1937); Riken Industrial Chemicals
(1938); Special Rubber Manufacturing (1939); Chōsen Riken Rubber (1939);
Riken Electrochemical (1940)

   6. *Precision Machinery and Electrical Components*
Riken Optical Instruments (1935); Riken Elelctrical Equipment (1937); Riken
Keiki (1938); Yamaga Works (1939); Tokoshi Precision Machinery (1939)

   7. *Miscellaneous Supplies and Sales*
Riken Corundum (1935); Tōyō Binding Strips (1937); Jōetsu Industries (Riken
Export Toys) (1937); Naniwa Machine Works (1937) and subsidiaries in Man-
churia (1939) and Korea (1939)

III. Foodstuffs (including Liquor) and Health Products
Yamato Brewing (1923); Dai Nippon Alcoholic Liquor (1925); Kashiwazaki Indus-
tries (1937); Riken Liquor (1938); Riken Nutritive Drugs (1938); Riken Fisheries
Processing (1939); Riken Nutritive Fodder (1940)

IV. Optical Equipment and Supplies
Riken Flashplates (1934); Ricoh (1936); Asahi Optical (1937); Nihon Optical (1938)

V. Miscellaneous
Riken Spinning (1935); Kagaku-shugi Kōgyō-sha (1937); Riken Science Films (1938);
Iida Machine Works (1939)

TABLE 9 Riken Group Investments by Industry, 1937 and 1946
(1,000 yen, paid-up capital)

Industry	1937	%	1946	%
metals	10,478	34.4	5,150	5.8
machinery/tools	5,545	18.1	74,385	83.8
chemicals	2,530	8.3	3,660	4.1
foodstuffs	4,400	14.4	1,500	1.7
other*	7,638	24.9	4,100	4.6
Total	30,591	100.0	88,795	100.0

Sources: For 1937, Takahashi Kamekichi and Aoyama Jirō, *Nihon zaibatsu ron* (1938), p. 196. For 1946, representing war's end (1945), Mochikabu Kaisha Seiri Iin-kai, ed., *Nihon zaibatsu to sono kaitai* (1951), I, p. 503; companies of whose shares the Riken holding companies held less than 10% are excluded.

*Other includes mining, rubber, textiles, paper, and non-industrial investments.

machinery factory that Rikagaku Industries managed and facilities belonging to 3 new subsidiaries, Riken Casting, Riken Chuck, and Riken Lathes, which together employed 5,000 workers by the end of World War II. A separate factory built in the Ojiya section of Tokyo during 1938 also produced lathes and employed 1,600 workers as of 1945. According to the estimates in Table 11, by 1942 Riken factories in Niigata prefecture alone had 18,500 employees, half of whom were women receiving low salaries. In neighboring Gumma prefecture, the plant that Riken Machine Tools had opened in 1938 at Maebashi to manufacture grinding machines, measuring instruments, piston rings, and parts for anti-aircraft guns, grew to 6,000 workers by 1942 and to 10,000 by 1945. At the end of World War II, Riken factories in Niigata, Gumma, and Tokyo thus employed nearly 40,000 workers. Most were young women between the ages of 16 and 20 who commuted from their homes in local villages; the government also conscripted 2,000 workers from nearby prefectures and housed them in dormitories while they worked in the Kashiwazaki plant.[49]

Simplified manufacturing operations, and specialized or single-function rather than universal machine tools, provided the basis for Riken's machine-industry ventures. In metallurgical or chemical fields, however, Ōkōchi advocated what he and other Japanese managers called the *"imo-zuru"* or "sweet-potato-root" style of operations. This name came from an alcohol manufacturer in Germany that

TABLE 10 Riken Piston Ring, 1934–1937
(1,000 yen)

Period	Paid-Up Capital	Profits	Profit Rate*	Dividend
1934.1	1600	157	19.6%	8%
.2	2456	256	20.8	10
1935.1	2700	317	23.5	"
.2	"	313	23.2	"
1936.1	"	286	21.2	"
.2	3250	335	20.6	"
1937.1	4167	612	29.4	"
.2	5187	733	28.3	"

Sources: Tōyō Keizai, *kabushiki kaisha nenkan,* 1938. Figures for 1934.1 from Saitō, p. 60, Table 8.
(Mistakes in profit rate calculations corrected from the Tōyō Keizai data.)
Note: *as a percentage of sales.

used a series of by-products to lower overall costs and increase revenues, as Ōkōchi explained in one of his essays:

In the case of alcohol production, needless to say, one should select a factory site where production operations can be easily rationalized—in other words, a location where production costs will be the least. For the sweet potato, one might choose a wide field and put a factory in the middle and then build pigsties on the periphery. Why? The sweet potatoes from the field serve as raw material for the alcohol, while the dregs left over from the distilling process make excellent pig feed. Pork can then be sold locally or pickled as ham and sausage. The hides can be tanned and sent to a leather factory or sold to another factory as raw material for broth . . . These all result from the manufacture of alcohol. But, whether pigs or alcohol are the main product, the basic idea is that a company can develop several industries around a single product and reduce production expenses as they mutually reinforce each other.[50]

Ōkōchi first tried the "sweet-potato-root" style of management in the production of metallic magnesium. In 1927, after two years of study, the Institute received a patent for extracting magnesium from sea water. Two years later, Ōkōchi received a grant from the Ministry of Commerce and Industry (the prewar predecessor of the Ministry of International Trade and Industry, better known as MITI) to build a factory in Kashiwazaki, which he completed in 1932. The plant had an annual capacity of 20 tons, twice the level of domestic demand for metallic magnesium, because Ōkōchi wanted to take

TABLE 11 Main Riken Group Factories, 1942 and 1945

Factory and Location*	Products	1942 Factory Workers			1945
		Men	Women	Total	Total
Kashiwazaki	piston rings, precision instruments, lathes, machine-gun mounts	3,000	4,000	7,000	11,000
Kakizaki	drills, cutters, screwdrivers	3,000	3,000	6,000	6,000
Miyauchi	machine tools, calculators, piston rings	2,500	1,500	4,00	5,000
Ojiya	small lathes	1,200	300	1,500	1,600
Subtotal: Niigata Prefecture		9,700	8,800	18,500	23,600
Maebashi	piston rings, grinders, anti-aircraft guns, measuring instruments	4,500	1,500	6,000	10,000
Hirai	steel, forging, rolling	500	–	500	500
Ōji-Steel	steel sashes	500	–	500	500
Ōji-Rolling	band steel, special steels	200	–	200	200
Adachi-Rolling	band steel, special steels	100	–	100	100
Kinegawa	saws	80	20	100	100
Ōji-Springs	steel springs	400	400	800	1,000
Arakawa	explosives, brass	800	100	900	1,500
Ōji-No. 1	aircraft piston rings	1,400	600	2,000	2,000
Ōji-No.2	rolling, forging	300	–	300	300
Total: Niigata, Gunma, and Tokyo		18,480	11,420	29,900	39,800

Source: Ushiyama Keiji, *Nomin-sō bunkai no kōzō* (1975), p. 236, Table 2-19.

*Note: The first 4 factories listed above were located in Niigata prefecture. Maebashi was located in Gunma prefecture. The others were in Tokyo.

advantage of economies of scale and guessed, correctly, that sales of the metal would increase as the Japanese Navy ordered more airplanes. He even opened a second factory in nearby Naoetsu during 1932 with an annual capacity of 70 tons, and formed a new company, Riken Magnesium, capitalized at ¥600,000.

The Japanese Navy wanted a still larger domestic supply of magnesium, even though it was cheaper to import than metal, and persuaded Ōkōchi in 1933 to merge the company into a joint venture, Nichi-Man (Japan-Manchuria) Magnesium (capitalized at ¥1,750,000). The South Manchurian Railway was the largest investor, followed by the Institute, although companies from the Sumitomo, Mitsubishi, and Furukawa zaibatsu also joined the venture. While Japan-Manchuria Magnesium tried both the Riken process and a technique developed at the railway's laboratories to extract magnesium from magnesite ore, neither was very efficient. The new company, renamed Riken Metals when Rikagaku Industries bought out the South Manchurian Railway's investment in 1938, averaged a profit rate on sales revenues of merely 6.5 percent during 1934–1942, as seen in Table 12. But the firm probably would have shown even lower earnings had it not found ways to supplement sales by collecting and marketing 8 by-products: soda ash, lime, and sodium bichromate from the Institute's brine process; and magnesium carbonate, solid carbonic acid, and materials for construction, insulation, and fireproofing from the magnesite ore process.[51]

A more profitable venture was Ricoh, Japan's largest manufacturer of copiers after World War II and a major producer of cameras and other optical and office equipment.[52] Ōkōchi founded this subsidiary in 1936 to produce sensitized paper for positive photographic prints. He had first seen this type of paper in Germany before World War I and then instructed one of the Institute's laboratories to study the technology beginning in 1917. The research finally resulted in a patent registered in 1926; Rikagaku Industries, established the following year, handled production and marketing operations. Sales of the sensitized paper did not rise substantially, however, until a distributor based in Kyūshū, Ichimura Kiyoshi (bn. 1900), convinced the South Manchurian Railway (which a division of the Japanese Army controlled) to buy the paper in large amounts beginning in 1931. Ōkōchi gradually increased Ichimura's responsibilities and, in 1935, made him head of Rikagaku Industries' sensitized-paper department. Ōkōchi then separated this department as an independent subsidiary in 1936. Ichimura served as the chief operating officer while Ōkōchi took the post of chairman, a position he also held at Rikagaku Industries, Riken Piston Ring, Riken Metals, and other firms in which he took a personal interest.

The new company, originally called Riken Sensitized Paper and capitalized at ¥350,000, quickly expanded into related product lines. Between 1936 and 1937, it merged with a blueprints manufacturer, began producing lenses, safety glasses, and other optical equipment developed at the Institute, and acquired a subsidiary to manufacture cameras, Asahi Optical (which Ricoh absorbed in 1953). Ichimura also made an important strategic move in 1938 when he signed a long-term contract with the Ōji Paper Company for paper supplies and then built a new factory in Tokyo to mass-produce the sensitized

TABLE 12 Riken Metals, 1934–1942
(units: 1,000 yen, %)

Period	Paid-Up Capital	Profits	Profit Rate*	Dividend
1934.1	1,750	43	4.9%	—
.2	"	54	6.2	—
1935.1	"	41	4.6	—
.2	2,423	26	2.1	—
1936.1	2,450	136	11.1	5.0%
.2	"	96	7.8	"
1937.1	"	106	8.7	"
.2	3,500	114	6.5	"
1938.1	"	146	8.3	6.0
.2	4,102	194	9.5	7.0
139.1	5,270	240	9.1	"
.2	7,000	297	8.5	"
1940.1	8,167	300	7.3	6.0
.2	8,750	318	7.3	"
1941.1	10,500	361	6.9	"
.2	11,300	47	0.8	—
1942.1	"	44	0.8	—

Source: Tōyō Keizai, *Kabushiki kaisha nenkan,* 1938–1942.

Note: *as a percentage of sales.

TABLE 13 Ricoh, 1939–1942
(units: 1,000 yen, %)

Period	Paid-Up Capital	Profits	Profit Rate*	Dividend
1939.1	3,000	206	13.7%	9.0%
.2	"	233	15.5%	"
1940.1	"	328	21.9	"
.2	"	379	25.3	8.0
1941.1	"	466	31.1	"
.2	"	517	34.5	"
1942.1	"	544	36.3	"

Source: Tōyō Keizai, *Kabushiki kaisha nenkan,* 1940–1942.

Note: *As a percentage of sales.

paper. To reflect its diversification, however, during 1938 the company adopted the name Riken Kōgaku (Riken Optics, shortened to "Ricoh" after World War II). A virtual monopoly on the market for sensitized photographic paper in Japan allowed Riken Optics to average a profit rate on sales revenues of more than 30 percent during the early 1940s (Table 13), although rising debt throughout the Riken group led the Institute and other holding companies to sell most of the shares they owned in Riken Optics prior to the end of World War II.

PROBLEMS: FINANCIAL MANAGEMENT AND PRODUCT QUALITY

During the 1930s, most firms in the Riken group, except for Riken Metals, consistently showed profit rates on sales revenues of between 15 and 35 percent.[53] Their performance made it possible for Ōkōchi to finance new investment through earnings from the Institute or subsidiaries and from sales to the public of shares held in group firms such as Rikagaku Industries, Riken Piston Ring, and Ricoh. After 1938, however, Ōkōchi wanted to expand the group faster than he was able to accumulate equity capital, which forced him to rely mainly on bank loans to finance new acquisitions. Group liabilities thus rose from a total of ¥37 million in 1938 to nearly ¥150 million by 1940, considerably more than the combined paid-up capital of all Riken subsidiaries and affiliates.[54] Profits also started to decline in the late 1930s, which made repayment of mounting debts impossible. To secure additional funds, the Institute, Rikagaku Industries, and Fukoku Industries sold stock, gradually reducing the control of Ōkōchi's holding companies over group subsidiaries.

An article in *Tōyō keizai* (The Oriental Economist) during April 1940 blamed the Riken group's financial predicament on Ōkōchi. It noted that, while he succeeded in commercializing several Institute patents, he exercised poor judgment and paid too little attention to financial analysis or strategic planning. His deficiencies as a financial manager then made it necessary for the Bank of Japan and the Industrial Bank, a semi-public institution founded in 1902 to provide long-term loans to manufacturing enterprises, to organize a syndicate of 8 banks (the Industrial Bank, Dai-Ichi, Mitsui, Yasuda, Dai-Hyaku, Sumitomo, Sanwa, and Nomura) to provide new credit during 1939.

In addition, the directors of the Industrial Bank felt compelled to send one of their financial experts, Sadao Shigeyuki, to serve as an executive director at Riken Heavy Industries and to supervise the reorganization of the entire group. Ōkōchi remained as chairman of the main Riken company but with much reduced authority.[55]

Debts were only one problem in the Riken group. Another was the small size of most subsidiaries, which made it difficult to gain maximum economies of scale, provide enough skilled managers, and compete with larger firms for supplies, labor, and credit under the wartime system of economic controls. Of the 60 or so companies in the group around 1940, 34 had capitalizations at or below ¥500,000 (about $150,000); only 22 had capitalizations of ¥1 million or more. In addition, while total paid-up capital in the combine grew 17-fold between 1935 and 1940, from around ¥7 million to ¥120 million, the number of subsidiaries grew far more rapidly than Ōkōchi had personnel to run them. As a result, many of the newly established or acquired firms proved to be financial drains rather than assets to the group's main business. Riken companies, whose shares once sold at a premium because of their ties to the Institute and high earnings, began to lose their attractiveness on the Japanese stock markets, forcing Ōkōchi to sell shares in the group's more popular subsidiaries and to take out more loans to continue his expansion plans. As indicated in Table 14, these policies brought down the average percentage of shares that group holding companies owned in subsidiaries to approximately 30 percent by 1940, including merely 23.4 percent in Riken Heavy Industries and 18.8 percent in Rikagaku Industries.

The banking syndicate pressured Ōkōchi to merge as many firms as possible to "rationalize" operations, even though this went against his strategy of maintaining specialized companies for specific product lines. The first major reorganization came in 1938, when Riken Piston Ring and Riken Special Steel combined to form Riken Heavy Industries. In 1940, this company absorbed Riken Headstocks-Ojiya and Riken Automobile Rebuilding. In addition, during 1940, Riken Chuck-Miyauchi, Riken Lathes-Miyauchi, and Riken Miyauchi Casting formed Riken Casting, while Riken Electromagnetic Instruments and Riken Hydraulic Machinery merged to create Riken Electric Machinery. Group bankers carried through another major reorganization in 1941 by arranging for Riken Heavy Industries to absorb Rikagaku Industries, Riken Forging, Riken Steel Materials,

TABLE 14 The Riken Group, March 1940: Main Companies and Shareholding (1,000 yen, number of shares, %)

Company	Paid-Up Capital	Total Shares	Riken Heavy Industries	Rikagaku Industries	Riken Institute	Fukoku Industries	Internal Shareholding Shares	%
*Rikagaku Industries	15,000	400,000	6,120	—	67,930	1,000	75,050	18.8
*Riken Heavy Industries	30,000	600,000	—	97,620	32,283	3,500	134,403	22.4
*Riken Forging	5,000	100,000	5,870	1,200	2,500	5,000	14,570	14.6
*Riken Steel Materials	6,000	120,000	8,720	1,500	4,000	950	15,170	12.6
*Riken Rolling	5,000	100,000	11,300	4,000	2,000	400	17,700	17.7
*Riken Machine Tools	4,000	160,000	14,000	10,000	10,000	8,000	42,000	26.3
Riken Machinery	3,900	90,000	52,935	—	—	21,905	74,840	83.2
Riken Springs	1,000	20,000	7,000	2,800	2,000	2,000	13,800	69.0
*Riken Hydraulic Machinery	1,500	30,000	6,500	2,800	2,000	1,000	12,300	41.0
*Riken Miyauchi Casting	2,000	40,000	3,160	3,470	1,270	4,850	12,750	31.9
*Riken Chuck	2,000	40,000	800	5,070	—	5,660	11,530	28.8
Riken Automobile Rebuilding	750	30,000	—	—	10,000	9,600	19,600	65.3
Riken Pneumatic	1,000	20,000	4,000	10,490	2,000	—	16,490	82.4
Aircraft Specialty Parts	725	20,000	6,850	4,000	—	2,400	13,250	66.3
*Ricoh	3,000	100,000	22,631	—	3,107	440	26,178	26.2
*Riken Rubber	2,800	160,000	—	32,100	1,500	7,060	40,660	25.4
*Riken Corundum	1,675	40,000	3,730	5,845	8,750	3,815	22,340	55.9
Riken Electrical Equipment	675	30,000	—	2,500	17,000	—	19,500	65.0
Riken Cable	1,500	30,000	960	6,870	2,200	6,170	16,740	55.8
*Riken Metals	8,750	360,000	—	65,500	10,000	100	75,600	27.0
*Riken Electromagnetic	1,500	30,000	9,870	3,000	3,000	3,000	18,870	62.9
Chōsen Riken Metals	7,500	300,000	10,000	52,300	13,350	28,000	103,650	34.6
Chōsen Riken Mining	1,500	60,000	1,000	1,000	600	8,500	11,100	18.5
Chōsen Riken Rubber	500	20,000	—	2,000	—	—	2,000	10.0
Tōyō Steel Works	1,000	20,000	7,000	10,000	1,000	—	18,000	90.0
Fukoku Industries	1,000	20,000	18,000	—	—	—	18,000	90.0
Total	109,275	2,940,000	200,446	324,065	197,490	123,350	846,091	28.8

Source: *Tōyō keizai*, 27 April 1940, p. 111.

Notes: Asterisks (*) indicate companies placed under syndicate direction. The above table includes only the 22 firms with capitalizations of ¥1 million or over, plus 4 of the other largest firms. Only shares held by the 4 holding companies listed above are included, although other firms held small numbers of shares.

Riken Machine Tools, Riken Rolling, and Riken Casting, creating Riken Industries (paid-up capitalization of ¥67 million). Ōkōchi remained as the chairman for one year, but the banking syndicate hired Yoshimi Seiichi, a former director of the Tōhoku Shinkō Electric Power Company, to serve as president and to run the new company. Sadao Shigeyuki from the Industrial Bank took on the post of executive director in charge of finance. Of Riken Industries' three managing directors, two came from the Industrial Bank and only one, Sugimura Ichibei, a PhD responsible for technology and a former researcher at the Institute, had previously worked in the Riken group. Company officials in subsidiaries resisted these reorganizations and personnel changes, although Ōkōchi owned few shares in group firms and had no alternative but to accept the instructions of his bankers and their decision to relieve him of nearly all managerial responsibilities.[56]

While these measures kept the Riken group from bankruptcy, Riken Industries still suffered from huge liabilities. Along with a doubling of the capitalization of the group's largest firm during 1940–1941, from ¥30 to ¥67 million, came a reduction in earnings and a deficit in the second half of 1941 totaling ¥2.5 million. This contrasted with profits of nearly ¥3 million in the second half of 1939, as seen in Table 15. To make matters worse, the liabilities of Riken Industries rose from ¥56 million to ¥134 million during this same period as it consolidated the debts from firms it absorbed.[57] The company stopped paying dividends in 1941, and retained earnings fell from nearly 73 percent in the first half of 1938 to zero by the end of 1941.

Other factors contributed to the declining performance of Riken companies. Rapidly increasing demand for armaments and government pressures to boost output encouraged Ōkōchi and executives in other firms to expand production capacity, integrate vertically, or acquire more suppliers. Much of this expansion after 1937 relied on bank credit, while economic controls imposed after 1938 restricted the freedom of managers to invest, dispose of profits, obtain funding, allocate materials, fuel, and power, reduce wages and prices, and transfer or hire technicians and other workers.[58] The difficulties that small and medium-size factories operating in rural areas had obtaining priority in the wartime rationing system exacerbated the structural problems of the Riken group, although it was logical to give priority to

TABLE 15 Riken Piston Ring to Riken Industries, 1938–1941
(units: 1,000 yen, %)

Period	Paid-Up Capital	Profits	Profit Rate*	Dividend	Retained Earnings
1938.1	9,000	1,749	38.9%	10.0%	72.6%
.2ᵃ	15,863	1,804	22.7	”	52.7
1939.1	22,932	2,218	19.3	”	45.1
.2	27,668	2,953	21.3	”	50.8
1940.1ᵇ	30,600	1,905	12.5	”	43.9
.2ᶜ	31,267	1,644	10.5	8.0	18.9
1941.1	40,123	621	3.1	3.0	3.2
.2ᵈ	67,000	-2,430	–	–	–

Source: Tōyō Keizai, *Kabushiki kaisha nenkan,* 1942.

Notes: *as a percentage of sales.

ᵃMerger of Riken Piston Ring with Riken Special Steel in October 1938 to form Riken Heavy Industries.

ᵇAbsorption of Riken Headstocks-Ōjiya, February 1940.

ᶜAbsorption of Riken Automobile Rebuilding, July 1940.

ᵈAbsorption of Rikagaku Industries, Riken Forging, Riken Steel Materials, Riken Machine Tools, Riken Rolling, Riken Casting, to form Riken Industries in July 1941.

firms such as Mitsubishi Heavy Industries, which had a paid-up capital at war's end of ¥750 million, or to Toshiba (466.5 million), Hitachi (437.5 million), or Kawasaki Heavy Industries (400 million), since they were far larger than the entire Riken group.[59]

The quality of Riken piston rings, which was only adequate during the early 1930s, also appears to have declined as the group expanded and began making its own machine tools. Maeda Riichi (bn. 1896), a professor of mechanical engineering at Osaka University who joined Nissan Motor in 1937 to head its testing section and retired in 1967 as a managing director in charge of research, studied the quality of domestically made piston rings during the late 1930s and early 1940s. He summarized his findings and presented a copy of his data to this writer during a 1982 interview. According to Maeda, Nissan (established in 1933) began using Riken piston rings during 1937–1938 in its line of standard-size trucks. Because dust from unpaved roads in Manchuria wore down the piston rings faster than expected, Maeda had Nissan's design department copy an air filter used in American farm trucks. After analyzing the composition and manufacturing process of the piston rings, however, he concluded that the Riken rings were "extremely bad" due to uneven surfaces resulting from sloppy production methods, even though Ōkōchi's manufacturing process was theoretically sound.[60] Maeda also served as the assistant director of the technology department in the Automobile Industry Control Association during World War II and submitted a report to the Association comparing Riken's piston rings with those made by Japan's other major producer, Nippon Piston Ring (established in 1934). The Association published this article in its 1941 proceedings.[61] After Maeda notified Ōkōchi of his findings, the quality of Riken's piston rings improved, but, in the meantime, Nissan shifted its orders to Nippon Piston Ring. Other users of piston rings in the motor vehicle and aircraft industries appear to have done the same.

Miyazaki Shōkichi (bn. 1913), a consultant to the Japanese machine-tool industry who graduated from the prewar predecessor of Hitotsubashi University and worked for Tokyo Gas and Electric and then Hitachi during the 1930s and 1940s, gave his opinion in a 1981 interview with this writer why Riken developed problems in manufacturing. According to Miyazaki, while Ōkōchi achieved the distinction of making his own machine tools, they were not comparable in performance to the more expensive Western machinery that wealthier companies imported. In addition, even though spreading out manufacturing operations in rural areas utilized unskilled agricultural workers at low wages, this practice too often resulted in products of low quality due to inadequate worker skills or training, and to a scarcity of engineers to supervise production operations at the myriad small firms that Ōkōchi created. Poor equipment only exacerbated the labor problem. At the same time, Ōkōchi appeared to be more interested in promoting his ideas and writing about scientific industry than in managing companies, and he failed to study the details of production management to help solve the group's difficulties.[62]

Since declining orders and profits added to the debts of the Riken group and forced holding companies to sell more shares in subsidiaries, Ōkōchi gradually lost control over individual firms and then over the entire concern. Riken Optics (Ricoh) was no longer a subsidiary at the end of World War II; in addition, the banking syndicate dissolved Chōsen Riken Mining, and sold Chōsen Riken Metals to

Shōwa Denkō and Riken Metals to Sumitomo Metals. Yet the total liabilities of Riken Industries, owed mostly to the Industrial Bank, still amounted to ¥240 million at war's end, compared to paid-up capital of approximately ¥100 million. Many subsidiaries were also heavily in debt and linked to the Riken group through extremely low percentages of shareholding.[63] As described in Table 16, the size of the combine when the American authorities designated Riken Industries for dissolution in December 1946, excluding firms in which internal group shareholding was under 10 percent, was 20 companies, representing paid-up capital of merely ¥88,795,000. At this point, the Institute owned only 9.4 percent of Riken Industries' outstanding shares and Fukoku Industries merely 3.5 percent. The Holding Company Liquidation Commission then dissolved Riken Industries and other group subsidiaries in 1949 and reorganized the combine into 11 independent firms, ending the formal existence of the Riken industrial group.[64]

The Institute, which had a paid-up capitalization of ¥10,482,000 at war's end, lost its status as a private foundation in 1948 but continued as a public corporation, independent of its former subsidiaries and barred from armaments research or production.[65] During the Korean War, it profited from making precision instruments and pharmaceuticals such as penicillin and streptomycin, although its directors decided to separate their product division as an independent firm in 1958.[66] The Institute subsequently came to rely on government funds channeled through the Science and Technology Agency and expanded its research in nuclear, solid state, and applied physics, as well as basic engineering, organic and inorganic chemistry, biochemistry, agricultural sciences, lasers, and solar energy. It also moved to a larger site in a Tokyo suburb during 1963, Wakō City (Saitama prefecture), although total staff in the early 1980s numbered only about 600, a third of the wartime peak.[67]

As for Ōkōchi, he resigned as chairman of Riken Industries in January 1942 to become head of the Industrial Machinery Control Association, a position he occupied until May 1944. Between 1942 and 1943, he held six cabinet-level positions, in addition to an appointment in March 1943 from Prime Minister Tōjō Hideki to the Cabinet Advisers Council to oversee wartime production. Ōkōchi ended his career in 1945 as an adviser to the Ministry of Munitions, the wartime counterpart to MITI. The U.S. Army investigated him for war

TABLE 16 The Riken Group, December 1946
         (1,000 yen, %)

Company	Paid-Up Capital	Internal Shareholding
Riken Industries	67,000	12.9%
Riken Machinery	2,500	14.2
Riken Cable	2,150	37.2
Riken Corundum	2,000	16.4
Riken Pneumatic Machinery	1,700	98.2
Riken Films	1,700	12.9
Riken Springs	1,500	82.3
Riken Fermentation	1,500	11.7
Riken Industrial Chemicals	1,480	13.7
Riken Synthetic Resins	1,200	16.7
Riken Crucibles	1,200	36.7
Tōyō Steel Works	1,000	100.0
Riken Optical Instruments	750	10.7
Riken Nutritive Drugs	630	30.0
Nihon Plating Machinery	600	50.0
Nihon Polished Steel Bands	500	19.6
Riken Electric Machinery	450	55.6
Riken Mining	400	55.8
Riken Pure Drugs	350	23.3
Tokyo Machinery	185	85.7
Subtotal	88,795	
The Institute	10,482	
Total	99,277	

Source: *Nihon zaibatsu to sono kaitai*, I, 503, and II, 17, 72.

Note: Internal Shareholding indicates the precentage of shares held in group firms by Riken Industries and the Institute, excluding firms in which this shareholding was less than 10%.

crimes and imprisoned him in December 1945, but released him in April 1946 following the dismissal of all charges. In October of the same year, he resigned as head of the Institute, after twenty-five years in the post, due to the purge of Japanese business and political leaders, but received appointments as a consultant to three former Riken subsidiaries after the purge ended in 1951. Ōkōchi died in 1952 at the age of 74.[68]

CONCLUSION

Had Ōkōchi been faithful to his writings, his actions as an entrepreneur and manager should have followed several specific strategies: high levels of investment in applied research, the commercialization of advanced technologies produced at the Institute to secure a stable source of revenues and to promote the general development of Japanese science and industry; a primary concern for long-term growth rather than short-term profits in operating companies; continuous introduction of the latest product technologies and mass-production techniques relying on worker specialization and simplified processes or single-function machine tools; employment of unskilled agricultural laborers at high wages; reductions in production costs through continual gains in productivity; utilization of by-products to increase revenues and profits; output of "low-price, high-quality goods." He founded or acquired too many small firms in the late 1930s and then had to abandon some of his principles during World War II to place greater emphasis on increasing production. But, by experimenting with new technologies and a strategy for commercialization and expansion, he set an example for postwar managers and constructed a diversified engineering concern that grew to be far larger than anyone could have imagined when Ōkōchi took over as head of the Institute in 1921.

The Riken group was not entirely faithful to Ōkōchi's concept of scientific industry. Subsidiaries did not pay high wages, for example, though many provided additional income for agricultural workers. Nor did Riken companies produce high-quality goods. They manufactured more or less adequate products at low prices, using cheap labor and domestic equipment, much of which Riken subsidiaries made themselves. Those employees who received little training or supervision and worked in small shops scattered throughout several of Japan's rural prefectures had trouble maintaining high standards for precision and quality, although these were problems that Riken companies would solve in time after 1945.

Ōkōchi probably contributed more to Japan's development into a modern industrial nation as a writer on technology and management, and as the director of a major research institution, than as an entrepreneur. It is particularly striking how commonly accepted many of his ideas became in postwar Japan. Toyota found that it was economical to combine universal machine tools with specialized equipment; this facilitated production in smaller lots, which reduced in-process inventories. Toyota also relied on unskilled "surplus" workers from agricultural villages, as did the Riken group, which became even more practical as increasing numbers of agricultural workers began taking second jobs or commuting to urban factories during the 1950s and 1960s. Rising wage levels also boosted domestic consumption and led to higher corporate profits, as Ōkōchi said they would. But perhaps his most important prediction was that Japan would someday capitalize on its human resources through education, concentrating on long-term growth, and investing more heavily in applied research and product development to manufacture inexpensive goods of high quality.

Few if any of Ōkōchi's theories were original. His critique of passive capitalism and British financiers had much in common with contemporary Marxist thinkers and Joseph Schumpeter, who also argued that innovation and entrepreneurship were necessary to "save" the capitalist system. The struggle between bankers and businessmen, and the call to engineers to take a more active role in management, were themes found in the writings of Thorstein Veblen. With regard to his ideas on production management, Ōkōchi was clearly a follower of Frederick Taylor and other Americans who pioneered techniques to "rationalize" manufacturing operations known as "scientific management." Ōkōchi also seems to have drawn much of his inspiration from German scientists and industrialists, as well as from Henry Ford, who adopted the strategy of increasing wages to stimulate higher productivity when he introduced the 8-hour, 5-dollar day in 1914. Mass production relying on simplified production processes and machine tools, utilizing the principle of "one factory, one product," were also Ford trademarks widely known and copied in Japan.[69] In addition, many Japanese businessmen shared Ōkōchi's basic views on management and his conviction that Japan had to improve the levels of technology employed in domestic industries. These men included not only his contemporaries in other new zaibatsu but also "old-zaibatsu" executives such as Mitsu's Dan Takuma (1858–1932) and Mutō Sanji (1867–1934), Mitsubishi's Iwasaki Koyata (1879–1945), and Sumitomo's Suzuki Masaya (1861–1921).[70]

Ōkōchi's writings prior to World War II reflected a belief that the greater application of science and technology to industry, and the principles of scientific management, would help Japan evolve into a modern industrial nation capable of competing with the United States and Western Europe. Since his ideas and companies were so useful to the military, however, Japanese scholars have disagreed on how to categorize Ōkōchi: as a benign industrialist, or as a technocratic "fascist." Most regard him as a leader in prewar Japan's movement toward "high-technology" industries while acknowledging that Riken and the other new zaibatsu took advantage of military contracts and therefore got "caught up in the imperial fascist system." Other Japanese writers, in contrast, insist that Ōkōchi was a combination technocrat and physiocrat, with ties to military figures such as Yamamoto Isoroku and Tōjō Hideki that made him little different from the Nazis in contemporary Germany.[71]

While this author found no indications in Ōkōchi's writings that he sympathized with the Nazis, it is undeniable that military contracts during the 1930s gave an enormous boost to the Riken group and other firms in the machinery, metals, and chemical industries. Furthermore, during his years in college and graduate school, and as a teacher at the University of Tokyo and a representative in the Japanese parliament, Ōkōchi developed a reputation as an armaments expert and encouraged the government to take a more active role in building up Japan's "defense" industries.[72] Yet, as suggested in his acquittal during the war-crimes investigation, Ōkōchi's misdeeds during the 1930s and 1940s probably did not exceed making piston rings for military aircraft and trucks, producing a few machine-gun mounts, and paying low wages to poor farmers' daughters while publicly extolling the virtues of a high-wage economy.

The Riken industrial group should be remembered as a novel experiment in strategic thinking, technology development, and entrepreneurial management that helped reduce prewar Japan's reliance on foreign engineers and technology imports from the West. Ōkōchi was also a major source of Japanese writings on production and operations management. As a founder of companies continuing after 1945, Ōkōchi's achievements were more modest. The Riken Corporation, which inherited the group's piston-ring business, became an important supplier of Nissan Motor, although, during the late 1980s, it had only 2,300 workers, far less than the Riken group employed in 1945. Ricoh grew to approximately 11,500 employees by the late 1980s and led all Japanese firms in the production of copiers, vying with Canon and other companies in Japan's highly competitive precision-machinery and office-equipment industries. Okamoto Riken Gōmu, Japan's largest maker of prophylactics with around 1,700 employees in 1988, also originated from a rubber-manufacturing subsidiary that Ōkōchi founded. But perhaps his memory survived best at the Institute and several of its former subsidiaries that, during the late 1980s, still had approximately 500 employees or less: Riken Vinyl (a maker of synthetic resins), Riken Cable (electric wires and cables), Riken Keiki (measuring instruments), Riken Vitamin (synthetic vitamins and other health products), Riken Kōki (steel construction materials), and Riken Corundum (grinding and polishing materials). These firms, as well as the history of the Institute and other Riken companies, demonstrate clearly that a drive to link human resources and an aggressive entrepreneurial spirit was not simply a postwar phenomenon in Japan.

CONTENTS

THEMES AND CONTROVERSIES

Aspects of the Firm
Comparative Dimensions: The Chandler Model
International Comparisons: The Family Firm and Industrial Structure
Industrial Organization and Industrial Policy: Further Comparisons

HISTORIOGRAPHY

Business History and Marxism in the Japanese Academic Setting
Business Historians, Societies, and Journals
The Company History
Notes for an Agenda
    Industry Studies
    Regional Industry and Proto-Industrialization
    Periodization

CHAPTER   NINE

Afterword: The Writing of Japanese Business History

WILLIAM D. WRAY

Although there has been a sudden spurt of books in business and industrial history in the last half-decade, there is every reason to suppose that this represents only a beginning of what is likely to be a continuing flow of publications. The importance of Japanese corporations in the world economy, the greater accessibility of business records in Japan, increasing contact with Japanese scholars, gradual development in the use of different methodologies from other fields of economic history, and advances in comparative business history should all expand the range of questions to be asked and enhance the quality of analysis in future work. Given these expectations, this volume is designed to present not just an integrated collection of papers but to give some direction to the field. In this Afterword I pursue that goal in several ways. First, I try to expand on several issues related to the company that were considered in the foregoing chapters. Second, I have raised large comparative questions, especially regarding company structure. Third, I have given some background to the emergence of business history in Japan. Although the *Japanese Yearbook on Business History* and other publications of the Japan Business Society (Keiei Shi Gakkai) have provided substantial bibliography on recent work, they have paid much less attention to historiography. Two issues in particular—Marxist historiography relating to business and the institutional context of business history in Japan—lack systematic treatment. This Afterword provides an introduction to these issues and makes suggestions for further research.

THEMES AND CONTROVERSIES

Aspects of the Firm

Aoki Masahiko has suggested that one of the three prerequisites of postwar Japanese management is freedom from "classical capitalist control" under which managers "passively serve the interests of owners."[1] He also indicates that this prerequisite had been met before World War II, a point clearly consistent with Morikawa's thesis. The question of ownership, however, is one aspect of company history touched on by most of the chapters in this volume but not given a principal focus. Morikawa argues that the key variable in whether firms promoted salaried managers to positions of authority was the degree of "owner progressiveness." The question of what made these owners progressive has received less attention. Morikawa basically suggests two answers, depending on the period when the transition to salaried managers occurred: For firms that experienced this shift after 1900—recognition of a more complex business environment; for large zaibatsu like Mitsubishi and Mitsui, which began the process roughly between the 1870s and the 1890s—the view that more recently educated personnel made better managers. Yasuoka has provided a somewhat different interpretation rooted more in the structure of ownership than in the outlook of individual owners. Most family businesses governed their family affairs by codes whose rules encompassed matters like inheritance, business activity of family members, and the relation between an individual member and the family unit. Codes varied with the firm, but some regulated family members in ways that made the firm more accommodating and flexible in the face of a new business environment.[2]

Some of the firms Morikawa examines had success in the Meiji period but did not promote salaried managers and subsequently declined in the 1920s. Another dimension from which to test Morikawa's thesis is the case of firms already large in the Tokugawa period, sharing some of the attributes of Mitsui and Sumitomo, but which failed in the Meiji period to develop into zaibatsu or even to keep pace with smaller rivals. Kōnoike was one such firm, which also illustrates Yasuoka's emphasis on the importance of family codes.[3] The Kōnoike family's principal business was banking. During the Meiji period, its securities became increasingly diversified, but it held these simply as portfolio investments. Its goal was to secure profits, and it did not become involved in the management of companies in which it invested. Until 1934, when Kōnoike merged with two other banks to form the Sanwa Bank, preserving the family fortune, rather than participating actively in the opportunities offered by industrial growth, was the hallmark of its banking business. During the rapid growth of the 1890s-to-World War I period, this passive attitude led to a decline in the bank's standing. In the late 1890s, Kōnoike still had the largest Osaka bank, but over the next two decades its share of deposits and loans in Osaka fell precipitously. Sumitomo established a bank only in the 1890s; it grew quickly, keeping pace with the general financial market in Osaka. But Kōnoike, failing even to increase its capitalization during World War I, sank to the level of a middle-ranking bank. This decline stemmed from the conservative strategy of concentrating on asset preservation, a policy pursued not only by the traditional managers who acted on behalf of branch families during the nineteenth century but also by the salaried manager, Harada Jirō, hired in 1897. He embraced the philosophy of asset preservation and turned the bank even more in the direction of family business.

Within the framework of Yasuoka's argument, a key structural variable in the Kōnoike case was the position of its branch families. They seem to have had considerable autonomy relative to other family firms and they hindered the development of a cohesive administrative structure. In contrast, though 11 families co-owned Mitsui, in practice ownership was collective, that is, the Mitsui code precluded autonomy in business affairs for individual families. This structure seems to have facilitated decision making, whereas the Kōnoike family adminstration acted as an obstacle to the development by appointees of independent policies. In some respects, Harada's position as a salaried manager makes this case a variant of Morikawa's thesis. Yet, the fundamental feature in Kōnoike's experience was the dominance of family strategy. In view of Kōnoike's decline, this suggests a basic consistency with both Morikawa's underlying arguments and Yasuoka's emphasis on family codes.

Another issue related to the problem of managerial authority within companies is the phenomenon of strong founder-executives who exercise long-term leadership. Noguchi Jun was a prime example, and Molony lists numerous postwar growth-firms that have had similar leadership. These include Sony and Matsushita in electronics, Toyota and Honda in autos, and Seikō in watch-making. Recent press accounts have also focused on the prevalence of "one-man" Japanese managers who have developed autocratic decision-making power, such as Suntory's Saji Keizō, Sumitomo Bank's Isoda Ichirō, and Fanuc's Inaba Seiuemon.[4] Morikawa comments on several large firms where the family continues to exercise strong leadership several generations beyond the founder, such as Suntory, Toyota, Ajinomoto, and Bridgestone Tire.[5] These three examples—founder-executives, one-man autocrats, and family enterprises—also seem to diverge from Morikawa's emphasis on salaried managers. Yet, a closer analysis would suggest that the variance is not so great. In the category of founder-executives, several firms (Sony and Honda) have passed on authority to salaried managers; Matsushita is gradually doing the same. Second, many one-man autocrats are essentially powerful salaried managers. Sometimes dubbed "emperor," as in Sumitomo's "Emperor Isoda," these leaders often encounter difficulty in assuring a smooth succession of authority; they may resort to a collective leadership as their power wanes with advancing age.[6] Third, most of the family enterprises are themselves managed through cooperation with salaried managers. A common element in the three formats is "expertise," not the "interfering owner" restraining innovative strategy. Relevant to this point is Aoki's comparison of founder-executives and career-managers in ex-zaibatsu firms. He suggests that the former tended to be "more technologically innovative and growth oriented," but within the general context of postwar managerial control he does not regard that as a qualitatively substantial difference.[7]

These comments refer to the top echelon of the firm. Most analysis of postwar Japanese management, however, has focused on the more general decision-making process in which deliberation at the middle-management level leads to recommendations usually accepted by top management, thereby showing the decisive role in policymaking played by middle or lower ranks of the company (the "decision-making-from-below" model). There are, however, important variations of this general model. In his study of the auto industry, Cusumano discusses several salaried managers in Toyota who were given major strategic roles when they were still young and of relatively low rank. In particular, before reaching top management, Ōno Taiichi developed Toyota's innovative assembly-line system which reversed the flow of General Motors' traditional production line.[8] His role was not typical of "decision making from below," usually described as a more diffuse process involving a large number of employees (the consensus, deliberative approach). Instead, it represents a different phenomenon in postwar Japan, that of a young and immensely talented *individual* who is given responsibility for making decisions governing the long-term strategy and production system of a firm. This case and others like it suggest that we need less social analysis and more documentation on the roles played by individual managers at every echelon of the company in specific and fundamental decisions.[9]

Most of the chapters in this volume examine the roles played by individual managers. However, they also consider the firm as a whole, that is, as an entity. In this respect the concept of autonomy can be utilized for analytical purposes. I use *autonomy* in an external sense, meaning the attempts by a firm to maintain its identity and to prevent excessive interference from outside institutions. Gordon's chapter, in its discussion of big business trying to retain its managerial prerogative against wartime government intervention, illustrates this dimension. In a different way, so too does Riken's experience, precisely because it lost its autonomy to banks, partly through Ōkōchi's ineffective management. The cases most relevant to the successful maintenance of a firm's autonomy are the N.Y.K. and Nitchitsu.

The concept of autonomy acts in a different structural context for a firm that is a member of a zaibatsu (or corporate group in the postwar period) than for an independent. Membership in a group has offered a certain protection to a firm's identity by insulating it against takeovers. This function became especially important during the 1960s when Japan's capital liberalization brought fears of foreign take-over attempts.[10] Such protection, however, is received at the cost of diminished autonomy in that all firms in the group are subject, in Aoki's words, to "reciprocal monitoring."[11] The basis for this system is the mutual stockholding within the corporate group.[12] Aoki's concept of "reciprocal monitoring" is similar, but not identical, to the term *vertical control* I have used to describe Mitsubishi's policy toward the N.Y.K. The differences are several: In the 1929–1932 years, at the height of Kagami's restorative mission to the N.Y.K., mutual stockholding was still in its early stages, and the holding company exercised authority at the top of the zaibatsu, in contrast to the "head-less groups" of the postwar period. Nevertheless, the N.Y.K.'s case suggests that there exists a limit to monitoring, whether mutual or vertical. In trying to merge the N.Y.K. with the O.S.K., Kagami was excessive. And the vigorous assertion of company autonomy by N.Y.K. career managers seemed to confirm that his actions violated informal rules of group behavior.

Nitchitsu's case was different in that it was independent and led by a founder-executive. Its problem was insufficient capital for rapid expansion. Thus, at critical junctures that required large investment, creditors could potentially constrict Noguchi's autonomy. He over-came this threat by adroitly establishing political connections, partic-ularly with Korean Governor General Ugaki Kazushige, which freed him from his original creditor, the Mitsubishi Bank. This case is inter-esting not just for its economic dimension but also for parallels with other institutional changes in modern Japanese history. It has a remarkable similarity to the case of Kitasato Shibasaburō, the medi-cal biologist who established the Institute of Infectious Diseases in 1892. The institute was originally under the Home Ministry, but throughout his tenure Kitasato struggled to prevent the Ministry of Education, which had a greater propensity for interference, from gain-ing control of it. When this ministry eventually succeeded against his wishes, Kitasato was able to raise sufficient capital through his political contacts to resign and set up his own institute. Both Nogu-chi and Kitasato had a strong independent streak and a superb capac-ity for political maneuvering. The comparison is even clearer if we regard Kitasato as a businessman, which in part he was.[13]

Several structural aspects of the firm discussed in foregoing chapters can perhaps best be illuminated though models developed by Aoki. Rejecting the neoclassical definition of the firm, he proposed the concept "efficient mediation postulate" to explain management behavior in postwar Japan. Under this system, management mediates between different constituencies within the firm, obtaining consent from employees for moderate wage increases in return for better career prospects. The commitment given to job security, which increases the firm's expenses, acts against the short-term interest of stockholders through lower dividends, but tax-free capital gains for stockholders more than compensate because of the long-term growth of the firm made possible by efficient use of internal human-capital resources. This model leads to a definition of the firm as "a complex organization within which the partly harmonious and partly conflicting interests of diverse constituents, including employees (and even suppliers), are brought into equilibrium."[14]

The prewar firm was different, but Aoki's concept of equilibrium is useful in elucidating its structure if we regard it as lacking the internal consensual systems (present in postwar firms) that could moderate internal disruption (the loss of equilibrium) in the event of external crisis. This model can be applied to the question of prewar stockholding, though more so in companies whose shares were fully traded than in zaibatsu firms insulated from the stock market, even if they were incorporated. Partly because the Meiji government promoted the idea of joint-stock companies, stockholders of that period often regarded large dividends as their right. They were thus asserting a prerogative that was quite different from Aoki's view of them in postwar Japan as "constituents" and not simply "owners" of the firm. Thus, economic "shocks" or even "bonanzas," with their accompanying speculation, could easily threaten a firm's equilibrium. At least three such crises are covered in this volume. Ericson shows how, during the financial panic of 1890, stockholder demands sometimes led to irrational managerial decisions. During World War I, stockholder interference in the financial planning of some firms was so disruptive that recovery took years. And during the Depression, concern by corporate stockholders led to unusual degrees of intervention.

Aoki's emphasis on "constituents" of a firm in his equilibrium model is also helpful in tracing certain continuities from pre- to postwar, especially in employment and financial policies. This is made possible by his revision in interpretations of the high debt-equity ratio in postwar Japanese firms. Until 1982, a large number of tax-free reserves in Japanese firms were not regarded as equity capital.[15] They were designated as long-term debt, though usable at management's discretion. These included pension reserves, with employee retirement compensation funds being particularly relevant for our purposes.[16] These funds were, first, *unportable*, that is, an employee leaving before retirement could not take all that was designated for him. The second feature, unique to Japanese firms, was that the funds were also *undiversifiable*. In the United States, professional pension managers administer such funds and they are "diversified in the capital market." In Japan, by contrast, they are kept within the firm and invested by management for business purposes.

Aoki's account is restricted to the postwar period, and he does not mention that this system has been in effect at some Japanese firms since at least the turn of the century. As early as 1914, the N.Y.K. pension fund equaled 4.5 percent of assets and 15.2 percent of capital stock, figures comparable to those in Aoki's postwar survey.[17] The system seems to have evolved from management bonuses to white-collar pensions and eventually to blue-collar retirement compensation. Gordon's account of the 1936 retirement-fund law suggests that its use became widespread by the late 1930s. One effect of this system was to discourage mobility, a point I have emphasized in comparing the Gordon and Morikawa chapters. Another more fundamental effect was employee participation in the firm's capital formation. Since the fund was employed within the firm, in a sense an employee purchased membership in his company when he joined and then sold it when he left and received his retirement compensation. The key point for the continuity of employment practice is that this reserve amalgamated the financial interests of both white- and blue-collar workers. More attention to accounting practices, then, may clarify such issues as the rise of enterprise unions.

Comparative Dimensions: The Chandler Model

While Aoki's work has clarified the economic rationale behind the behavior of firms, most of the comparative analysis of Japanese companies in recent years focuses on organization in large-scale firms. The basis for this trend has been the models of big business organization, specifically in capital-intensive industries, developed by

Alfred Chandler out of the American experience but increasingly utilized as explanatory devices for European company structure and, more recently, for Japan's. Though Chandler's model is complex, with many sub-levels of analysis, its essence can be summarized briefly. In the nineteenth century, new technology brought improvements in transportation and communication and laid the basis for innovations in marketing and in the organization of production. These changes greatly increased the scale of business operation, rendering their administration too complex for a family enterprise and necessitating the rise of salaried managers, who proceeded to build giant enterprises. These enterprises were multi-unit firms. Their managers determined strategies and performed the functions of coordinating, monitoring, and allocating resources to the operating units of the firm.

This summary provides only the skeleton of the model, which is incomplete without two further essential features. First, the managers formed hierarchies, hence the term "managerial hierarchies" for the organizational structures which performed the aforementioned functions. Second, the large firms were not simply producing enterprises. They expanded through vertical integration, first forward into distribution, then later backward into purchasing. This integration, an internalization of functions previously carried out between separate enterprises, provided savings through the routinization of transactions and administrative coordination.[18] Beyond these innovations, many such firms diversified into new products (thereby adding new units, or divisions); then, as conglomerates, they diversified into products unrelated to their original business; and eventually, after establishing overseas marketing networks, they began to produce abroad as multinational corporations.

In comparing the Chandler model to the Japanese experience my concern is with the two essential features: managerial hierarchies and vertical integration. Stated briefly, Japanese firms generally did not expand by vertical integration, and their managerial hierarchies operated at levels lower than those in American companies. At least until World War II, two basic differences from the American experience characterized the managerial hierarchies of Japanese firms. First, the head offices of Japanese companies tended to be thinly staffed compared with the top management of American firms, which oversaw the coordination and other functions mentioned by Chandler.

Second, the American hierarchies included both top- and middle-salaried managers who were senior to executives (labeled "lower-level managers") in charge of the factories and sales offices within the firm's operating units. By contrast, in Japan the hierarchies extended *downward into* the operating units where salaried managers served first as members and then as heads of the section within the units.[19]

This type of "organizational" analysis is essential for understanding how frequently noted Japanese practices (for example, "management from below") actually functioned and for clarifying issues like the nature of strategic planning and new-product development. What follows is an attempt to explain these issues within the framework of the Chandler model (or in contrast to it) through the cases of individual Japanese firms, some of them drawn from the chapters in this volume. These examples show a close link between the difference in managerial hierarchies and the lack of vertical integration.

In the postwar period, many of the large firms in Japan have been either members of corporate groups (*kigyō shūdan*) or heads of their own groups (manufacturing *keiretsu*). The heads of the manufacturing groups have grown faster than the ex-zaibatsu firms, but they have expanded not by vertical integration but by establishing a network of subcontractors (or what are sometimes called quasi-autonomous subsidiaries) for supplying parts, for developing new products, or for marketing.[20] Some of these firms, most notably Toyota and Matsushita, originated in the interwar years. The pattern of their early growth set a strong precedent for the later development of their group-style organization. In one pattern of growth in the large American firms, integration occurred *in the course of* its development rather than at its *beginning*. It might, for example, integrate backward by making intermediate products *previously* purchased from outside suppliers. Alternatively, as in the case of Ford, once a firm had moved into mass production, backward integration might occur as a means to ensure supplies. When these became readily available, however, such firms might begin to "dis-integrate." Toyota's history reveals a different pattern. Though at first it imported parts (the automobile law allowed for such by keeping tariffs on imported parts low), it soon tried to replace them with domestically produced parts. Since, however, domestic manufacturers could not supply them, Toyota began to make its own. Then, rather than internalizing the part-manufacturing process, it spun it off in the form of subsidiaries (which it retained rather than going through a subsequent process of "dis-integration"). Developing such part production so quickly required employment of many engineers to supervise production at the factory level. These engineers, known as "engineer-administrators," account for the "downward penetration" of the managerial hierarchy.[21]

In the postwar period, groups like Toyota have continued to utilize subsidiaries in the manufacturing process, but, in the 1980s, in a kind of "reverse integration," they have begun internalizing their marketing arms which had previously been subsidiaries, as in Toyota's merger with Toyota Motor Sales, its sales subsidiary. Of course, this corporate distinction in Toyota's experience has been primarily legal and financial. However, Matsushita's recent merger with Matsushita Trading, which handled most of the group's exports, may have been more of an administrative reform, prompted by changing trade patterns. It was motivated by the increasing shift to overseas production by both Matsushita and its industrial customers and the consequent need to combine domestic and overseas sales operations. Matsushita's reform, in turn, spurred Hitachi to take similar measures. It has integrated its home electronics sales subsidiary with its Product Planning Division within the head office's Home Electronics Enterprise Division and given it expanded functions for the Hitachi Group's sales in the information and communications fields.[22]

In the case of the zaibatsu, Mitsubishi represents a devolution from the Chandler model. It set up operating divisions in 1908, which gave the zaibatsu an increasing resemblance to the multi-unit enterprise described by Chandler. It abandoned this structure in 1917, however, by incorporating the divisions as separate joint-stock companies. The subsequent structure had two characteristics relevant to the present discussion. First, since some of its new firms (in electrical equipment and aircraft) required new technology, Mitsubishi undertook a rapid expansion in hiring, recruiting supervisory staff and engineer administrators for new production processes.[23] As in Toyota's case, this resulted in an intensive lower-level hierarchy. Second, though Mitsubishi's overall strategic planning was handled cooperatively between the salaried managers (mostly from the subsidiary firms) and Mitsubishi's president, Iwasaki Koyata (who had unusual expertise for a zaibatsu family member), the head office (that is, the holding company) under the president was still thinly staffed. Though it underwent more frequent change than Mitsubishi, Mitsui's head office was likewise small. Its subsidiaries had larger research staffs, and they made the strategic decisions, which were submitted for approval to the head office. It did not function as a centralized policymaking unit but rather as a loose, informal coordinator among the subsidiary companies.[24]

Hitachi's development as an electrical-equipment manufacturer in the interwar years offers a similar contrast to the Chandler model. Its head office was relatively small, but its factory-level organizations were large. They took on a full set of managerial functions including planning. Only sales and some monitoring functions were concentrated at the top. Production, however, was decentralized in what Yui Tsunehiko has called a "strongly bottom-up style of production." What was "missing" in Hitachi relative to the Chandler model was not only the extensive coordination by a head office but also the multi-divisional form. It was the decentralized factories that performed the managerial functions associated with production lines. These were not centralized in division-level offices. Hitachi's structure was quickly adopted by Mitsubishi Electric and later by Shibaura.[25]

The above examples provide at least three additional general comparisons with other organizational forms. First, the literature on management is replete with contrasts between M-form and U-form structures. M-form refers to a multi-divisional firm which allows for an efficient and rational separation between strategic decisions reserved for the general (that is, head) office and operating decisions made at the divisional level. The U-form, though it could be "functionally departmentalized," has a centralized decision-making structure which runs the danger of "communications overload" for top executives as the firm expands.[26] The examples considered above seem to fit neither of these forms. They solved "overload" problems by delegating substantial strategic authority from the top level. At least until after World War II, however, most of the subsequent decentralization occurred at the level of factories or subsidiary companies, not in internal divisions within the parent firm. Second, one of the reasons for the internalization of functions by growing American firms was the advantage derived from economies of scale under which average costs for a "single line of commerce" decline with increasing output. However, Japanese firms, as the Hitachi example suggests, benefited more from economies of scope. These are realized when combining two or more product lines in one firm becomes cheaper than producing them separately.[27] The decentralized factory system was ideally suited to exploit such economies, a point that helps explain the diversified product lines of postwar Japanese electronics firms. Third, the two contrasts above are derived from the Western literature on management; it may also be instructive to look for comparisons within Japanese history. For example, is it a coincidence that the structure of many modern Japanese companies, with thinly staffed head offices and intensive middle and lower management, seems to resemble the contrast between the "thin" bureaucracy of the Bakufu and the "intensive" government of the domains in Tokugawa Japan? To my knowledge, no one has attempted any rigorous analysis of this resemblance, but it suggests the need for comparison between Japanese companies and other Japanese institutions.

This last comparison has direct relevance to some of the issues discussed here. Chandler has suggested that another difference between Japanese and Western firms lies in the degree of "managerial intensiveness" in Japan.[28] One reason for this intensiveness was the use of engineer-administrators in the 1920s to supervise the rapid transfer of technology. However, big Japanese firms, especially Mitsubishi, in the Meiji period already had a relatively large number of salaried managers. In commenting on the employment of these managers in early Meiji, many scholars have referred to the *bantō*, debating whether they represented a precedent for the rise of salaried managers or an obstacle to it. Yet, the *bantō*, coming from the merchant firms, represented only one kind of managerial tradition. A different, though admittedly short-lived, tradition can be found in the commercial enterprises of the domains. As is well known, Mitsubishi evolved directly out of such an enterprise in Tosa. This was a bureaucratic agency with a kind of primitive departmentalization that covered functions ranging from whaling to currency management. Though its short history is not well documented, this "organizational transition" seems to be of fundamental importance in understanding why Mitsubishi, almost from its beginnings, hired salaried managers and adopted diversified business strategy.[29]

There were several more general reasons why Meiji business firms needed salaried managers. First, the social distance between ex-samurai government bureaucrats and the "merchant" representatives of companies made effective communication difficult during daytime hours. This was one reason for the prevalence of nighttime consulta-tion over *sake*. Even there, companies needed qualified representatives to match the generally well-educated samurai. Second, in the nine-teenth century, graduates in technical fields preferred the military or government ministries to employment in a private company. In this sense Japanese firms had to catch up with their own government.

The Chandler model raises questions about two other issues of great importance in Japanese business history. One concerns trading companies and their relation to the issue of vertical integration; and the other, industrial structure. One reason often given why Japanese firms did not follow strategies of vertical integration is the presence of trading companies.[30] A full treatment of this issue would require an examination of many varied relations, some zaibatsu-connected and others not. Cotton spinning companies—single-function produc-ing firms—relied on trading companies, though before World War I Mitsui Bussan was the only major one from a zaibatsu. The rest were specialized cotton traders. Another question concerns coordination and transactions within the zaibatsu; specifically, were the intra-zaibatsu services provided by trading companies functionally equiva-lent to vertical integration? Mitsui Bussan, for example, performed distribution, marketing, and purchasing services not only for the main subsidiaries in its zaibatsu but also for companies only partially owned by the Mitsui. It is probably inappropriate, though, to view these services as functional vertical integration, for Mitsui Bussan's business in such cases was more akin to contracts between separate firms. To regard this relationship as a kind of functional substitute, two conditions would have to obtain. First, the business conducted would resemble an internalized transaction more than a contract. Second, vis-à-vis the zaibatsu firm it serviced, the trading company would function more like an internal sales organization than an out-side "intermediary." (Chandler defines the commercial intermediary as a distributor or marketing agent that gained cost advantage by handling (1) "a single line of products" from many manufacturers, that is, through economies of scale, and (2) "a number of *related* prod-uct lines through a single set of facilities," that is, through economies of scope).[31]

In the late 1910s and early 1920s, when Mitsubishi was incorpor-ating its divisions, its trading company, Mitsubishi Shōji, tempo-rarily had the function of a sales division for each of the new subsidiaries. For example, the year after Mitsubishi Electric was established, Shōji signed an exclusive marketing agreement with it. Within a few years, though, this became a joint agreement, as the electric firm began to build up its own sales staff through which it marketed electric fans. Meanwhile, Shōji began marketing for other electrical firms as well.[32] Thus, in this case, the trading company's role seems closer to what Chandler called an intermediary than an internal sales organization. Mitsubishi Electric, however, did not move far in the direction of vertical integration. Its relationship with Shōji was by no means temporary. Their agreement lasted until 1947 when the Occupation dissolved both Mitsubishi Shōji and Mitsui Bussan, a move that deprived Mitsubishi Electric of much of its marketing arm and forced it to set up its own sales division.[33]

In general, Mitsubishi Shōji carried out a greater percentage of its business within the Mitsubishi zaibatsu than Mitsui Bussan did within the Mitsui zaibatsu. Mitsubishi Shōji played a major strategic role by importing new technology. Certainly Mitsui Bussan also imported technology, but this role was less substantial than that performed by its worldwide commercial network. That was strongest in commodities and tended to service firms that had only a small, or no, equity relationship to Mitsui. Bussan also marketed products of more technology-intensive firms loosely connected to its zaibatsu, but this distribution, though economically strategic, was not worldwide. It was often restricted by territorial marketing agreements. In one involving automatic looms between Toyoda (the precursor of Toyota) and the successor to the Platt Brothers of England, Toyoda had the upper hand; in another, between General Electric and Toshiba (the successor to Shibaura), the American firm had the advantage.[34] In these examples, the Mitsui-related firms that Bussan serviced had a much looser tie with the Mitsui zaibatsu than Mitsubishi firms had with their zaibatsu. Ironically, insofar as Bussan acted as a mechanism of growth for the firms it serviced, these firms quickly built up their capacity and became more inclined to independence. During the interwar years, then, as a trading company Bussan had less of a long-term integrative role in the Mitsui zaibatsu than did Shōji in Mitsubishi.

Though vertical integration could not be found within the zaibatsu in a structural sense or even in the form of a truly parallel function (given the essentially contractual relationship between separate firms), as a phenomenon it was not entirely absent from prewar Japan. Though Hitachi lacked a multi-divisional structure, the centralized sales function of its head office suggests a form of vertical integration. Nitchitsu provides a slightly different example. Since its subsidiaries were legally separate (though wholly owned), in a strict structural sense it did not follow vertical integration. However, its policy of incorporating subsidiaries seems to have been motivated more by tax considerations than by any disinclination against a vertically integrated strategy. Functionally, this strategy was followed by the head office through its marketing and supply services performed for subsidiaries. Admittedly, trading companies handled its fertilizer distribution, but this probably resulted more from their strength in the domestic market than from any "lapse" in Noguchi's strategy. Furthermore, Nitchitsu as a whole had a kind of hierarchical, multi-unit form. As Molony states, its diversification led to the establishment of "separate facilities for different types of products." Since these were chemically related, some were intermediate products and others by-products, but all moved in a vertically integrated flow that required coordination and monitoring.[35]

Implicitly, the Chandler model also has a close bearing on the issue of industrial structure change, for he treats the large firm as an internal capital market. He states that the "continuing growth of the firm rested on the ability of its managers to transfer resources in marketing, research and development, and production (usually those that were not fully utilized) into new and more profitable related product lines."[36] Nitchitsu's move all the way from fertilizers (which represented a declining portion of its sales) to explosives typifies this transformation. Chandler also argues that such a transformation occurred only after a firm had first integrated production and distribution. Certain Japanese cases represent exceptions to this argument. Toyota, for example, diversified from automatic-loom production to motor vehicles. Its experience is clearly relevant to Chandler's statement if we take the term "related product lines" to include the meaning "technologically convergent," for the production systems Toyota used in making looms shaped its approach to automobile manufacturing. Nevertheless, as a loom maker Toyota did not integrate forward into distribution. It relied instead on Mitsui Bussan, especially for overseas sales. Its diversification is best explained by circumstances within the Toyoda family, the firm's owner.[37]

Most of the examples considered here that differ from the Chandler model are drawn from the prewar period. It is generally conceded, however, that his model is much more applicable to postwar Japan. In particular, there has occurred a strengthening of the managerial hierarchy at the top level as firms have expanded their head offices and committed more to research and development. This trend, together with organizational reforms creating semi-autonomous divisions, as at NEC, and the increase in marketing by manufacturing firms, has brought the structure of postwar firms close to the Chandler model. The case of NEC represents a structural reform designed to exploit new opportunities in a growing market. Since the yen began to rise in value in 1985, however, different trends have motivated structural change. Companies have rapidly diversified to lessen dependence on their traditional products now subject to competition from NICs. The structural outcome of this diversification differs from that of the earlier postwar growth period. A particularly interesting change now underway at New Japan Steel seems to represent a hybrid between a multi-divisional conglomerate and something approaching a prewar-style holding company.[38] The company is setting up 5 semi-autonomous divisions which will maintain their own profit-and-loss accounts and balance sheets. The 5 divisions are: (1) engineering, (2) new materials, (3) electronics, information, and communications, (4) biotechnology, and (5) "life service."[39] Each division will pay dividends on its profits to the head office and interest on loans from it. Apart from the obligation to submit its accounts twice yearly to the executive committee of the company's board, decision-making power on all matters pertaining to each division has been delegated to the division head. The ultimate intent, which is to turn each division into a separate company, invokes the prewar holding-company model.

International Comparisons:
The Family Firm and Industrial Structure

The preceding consideration of the Chandler model has focused more on the internal structure of the firm than on its broader economic context or on the issue of why it evolved as it did. This latter question can be approached though international comparison. Here, too, Chandler's model provides a useful framework. In recent years, his analysis of the large firm has aimed at a comparison of the United States, Britain, and Germany, with some attention to Japan as well. One way of briefly summarizing these concerns is to focus on the interrelated question of the role of the family in big business, the effect that role had on the organization and scale of the firm, and the way the firm has been shaped by the industrial structure. To begin with, the role of the family as a central variable provides a clear contrast among the four countries mentioned here. Family control was relinquished earliest in America. The rate at which it gave way to salaried managers was comparatively rapid in Japan. However, at least in the case of the zaibatsu, the retention of a form of family control, despite the delegation of strategic decision-making authority to salaried managers, resulted in certain contrasts in the makeup of the board of directors. The one most frequently noted is that, in America, salaried managers serving as inside directors appointed outside directors to the board (to represent stockholders), whereas, in Japan, the family (or the holding company as its representative in the case of the zaibatsu) appointed outside directors to the boards of subsidiaries. Since inside managers had come to make the basic strategic decisions, there is some debate about how significant that distinction was. There is general agreement, however, that, of the four countries, family control persisted longest in Britain. Family influence was also strong in Germany, but there it was shared with banks, especially in the nineteenth century, and increasingly thereafter with salaried managers.

The contrast in the degree of family influence around the turn of the century reflects the different types of industries in which each country developed advantages. In the United States, the largest manufacturing firms appeared in industries characterized by mass production and enjoying economies of scale. These included light machinery (which produced for consumers, as in sewing machines, as well as for agriculture and industry), metals, chemicals, and branded and packaged products. Economies of scale in these industries could be achieved through vertical integration, made feasible by the improved transportation system, the rise of managerial hierarchies within the firm, and large market demand. Since these industries grew quickly, retained earnings both lessened the need for external financing and weakened family control. In Germany, the largest firms arose in relatively more capital-intensive industries, such as complex machinery and industrial chemicals. These industries depended more on banks, but they also developed large enough hierarchies that the influence of salaried managers increased. The pattern of German investment also differed from that of the United States in that diversification emerged earlier.[40]

Because family control was strongest in Britain, I have used it as a focus for comparison with Japan, especially with regard to the effect of its persistence on company investment patterns, strategy, and performance. The issue of whether there was a causal connection between the family firm and declining economic performance in Britain continues to spark debate. Views tend to vary considerably with the period under study. There is general consensus that family control delayed a needed restructuring of the economy before World War I, but assessments differ over whether recovery after World War I was sufficient to remove the earlier obstacles. I have divided the following comments, then, by period, touching first on some general patterns from the late nineteenth century to World War I.

Chandler argues strongly that Britain's falling behind the United States in industries of mass production was an "entrepreneurial failure," resulting from the reluctance to make structural changes in the firm which would have led to more integration and the development of managerial hierarchies. Such change, however, would have loosened family control; ingrained tradition militated against that. Even in family firms that did create hierarchical organization, the degree to which authority was actually delegated was greatly restricted by myriad and precise rules. These reflected a kind of U-form structure with continued control from the top, inhibiting—by its potential for "overload"—an extension of the firm's limits.[41]

Examining why such control persisted requires attention to the market, particularly the role of consumer demand. In the late nineteenth century, the large firms in Britain were concentrated in light consumer industries which manufactured clothing or made branded and packaged goods such as soap and foodstuffs (including whiskey and tobacco). One reason family control persisted in these industries was that they did not require large hierarchies or overly substantial amounts of capital. Furthermore, there was no pressing incentive to enlarge the size of the firm by integrating forward, for Britain possessed an efficient network of marketing middlemen whose distribution included both domestic and international spheres.[42]

These characteristics have several superficial parallels in Japan during the same period. There, consumer-related firms producing textiles dominated the list of large manufacturing companies, and the strength of the country's distribution system was such that it acted as a barrier to investment in marketing by producing firms. However, although several other consumer-related industries like food and paper received substantial private investment, most Japanese enterprises in this field were still extremely small. Furthermore, unlike Britain, at the time most consumer goods were "undifferentiated," that is, they were neither branded nor advertised. Though there were exceptions such as Kikkoman soy sauce and Hattori watches, which bore their firm's brand, most branding that did occur was done by the distributor, not by the producer.[43] Also, the Japanese distribution system, with its multi-tiered network of wholesalers, was hardly efficient. There was, too, more of a distinction in Japanese marketing between the domestic and international spheres (a result, of course, of Japan's long isolation), though trading companies had begun to bridge that gap by the 1890s.[44]

These structural and organizational contrasts in consumer industries are dwarfed in significance by the major difference, which was one of demand. Around the turn of the century, Britain was in the middle of a long-term and substantial increase in real consumer expenditure, as food prices were falling and wages and salaries were increasing as a portion of the national income. This trend underlay the rise of large-scale consumer industries and tended to defer any sense of urgency that the country's economy could benefit from restructuring.[45]

Whereas some scholars view this lack of restructuring as an entrepreneurial failure stemming from family control of the firm, Barry Supple suggests that it was a rational short-term response to market choices. His statements offer a striking contrast to Japanese business strategies. He questions "the view that it may have been profitable to avoid radical restructuring of the economy, but that it was ultimately weakening," arguing instead that

just as it is no part of the individual business man's role to anticipate unpredictable developments, so it would hardly have been "natural" for him to forgo [in the 1870–1914 period] opportunities of substantially profitable enterprise in the production of textiles, shipbuilding, and coal at a time when he could do these things extremely well—and profitably. Nor for that matter would it have been "rational" to ignore the potential of overseas investment.

He also qualifies the "entrepreneurial-failure" thesis by contending that the poor performance of an industry "can also derive from an 'exogenous' cause—namely the slow rate of growth of the market."[46] Granted this is a strong statement of classical business principle, even in 1900 many Japanese businessmen, and certainly Japanese economic bureaucrats, were prepared to take a longer-term view of the need for strategic planning. Fundamentally, though, the proposition that there was too small a market for alternative products is contrary to the assumptions on which the entrepreneurial-failure thesis is based. Chandler makes a telling point about the British textile industry which emphasizes the failure to respond to potential demand. In the 1870s, it constituted the world's largest market for dyes, but, within a brief period, Germany had come to dominate the new dye industry. Supple's argument also reflects the laissez-faire mentality of the 1900 era in overlooking the possibility that government promotional policies might trigger demand. This is perhaps his statement's clearest contrast with Japanese policies of that period.[47]

The sense of security that the wealth of Britain's consumer industries generated raises basic questions about investment decisions and what they meant for the long-term organization of the firm, national competitiveness, and industrial structure. Britain certainly had the funds to undertake restructuring toward more science-based and technologically advanced industries, but, as a leading scholar of British industrialization has observed, "capital formation does not matter as much as capital utilization."[48] This view raises questions, first, about the role of the British capital market and whether it was less effective in encouraging innovation than were large corporations in America and industrial banks in Germany. Britain's capital market was not only large and highly developed but also diverse. Options available to a firm for raising capital ranged from stock-exchange issues, to insurance companies, and even to family managers with special financial skills. In contrast to Germany and the United States, at least until the 1930s there was less need to rely on investment bankers or industrial banks which might have attained a controlling interest over a family firm. Hence, the range of financial options may have sustained family control.[49]

Second, as noted above, family control was strong in Britain's consumer industries. By contrast, Japan's leading textile firms were joint-stock companies and largely free of zaibatsu ownership. As Morikawa indicates, by 1900 they had become increasingly dependent on the expertise of salaried managers. Yet, they were often hard-pressed for funds, especially in the 1890 crisis when banks cut off the supply of short-term financing. At that point, trading companies began providing trade credit, but in general Japan's capital market was small by international standards. One effect of the difficulty of raising large sums was to induce cooperation between producing firms and both suppliers of raw materials and distributors. This type of cooperation, often referred to as organized entrepreneurship and especially important in overseas trade, can be thought of as organization substituting for capital. For the firm, too, it acted as a substitute for investment in internal facilities and thus is related to the lack of vertical integration. This point is important for the issue of capital utilization noted above. For example, Leslie Hannah suggests that British textile firms, despite their standing as among the largest in the world, were relatively unsuccessful "in integrating the various vertically related activities to achieve cost reduction and marketing success."[50] This seems to strengthen the thesis that effective Japanese organization sometimes canceled out Britain's advantages in access to capital.

The interwar years, however, present a more ambiguous picture. One perspective sees Britain as a "latecomer" in technical industries that was catching up in the interwar period.[51] Others recognize improvements but emphasize the persistence of conservative business organization. In the 1920s, rapidly growing industries emerged, especially in rayon, automobiles, electrical engineering, and the modern sectors for the chemical trade. In automobiles, Morris increased its share of the domestic market from 5 percent in 1919 to 41 percent in 1925, while overall the country's growth rate exceeded that of the "stagnant" decades before World War I. There seem to have been two major factors behind this growth. One was a rapid change in industrial organization which saw greater concentration and reduced competition. This led to a rationalization of old plant and new investment. A large number of mergers created economies of scale, making British firms more competitive not only against foreign companies in the domestic market, but also overseas as multinationals. A second factor, to some extent made possible by the first, was business reorganization, as some firms developed hierarchies by recruiting managers from outside and by investing in non-manufacturing facilities. Hannah, stressing these "qualitative innovations," argues that "the case for a clear shift in industrial practices in the 1920s is overwhelming."[52]

Despite these innovations, another scholar contends that the negative impact of the family firm on Britain's economic vitality was felt decisively not in the late nineteenth century but in the interwar years.[53] This view stresses ambivalent features of the merger movement which are seen as undermining some of the positive results of increased concentration. In particular, rather than leading to rationalization, many mergers took the shape of federations where the family firm as a constituent continued many of its former practices. This type of merger seems to have been more common just before, rather than after, World War I when centralized structures became more evident. The question, then, centers on the lingering effect of the family. Even in some of the largest firms, such as Courtaulds, the world leader in rayon, family influence remained substantial down to World War II. This, then, may be related to the view that Courtauld's management organization was inadequate. On a more general level, critics of the time noted a continued lag in science-based industries. The evidence from the 1930s remained mixed. During the decade, Britain achieved a growth rate considered high relative to leading Western industrial nations. But questions remain about its leading industries. The two fastest growing were electrical engineering and automobiles. Of these, the former had a substantial American component and the latter appears to have bypassed opportunities to reduce costs. The second tier of growth firms included traditional industries such as food and tobacco that had a consumer orientation and strong family influence. Finally, there were some promising trends, for example, financial interests turning away somewhat from overseas investments and focusing more on domestic industry. The government also played a helpful role in the reorganization of the steel industry in the 1930s; however, that industry, too, remained small by American and German standards.[54]

Industrial Organization and Industrial Policy:
Further Comparisons

Japan's industrial organization and policies shared certain common phenomena with Europe during the 1920s and 1930s. These included rationalization movements, increased industrial concentration, and tariff hikes. The effects and characteristics of these phenomena in some cases were similar, in others different. As in Britain, the trend toward concentration in Japan brought some reduction in competition. This was manifested in the form of cartels, especially in the early 1930s. Cartelization did not, however, develop nearly as strongly as in Germany, partly because the presence of the zaibatsu discouraged strong independent industrial cartels. In a similar vein, the merger movement in Japan among large firms was less extensive than in Britain, again partly because of the zaibatsu. The legal context explains much of the difference between Germany and Britain on this issue. In Germany, the government not only encouraged cartels; the courts removed obstacles to them. In Britain, the large number of mergers was in part a reaction to restrictions against cartels.

Amalgamations seem to have occurred in three forms in Japan. One was akin to takeovers of bankrupt firms in consequence of the 1923 earthquake and especially the 1927 bank crisis. The circumstances of these mergers meant that some rationalization had already occurred before ownership changed hands, while the purchasing firm probably had more leeway to effect further measures than in the case of many of the British mergers. A major cause of these developments was the bankruptcy of Suzuki Shōten. It had a counterpart in Britain in the collapse of the Royal Mail Line. Both these bankruptcies grew out of an overestimation of the postwar shipping market, both were characterized by scandal and financial manipulation, and both firms had been strongly owner- or family-dominated.[55] However, Suzuki probably left behind more enterprises with long-term growth potential, especially in chemicals and synthetic fibers. A second type of merger followed a long-term trend toward horizontal concentration, as in the cotton spinning industry and electric utilities. A third type was the result of prolonged negotiations with an explicit motive to effect rationalization. In the steel industry, this process was indeed more effective in Japan than in Britain, though much of the rationalization had already occurred before the formation of Japan Steel in

1934.[56] The Japanese policy during the interwar years of attempting to implement rationalization and increase competitiveness by establishing large firms through mergers was itself heavily influenced by foreign models. Its attractiveness as a policy stemmed perhaps more from the strong precedent for it overseas than from any genuine necessity for it at home. The influence of the foreign, especially German, model certainly helps to explain Kagami's attempt to merge the N.Y.K. and the O.S.K.

Of greater long-term importance to Japan than cartel or merger policy was the rise of new firms during this period, such as Nitchitsu, Hitachi, Nissan, and Toyota. Like older enterprises, these young companies benefited from new ideas concerning technological improvement and production management promoted during the rationalization movement. Britain had its share of new post-World War I growth firms as well, but their impact on the business world came earlier, in the 1920s, than the Japanese enterprises mentioned here. Given some of the reservations about the efficiency and management of these British firms during the 1930s, it may be that the rationalization movement was more effective in Japan than in Britain.

Another contrast between Britain and Japan involved foreign capital. On the one hand, in both countries its effects were clearly favorable. In Britain, the influx of American capital and technology was partly responsible for the productivity improvements and technical progress achieved by the growing firms of the 1920s.[57] Still, no matter how beneficial there, the impact of foreign technology was clearly less decisive in Britain than in Japan. Especially during the 1920s, it was absolutely indispensable for development in Japan's electrical industry. This makes all the more ironic the autonomous route Japan chose in the 1930s in trying to reduce the presence of foreign capital. It also points to an ambivalence in government industrial policy. In the 1920s, both the movement to encourage domestic production (*kokusanka*) and access to foreign capital and technology were part of the government-promoted rationalization movement. This explains why the movement had the strong support of pro-Western government leaders like Inoue Junnosuke. Apropos of this, Kozo Yamamura has argued convincingly that the types of protectionist policies Japan adopted in the 1920s, the development of more autonomous, nationalistic measures in the 1930s, and the growth of military capability were all necessarily dependent on the increased competence gained by the electrical industry through the tie-ups with Western firms in the 1920s.[58]

A related question, hinted at but not pursued by Yamamura, is the role of tariff policy. Granted that the foreign-inspired technological competence to which he refers was a necessary condition for the nationalistic policies of the 1930s, was it also sufficient? Or, was sufficiency attained only through tariffs? Even the short-term impact of the substantial 1926 tariff increase on the electrical industry (especially on electric generators and electric motors) is hard to evaluate because of the statistical aberration created by the earthquake that preceded it and the 1927 bank crisis that followed it. By 1928, however, domestic production of heavy electrical machinery was at about the same level as in 1926, but imports were off by half. The tariff certainly affected marketing patterns. Through the mid-1920s, Mitsui Bussan marketed for both General Electric and its Japanese partner, Shibaura. The 1926 tariff was one important reason why Mitsui and other trading companies shifted their marketing more toward domestic firms. Thus, the share of domestic firms in Mitsui's distribution of electrical products increased from 25 percent in 1921 to 70 percent in 1928.[59] A further round of tariff hikes followed in 1932, the same year that Britain departed from some of its laissez-faire principles to impose import duties.

The study of Japanese tariff policy during the 1920s requires a closer look at the influence of Germany, the leader in the use of protective tariffs. Recent Western historiography has paid considerable attention to the impact of German social and economic thought on Japan's social and labor policies.[60] It is arguable that the German influence may have been even greater on Japanese industrial policy. However, this particular influence has received little emphasis in studies written in English. The German model extended beyond specific policies like rationalization, cartels, trusts, and tariffs to the more general realm of government-business cooperation. Particularly important was the German concept of "organized capitalism." This was rooted in the ties between private business monopolies and the state. Analysis of it embraced issues like protectionism, the role of business federations and cartels, and the dominating influence of large financial institutions. Much of the writing about this concept had a strong Marxist element, and in fact the term itself had been coined in 1915 by a leading Marxist theorist, Rudolf Hilferding. This background may help to explain the confluence in Japan of bureaucratic planning and Marxist ideology which became important in economic policy formation in the 1930s.[61]

Industrial policies Japan pursued in the 1920s, such as tariff increases, cartels, rationalization, and support for the use of domestic products, had their Western counterparts. Some extensions of these policies in the 1930s also resembled measures taken abroad. Yet, the comprehensive intensity of industrial policy after 1931 was at least distinctive, if not unique. This included tax laws, foreign-exchange controls, cartels, the rollback of foreign capital, numerous other measures to promote strategic industries, and, of course, the devaluation of the yen, which, together with the rationalization measures of the 1920s, prompted the subsequent export boom. After 1937–1938, comparison with other countries is complicated by the common need for mobilization. Other countries may have implemented that more effectively, but the broad phalanx of industrial policy that accompanied Japan's mobilization left a stronger institutional legacy for the postwar period. The effect of the measures taken between 1931 and 1945 will long be debated because their causative implications are ambiguous. To take one example, Toyota benefited from military-inspired protectionism in the mid-1930s but, in the late 1930s, the military stopped it from doing what it wanted, which was building passenger cars.[62]

The study of the history of Japanese industrial policy is still young, especially in the West. On the one hand, analyses of the prewar period have probably not incorporated, at least in a systematic way, sufficient comparative perspective, say along the lines suggested above regarding Germany. On the other hand, postwar studies seem rooted in general dichotomies which reflect the comparative dimension. Specifically, American government policies toward industry are regarded as regulatory, in contrast to Japanese policies which are viewed as promotional or developmental. One can accept the general thrust of this argument while noting important exceptions. In certain cases, Japanese industry-specific policies have had a strong regulatory component, while U.S. measures have suffered from the absence of regulation integrated with comprehensive policy goals. A comparison between the Japanese shipping industry and the U.S. automobile industry can illustrate this point. Since the 1870s, Japanese subsidies to shipping have been accompanied by restrictions on diversification. In the postwar period, these have taken the form of limitations on the capital that may be invested in non-related business enterprise. Overall, one might say that this regulation has been good for shipping but not so good for the individual firm. The restriction on investment strategy has meant a gradual decline in the size of shipping companies relative to other Japanese firms. In the 1980s, quotas on imports of Japanese automobiles, a kind of industry-specific American industrial policy, enabled U.S. firms to reap huge profits. Perhaps the major consequences of this policy, especially for General Motors, were an increase in its *overseas* auto production and diversification into non-related business, especially its purchase of Hughes Aircraft. Had "Japanese-style" industrial policy been applied in this case, it probably would have included regulation to restrict General Motors' use of profits generated by quotas by confining them more to the auto industry. Thus, in contrast to the Japanese shipping industry, the American policy may have been good for the firm but bad for the industry.[63]

HISTORIOGRAPHY

Business History and Marxism in the Japanese Academic Setting

Over the past two decades, business history in Japan has succeeded in establishing its own identity separate from that of other branches of economic history. However, no one studying Japanese business or economic history can afford to overlook Marxist historiography, either for its influence over much of this century or for the large amount of excellent work being published by its current practitioners. Marxism is still the most commonly used methodology among economic historians in Japan. Thus, it is necessary to have some knowledge of Marxist theory, in particular the technical meaning of certain terms, to understand interpretations presented and to avoid distortion in the meaning of factual detail which can easily be pulled out of its interpretive context. The intent of this section is not to provide an evaluation, critique, or even explanation of Japanese Marxist historiography but rather to highlight certain ways in which it may have inhibited an earlier development of business history and to give some examples of its approaches to problems of concern to business historians.

The starting point for any discussion of Marxist historiography is the classical prewar debate over the significance of the Meiji Restoration between the two factions known as the Kōza-ha (Lectures Faction) and the Rōnō-ha (Labor-Farmer Faction). Having been treated elsewhere, however, this requires only a brief comment here.[64] The Kōza-ha contended that Japanese capitalism was too backward to effect a bourgeois revolution during the Restoration. Instead, in a kind of transitional phase which they called absolutism, it had to share power with feudal elements which, among other phenomena, included the emperor system and an oppressive landlord system. The Rōnō-ha, on the other hand, argued that Japan had indeed experienced a bourgeois revolution and that capitalism was sufficiently advanced to have obtained a primacy over the state, which was its "instrument." The Kōza-ha's emphasis on feudal elements led it over the years to stress Japan's distinctive features, whereas the Rōnō-ha paid more attention to the universal aspects of Japanese capitalism.[65] Generally, Kōza-ha interpretations were seen as offering a more convincing explanation of Japan's interwar crisis that led to war, and it became the majority faction. Over the last few decades, the concerns about the Restoration era have given way to debates about later periods, which focus on issues of timing, such as when the development of modern capitalism reached the stages defined by Marxist theory (industrial capital and finance capital, for example).

Though there was substantial diversity within the prewar Kōza-ha, in postwar Japan the Rōnō-ha has experienced more ideological innovation, perhaps because of its eclectic nature. In recent years, the influence of the Kōza-ha within the field of economic history has been in decline, in large part because of the statistical work of quantitative economic historians, especially Nakamura Takafusa.[66] In subjects like political history, though, the Kōza-ha has maintained its strength. Even within economic history, despite increasing diversity of views, it retains the loyalty of many scholars, who in the introductions to their books continue to refer to the prewar debate as a kind of permanent standard which defines the fundamental issues.[67] In the West, however, time quickly bypassed the original participants in these prewar debates and what remained influential after the war were works of popularizers: for example, Takahashi Kamekichi, who had criticized the prewar left by applying a Marxist framework to the problem of Japan's "encirclement" by Western powers;[68] and Suzuki

Mosaburō, a Rōnō-ha financial specialist, journalist, and politician who later became Chairman of the Socialist Party. Both wrote numerous books about the zaibatsu which included useful information on internal finances, market shares, and individual zaibatsu managers, though both saw the zaibatsu as representatives of "finance capital" without recognizing the decision-making powers of these managers. Their works, together with numerous early postwar studies, especially by Rōnō-ha writers like Tsuchiya Takao and Kajinishi Mitsuhaya, constituted the main sources for what business history there was in the West prior to 1970.[69]

The dominance of Marxism within Japanese universities during the early postwar years constituted an inhospitable intellectual environment for the emergence of business history. Several issues can illustrate the way Marxism has relegated questions important to business historians to sub-categories peripheral to theoretical approaches to the development of capitalism. First, the Kōza-ha emphasis on Japan's "backwardness" tended to channel historical inquiry more toward the political or social dimension of economic history. Yamada Moritarō, the Kōza-ha author frequently cited as the faction's most representative writer on the late Meiji period, viewed Japanese capitalism as based on a semi-feudal landlord structure and the military-led character of the emperor system. Private monopoly, he argued, had yet to overcome its fundamental dependence on the state. Thus, the combination of state capital (kokka shihon) and the military was dominant, while private capital fell short of an autonomous existence. This thesis tended to deflect inquiry away from private business, and, in his own discussion of zaibatsu capital, Yamada provided little in the way of specific detail.[70]

A second issue, stage theory, deserves more attention, because it is common to all Marxist approaches and because it has undergone important theoretical changes among Rōnō-ha scholars. Marxist convention usually periodizes the development of capitalism in three stages: commercial capitalism (the period of primitive accumulation), industrial capital, and finance capital (the stage of monopoly, or imperialism). The Kōza-ha has tended to subdivide the industrial-capital stage into a period of formation (seiritsu-ki) and a period of establishment (kakuritsu-ki).[71] (Yamada dates the establishment period of industrial capital as 1897–1907 and the early phase of finance capital as 1906–1917.)

New approaches to stage theory were developed in the 1930s by Uno Kōzō, a scholar who shared the Rōnō-ha's assessment of the Restoration but who was actually a critic of both factions. Partly because of censorship, he did not publish much before the war, but his postwar writings so influenced the Rōnō-ha that the term Uno-faction (Uno-ha) is now frequently used instead of "Rōnō-ha." Uno's main contribution to this issue was to move it into a more worldwide dimension that would accommodate diversity of experience in different countries.[72] His stage theory sought to find the historically dominant type of capital accumulation, and for each stage he chose a classical type, that is, a representative industry most characteristic of the particular stage.[73] He identified the three stages as (1) mercantilism (the period of primitive accumulation), represented by British wool manufacturing because of the way merchant capital accumulated through the organization of manufacturing as a putting-out system that gradually became separate from agriculture but that relied on state support for its interest in international trade; (2) liberalism (period of industrial capital), represented by British cotton manufacturing which saw the "commodification" of labor, the development of the factory system, and reliance on the market mechanism; (3) imperialism (period of finance capital), represented by the German steel industry, which led to the development of monopolies that began to supplant the market mechanism but that required state intervention to protect their large long-term investments. The resulting state economic policies led to imperialism.

In Uno's typology, however, the effort to *characterize* each stage seems to forego analysis of movement between stages, change that could be illuminated by reference to business strategy. Within Uno's framework, inquiry is governed too exclusively by the concepts of stage and dominant type. For example, "stage theory is essentially static since it aims to grasp the dominant type of capital accumulation and not actual historical change and development."[74] One effect of this is expressed as follows:

"Finance-capital" is a pure-type concept in the sense that the historical reality of finance-capital always involves local peculiarities. Although German steel may be the purest example, in its empirical concreteness it involves its own peculiar details and irrelevant contingencies. So we theorize the German steel industry as a *type* of organization and operation of capitalist accumulation and not as a detailed descriptive history.[75]

Stage theory, as defined here, had led Japanese historians to focus on the zaibatsu and to assess the strength of their financial power in judging whether this had led Japanese capitalism at a given time into a particular stage. The concern with stages encouraged the tendency to identify a "classical type." At least until recently, this has concentrated inquiry on monopolies at the expense of other industrial issues. Finally, in both the "backwardness" theme of Yamada and the stage theory of Uno, analysis of company decision making—the heart of business history—has no central place. In particular, the basic issue of the decision-making role of managers is ignored within the principal category of financial capital and control.

These theoretical considerations represent reasons why Marxism may have discouraged the emergence of business history. In addition, there are certain institutional features that help to explain the continued influence of Marxism in Japanese economic history. Some of these are associated with Tokyo University, a bastion of Marxism in economic history. This statement applies to the Economics Faculty, the Institute of Social Science, and the Historiographical Institute. Such a large faculty representation also means that most books on economic history published by the university's press incorporate a Marxist approach. Finally, unlike certain universities where business history is popular within faculties of business administration, Tōdai has no such separate faculty. Business historians (what few there are) at Tōdai teach in the Economics Faculty where their influence seems to be a kind of second rank, despite the facts that two of the four chairmen of the Japanese Business History Society hailed from the faculty and that the society's offices are located there. A more general point in a similar vein concerns academic exchange. Although there are a substantial number of important exceptions, in general, relative to other groups of economic historians, such as quantitative economic historians or business historians, Marxists have had less long-term experience, institutional affiliation, or informal scholarly contact at the international level. This may have discouraged a broadening of their perspective and, as I will argue below, deprived Westerners of valuable insight.

While it seems undeniable that Marxism has, in an absolute sense, inhibited the rise of business history in Japan, there remains considerable doubt about how much of a lag this has caused relative to other countries. For example, in Britain, the first university post exclusively in business history was created in 1959; the British journal *Business History* began its publication in 1958. In Japan, the first university course in business history was given in 1951, and the *Japan Business History Review* (*Keiei shigaku*) was first issued in 1965.[76] Though American business history could be said to have started several decades earlier, the comparison with Britain does not indicate a very considerable Japanese delay by some international standards. On the other hand, comparison at the national level suggests not so much that Japanese business history alone was a "late-developing" discipline but rather that Marxism tended to create a lag in all forms of non-Marxist economic history in Japan. Even today, although quantitative economic historians have a decade or two of experience behind them, they are still small in number relative to Marxist economic historians.

In business history, however, this lag cannot be attributed to Marxism alone. In Western Japanese studies, where Marxism has negligible influence, business history has emerged much more slowly than in Japan. A case can be made that modern economists, writing as historians, have also inhibited the development of business history, especially with their concentration on macroeconomics and aggregate analysis and their commitment to the neoclassical view of the firm. To business historians, the work of Aoki in modifying this view seems less a conceptual breakthrough than an insight long overdue. In this sense, there has been a considerable "lag" within modern economic theory itself—so much so in fact that, despite the above remarks on Marxist theory, the concerns of business historians have often been closer to the subject matter of Marxists historians than to that of the modern economists. Generally speaking, Marxists tend to deal more with the "history" side of economic history, while modern economists focus on its "economic" side; however, virtually all Westerners presently studying Japanese business history come from history departments. Furthermore, within Japan there are a number of Marxist historians whose primary field of research is business history, and in recent years the younger, more flexible economic historians who write within the Marxist framework have begun to incorporate the findings of business historians into their own work.[77]

These last points are unlikely to lead to an "historical reconciliation," but they suggest that, despite the differences between business historians and Marxists in their modes of questioning, their paths of inquiry sometimes meet at a junction at which conclusions, though expressed in different terminologies, can be mutually supporting. This can be illustrated through the work of Shibagaki Kazuo, a Rōnō-ha scholar who published a major "Analysis of Japanese Finance Capital" in 1965.[78] As the first academic work to use the Mitsubishi Company Records[79] and several new sources from Mitsui, this book was widely acclaimed for the new information it provided on the zaibatsu. In this work, Shibagaki applied Uno's stage theory to the development of Japanese capitalism. On the one hand, Shibagaki recognized the zaibatsu as a Japanese form of finance capital, but his other conclusion, which has been more debated, saw cotton manufacturing as independent of the zaibatsu, as a "second pole" of finance capital, the horizontal-style industrial monopoly organization which grew out of the cotton spinners cartel. It thus differed from the organizational structure of the zaibatsu, but its horizontal-style monopoly structure within a specific industry was a feature common to German and American finance capital. In Japan, however, this structure arose in the light industrial sector. Drawing on Uno's stage theory, Shibagaki concluded that "generally in advanced countries a textile industry such as cotton manufacturing reaches a position of controlling influence in the stage of liberalism and has fallen into decline with the transition to the stage of imperialism. However, in Japan, even in this latter stage, together with the zaibatsu it formed one of the two poles of dominant capital."[80]

Shibagaki's critics, who included both business and Kōza-ha historians, charged him with confining his analysis to Uno's stage theory and ignoring (1) the role of state capital, especially its ties with zaibatsu capital in the connection between the latter's coal monopoly and the government-funded steel industry, which was seen as a major factor in Japan's imperialism; and (2) the influence the zaibatsu had over the cotton industry through equity, financing, purchasing and distribution, and transport.[81] Shibagaki's central thesis was soon labeled "cotton imperialism" (*mengyō teikokushugi*) as it was developed in his later work and in the writing of Nishikawa Hiroshi, who collected more documentation abroad on the industry's exports and direct investments and focused on what he viewed as the transition from the industry's monopoly capital structure to its surplus capital and capital exports to China.[82]

As discussed in Steven Ericson's paper, Chandler defined modern enterprises in three ways: as (1) personal, family, or entrepreneurial, (2) financial, in which outside representatives exercise considerable influence, and (3) managerial, in which managers have control.[83] Now, if for the sake of argument, we accepted the views of Shibagaki's critics, then, because of the evidence of control from outside, we might have to regard the cotton spinning industry as an example of a financial enterprise rather than an entrepreneurial, or fledgling managerial, enterprise. On the other hand, if we recognized Shibagaki's position that cotton spinning capital was independent, then we could regard the industry's firms as managerial enterprises, or at least moving in that direction as salaried managers increased their influence vis-à-vis the original entrepreneurs or current stockholders and creditors. Some see this issue less as a dichotomy, as expressed here, than as a process through two stages. In the first stage, beginning in the 1890s, the industry was characterized by a pattern of dependency not only on services provided by zaibatsu-affiliated enterprises (especially Mitsui Bussan and the N.Y.K.) but also on state support in the form of shipping subsidies, railway rebates, Yokohama Specie Bank trade finance, bill rediscounting by the Bank of Japan, and emergency relief financing (1898) from the Japan Hypothec Bank. Frequent mergers between 1900 and World War I, however, reduced the number of firms, creating economies of scale (through the formation of monopoly structure) that improved export performance. Return from this increased retained earnings and the percentage of owned capital and reduced dependence on financing from banks and trading companies as well as the share of zaibatsu-held equity (Mitsui's share in Kanegafuchi had fallen to 2 percent by 1909, for example). With increasing advantages of monopoly, the industry strengthened its cartel organization, began to export capital in the form of direct investments in China, and developed a monopolistic structure that was independent of zaibatsu control.[84]

There is, however, a limit to the extent to which we can regard the Marxist framework in this case as operating parallel to the questions of business historians. The key variable is in the Kōza-ha assumption that the various contracts with zaibatsu-related trading companies and shipping firms automatically put the cotton spinning industry in a position of dependency or subordination. Business historians are more likely to view these contracts as a relationship of mutual advantage. If mutuality rather than dependency was their principal characteristic, these contracts could still accommodate the view that, even in the first stage mentioned here, cotton spinning firms were becoming, albeit haltingly, managerial enterprises. Still, this distinction is probably fine enough that the evidence and arguments of both schools can be mutually helpful.

Two other related controversies that concern the issues discussed in this volume can be noted briefly. First, Matsumoto Hiroshi has argued that Mitsui Bussan acted as an "organizer" of Japan's "late developing industrial capital." In the process, the distribution monopoly it established strengthened the financial base of the Mitsui zaibatsu, which in turn was instrumental in the transformation of zaibatsu capital into a monopoly structure.[85] Despite the Marxist terminology, the underlying phenomena in this case are clearly related to the issue of vertical integration (or lack thereof) and the extent of Mitsui Bussan's coordinating role within the Mitsui zaibatsu. Second, a sub-controversy of the "cotton-imperialism" debate concerns the views of Shibagaki and others that Japan's heavy and chemical industries were weak and backward. (This assumption partly explains their focus on cotton manufacturing as the representative industry in the stage of imperialism.) As opposed to this, Hashimoto Jurō has placed more emphasis on the strength of Japanese heavy industry and its role in changing the industrial structure in the 1930s. Hashimoto also draws the important distinction between the export dependency of the textile industry and the domestic demand-led growth of heavy industry.[86] For this volume, this controversy is especially relevant to Molony's paper, which draws on work by Hashimoto on the chemical industry.

A final dimension of Marxist influence concerns regional variations within Japanese historiography. In the 1930s, partly as a reaction to the debate on capitalism, there arose a school of economic history known as the "Kyoto School." The leaders of this group were Honjō Eijirō and, later, Horie Yasuzō, who are well known to Western scholars through translations. This school has had an important influence in the development of business history in Japan, though less because of a particular ideological stance than by a continuity of interest through several generations of professors. Some view the emergence of this school partly as an anti-Kantō reaction in the sense that Marxism was stronger in the Tokyo area. However, it did not entirely reject Marxist categories. For example, it retained the stage approach, focusing on the transition from commercial to industrial capitalism in its studies of Tokugawa and early Meiji economic history. The school's two principal subjects were Tokugawa commerce and social dimensions of early business organizations. These fields of interest are associated especially with Miyamoto Mataji (the representative "successor" to Honjō), who was also the second chairman of the Japan Business History Society, and Yasuoka, the fourth, and present, chairman. This background is important for explaining why Yasuoka and the Kantō-based Morikawa have developed somewhat different views about the relations between owners and managers. Yasuoka's outlook was shaped by the emphasis within the Kyoto School on social history and social continuities to the modern period. These concerns influenced his early book on zaibatsu history, which was the first example of a major work in Japanese business history.[87] On the other hand, Morikawa's views represent more of a reaction against Marxism and its emphasis on finance capital, which assumes owner control over management.

Business Historians, Societies, and Journals

As suggested above, one way to examine the rise of business history in Japan is to consider the careers of the chairmen of the Business History Society. So far, the chairmanship has alternated between the Kantō and the Kansai. Miyamoto and Yasuoka represented the latter. The first and third holders of the office were Wakimura Yoshitarō and Nakagawa Keiichirō.

Wakimura taught the first course in Japan in business history in 1951, but he is important more for the way his scholarly and public careers have been intertwined, both before and after the war.[88] Though he is not well known in the West, he has been one of the most politically influential economics professors in postwar Japan. This can be understood only in the context of his prewar career. As a scholar he was known for his eclectic interests, and he never stayed with one subject long enough to produce a major book. Perhaps his greatest strength was his knowledge of the mutual ties between different industries and his emphasis on the technical and technological features of each industry he taught. Nakagawa, who was briefly his student in the late 1940s, was influenced by these approaches, especially as he developed the concept of organized entrepreneurship in the 1960s.[89] As an assistant professor at Tokyo University in the 1920s, Wakimura studied mainly trade, shipping and marine insurance. He had also begun, however, to examine the problem of trusts and cartels in both America and Germany. His work on monopolies and the American anti-trust movement led him naturally to the role of oil. The subject of oil became the fulcrum that united his earlier research on shipping with his new interests in trusts.[90] This was at a time of technological change in shipbuilding, as diesel ships were being introduced, which used oil for fuel. This research, which had soon embraced the technologies of shipbuilding and several related industries, came to a halt in February 1938, shortly after he had returned to Japan from two years of study abroad, when he was arrested in the Professors' Group Incident, an offshoot of the government's attack on the Rōnō-ha-affiliated Popular Front Movement in late 1937.[91]

Because of this incident, Wakimura was suspended from Tōdai, but, during the war, he worked in the Foreign Ministry doing research on oil, shipping, and fuel policy. Later, observing the Allied policies toward monopolies in the occupation of Germany after its surrender in May 1945, he began to anticipate the policies that an American occupation might take toward Japan's zaibatsu. Thus, as a Foreign Ministry official he held discussions with Mitsui and Mitsubishi, which sought his advice in September 1945, before the Occupation took its first steps against the zaibatsu. From this position, and with his earlier research, it was a short step toward his appointment as one of the two Japanese academic members of the Holding Company Liquidation Commission (the other being Minobe Ryōkichi), which subsequently administered the dissolution of the zaibatsu holding companies and the reorganization of some of the operating companies. While his colleague Minobe later became famous as the Socialist governor of Tokyo, Wakimura gravitated to the Liberal Democratic Party where he was sometimes known as an adviser to Miki Takeo. His most important government role, however, was in advisory commissions, especially in the mid-1960s when he was primarily responsible for the plan adopted to reorganize the shipping industry. Work in these official capacities points to a key dimension of Wakimura's career, namely, that both as a scholar and an official he straddled the two fields of business history and industrial organization. Very few scholars achieve that combination of fields today.

Wakimura's activity in the shipping industry was undertaken shortly after he retired from Tōdai and at about the same time that he became the first chairman of the Business History Society. In subsequent years he retained a strong influence among many company presidents across a range of industries. Without these contacts it is hard to see how, for example, the society's annual International Conference on Business History (popularly known as the Fuji Conference) could have been inaugurated in 1974.

If Wakimura acted as a kind of godfather to the society, Nakagawa Keiichirō became its principal organizer. He took the initiative in planning for various conferences, programs for international exchange, and publishing projects. As a business historian, Nakagawa was influenced by two approaches developed at Harvard University in the 1950s. The first concerned research in entrepreneurial history, stressing an interdisciplinary methodology but focusing particularly on cultural factors. The second was an organizational approach which later came to be associated primarily with Alfred Chandler. As an economic historian, in his choice of research topics which emphasized trade, the mutual ties among industries, and technology, Nakagawa borrowed heavily from Wakimura. In his early years, however, Nakagawa was known primarily as a comparative historian. While his experience in the United States and under Wakimura both contributed to this, perhaps the most decisive influence derived from his seminar professor, Ōtsuka Hisao, a Kōza-ha scholar who applied Weberian methodology to economic, social, and cultural history within a comparative perspective.[92] Nakagawa thus had a diverse intellectual heritage. Never a confrontational scholar, rather than exclusively adopting one of these methodologies, he tried to accommodate all of them (except the Marxism of Ōtsuka) in developing an integrated approach.[93] He thus acquired a broader range as an economic historian than most of today's younger business historians.[94]

Another influence on Nakagawa, the model of late development associated with Alexander Gerschenkron, deserves mention not just for how Nakagawa used it but for how others have applied it to Japan. The Gerschenkron model was formulated primarily to show how the pattern of development in "backward" European countries differed from that of earlier-developing economies, especially Britain's.[95] Among other points, the model suggested that "backwardness" would lead to a greater role for the state in the process of development and would encourage the choice of certain technologies (modern and labor-saving ones). Some economic historians have expressed frustration that Gerschenkron's highly generalized arguments are not easily susceptible to quantitative testing. However, in European history, statistical tests that have been conducted frequently conclude that the model does not apply.[96] In the case of Japan, even a scholar like Minami Ryoshin, who generally supports the use of the model, finds numerous examples in the adaptation of technology and the choice of industry (textiles) in early development which either differed from the model or placed Japan closer to the British than the continental European pattern.[97] The point that needs emphasizing is that many non-Marxist Japanese business and economic historians found the Gerschenkron model attractive in part because it shared with the Kōza-ha, though with different assumptions, a focus on backwardness. Though business historians welcomed it as freeing them "from the restraints of traditional stage theories,"[98] the Gerschenkron model too has a deterministic quality in the sense that it tends to encourage a fixed or preset way of asking questions about Japan's development. Furthermore, often Western scholars who use late-development models to interpret Japanese history derive their original inspiration from Gerschenkron but their factual evidence from Kōza-ha writing, without realizing that the general framework of Kōza-ha analysis, which governed the selection of facts, may already have been rejected by subsequent Japanese scholars.

The Business History Society's organ, *Keiei shigaku*, is one of two periodicals that provide coverage of business history in Japan. The second, the *Journal of Social and Economic History* (*Shakai keizai shigaku*) offers a broader range of subjects in the history of trade and in industrial and economic history. That Nakagawa himself was its editor from 1965 to 1971 testifies to his range of interests. This journal also accommodates a wider variety of views, methodology, and ideology than the *Keiei shigaku*. One way of demonstrating this is to consider the diverse specialties of the three editors the journal has had over the past decade. Hayami Akira is the leader of Japan's school of quantitative demographic history with a strong influence in the West. Yonekawa Shin'ichi, a comparative business historian whose principal work is in cotton manufacturing, seems equally at home in either of the two journals. Unlike his two predecessors, the present editor, Ishii Kanji, writes within the Marxist framework. Over the past fifteen years, he has been one of Japan's most prolific and diversified economic historians with work on finance, banking, industry, industrial structure, and trade. His principal research, which provides a focus combining the international context of Japan's trade with the country's industrial structure and distribution system, especially at the time of the Restoration, is likely to encourage similar studies not only because of its depth of archival research and complex argumentation but for its thematic resonance with present international issues.[99]

The Company History

A scholar entering the field of Japanese business history should have no trouble gaining basic preliminary information about his subject because of the large number of company histories now available. In the postwar period, the writing of these histories has gone through two stages. Most appearing in the first stage, which lasted till roughly the early 1970s, were compiled as in-house publications. In the second stage, companies began to commission scholars. This tendency has become so common that now relatively few histories are compiled in house. It has resulted in a more liberal access to company archives and the appearance of numerous well-researched company histories. In industries where a large percentage of companies have published histories, analytical comparison between these firms and generalizations about the industry as a whole have been facilitated. These histories, however, remain subject to considerable controversy. Typical of attitudes toward them still prevailing among Western scholars is a view offered a decade ago by Yoshi Tsurumi: "Many Japanese firms publish anniversary issues of their firm's history. But these accounts are invariably chronologies of events, anecdotes, and personalities. While they are rich in information, they seldom provide analytical accounts of the firm's growth or its interaction with its markets, the government, or its competitors at home and abroad."[100] The last part of Tsurumi's assessment still has a ring of truth. The first part was probably already outdated when published in 1978 thanks to the Japan Business History Institute (Nihon Keiei Shi Kenkyūjo), which has compiled most of the better company histories over the past fifteen years. The quality of scholarship evident in these works, their careful attention to detail throughout the roughly one thousand pages (the typical length), and the use of hitherto virtually unknown primary archival materials make the recent company history vastly superior to efforts published before the mid-1970s. Yet, the way these histories are compiled still leaves room for skepticism about their worth.

The Japan Business History Institute is an agency that signs contracts with companies to produce a company history and then hires scholars to do the work. Essentially three groups participate in the project: the committee of scholars; a small number of company staff members; and several assistants, usually graduate students hired by the Institute to record data or handwriting experts who copy minutes and reports which even Japanese scholars find difficult to read. The committee consists of from six to eight scholars of varied specialization and sometimes quite different philosophy. Marxists often participate. (Shibagaki Kazuo is an example.) Even if the structure of the volume permitted, this diverse representation thwarts the likelihood of a unified interpretation. Instead, the goal is descriptive, with each participant usually writing one or two chapters.

Another problem with these histories is that company policy often limits objectivity. If two companies in the same industry are having their histories written at the same time, they will not allow a scholar to participate in both projects. This clearly impedes the development of intra-industry comparisons based on archival material. Furthermore, some issues are always regarded as off limits to the committee. These would include political donations, controversial matters involving conflict among executives, or past incidents that might adversely affect the company's current trade with another country. Usually these issues are spelled out to the Institute before the work begins. However, in the mid-1970s, Mitsui Bussan imposed new restrictions *after* a 2-volume set of close to 2,000 pages had been finished. Since it was completed during a period of revived trade with China, Mitsui worried about the detail on its activities in Manchuria in the 1930s and decided to suppress the book. They printed only a small number of copies (rumored to be about 30) and made the binding firm enough to prevent the books from being opened wide enough for photocopying. Officially, Mitsui Bussan claims the work is only a draft, though Yonekawa Shin'ichi calls it "one of the most useful company histories ever written in Japan."[101] It is difficult to obtain, for Mitsui extracted a promise from the participating scholars not to lend the copies they were given.[102] This incident embarrassed the Institute and it has since tightened up its agreements prior to commencement of its projects. In recent years, the Institute, as a business, has undergone what might be called both diversification and expansion. First, it no longer writes for companies exclusively, but for labor unions as well. Also, foreign companies in Japan have employed it, most notably IBM Japan.[103] Second, there has also been both an increase in the number of commissioned histories and an improvement in their quality.[104] This last point can be attributed to a number of factors. Many firms are reaching their 100th anniversary. That the Business History Institute produces superior histories is widely enough known to induce a sense of competition. An inferior, in-house history can cause a loss of face. One effect of this competition is gradually to lessen the number of issues that can be considered off limits. Finally, there are probably more company presidents and chairmen with a sensitivity to academic and intellectual concerns than was the case even a decade ago.

Still, the major variable in whether a firm commissions its history remains the political environment of an industry's market. My impression is that the histories of shipping firms, banks, and insurance companies are much better than those of electrical or auto companies. Trading companies, meanwhile, still do not seem to have recovered from the rash of criticism they received in the mid-1970s. Overall, though, Japanese firms are probably as "open" to historical research as American firms and almost certainly more so than British companies. Most company histories in Britain are quite different from the Japanese variety. British firms usually commission a single scholar. This has not prevented the appearance of some huge multivolume works. The "commissioning boom" in Britain, however, has placed restraints on the work of scholars, leaving them in a classical dilemma, as expressed by Donald Coleman: "Business history, by definition, must use the records of business companies. The only way that business historians can normally get access to those records, however, is to be commissioned to write company histories."[105] The committee system in Japan ensures a slightly wider dispersal of information. It also constitutes another contrast with Britain, in that for years the Japanese participants in these committees received no public recognition for their work. However, in the the past decade companies have begun to acknowledge authors' identities at the back of the book. The reasoning behind the widespread participation of scholars in these projects is their feeling that it is the easiest way to get access to documentation they can later use for their own research. For a long time this seemed an inadequate excuse. However, in the last few years more evidence of such independent use has emerged; thus the rationale seems more justifiable.

Foreign scholars' criticism of the passive approach taken by Japanese scholars in obtaining material reflects their own experience. It is said that the company approaches the Japanese scholar, whereas the foreigner approaches the Japanese company. In the former case, the company controls the terms of research; in the latter, the foreigner does. There is a strong feeling that Westerners have an easier time than Japanese scholars in gaining access to documents for independent research. This is partly because the Japanese company may find it useful to have its history written in English by a Western scholar. Also, Westerners are more likely to be permitted to do archival research in different companies within the same industry.

The foreign scholar who has gained access to company records will probably feel a sense of competition with his Japanese counterparts and will want to write for the Japanese market. Addressing a similar syndrome among medieval historians, Jeffrey Mass has commented that, "if Western scholarship is to win the respect of historians in Japan, it will be necessary to master the same sources that they use, and also to show greater confidence in our own capacities for originality." Making "this task doubly difficult," says Mass, "is that medievalists writing in English must aim for a 'general' audience."[106] Mass writes of competition with historians in Japan. The situation is slightly different for the business historian. Most Westerners writing Japanese business history teach in history departments, whereas most Japanese business historians are in faculties of economics or business administration. Our general background in history starts us off with a concern for broader issues, but we are pulled toward more specialized topics by (1) the pressure to compete with our Japanese colleagues and (2) the prodding of business and industrial historians outside the Japan field who, for their own comparative study, are anxious to obtain substantial detail about Japanese firms, some of it of a semi-technical nature that is of minimal interest to non-economic historians of Japan in the West.

This problem of specialization is exacerbated by the generally negative impression that "business history" conveys both in Japan and the West. For many years, Japan's major historical journal, *Shigaku zasshi*, virtually ignored the output of business historians in its bibliography section. In a recent review, Nagahara Keiji noted the shift in interest among Japanese historians away from the Industrial Revolution to the interwar years. "What is being studied," he stated, "are the processes of the development of major industries and the business history of individual firms, against the background of the continuing growth of monopoly capitalism."[107] Beyond the fact that most business historians in Japan are no longer concerned with the Marxist category of monopoly capitalism, in the works he cites Nagahara fails to do justice to writing by business historians. These works contain essays by Miwa Ryōichi and Hashimoto Jurō, both of whom have participated in writing company histories for the Business History Institute, but by their own reckoning they are scholars of industrial policy, cartels, and government economic policy more than they are business historians.

Nagahara's comments come from a scholar outside the field of business history. Perhaps more important are assessments within it. These, however, must be placed within their national contexts. For example, in Britain Leslie Hannah has been the most vocal in criticizing the "inveterate" empiricism of company histories and the "enthusiasm for demarcating business history" as opposed to "integrating it within the mainstream of history."[108] Hannah's views, however, have surely been influenced by a several-decades-long tradition of commissioned scholarship in which British business history *has* been company history, with at least some of it written in annoyingly laudatory and apologetic tone. In Japan, Morikawa himself has criticized the overemphasis on individual company history among business historians.[109] There needs to be a distinction, though, between independent research and research carried out by scholars while in the employ of the Business History Institute. The "overemphasis" to which Morikawa refers applies to the latter type of research. One could argue that, because relatively little independent research has been undertaken in this area, there are very few good book-length analyses with integrated interpretations of individual firms in Japan.

In contrast to Britain and Japan, one hears less criticism of company history in America. There academic business history extends back to the interwar years, the amount of commissioned scholarship relative to independent work is small, and Americans have produced a strong body of theoretical models which show the value of research in companies. The circumstances facing Western business historians of Japan are, if anything, even further removed from the historiographical context in Britain and Japan. Within Western Japanese studies, prior to the 1980s there was virtually *no* business history. What little existed was subsumed under economic or social history. Before it can be "integrated into the mainstream of history" its theoretical models, its style of questioning, and its potential contributions have to be more widely understood among Japan specialists. Finally, although Westerners in certain cases may have been able to gain access to company records more easily than their Japanese counterparts, they are pursuing their research independently without company restrictions on what they write.

Yet the writing of individual company histories is only one part of business history. It is certainly not its main goal. In fact, business history will not achieve its potential (commensurate with the growth of newly opened material) unless it can shake off the image in which it is cloaked—that of being simply company history. Some of the chapters in this volume focus on individual firms, but the scholars represented here are all primarily interested in the broader issues that a company study can illuminate. The heart of business history lies less in the individual company study than in the conviction that modern Japanese economic history, and issues like the role of the government in implementing industrial policy, the nature of industrial organization, and Japanese strategies in international trade, cannot be properly understood without reference to the history of individual companies. Their archives may contain the most illuminating evidence of these issues. Thus, studies of Japanese business history in the West are likely to proceed in two ways: (1) through investigation of issues like the above based on an individual company, an industry, or a representative selection of firms; (2) through comparison of companies and industries to build general propositions about the history of Japanese firms.[110]

Notes for an Agenda

The burgeoning number of company histories in Japan and the data that are often published with them provide an almost unlimited range of research options. Here I have chosen to highlight three broad areas that are touched on briefly or implicitly in several of the foregoing chapters but have been marginal to the preceding discussion in this Afterword. They are (1) specific industries that have been neglected by Western scholars, (2) connections between local industries, distribution patterns, and international trade, and (3) issues of periodization relating especially to "great divides" like the Restoration and the two world wars.[111]

INDUSTRY STUDIES. Relative to its importance in Japan's industrialization from the 1880s to the 1930s, the textile industry remains the least studied industry among Western scholars. Except for several papers on technology, almost all the work being done in the West on cotton spinning centers on female labor. The business operations, strategy, and organization of the industry have hardly been touched. One "barrier to entry" into the study of this industry is the fact that its company histories are generally old and inferior in quality. This may be attributable to the disposal of documents during the frequent mergers between 1900 and 1930 and to the industry's decline, and hence lack of financial resources, in recent decades. Still, the Cotton Spinners Association (Bōren) had perhaps the best publishing arm of any industry association. This provided data on its own firms and their relations with other industries. Coverage of mining suffers from a fate similar to that of textiles. Despite its strategic role in Japan's development before World War I, it too has been neglected (except, again, for the labor dimension), even though three of the largest six industrial companies (among joint-stock enterprises) in 1918 were mining concerns.[112]

There are several strategic heavy industries that have a multitude of good company histories and a well-developed historiography in Japan but that have been studied only in a peripheral way in the West. These include shipbuilding, steel, and electrical equipment.[113] These industries offer interesting research possibilities not only for their own development (in technology, organization, labor management, and financing) but for their connections with zaibatsu. All three also had (1) close mutual ties, with both commercial shipbuilding and the military acting as markets for steel and electrical equipment, and (2) connections with trading companies, which supplied them with raw materials and distributed their products. Trading-company histories provide some documentation of these activities. Generally, trading companies have received more attention than specific manufacturing industries, but they too await full historical treatment. Despite the suppression of its history, Mitsui Bussan remains the best candidate for study because of the substantial documentation on it in the Mitsui Bunko in Tokyo. In the last few years, Mitsubishi companies in general have become somewhat more open to researchers, at least with regard to materials in the Mitsubishi General Research Institute. This is partly because of the recent publication of Mitsubishi Shōji's official history.[114] Despite its bulk, this history (done in house) is below the standards set by the Business History Institute.

In the near future, the industrial theme that promises to receive the most attention is the issue of industrial organization. Though perhaps only in embryonic form, a lively debate seems to be emerging, especially over the role of cartels, between scholars of industrial organization who write on postwar Japan and business historians concerned with the prewar years. The starting point for this is a recent article by Kikkawa Takeo.[115] Most research on cartels focuses on how they restrict competition. While agreeing that the export orientation of the Japanese Cotton Spinners Association led to restraints on domestic production, Kikkawa argues that generally the functions performed by this cartel were designed more to strengthen the competitive power of the industry than to restrict competition. These functions included joint-purchasing agreements, stabilizing the supply of workers, reporting data, and cooperation in marketing strategy and in negotiations over financial terms for credit (which enhanced the industry's bargaining power with trading companies, shipping firms, and the Yokohama Specie Bank). After surveying many other cartels, Kikkawa suggested that: (1) competition remained even after cartels were formed; (2) actions to restrict competition were effective only in depressions and were usually of short duration; and (3) stability, which cartels provided during depressions, enabled their industries to follow long-term strategies that both enhanced growth and tended to shorten the duration of depressions in Japan.

As opposed to this assessment, the standard argument against cartels is that they increase inefficiency in the allocation of resources. Even in the case of research, cooperation that lessens risk is said to suppress innovation.[116] On the other hand, Ronald Dore contends that cartel arrangements that lead to over-investment during boom periods can also facilitate changes in industrial structure by encouraging, where appropriate, diversification into new lines of activity or the scrapping of a plant.[117] The postwar debate on this issue is likely to have a productive influence on prewar historiography only if (1) enough data can be uncovered to support an economic analysis and (2) historians can first provide a full account of the context in which cartels operated.[118]

REGIONAL INDUSTRY AND PROTO-INDUSTRIALIZATION. Ericson's treatment of railways in this volume focuses mainly on finance. However, in his reference to local residents and industrialists and their interests in railways, he implicitly suggests links between distribution patterns and the economic impact of railways on local industry. Assessment of that impact is itself part of two larger questions, namely, whether there was an Industrial Revolution in Japan before World War I and how that issue, in turn, is related to the increasingly popular concept of proto-industrialization. As a systematic form of analysis, this concept is only about a decade and a half old. Applied first to the "long period" of European history leading up to industrialization, it is being used as a new model for the interpretation of Japanese history, especially through the writings of Saitō Osamu.[119]

The concept of proto-industrialization is concerned with the development of rural cottage industry in which peasants participate through a putting-out system in the production of handicrafts or other non-agricultural goods within a *region* (the unit of reference) where their activity is linked to commercial agriculture and from which their goods are exported, either to another region or, in certain cases in Europe, across national boundaries. There is also a neo-Marxist version of the concept which sees proto-industrialization as an intermediate stage between feudalism and capitalism.[120] Generally, however, the advocates of this approach have reacted against stage theory or the emphasis on discontinuities like "take-offs." They share with many economic historians an inclination to analyze economic growth "with biological rather than aeronautical metaphors."[121]

In applying this theory to Japan, Saitō has combined it with concepts of time proposed by Fernand Braudel, namely, *longue durée* (a "long period" characterized by constant repetition and ever-recurring cycles), conjuncture, and event.[122] Most relevant to this volume is Saitō's contention that the century from the 1820s to the 1920s constituted a single "long period." In Saitō's analysis, each long period, or "phase of expansion," is typically characterized by a new form of economic activity which becomes an "engine of growth." In the seventeenth century, it was an expansion of arable farmland; the phase that began in the 1820s "saw a proliferation of non-agricultural economic activity in rural areas" in which "each region now tended to have its own specialties . . . which were 'exported' to other regions through the commercial centre of Ōsaka." This phase, the early years of which had a rough parallel to eighteenth-century Europe, lasted in Japan till after World War I. Saitō bases this assertion on the following: (1) the traditional sector (mostly the putting-out system separate from large factory production) kept growing till the 1920s; (2) the leading modern industry in the Meiji period, cotton spinning, still had only a 10-percent share of total manufacturing output by 1914; and (3) full-fledged industrialization, characterized mainly by heavy and chemical industries, "gained momentum" only after World War I. Thus, there was no Industrial Revolution in the Meiji period.[123]

Saitō's thesis has much to recommend it, but I would point to at least three ways in which it is inadequate to explain Meiji economic history. First, Saitō supports his case with the assertion "that virtually no traditional industries were replaced by modern counterparts during the Meiji period."[124] This overlooks the fact that many industries that began in the Meiji period had no Tokugawa precedent. These ranged from railways to the output of modern weapons in military arsenals. Actually, one of the standard arguments against the theory of proto-industrialization is that it ignores the fact that many industries, in the technical form in which they developed during "industrialization," had no real traditional counterpart. Critics also slight it for overlooking industrial processes that arose in towns (as opposed to rural regions) or which were distinct from cottage industry. Thus, they contend that the theory is "concerned with only one small part of what we call industrial revolution."[125] Second, since the interwar years represent a new phase of expansion in Saitō's view, one should note that most of the growth industries of that period had at least begun in the Meiji period. These included steel, chemicals, electrical engineering, though obviously not aircraft. (The growth of automobiles before World War II was probably too insubstantial to be relevant to the debate.) Most important, perhaps, is that shipbuilding grew more quickly between, say, 1900 and 1914 than it did in the 1920s (though by how much depends on the base years chosen). On the other hand, more consistent with Saitō's argument is the fact that most of the key technologies necessary for longer-term growth were introduced only in the 1920s (diesel engines in ships, imports of American technology for the electrical industry, for example).

A third, and more general, point relates to innovations in distribution and trade. We cannot limit our discussion of "engines of growth" simply to production. Certainly the confluence in the arrival and development between the 1870s and the 1890s of trading companies, better credit facilities through banks, the steamship, railways, the construction of ports, and the telegraph brought substantial change to the distribution of products in the domestic market and an even greater transformation in the pattern of foreign trade. Without the support of most of these categories, cotton spinning, with its export dependency, would have been a much smaller industry. Coal (the production of which also grew more quickly from 1880 to 1910 than it did in the 1920s) could not have been exported to the extent it was. And, from the traditional sector, the products of sericulture, the country's major export industry, would have been less competitive without the steamship. (For the American market, speed of delivery, in holding down interest and insurance charges, was absolutely essential to the rapid growth of raw silk exports.) It is true that railways had less impact in Japan than they did, say, in America. This was because of the availability of other forms of transport, namely, coastal shipping, and geographical factors of both the size and shape of the country.[126] Even so, railways and other technical changes mentioned here prompted organizational reforms in the business activities of traditional Japanese merchants.[127] The key point here is that these technical changes in distribution not only prepared the way for the heavier industries of the interwar years, at least those dependent on trade, but also encouraged more production from the traditional sector.

The above innovations in distribution, though resulting partly from technical development, can be categorized as a form of institutional change. Saitō's mathematical analysis, which treats manufacturing output, cannot accommodate this. The lack of attention to institutional analysis is another feature of proto-industrialization theory that even supporters of the concept criticize. For example, Patrick O'Brien, in commenting on how producers goods and some consumer goods were not manufactured under the putting-out system, argues that if the research on the concept "is to fulfill its promise we need to know more about the varieties and adaptabilities of *organizational forms* that are encompassed under the heading of proto-industrialization."[128] Certainly, in assessing the issue of industrial revolution in Japan, we can no longer refer simply to organizational change in the form of joint-stock companies during the 1880s as proof that a revolution occurred. But this change (and the rapid growth of the companies concerned before 1914) certainly must be included in any such assessment. As Donald Coleman argues, the value of the concept "industrial revolution" lies in its vagueness, in its lack of precise definition. "We cannot measure the industrial revolution," he states. "We measure component bits . . . but not the totality."[129] The institutional changes mentioned here were part of that totality, just as were the growth of new industries and the contribution the traditional sector made to new developments, ranging from taxes paid to the government investments in railways by silk merchants. Together they suggest there was indeed an industrial revolution in Japan between the late 1880s and 1914.

Although it may not be readily apparent from the foregoing discussion, my intent is less to criticize Saitō and his fellow advocates than to try to link their findings with analysis of other specific issues. On the one hand, we can recognize the great value of their analysis (certainly it should lead to many new innovative proposals for research on the whole nineteenth century, or the 1820–1914 period) while still contending that, if they try to place the whole economy under the rubric of measurement, whether it be of manufacturing output or living standards, they overlook a good part of history, including other, non-quantifiable engines of growth. On the other hand, if we can formulate research topics that integrate the focus on regions and local industry with issues of organizational change, business practices, and distribution patterns, then progress might be made in breaking down the demarcation between different schools of history and achieving more comprehensive conclusions.

The following are some possible topics that are suggested both by Ericson's chapter and by the concern with regions in proto-industrialization theory:

(1) Despite a multitude of books on peasants, landlords, and tenants in recent years, analysis of the commercial activities of these classes has taken a back seat to social conflict. Yet, agricultural business through analysis of landlord investment, putting-out systems, or distribution patterns remains an open area. Richard Smethurst introduces some information of the connection between traditional industries and the electrification of railways in the interwar years which facilitated transport between urban areas and neighboring distribution points (a point relevant to Saitō's emphasis on the "spurt" in the interwar years). However, the work that he criticizes by Nakamura Masanori contains more information on landlord business activity.[130] A topic in this vein could also include analysis of new forms of credit backed by the government and official programs to promote agricultural business.

(2) The study of local industry could focus on specific enterprises producing goods that ranged from seasonings to cement, with attention to the role of wholesalers and retailers. Much work could be done on the business organization of such local enterprises. Another approach would be to examine rural subcontracting for urban-based firms.[131] Among new urban enterprises, the watch and clock industry has a rich historiography.[132]

(3) A topic with perhaps the best potential from the viewpoint of new material would be the distribution of commodities in early and mid-Meiji. A recent work edited by Yamaguchi Kazuo and Ishii Kanji contains a wealth of suggestions along this line. It deals with both the movement of goods and new developments in transport.[133] This analysis is backed by the massive statistical record of *Kindai Nihon shōhin ryūtsū shi shiryō*.[134] Similarly, the Mitsubishi General Research Institute in Tokyo possesses records of Mitsubishi's branches in many ports throughout Japan during the 1870s and early 1880s. The most important (and legible) of these have been published in conjunction with the N.Y.K.'s company history.[135] With respect to transport, these Mitsubishi materials deal mostly with shipping, but a topic of this nature could be integrated with port construction, railway development, and other forms of land transport.[136] The role of wholesalers and trading companies at the level of both regional eco-

nomic activity and national integration could also be considered. Thus, one could undertake an intensive analysis of the movement of a specific commodity or make a general assessment of the overall distribution process.

(4) Along more political lines, Ericson offers ideas for combining business, social, and regional history in his discussion of the clash of interests over railways involving urban capitalists, local landowners and businesses, representatives in the Diet, the government, big investors, and local residents.

(5) The growth of regional commerce and industry might be studied in the context of urban change. One type of analysis might examine how firms or industries took advantage of new distribution patterns to build on an existing urban base. Another approach would be to analyze the impact of new industry, which in effect was imposed on a region, as in the case of Yawata Iron and Steel Works in northern Kyushu. A recent study of Okayama, which is closer to the former type, considers the changes in the region's industrial structure during the 1870s and 1880s, its distribution patterns, and shipments in and out of the prefecture.[137]

(6) A final topic would embrace international trade and link the production of local enterprises with overseas marketing by trading companies. This could be done for both a new industry like cement (Onoda Cement, for example, with its ties to Mitsui Bussan) or a traditional industry like matches, where most production was still under a putting-out system or in small factories. Mitsui tried to impose standards of quality on this industry, branded its products, and marketed them overseas.

I have listed these topics in a vertical manner from the local to the international. Thus, it might be possible to take an individual industry, enterprise, or even family and trace its business activity in a "vertical" order through each of these categories. An example of this approach is a recent study of the Hattori, a large landowning family in Okayama prefecture. This study covers the period from the Restoration to World War II and examines the family's transition from brewing activity in late Tokugawa to increasing purchase of land in early Meiji, which led to an extensive leasing business. It considers the family's subsidiary operations in salt farming, compares its management strategy with that of neighboring landlord families, and provides background on the social and economic change in the southeast part of Okayama prefecture where the Hattori were based. The family's wealth also accumulated through moneylending and investment in securities, and it was able to expand its landholding into Korea. Records left are so extensive that the work provides an analysis of accounting and management for each of the family's operations.[138]

The secondary works cited under the above topics are diverse. Some are written by Marxist economic historians; others are closer to the work of business historians or the concerns of proto-industrialization theorists. Thus, a scholar attempting such research would have to be cognizant of the different methodologies employed. Again, several options present themselves. One could examine these issues within the framework of business history, drawing where appropriate on the insights of the other schools. Or some sort of methodological comparison itself could be attempted that would test the propositions of the different schools.

PERIODIZATION. The final section of this agenda concerns a major tendency in recent historiography: the search for continuities across great divides. In the case of the Restoration, two approaches seem characteristic of present work in Japan. One treats broad changes in trading patterns and their impact on society, covering some local issues as well. A second is institutional and focuses on the fate of business enterprises in the transition from Tokugawa to Meiji. The major work in the first category is Ishii's study of Jardine, Matheson, which covers the period from 1859 to 1888.[139] This is indispensable not only for the foreign impact on Japan in general but for specific issues like the organization of early trade (mainly in commodity exports and machinery imports), the response of Japanese merchants, and the background it provides on trade-related banking facilities and the distribution patterns mentioned in the previous list of topics. Insofar as it focuses on a Western business firm and stresses the strength of the foreign impact, it differs from a recent minority view that emphasizes (1) the intra-Asian character of Japan's trade as autonomous, that is, as arising separately from the Western impact but prompting a greater demand for Western products, and (2) the view that the economic impact of the West has been exaggerated, especially in the cotton trade, because Western imports could not overcome Japanese preference for traditional thick cloth.[140] Among institutional studies, the major works on big business are Yasuoka's study of Kōnoike and Mitsui and two recent assessments of Sumitomo, the first of which touches on political and social background from the 1830s to the 1870s, while the second concentrates on the Besshi Copper Mine.[141] The response to economic change in the Restoration years by rural enterprises and regional merchants has also received more attention lately, especially the activity of the Ōmi merchants.[142] Few of the above issues have been studied by Western scholars.

More work has been done in English on the World War II "divide." This focuses on the transition in heavy industry between the 1930s and 1950s or the effects on business of the reverse course during the Occupation.[143] While studies of labor and industrial policy are coming to dominate research on the Occupation, apart from earlier work on zaibatsu dissolution (itself concerned mainly with American policy) there has been little research in English on managers or the development of company strategy during the late 1940s. Most work stresses management's fears of the loss of its prerogatives to labor. During the first three years of the Occupation, however, numerous companies had to partially suspend operations (because of imposed restrictions and threatened dissolution). One could argue that these measures caused even more anxiety than the rise of labor. The managers of these restricted firms who were not purged enjoyed a kind of enforced sabbatical.[144] The planning and strategic formulation they undertook at this time probably constitutes a missing link in our understanding of business development in the 1950s. A study of the younger managers of this era, whether their firms were on the restricted list or not, would bring a new perspective to the reverse-course phenomenon. Credit, if such it can be called, for leading the reverse course in Occupation policy has usually been given to American businessmen or government officials, who struggled against MacArthur's reforms, or to the persuasive influence of Japanese officials like Finance Minister Ikeda Hayato. Younger Japanese managers were in an ambiguous situation. Many had benefited from the reforms in that their superiors had been purged. Some tried to develop new approaches through organizations like the Keizai Dōyū-kai. Others in firms outside the old zaibatsu had benefited from the opening up of a more competitive business environment. Virtually all, though, sought to improve conditions for their firms through removal of restrictions in areas like heavy industrial production, foreign trade, and inter-company transactions. Relative to the well-researched policy shifts in Washington, the momentum that developed out of these managerial priorities in Japan deserves more attention. This is especially so with regard to strategic planning for post-Occupation policy.

Finally, generalizations about the Occupation must accommodate the diversity of experience among companies. Some manufacturing firms obviously had large confrontations with labor's offensive (Tōshiba, for example). Others had to contend not only with labor but also with restrictions on production and the threat of reorganization or dismemberment (Japan Steel, for example). Relative to manufacturing firms, service industries probably suffered less from labor demands but more from Occupation restrictions. Large shipping firms had three strikes against them: severe restrictions on the size of ships, threats of dissolution, and Occupation controls on foreign trade. And, of course, in the realm of trading, Mitsui Bussan and Mitsubishi Shōji were dissolved. Generally, Occupation policy until 1948–1949 kept under suppression a great deal of latent industrial potential. To a large extent, this issue is separate from institutional questions of labor reform and zaibatsu dissolution. Emphasis is often placed on favorable American policies in the late Occupation (aid, "economic cooperation," support for export and development banks) in assessments of recovery. But more attention must be paid to the release of that "latent potential." In another respect, however, the Occupation positively benefited some firms, even in its early stages. NEC, for example, was in dire straits after the closing of its military-related business. The Occupation rescued it with large orders for its telephones.

The great divide that has been least studied in English is World War I. Our general image of it is clear enough—huge profits, massive dividends, the emergence of nouveaux riches, and then sudden collapse in 1919 and 1920. Yet, too much research seems to end in 1914 or to begin in the early 1920s. On the other hand, the case-study approach often treats war as just a phase, albeit a major one, in the longer history of a firm or industry. What we need is a more intensive examination of the war and its consequences for Japan, employing comparative research to embrace many industries and firms and spanning the years from roughly 1910 to 1927. The verdict will clearly vary with the firm. Nitchitsu, for example, was one of the major beneficiaries. But, from a general perspective, the speculative character of commercial opportunity, followed by the severe recession and coupled with the expansion experienced by many industries from 1910 to 1914, may call for some revision in the common view that World War I was Japan's "best war."

Notes
Index

1. Introduction, by William D. Wray

1. Recent works in business history include W. Mark Fruin, *Kikkoman: Company, Clan, and Community* (Cambridge, Harvard University Press, 1983) and the following in the Harvard East Asian Monograph series: William D. Wray, *Mitsubishi and the N.Y.K., 1870–1914: Business Strategy in the Japanese Shipping Industry* (1984); Andrew Gordon, *The Evolution of Labor Relations in Japan: Heavy Industry, 1853–1955* (1985); Michale A. Cusumano, *The Japanese Automobile Industry: Technology and Management at Nissan and Toyota* (1985); Marie Anchordoguy, *Computers, Inc.: Japan's Challenge to IBM* (forthcoming); and Barbara Molony, *Technology and Investment: The Prewar Japanese Chemical Industry* (forthcoming).

2. For two succinct summaries of the methodology of this school, see Kozo Yamamura, "Introduction," *Explorations in Economic History* 15.1:1–10 (January 1978), and "Introduction to Part Four," in Marius B. Jansen and Gilbert Rozman, eds., *Japan in Transition: From Tokugawa to Meiji* (Princeton University Press, 1986), pp. 377–381.

3. See my "agenda" in the Afterword to this volume for some possible topics that might benefit from the integration of these two schools.

4. For a list of works on industrial policy divided according to these two perspectives, see Geroge C. Eads and Kozo Yamamura, "The Future of Industrial Policy," in Yamamura and Yasukichi Yasuba, eds., *The Political Economy*

of *Japan*, Vol. I, *The Domestic Transformation* (Stanford University Press, 1987), pp. 635–636n1. For a fuller list, see William D. Wray, *Japan's Economy: A Bibliography of its Past and Present* (New York, Markus Wiener, 1989). Johnson's principal work on the subject is *MITI and the Japanese Miracle: The Growth of Industrial Policy, 1925–1975* (Stanford University Press, 1982).

5. In my own study, *Mitsubishi and the N.Y.K.*, I found much to support in both of the above perspectives, but the approach of each seemed like an attempt to balance a seesaw by sitting a sumo wrestler at one end and a jockey at the other. For historical material on the early years of industrial policy, see Harada Mikio, ed. *Tsūshō sangyō seisaku shiryōshū: Dai ichiji taisenki*, 5 vols. (Tokyo, Kashiwa Shobō, 1987).

6. Among Western specialists, the standard work is Eleanor Hadley, *Antitrust in Japan* (Princeton University Press, 1970). See also the important article by Uekusa Masu, "Effects of the Deconcentration Measures in Japan," *Antitrust Bulletin* 22:687–715 (Fall 1977); and the same author's *Sangyō soshiki ron* (Chikuma Shobō, 1982), pp. 248–292.

7. Aoki Masahiko, "Aspects of the Japanese Firm," in Aoki, ed., *The Economic Analysis of the Japanese Firm* (Amsterdam, North Holland, 1984), pp. 3, 5.

8. For an excellent treatment of Japanese technological induction during this period, see Erich Pauer, "Traditional Technology and its Impact on Japan's Industry during the Early Period of the Industrial Revolution," *Economic Studies Quarterly* 38.4:354–371 (December 1987).

9. The international context of this problem is treated succinctly in Claudio Zanier, "Japan and the 'Prebrine' Crisis of European Sericulture During the 1860s," in Erich Pauer, ed. *Silkworms, Oil, and Chips. . . . Proceedings of the Economics and Economic History Section of the Fourth International Conference on Japanese Studies*, Japan Seminar, University of Bonn, 1986, pp. 51–63.

10. See the account of vacillation in government shipping policy prior to 1875 in my *Mitsubishi and the N.Y.K.*, pp. 30–86.

11. Saitō Osamu, "Scenes of Japan's Economic Development and the 'Longue Durée,'" in Pauer, ed., *Silkworms, Oil, and Chips*, pp. 15–27, esp. p. 17.

12. Sugiyama Shin'ya, "Higashi Ajia ni okeru 'gaiatsu' no kōzō," *Rekishigaku kenkyū* 560.128–138 (October 1986), pp. 137–138. In English there is Sugiyama's "The Impact of the Opening of the Ports on Domestic Japanese Industry: The Case of Silk and Cotton," *Economic Studies Quarterly* 38.4:338–353 (December 1987).

13. Ishii Kanji, "Ishin henkaku no kiso katei: taigaiteki keiki to 'henseikae,'" *Rekishigaku kenkyū* 560.138–148 (October 1986); and especially *Kindai Nihon to Igirisu shihon: Jādein Maseson Shōkai o chūshin ni* (Tokyo Daigaku Shuppankai, 1984). In English, see the review of the latter by Takeda Haruhito in *Japanese Yearbook on Business History* 3.187–189 (1986). Also, for subsequent developments in the silk industry, see Stephen W. McCallion, "Silk Reeling in Meiji Japan: The Limits to Change," PhD dissertation, Ohio State University, 1983.

14. Yen-p'ing Hao, *The Commercial Revolution in Nineteenth-Century China: The*

Rise of Sino-Western Mercantile Capitalism (University of California Press, 1986), 327–344. As background to the crisis, Hao refers to natural disasters, the fall in silver prices which hurt the balance of China's trade, and anxiety over an impending war with France, but he still contends that the basic reason for the crisis was market speculation.

15. Jan C. Bongaerts, "Financing Railways in the German States, 1840–1860: A Preliminary View," *Journal of European Economic History* 14.2:331–345 (Fall 1985).

16. For a study of the Imperial House and the peers in the N.Y.K., see my *Mitsubishi and the N.Y.K.*, pp. 235–244; for their role in the insurance business, see *Tokyo Kaijō Kasai Hoken Kabushiki Kaisha 100 nenshi*, I, edited by Nihon Keiei Shi Kenkyūjo (Dōsha, 1979).

17. See Imuta Yoshimitsu, "Kazoku shisan to tōshi kōdō: kyū daimyō no kabushiki tōshi o chūshin ni," *Chihō kin'yū kenkyū* 18:1–49 (March 1987), which contains further bibliography.

18. Takeda Haruhito, "Meiji zenki no Fujita-gumi to Mōri-ke yūshi," *Keizaigaku ronshū* (Tokyo University) 48.3:2–22 (October 1982).

19. Yonekura Seiichirō, "Seifu shizoku jusan seisaku to Onoda Semento," *Hitotsubashi ronsō* 87.3:377–394 (March 1982); *Onoda Semento 100 nenshi*, ed. Nihon Keiei shi Kenkyūjo (Dōsha, 1981); Imuta, "Kazoku shisan," p. 25.

20. Senda Minoru, "Kazoku shihon no seiritsu, tenkai: Ippanteki kōsatsu," *Shakai keizai shigaku* 52.1:1–37 (April 1986).

21. Calculated from Imuta, "Kazoku shisan," p. 10.

22. For background on the Japanese board, see Yui Tsunehiko, "The Development of the Organizational Structure of Top Management in Meiji Japan," *Japanese Yearbook on Business History* 1:1–23 (1984).

23. See the autobiographical comments on this point in Morikawa Hidemasa, *Zaibatsu no keiei shiteki kenkyū* (Tōyō Keizai Shinpōsha, 1980), pp. 307–311.

24. See the book reviews in *Japanese Yearbook on Business History* 1.176–181 (1984). For more extensive discussion of the issues raised here, see Kobayashi Kesaji and Morikawa Hidemasa, eds., *Development of Managerial Enterprise*, (University of Tokyo Press, 1986).

25. For two excellent studies of this transition, see Shiba Takao, "Succeeding Against Odds, Courting Collapse: How Mitsubishi Shipbuilding and Kawasaki Dockyard Managed the Post-WWI Slump," *Japanese Yearbook on Business History* 2.100–118 (1985); and "A Comparative Study of the Managerial Structure of Two Japanese Shipbuilding Firms: Mitsubishi Shipbuilding and Engineering Co. and Kawasaki Dockyard Co., 1896–1927," in *Managerial Enterprise*, pp. 211–229.

26. For brief comments on these disputes, see Morikawa Hidemasa, "Prerequisites for the Development of Managerial Capitalism: Cases in Prewar Japan," in *Managerial Enterprise*, pp. 19–21.

27. The telecommunications case mentioned differed from both the chemical and electrical machinery examples in that the NEC joint venture was more the product of Western Electric strategy than of Japanese initiative. Western Electric's Japanese partner in NEC was Iwadare Kunihiko, the American firm's former agent in Japan. *Nippon Denki Kabushiki Kaisha 70 nenshi*

(Dōsha Shashi Hensan Shitsu, 1972), pp. 24–50. For further comment, see Uchida Hoshimi, "Western Big Business and the Adoption of New Technology in Japan: The Electrical and Chemical Industries, 1890–1920," in Okochi Akio and Uchida, eds., *Development and Diffusion of Technology: Electrical and Chemical Industries* (University of Tokyo Press, 1980), pp. 145–172.

28. For further background on the N.Y.K.'s cartel, which provides useful comparison with Molony's chapter, see my "NYK and the Commercial Diplomacy of the Far Eastern Freight Conference, 1896–1956," in Yui Tsunehiko and Nakagawa Keiichiro, eds., *Business History of Shipping: Strategy and Structure* (University of Tokyo Press, 1985), pp. 279–311. For cartels in the electrical industry during this period, see Hasegawa Shin, "Satsukikai (jūdenki karuteru)," in Hashimoto Jurō and Takeda Haruhito, eds., *Ryōtaisen kanki: Nihon no karuteru* (Ochanomizu Shobō, 1985), pp. 273–322.

29. Moritani Masanori, *Gijutsu kaihatsu no Shōwa shi* (Tōyō Keizai Shinpōsha, 1987), pp. 2–15. For further background, see Nakaoka Tetsurō, Ishii Tadashi, and Uchida Hoshimi, *Kindai Nihon no gijutsu seisaku* (Kokusai Rengō Daigaku, 1986), pp. 213–231.

30. *Kyūshū shin jidai,* ed. Nihon Keizai Shinbunsha (Editor, 1987), pp. 16–21.

31. For discussion of government tariff protection for other branches of the chemical industry (dyestuffs and soda), see Motomiya Kazuo, "1920 nendai ni okeru kagaku kōgyō hōgo seisaku: Shōkōshō 'sandai seisaku' no rekishiteki igi," *Shigaku zasshi* 95.11:1–39 (November 1986).

32. Taking a similar position is Ōshio Takeshi, "Shinkō Konzern," *Shakai Keizai shigaku* 47.6:71–90 (June 1982).

33. For general background on these federations, see Miyamoto Matao, "The Development of Business Associations in Prewar Japan," in Yamazaki Hiroaki and Miyamoto, eds., *Trade Associations in Business History* (University of Tokyo Press, 1988), pp. 1–45.

34. Actually, the membership of the leading business federations consisted almost exclusively of salaried managers. However, in Morikawa's terminology a large number of them could be classified as "managers become capitalists." For a study of the composition of Keizai Renmei, see Takahashi Kyūichi, "Senjiki Nihon Keizai Renmeikai no yakuwari," *Keizai keiei kenkyū* (Kobe Daigaku) 28.2:89–141 (1978).

35. A useful follow-up to Gordon's paper is Hideo Ōtake, "The *Zaikai* Under the Occupation: The Formation and Transformation of Managerial Councils," in Robert E. Ward and Yoshikazu Sakamoto, eds., *Democratizing Japan: The Allied Occupation* (University of Hawaii Press, 1987), pp. 366–391. This also discusses managerial prerogative with regard to labor.

36. The following is based on Sanford M. Jacoby, *Employing Bureaucracy: Managers, Unions, and the Transformation of Work in American Industry, 1900–1945* (Columbia University Press, 1985), pp. 241–285. The term *bureaucracy* in the title refers not to the government but to the corporate bureaucracy of personnel management. This work is a must for anyone who has read Gordon's book, *The Evolution of Labor Relations.*

37. Jacoby, *Employing Bureaucracy,* pp. 265, 282, 284.
38. Takahashi, "Keizai Renmei," p. 117n16, provides one concrete parallel to Gordon's account. In commenting on the labor inspection system under the Welfare Ministry in the early wartime period, Gordon notes that private firms supplied some of the inspectors. On the matter of industrial production, a March 1943 imperial ordinance created the Administrative Inspection System to carry out observation of factories and installations in essential industries like aircraft production, steel, shipbuilding, mining, and wooden shipbuilding. Members of the inspection teams came from both the government and private sector. Also, three of the four missions carried out in 1943 were headed by Keizai Renmei leaders then serving as government advisers or cabinet ministers (Fujiwara Ginjirō and Gotō Keita).
39. See, however, Richard Rice, "Economic Mobilization in Wartime Japan: Business, Bureaucracy and the Military in Conflict," *Journal of Asian Studies* 38.4:689–706 (August 1979). The view here corresponds to Gordon's statement that "the zaibatsu lost little, if any, autonomy to the economic bureaucrats" during the wartime period.
40. Johnson, *MITI.*

2. The Increasing Power of Salaried Managers in Japan's Large Corporations, by Morikawa Hidemasa

1. Hiratsuka Masatoshi, *Besshi kaikō 25 nen shiwa* (Osaka, Kabushiki Kaisha Sumitomo Honsha, 1941), p. 305.
2. Shioda Taisuke, *Jijoden* (Private publication, 1938), p. 92; *Mitsubishi Sha shi* (Tokyo Daigaku Shuppankai, 1980), XII, 413.
3. Ibid., XV, 242.
4. *Shashi Sumitomo Denki Kōgyō Kabushiki Kaisha* (1961). p. 95.
5. *Ōji Seishi Shashi* (1956), I, 153–154.
6. Ishikawa Yasujirō, *Kōzan no henei* (1923), p. 128.
7. Although there are various predecessors of Teikoku Daigaku (Imperial University) and the Faculty of Technology, each with different names, I have avoided writing out their formal names each time they appear in this paper.
8. According to the *Gakushikai shimeiroku;* Morikawa Hidemasa, "Meijiki Kōka Daigaku sotsu kaisha gishi no list," *Hōsei Daigaku Keiei shirin* 11.2 (1974).
9. Fukuzawa Yukichi, "Jitsugyōron," *Fukuzawa Yukichi zenshū* (Iwanami Shoten, 1959), Vol. VI.
10. *Mitsui jigyōshi* (Mitsui Bunko, 1980), Vol. II, Chapters 3 and 5.
11. Ibid., pp. 464ff.; *Nakamigawa Hikojirō denki shiryō* (Tōyō Keizai Shinpōsha, 1969), Chapter 5.
12. *Sumitomo Shunsui* (Osaka, 1950), pp. 240–261.
13. Ishikawa, *Kozan,* pp. 122ff.
14. Nitta Naozō, *Kikuchi Kyōzō den* (Osaka, 1948), pp. 70ff., 146ff.
15. Morikawa Hidemasa, *Nihon keieishi* (Nihon Keizai Shinbunsha, 1981). The

translated source mentioned in this paragraph is *Nihon zenkoku sho kaisha yakuinroku* (Shōgyō Kōshinjo, 1905, 1913, 1930).

16. Kinukawa Taichi, *Honpō menshi bōsekishi* (1939), IV, 134–136; Nitta, *Kikuchi*, p. 199.
17. Nitta, *Kikuchi*, pp. 232–233.
18. *Shibusawa Eiichi denki shiryō* (Ryūmonsha, 1956), X, 50.
19. Sugiyama Kazuo, "Keieisha no soshutsu to hoju," *Nihon keieishi kōza* (Nihon Keizai Shinbunsha, 1977), VI, 112.
20. Morikawa, *Nihon Keieishi*, p. 69.
21. Yui Tsunehiko, "Meiji jidai ni okeru jūyaku soshiki no keisei," *Keiei shigaku* 14.1:1–27 (September 1979).
22. Ibid.
23. *Tōyō Kisen Kabushiki Kaisha 64 nen no ayumi* (1964), Chapter 6.
24. *Fujiyama Raita den* (1939), Chapters 10 and 11; *Nitto saikin 25 nenshi* (1919).
25. *Hiraga Bin den* (1931).
26. *Ōji Seishi Shashi* (1958), Vol. III, Chapter 5.
27. Takahashi Junjirō, *Mitsukoshi 300 nen no keiei senryaku* (Sankei Shinbunsha, 1972).
28. Maeda Kazutoshi, "Kobayashi Ichizō," in Morikawa Hidemasa, et al., *Nihon no kigyōka (3): Shōwa hen* (Yūhikaku, 1978), pp. 89–131.
29. Mutō Sanji, *Watakushi no minouebanashi* (1934), pp. 193ff.
30. Kobayakawa Yōichi, "Mutō Sanji," in Yui Tsunehiko, et al., *Nihon no kigyōka (2): Taishō hen* (Yūhikaku, 1978), pp. 73–105.
31. *Mutō Sanji zenshū* (Shinjūsha, 1963), II, 802.
32. Shiba Takao, "Kin'yū kyōkōji ni okeru keiei senryaku no hatan to sono seiri: Kawasaki Zōsenjo no baai," *Keiei shigaku* 15.1:28–53 (April 1980).
33. Yamazaki Hiroaki, "1920 nendai no Mitsui Bussan," in Nakamura Takafusa, ed., *Senkanki no Nihon keizai bunseki* (Yamakawa Shuppansha, 1981), pp. 303–329.
34. Morikawa Hidemasa, "Meijiki senmon keieisha no keisei no sono haikei," *Keizaikei*, Kanto Gakuin Daigaku, no. 100 (1974).

3. Business and the Corporate State: The Business Lobby and Bureaucrats on Labor, 1911–1941, by Andrew Gordon

I presented an earlier version of this chapter at a panel on Labor Policy under Authoritarianism at the meeting of the Association for Asian Studies of 2–4 April 1982. I should like to thank fellow panelists Gary Allinson and Sheldon Garon for their extensive and helpful written comments.

1. Sumiya Mikio, "Kōjōhō taisei to rōshi kankei," in Sumiya, ed. *Nihon rōshi kankei shi ron* (1977), p. 7, cites *Kōjōhō an no setsumei* (1910).
2. Andrew Gordon, "Workers, Managers, and Bureaucrats in Japan: Labor Relations in Heavy Industry," PhD dissertation, Harvard University, 1981, pp. 113–114.
3. Sumiya, "Kōjōhō," p. 30.
4. Ibid., pp. 33–34.

5. The Tokyo Chamber of Commerce actually supported a factory law in 1883.
6. Sumiya, "Kōjōhō," pp. 12–17.
7. Ibid., pp. 14–15, cites Hara Kei's diary on a meeting with textile industrialists over this issue.
8. Sheldon Garon, "Parties, Bureaucrats, and Labor Policy in Prewar Japan, 1918–1931," PhD dissertation, Yale University (1981), pp. 23–24. See also Garon, *State and Labor in Modern Japan, 1868–1952* (Berkeley, University of California Press, 1987).
9. Sheldon Garon, *State and Labor,* Chapters 2 and 3, offers a rich picture of the background and motives of the bureaucrats and politicians, from which the description in this paragraph is drawn.
10. Gordon, "Labor Relations," pp. 412–413.
11. *Nihon kōgyō kurabu 50 nen shi* (1972); Morita Yoshio, *Nihon keieisha dantai hattatsu shi* (1958), pp. 63–64 and passim.
12. *Nihon rōdō nenkan,* 1920, p. 905, cited in Garon, "Labor Policy," p. 44.
13. Garon, "Labor Policy," pp. 45–46.
14. *Tokyo asahi shimbun,* 15 March 1920, p. 9.
15. Garon, "Labor Policy," pp. 236; Morita, *Keieisha dantai,* p. 62.
16. Garon, "Labor Policy," pp. 155–157.
17. Morita, *Keieisha dantai,* pp. 54–56, 117–124.
18. Ibid., pp. 124–131.
19. Ibid., pp. 174–178.
20. Garon, "Labor Policy," pp. 241–244, and Appendix III, p. 276.
21. Ibid., pp. 258–260.
22. Morita, *Keieisha dantai,* p. 174.
23. Ibid., p. 180.
24. Ibid., pp. 173–186.
25. Ibid., pp. 186–189.
26. Naisei Shi Kenkyū Kai, ed., *Matsumoto Gaku shi danwa sokkiroku,* II, 69.
27. This account of the political debate and struggle over the Retirement Fund Law is drawn primarily from *Nihon rōdō nenkan,* 1937, pp. 404–414. The text of the law is reproduced on pp. 415–422. Information on the creation and membership of the Home Ministry committee is taken from the 1931–1937 volumes of the *Shokuin roku* and from Rōdō shō, ed., *Rōdō gyōsei shi,* pp. 310, 576–577.
28. *Nihon rōdō nenkan, 1937,* pp. 379–381, prints the text of the Zensanren statement and the press reaction.
29. Gordon, "Labor Relations," p. 435.
30. Morita, *Keieisha dantai,* pp. 226–227, claims that Zensanren accepted the law in deference to the "new social situation" after the 26 February incident.
31. Gordon, "Labor Relations," pp. 435–436.
32. Morita, *Keieisha dantai,* p. 225. *Shokuin roku,* 1931–1937.
33. Philippe Schmitter, "Still the Century of Corporatism?" *The Review of Politics* 36.1 (January 1974).
34. The account here of the Sanpō movement is drawn from the following sources: Morita, *Keieisha dantai,* pp. 244–280, including excellent detail on

the role of Zensanren; Yoshii Yukiko, "Sangyō hōkoku undō: sono seiritsu o megutte," *Hitotsubashi ronsō* 73.2 (February 1975), with an insightful, slightly revisionist assessment that casts Zensanren as skillful manipulator rather than opponent of Sanpō; Ujihara Shōjirō, "Sangyō hōkokukai undō no haikei," Tokyo Daigaku Shakai Kagaku Kenkyūjo, ed. *Undō to teikō* Vol. I, (1979).

35. Yoshii, "Sangyō hokoku undo," p. 44.

36. Morita, *Keieisha dantai*, pp. 208–212.

37. *Rōdō jihō*, March 1942, pp. 72–79. This monthly publication of the Welfare Ministry printed the text and official explanation of the regulation.

38. *Dayamondo*, 16 October 1941, pp. 18–21, article by Satō Masayori, the general manager (*sōmu bucho*) of Nihon Seitetsu. The article is dated 16 September 1941.

39. *Shakai seisaku jihō*, February 1942, pp. 37, 141, 172, 188–189, for this and other similar evaluations.

40. Naikaku insatsu kyoku, *Shokuin roku* for 1930s has information on the number and size of these regional offices. Kawasaki Jūkōgyō Kabushiki Kaisha ed., *Kawasaki Jūkōgyō Kabushiki Kaisha Shashi*, pp. 97–99 details the rare sort of case when the naval inspectorate played an active role in the internal affairs of a company before 1940. The threat of bankruptcy in 1927 drew in the naval inspectorate here, for Kawasaki was at work on several naval vessels.

41. Shūgiin, Sangiin, eds. *Gikai sei 70 nen shi: Teikoku Gikai anken meiroku* (1961), p. 264.

42. *Asahi shimbun* 15 January 1938, p. 3; 17 January 1938, p. 2; 6 May 1938, p. 2.

43. Ishikawajima Jūkōgyō Kabushiki Kaisha Shashi Henshū Iinkai, ed. *Ishikawajima Jūkōgyō Kabushiki Kaisha 108 nen shi* (1961), p. 446, and Uraga Dock Co., ed., *Uraga dokku 60 nen shi* (1957), pp. 297–298.

44. 12 October 1980 interview with Ōhashi Takeo; Yoshitake Eiichi testimony reported in Ishida letter.

45. Ōhashi interview.

46. *Tokyo asahi shimbun*, 29 August 1941, evening, p. 1.

47. Rōdōshō, ed., *Rōdō gyōsei shi* (1961), I, 1199–1205.

48. *Tokyo Asahi shimbun* 1 July 1938, p. 1, for list of Council members; *Jinji kōshinroku* (1939), for brief profiles of the business members.

49. *Tokyo asahi shimbun*, 16 July 1941 through 3 August 1941.

50. Ibid., 4 September 1941, p. 1.

51. Ibid., 31 July 1941, 1, 2, 3 August 1946.

52. Ibid., 12 September 1941, p. 2; 13 September 1941, p. 2.

53. Ibid., 24 September 1941, p. 1.

54. Morita, *Keieisha dantai*, pp. 295–297.

55. Ibid., pp. 325–326.

56. Ōhashi Takeo interview, 12 October 1980; Kaneko Yoshio interview, 28 October 1980; Letter from Ishida Tsutomu of Labor Ministry, December 1981, reporting on conversations with Kaneko and Yoshitake Eiichi, both of the Welfare Ministry in 1941.

57. *Dayamondo*, October 1941, pp. 18–21.

58. Hattori Eitaro, "Senji rōdō tōsei no tenkai to 'nōritsu' mondai," *Shakai seisaku jihō*, March 1942, pp. 172–193. The essay was actually written in February.
59. Masuda Tomio, "Rinsen taisei ka no rōryoku haichi to rōmu kanri," *Shakai seisaku jihō*, December 1941, pp. 115–120.
60. *Daiyamondo*, 11 February 1943, p. 13.
61. Gordon, "Labor Relations," pp. 477–479.
62. Ibid., pp. 473, 482–485.
63. Kaneko Yoshio interview, 28 October 1980, and Tomiyasu Nagateru interviews, 21 August and 28 August 1979. Tomiyasu was the NKK manager.
64. Morita, *Keieisha dantai*, pp. 297–306.
65. Schmitter, "Corporatism," pp. 105–108.
66. Ernest James Notar, "Labor Unions and the *Sangyō Hōkoku* Movement, 1930–1945: A Japanese Model For Industrial Relations," PhD dissertation, University of California, Berkeley, 1979.
67. See Gordon, "Labor Relations," Pt. IV, for a more detailed discussion of these issues.

4. Trial and Error: The Model Filature at Tomioka, by Stephen W. McCallion

1. Based on figures in Takahashi keizai kenkyūjo, ed., *Nihon sanshigyō hattatsu shi* (Tokyo: Seikatsusha, 1941), I, 61, 200, 212.
2. Based on figures in Gumma-ken sanshigyōshi hensan iinkai, ed., *Gumma-ken sanshigyōshi* (Maebashi: Gumma-ken Sanshigyō Kyōkai, 1954), I, 638 and Hirano Murayakuba, ed., *Hirano sonshi* (Hirano: Hirano Murayakuba, 1933), II, appendix.
3. The full text is in Ōtsuka Ryōtarō, ed., *Sanshi* (Tokyo: Fusōen, 1900), I, 249–250.
4. Comparative expenditures for state-run factories through 1885 can be found in Kobayashi Masaaki, *Nihon no kōgyōka to kangyō haraisage* (Tokyo: Tōyō Keizai Shinpōsha, 1977), p. 139.
5. As of the summer of 1871, the supreme decision-making body of the Meiji government was the Council of State (Dajōkan); the council was headed by the chancellor (*dajō daijin*) and subdivided into the Central Board, the Right Board, and the Left Board. Policy decisions, including those pertaining to Tomioka Filature, were usually made by the Central Board and the Right Board (whose memberships were increasingly the same and were mostly the heads of ministries), and were issued in the name of the chancellor. This structure was retained until the adoption of the cabinet system in 1885.
6. Ōtsuka, *Sanshi*, I, 254–256. This sequence of events is based on the recollections of Shibusawa Eiichi.
7. Tomioka seishijōshi hensan iinkai, ed., *Tomioka seishijōshi* (Tomioka: Tomioka-shi Kyōiku Iinkai, 1977), document no. 4, I, 139, 147–150 (hereafter cited as *TSS*).
8. Brunat's contract is included in ibid., pp. 150–152.

9. Tomioka's establishment costs were estimated at ¥200,000. For details, see *TSS,* document no. 3, I, 134–135.

10. See *TSS,* document no. 5, I, 157.

11. Sano Akira, *Dai Nihon sanshi: seishi* (Tokyo: Dai Nihon Sanshi Hensan Jimusho, 1898), pp. 242–243.

12. *TSS,* document no. 39, I, 227–239.

13. *TSS,* document no. 5, I, 156–158; Fujimoto Saneya, *Tomioka seishijōshi* (Tokyo: Katakura Seishi Bōseki Kabushiki-Kaisha, 1943), pp. 16–17.

14. Fujimoto, *Tomioka seishijōshi,* p. 16.

15. *TSS,* document no. 5, I, 158.

16. Fujimoto, *Tomioka seishijōshi,* pp. 18, 24.

17. *TSS,* document no. 3, I, 134–138. Odaka referred to his alternative approaches in an article he wrote in 1893 but in a form different from what he had originally written. For specifics, see *TSS,* document no. 10, I, 171.

18. *TSS,* document no. 10, I, 172.

19. *TSS,* p. 44.

20. The most sensational rumor about the French was that they drank Japanese blood. This apparently began when a Tomioka resident saw the French drinking red wine. For details, see *TSS,* document no. 5, I, 159.

21. The full text of the announcement is in Sano, *Dai Nihon sanshi: seishi,* pp. 289–290.

22. Fujimoto, *Tomioka seishijōshi,* pp. 25–26.

23. The notice is found in *TSS,* document no. 134, I, 321–322. The prefectures' response is based on figures in *TSS,* document no. 165, I, 357–358.

24. Fujimoto, *Tomioka seishijōshi,* pp. 25–26.

25. *TSS,* document no. 165, I, 357–358. For an example of the response of the samurai to the situation, and an illustration of the pressure they were under, see Wada Hide, *Tomioka nikki,* ed. Kamijō Hiroyuki (Tokyo: Sōjusha, 1976), pp. 9–10.

26. For the number of women at Tomioka, and their origin, for selected years through 1884, see *TSS,* document no. 165, I, 357–358.

27. Wada, *Tomioka nikki,* pp. 21–22.

28. The regulations for the women trainees are included in *TSS,* document no. 4, I, 153–154.

29. For the names and salaries of the French employees, see Fujimoto, *Tomioka seishijōshi,* p. 32.

30. Wada, *Tomioka nikki,* pp. 21–22.

31. The two accounts are Wada, *Tomioka nikki,* and a much briefer one in *TSS,* document no. 339, I, 819–821.

32. Based on information in *TSS,* document no. 176, I, 383–384. Spending of this magnitude was not unique to Tomioka; salaries for Western advisers in the Ministry of Industry, for example, amounted to 42% of the Ministry's total expenditures between 1870 and 1888. See Hisashi Kawada, "Industrialization and Educational Investment in the Meiji Era," in *Educational Investment in*

the *Pacific Community* (Washington, D.C., American Association of Colleges for Teacher Education, 1963).

33. *TSS,* document no. 5, I, 161–162.
34. *TSS,* document no. 18, I, 194 and document no. 22, I, 195–196.
35. *TSS,* document no. 25, I, 196.
36. *TSS,* document no. 31, I, 216–218.
37. According to Odaka, when Brunat's contract finally expired, there were some in the government who thought it desirable to extend it or, alternatively, to hire another French director. Odaka said the idea was dropped when he protested strongly and insisted that the Japanese had to run Tomioka themselves at that point. See *TSS,* document no. 5, I, 161.
38. Fujimoto, *Tomioka seishijōshi,* pp. 28–30.
39. *TSS,* document no. 180, I, 394–395.
40. *TSS,* document no. 221, I, 503. Through fiscal 1884, the fiscal year ran from July of the year designated through June of the following year. As of fiscal 1885, the period was changed to run from April to the following March.
41. For Hayami's full report, see *TSS,* document no. 187, I, 401–403. Such problems were apparently typical of government industries in general. In 1876, the Ministry of Industry complained that officials at public factories received disproportionately high salaries, were less efficient than their counterparts in private business, and were trapped by red tape. See Kobayashi, *Nihon no kōgyōka to kangyō haraisage,* p. 123.
42. The merchant also gave his opinion of the state of the silk industry in general, and his report is interesting in that respect as well. See *TSS,* document no. 188, I, 403–406.
43. *TSS,* document no. 5, I, 162–163.
44. *TSS,* document no. 193, I, 425.
45. *TSS,* document no. 222, I, 515. The money was to be used for the purchase of cocoons, and was to be repaid each year after receipts for the sale of raw silk on the Lyon market arrived.
46. Ōtsuka, *Sanshi,* I, 398.
47. Fujimoto, *Tomioka seishijōshi,* p. 46.
48. *TSS,* document no. 219, I, 482–483. At the government's request, Hayami continued to act as an adviser on matters concerning Tomioka. See Ōtsuka, *Sanshi,* I, 434.
49. For the complete announcement, including terms of disposal, see Kobayashi, *Nihon on kōgyōka to kangyō haraisage,* pp. 182–183.
50. For the complete report, written by Maeda Masana and dealing with the silk industry in Gumma as a whole, see *TSS,* document no. 204, I, 458–463.
51. *TSS,* document no. 218, I, 482.
52. *TSS,* document no. 261, I, 635–636.
53. *TSS,* document no. 263, I, 638–645.
54. *TSS,* document no. 264, I, 662.
55. *TSS,* document no. 234, I, 542.
56. This was true of the silk-reeling industry as a whole; exports to the United States were insignificant until about 1880, at which point they increased

spectacularly and continued to increase thereafter. For figures, see Yoko-hama-shi, ed., *Yokohama shishi* (Yokohama: Yūrindō, 1951), III, pt. I, 470.

57. *TSS,* document no. 244, I, 579; Ōtsuka, *Sanshi,* II, 10–11.

58. *TSS,* document no. 233, I, 539.

59. For examples, see *TSS,* document no. 241, I, 566–572 and document no. 242, I, 572–573.

60. For examples of this way of thinking, see *TSS,* document no. 218, I, 477–482 and document no. 233, I, 539–542.

61. Based on figures in *TSS,* document no. 237, I, 556 and document no. 245, I, 585.

62. Based on figures in *TSS,* document no. 237, I, 556, document no. 243, I, 575, and document no. 244, I, 580. At the same time, it should be noted, this reputed champion of private enterprise raised the salaries of the officials at Tomioka.

63. Quoted in Fujimoto, *Tomioka seishijōshi,* p. 52.

64. Ibid., p. 54.

65. Kobayashi, *Nihon no kōgyōka to kangyō haraisage,* p. 299.

66. Fujimoto, *Tomioka seishijōshi,* p. 56.

67. TSS, document no. 258, I, 617.

68. The surplus is based on figures in Fujimoto, *Tomioka seishijōshi,* p. 56, and *TSS,* document no. 3, I, 134 and document no. 258, I, 617–618. For Tomioka under civilian management, see Fujimoto, *Tomioka seishijōshi,* pp. 57–78; Kobayashi, *Nihon no kōgyōka to kangyō haraisage,* pp. 301–306; and *TSS,* pp. 76–93.

69. *TSS,* document no. 258, I, 618.

70. Works that stress Tomioka's importance include Hirano Murayakuba, *Hirano sonshi;* Andō Yasuo, "Tomioka seishijō," in Chihōshi Kenkyū Kyō-gikai, ed., *Nihon sangyōshi taikei,* IV (Tokyo: Tokyo Daigaku Shuppankai, 1959); and Ueda Shishi Hensan Iinkai, ed., *Ueda kindaishi* (Ueda: Ueda-shi, 1970). Those that regard Tomioka as of little consequence include Yagi Akio, *Nihon kindai seishigyō no seiritsu,* 2nd ed. (Tokyo: Ochanomizu Shobō, 1978) and Kajinishi Mitsuhaya, *Gendai Nihon sangyō hattatsu shi,* XI (Tokyo: Kojunsha Shuppan-Kyoku, 1964).

71. Quoted in Fujimoto, *Tomioka seishijōshi,* p. 47.

72. *TSS,* document no. 258, I, 618.

73. Shibusawa Eiichi, "Yo wa ika ni shite Tomioka seishijō sekkei kantoku no nin ni atarishika," *Dai Nihon sanshikaihō* 200:14 (January 1909).

74. Based on figures in *TSS,* document no. 165, I, 357–358 and document no. 237, I, 556. The women are assumed to have stayed at Tomioka for an average of one year (a rather generous assumption).

75. Based on figures in Yokohama-shi, *Yokohama shishi,* III, pt. I, 516.

76. See *TSS,* I, 821–831 passim.

77. The figures are in *TSS,* document no. 165, I, 357–358.

78. Nōshōmushō Kannō-Kyoku and Shōmu-Kyoku, eds., *Kyōshinkai hōkoku: kenshi no bu* (Tokyo: Yūrindō, 1880), pp. 67–69; Nōshōmushō Nōmu-Kyoku,

ed., *Seishi shijunkai kiji* (Tokyo: Nōshōmushō nōmu-kyoku, 1883; reprint ed., Tokyo Daigaku Shuppankai, 1965), p. 77.

79. Ibid., p. 49.
80. Based on information in *TSS,* document no. 164, I, 338–357.
81. Wada, *Tomioka nikki,* pp. 56–57.
82. *TSS,* document no. 195, I, 444.
83. The practice of hiring local women actually began in 1875, according to the filature's financial statement for that fiscal year; but there are no figures for this until 1884, at which point commuters and day laborers accounted for over one-third of the work force. See *TSS,* document no. 195, I, 444 and document no. 165, I, 358.
84. The best source for information on Rokkusha (also referred to as Rokkōsha) is Dai Nihon Sanshikai Shinano Shikai, ed., *Shinano sanshigyōshi* (Nagano: Dai Nihon Sanshikai Shinano Shikai, 1937), especially III, 162–186. See also *TSS,* document nos. 374, 375 and 376, I, 833–839.
85. Wada, *Tomioka nikki,* pp. 72, 78.
86. For examples, see Dai Nihon Sanshikai Shinano Shikai, *Shinano sanshigyōshi,* III, 202–203 and Honda Iwajirō, *Nihon Sanshigyōshi* (Tokyo: Dai Nihon Sanshikai, 1935), pp. 69–83 passim. There was at least one case where someone was refused admission to Tomioka; see Ishii Kanji, *Nihon sanshigyōshi bunseki* (Tokyo: Tokyo Daigaku Shuppankai, 1972), p. 74.
87. Honda, *Nihon sanshigyōshi,* pp. 69–71.
88. Ibid., p. 77.
89. Ōtsuka, *Sanshi,* I, 402.
90. The 1883 prefectural survey is in Dai Nihon Sanshikai Shinano Shikai, *Shinano sanshigyōshi,* III, 584–616. For a study of Nagano filatures based on Tomioka's technology, see Takeda Yasuhiro, "1870 Nendai Nagano-ken kikai seishi no tenkai katei no kentō," *Shinano* 30.2:111–128 (February 1978) and 30.3: 213–227 (March 1978).
91. Shibusawa, "Yo wa ika ni shite Tomioka seishijō sekkei kantoku no nin ni atarishika," p. 14.
92. Based on figures in Dai Nihon Sanshikai, *Nihon sanshigyō shi* (Nagano: Dai Nihon Sanshikai Shinano Shikai, 1937), p. 428.
93. Ehado Akira, *Sanshigyō chiiki no keizai chiriteki kenkyū* (Tokyo: Kogon Shoin, 1939), pp. 72–73.
94. Based on statistics in Hashimoto Jūhyōei, *Kiito bōeki no hensen* (Tokyo: Maruyamasha Honten, 1902), pp. 102–104.
95. Mitsui, in fact, replaced Tomioka's machinery shortly after taking over. See Kobayashi, *Nihon no kōgyōka to kangyō haraisage,* pp. 76–93.
96. Figures are in Nōshōmushō nōmukyoku, *Sanshigyō ni kansuru sankō shiryō* (Tokyo: Nōshōmushō, 1916), pp. 60–62.

5. *Railroads in Crisis: The Financing and Management of Japanese Railway Companies during the Panic of 1890, by Steven J. Ericson*

1. Kozo Yamamura, "Entrepreneurship, Ownership, and Management in Japan," in Peter Mathias and M. M. Postan, eds., *The Cambridge Economic History of Europe* (Cambridge, Cambridge University Press, 1978), Vol. VII, pt. 2, p. 243. In fairness to Yamamura, he does consider the experience of companies in several other industries as well in his more detailed study, "Japan, 1868–1930: A Revised View," in Rondo Cameron, ed., *Banking and Economic Development: Some Lessons of History* (New York, Oxford University Press, 1972), pp. 178–181.

2. Takafusa Nakamura, *Economic Growth in Prewar Japan*, tr. Robert A. Feldman (New Haven, Yale University Press, 1983), pp. 108, 111.

3. Alfred D. Chandler, Jr., *The Visible Hand: The Managerial Revolution in American Business* (Cambridge, Harvard University Press, Belknap Press, 1977), p. 9.

4. Ishii Kanji, "Kigyō bokkō," in Ōishi Kaichirō and Miyamoto Ken'ichi, eds., *Nihon shihonshugi hattatsushi no kiso chishiki* (Yūhikaku, 1975), p. 105; Masaho Noda, "Corporate Finance of Railroad Companies in Meiji Japan," in Keiichiro Nakagawa, ed., *Marketing and Finance in the Course of Industrialization: Proceedings of the Third Fuji Conference*, The International Conference on Business History (Tokyo, University of Tokyo Press, 1978), p. 88.

5. Nagaoka Shinkichi, *Meiji kyōkōshi josetsu* (Tōkyō Daigaku Shuppankai, 1971), p. 21. On the installment payment system and stock-collateral lending by banks in connection with private railways, see Noda Masaho, *Nihon shōken shijō seiritsushi: Meiji ki no tetsudō to kabushiki kaisha kin'yū* (Yūhikaku, 1980), pp. 189–231, and "Corporate Finance of Railroad Companies," pp. 90–96.

6. *Meiji shijū nendo Tetsudō kyoku nenpō*, ed. Teishin Shō Tetsudō Kyoku (Tetsudō In, 1909), Appendix, p. 44; *Nihon teikoku dai jūsan tōkei nenkan*, ed. Naikaku Shokikan-shitsu Tōkei-ka (By the Editor, 1894), p. 655.

7. The market prices of only a handful of the stocks listed on the Tokyo and Osaka stock exchanges did not fall below their paid-up values in 1890. *Tōkyō kabushiki torihikijo gojū nenshi*, ed. Tōkyō Kabushiki Torihikijo (By the Editor, 1928), p. 126; *Ō-kabu gojū nenshi*, ed. Ōsaka Kabushiki Torihikijo (By the Editor, 1928), p. 589.

8. *Nihon tetsudōshi*, ed. Tetsudō Shō, 3 vols. (By the Editor, 1921), I, 663; *Japanese Railways: Annual Report of the Imperial Railway Department for 21st Fiscal Year of Meiji (April 1888 to march 1889)*, p. 24, Transportation Museum Archives, Tokyo.

9. *Nihon Kokuyū Tetsudō hyaku nenshi*, ed. Nihon Kokuyū Tetsudō, 14 vols. (By the Editor, 1969–1974), II (1970), 390–391, hereafter cited as *Hyaku nenshi*.

10. Noda, *Nihon shōken shijō*, p. 75.

11. M. C. Reed, *Investment in Railways in Britain, 1820–1844: A Study in the Development of the Capital Market* (London, Oxford University Press, 1975), p. 96.

12. *Tetsudō Kyoku nenpō* (1909), Appendix, p. 44.

13. Ibid., p. 31, Appendix, pp. 22–46 passim.
14. *Tetsudō iken zenshū*, ed. Otani Matsujirō (By the Editor, 1892), pp. 397–398.
15. *Tōkyō Kabushiki Torihikijo*, Table 5; *Ō-kabu*, Statistical Appendix.
16. Nakanishi Ken'ichi, *Nihon shiyū tetsudōshi kenkyū; toshi kōtsū no hatten to sono kōzō*, 2nd ed. (Minerva Shobō, 1979), p. 40.
17. Noda, *Nihon shōken shijō*, pp. 83–85, 263.
18. *Nihon tetsudōshi*, I, 899.
19. "Shin jigyō no shihonkin roku oku en ni noboru," *Tōyō keizai shinpō*, no. 15 (5 April 1896), cited in Noda, *Nihon shōken shijō*, p. 98.
20. *Nihon tetsudōshi*, I, 878.
21. Takamura Naosuke, *Nihon bōseki gyōshi josetsu*, 2 vols. (Hanawa Shobō, 1971), I, 169–170, 172n28. Takamura notes that, in both semesters of 1890, over 40% of the spinning companies whose dividend rates could be determined offered no dividends whatsoever.
22. Vols. VII–IX of the Teishin Shō Kōbunsho, Japanese National Railways Archives, Tokyo, contain an extensive collection of railway-company business reports, many with appended stockholders' lists, for 1894–1895. Rakechi has analyzed lists of major stockholders primarily for 1895–1896 and Sugiyama, for 1902–1903 and 1905–1906. Takechi Kyōzō, "Nisshin sensōgo tetsudō kaisha no dai kabunushi to sono keifu," *Seitō joshi tanki daigaku kiyō* 6:1–61 (September 1976); Sugiyama Kazuo, "Meiji 30 nendai ni okeru tetsudō kaisha no dai kabunushi to keieisha," *Seikei daigaku keizai gakubu ronshū* 7.2:153–181 (1977).
23. Hoshino Takao, "Nippon tetsudō kaisha to Dai jūgo kokuritsu ginkō (2)," *Musashi daigaku ronshū* 19.1:9 (August 1971).
24. Ishii Tsuneo, "Ryōmō tetsudō kaisha ni okeru kabunushi to sono keifu," *Meidai shōgaku ronsō* 41.9–10:142–143, 147 (July 1958).
25. "San'yō Tetsudo kaisha kabunushi meibo," September 1891, in *Nakamigawa Hikojirō denki shiryō*, ed. Nihon keieishi kenkyūjo (Tōyō Keizai Shinpōsha, 1969), pp. 170–174.
26. Takechi, pp. 44–45. Several of Takechi's other categories include bank executives who were concurrently merchants, landlords, brokers, and the like.
27. Ishii, pp. 142–146.
28. "San'yō kabunushi meibo," p. 170.
29. See Hoshino, "Nippon tetsudō (2)," p. 22, on the Fifteenth National Bank's conversion to ordinary bank status in 1897 and its appearance from that year on Nippon Railway stockholders' lists; and Sugiyama Kazuo, "Kabushiki kaisha seido no hatten: bōseki, tetsudō gyō o chūshin ni," in Kobayashi Masaaki et al., eds., *Meiji keieishi*, Vol. I of *Nihon keieishi o manabu*, Yūhikaku sensho (Yūhikaku, 1976), pp. 117–118, on the rise of institutional investors in railway companies after the turn of the century.
30. "San'yō kakbunushi meibo," pp. 170–171.
31. See Hoshino Takai, "Nippon tetsudō kaisha to Dai jūgo kokuritsu ginkō (1)– (3)," *Musashi daigaku ronshū* 17:77–109 (June 1970), 19.1:1–22 (August 1971), 19.5–6:117–183 (March 1972).
32. Hugh Patrick, "Japan, 1868–1914," in Rondo Cameron et al., *Banking in the Early Stages of Industrialization: A Study in Comparative Economic History*

(New York, Oxford University Press, 1967), pp. 258–259; Kozo Yamamura, *A Study of Samurai Income and Entrepreneurship: Quantitative Analyses of Economic and Social Aspects of the Samurai in Tokugawa and Meiji Japan,* Harvard East Asian Series, 76 (Cambridge, Harvard University Press, 1974), pp. 174–176; Yamamura, "Revised View," p. 175.

33. Hoshino, "Nippon tetsudō (3)," pp. 155–156, 182.

34. Ibid., pp. 164–165; *Tetsudō Kyoku nenpō* (1909), Appendix, pp. 44–45.

35. Hoshino, "Nippon tetsudō (3)," p. 155.

36. Ibid., pp. 164–165.

37. Ibid., p. 155.

38. The bank would acquire an interest—a relatively minor one—in only one other railway company, the medium-sized Iwagoe, founded in 1897. At the time of the Iwagoe's purchase by the government in 1906, the Fifteenth National held 5,000 shares in the railway. Ibid., pp. 180–181.

39. "San'yō kabunushi meibo," p. 170; Hoshino, "Nippon tetsudō (2)," pp. 11, 19–20, "Nippon tetsudō (3)," p. 166; Kansai Tetsudō Kabushiki Kaisha, *Dai jūnikai hōkoku* (1894), p. 36; "Kaku shisetsu tetsudō dai kabunushi ichiran-hyō (1)," *Tetsudō zasshi* 5:22 (June 1896); *Chikuhō tetsudō kabushiki kaisha kabunushi jinmeihyō* (1895). Noda has shown that the aggregate turnover in railway shares on the nation's stock exchanges declined dramatically during the panic and recession and remained at a moderate level through 1895. Noda, *Nihon shōken shijō,* p. 238. In most cases, therefore, one can probably regard the number of first-issue shares held by an investor, say, at the end of fiscal-year 1895 as a fairly accurate approximation of the number he possessed during the financial crisis (most railways did not issue new shares until after 1892).

40. In 1905–1906, the Fifteenth National held 308,773 shares of railway stock; Mitsubishi (Iwasaki Hisaya and Iwasaki Yanosuke), 157,122 shares; Mitsui (Mitsui Bank and Bank President Mitsui Takayasu), 126,752 shares; and the Imperial Household, 63,326 shares. Sugiyama, "Meiji 30 nendai," pp. 156–157, 160–161, 170.

41. Hoshino, "Nippon Tetsudō (2)," pp. 10, 19–20, "Nippon Tetsudō (3)," p. 166; Ishii, p. 143.

42. Takechi, p. 10; "San'yō kabunushi meibo," p. 170.

43. "Dai kabunushi ichiranhyō (1)," p. 22; Takechi, p. 22.

44. Takechi, p. 44.

45. Ibid., pp. 10, 15, 30; Hoshino, "Nippon Tetsudō (2)," pp. 19–20, "Nippon Tetsudō (3)," p. 166.

46. Hoshino, "Nippon tetsudō (2)," p. 16n4.

47. Sugiyama Kazuo, "Kigyō no zaimu-tōshi katsudō to bunkateki haikei: Meiji ki no tetsudō gyō, men-bōseki gyō o jirei to shite," *Keiei shigaku* 10.1:57 (August 1975).

48. Takechi, p. 10; Kōbu Tetsudō Kabushiki Kaisha, *Dai jūnikai hōkoku* (1894).

49. Takechi, pp. 44, 47–49.

50. Ibid., p. 45.

51. In 1902–1903, Tanaka, with a total of 27,217 shares, appears to have been the

fifth largest railway stockholder after the Fifteenth National Bank, Mitsubishi, Mitsui, and the Imperial Household. Sugiyama, "Meiji 30 nendai," pp. 155–156.

52. Takechi, pp. 44–46.
53. Sugiyama, "Kabushiki kaisha seido," p. 116.
54. "San'yō kabunushi meibo," p. 170.
55. Ishii, pp. 142–147.
56. Ono Kazushige, "Kōbu Tetsudō to Tachikawa," *Tachikawa-shi shi kenkyū* 2:116 (December 1965).
57. Ishii, pp. 141–142.
58. Takechi, pp. 53–55; Ishii, pp. 143–145.
59. Sugiyama, "Meiji 30 nendai," p. 159n1.
60. Murakami Teiichi, *Minami Kiyoshi den* (Hayami Tarō, 1909), pp. 69–70.
61. Tagawa-shi, ed., *Tagawa-shi shi*, 3 vols. (Tagawa, Tagawa Shiyakusho, 1976), II, 912–913.
62. Sugiyama, "Kigyō no zaimu-tōshi katsudō," p. 57.
63. Albert Fishlow, *American Railroads and the Transformation of the Antebellum Economy*, Harvard Economic Studies (Cambridge, Harvard University Press, 1965), p. 308.
64. "Kyūshū Tetsudō Kabushiki Kaisha chōsa hōkokusho," February 1900, in *Shibusawa Eiichi denki shiryō*, ed. Shibusawa Seien Kinen Zaidan Ryūmonsha, 68 vols. (Dō Shiryō Kankōkai, 1955–1971), IX (1956), 278.
65. Kikuchi Takenori, *Nakamigawa Hikojirō-kun* (Jinmin Shinbunsha Shuppanbu, 1903), pp. 57–59.
66. "Kyūshū tetsudō hōkokusho," p. 278.
67. *Hyaku nenshi*, II, 582–584.
68. Kikuchi, p. 60.
69. Murakami Sadamu, "Keiroku," in *Nakamigawa denki shiryō*, p. 185. The number of cars fell from 684 in 1891 to 462 in 1892. *Hyaku nenshi*, II, 582.
70. Memorandum from Matsukata to Prime Minister Yamagata Aritomo, 25 April 1891, Kōbun ruiju, 15th ser., Vol. XXXVII, no. 8, Kokuritsu Kōbunshokan, Tokyo.
71. Cited in memorandum from Home Minister Soejima Taneomi to Prime Minister Matsukata Masayoshi, 9 April 1892, Kōbun Ruiju, 16th ser., Vol. XXXVIII, no. 4.
72. *Nihon teikoku dai jū-dai jūni tōkei nenkan*, ed. Naikaku Tōkei Kyoku (By the Editor, 1891–1893), pp. 330 (1891), 680 (1892), 673 (1893); *Tetsudō kyoku nenpō* (1909), Appendix, p. 41.
73. Patrick, p. 283.
74. Ibid.
75. *Tetsudō kyoku nenpō* (1909), Appendix, pp. 44–45.
76. Patrick, p. 285.
77. In 12 of the 21 railways licensed before 1893, 42 of the 75 directors in June 1896 appear on their companies' major stockholders' lists for either March or September 1896. "Dai kabunushi ichiranhyō," *Tetsudō zasshi* (retitled *Tetsudō* from no. 19) 5:21–23 (June 1896); 7:23–24 (July 1896); 8:22–24 (July 1896);

26:30–32 (November 1896); "Jūyaku kachō ichiranhyō," *Tetsudō zasshi* 9:29–31 (July 1896), 10:23–26 (July 1896). (The definition of "major stockholders" ranges from owners of 100 or more shares in the case of the smaller companies to owners of 1,000 or more in that of the largest firms.) The data analyzed by Sugiyama, however, indicate that the situation had changed little, if at all, by the early 1900s. Whereas 39% of the directors in the 1896 sample appear among the top 10 shareholders in their firms, 37% of those in Sugiyama's 1902–1903 sample do so as well. Furthermore, directors listed among the major stockholders held, as a group, 10% or more of the total shares in 26% of the railways in Sugiyama's 1902–1903 sample and 34% of those in his 1905–1906 sample, compared to 33% of the companies in the 1896 group. Ibid.; Sugiyama, "Meiji 30 nendai," pp. 157–158.

78. Hoshino, "Nippon Tetsudō (1)," p. 105.
79. "San'yō Tetsudō Kaisha teikanchū kōsei no ken," Kōbun Ruiju," 13th ser., Vol. XLVI, no. 36.
80. "San'yō kabunushi meibo," pp. 170–174.
81. *Nakamigawa denki shiryō*, p. 135.
82. Sugiyama, "Kigyō no zaimu-tōshi katsudō," p. 71.
83. Ishii, pp. 137, 145.
84. "San'yō kabunushi meibo," pp. 170–174.
85. Tsunehiko Yui, "The Personality and Career of Hikojirō Nakamigawa, 1887–1901," *Business History Review* 44.1:45 (Spring 1970).
86. Ibid.
87. Murakami, "Keiroku," p. 183; Kikuchi, p. 57.
88. Ida Seiza, "San'yō tetsudō jidai," in *Nakamigawa denki shiryō*, p. 178.
89. Kikuchi, p. 63.
90. *Imanishi Rinzaburō ibunroku*, ed. Komatsu Mitsuo, 3 vols. (Osaka, Imanishi Yosaburō, 1925), Vol. I, Suppl., p. 4.
91. Yui, p. 47.
92. *Hyaku nenshi*, II, 585; "San'yō kabunushi meibo," pp 170–174.
93. *Imanishi ibunroku*, Vol. I, Suppl., p. 4b.
94. *Tōkyō nichinichi shinbun*, 17 June 1892, cited in *Hyaku nenshi*, II, 587.
95. *Hyaku nenshi*, II, 379–380.
96. Adachi Ritsuen, *Imamura Seinosuke-kun jireki* (Otani Matsujirō, 1906), p. 177.
97. Ibid., p. 179.
98. Ibid., pp. 178, 181. At the end of fiscal-year 1895, Imamura held 1,100 shares of the Kyushu Railway's first stock issue. "Dai kabunushi ichiranhyō (1)," p. 23.
99. *Tetsudō senjin roku*, ed. Nihon Kōtsū Kyōkai (Nihon Tishajō Kabushiki Kaisha, 1972), pp. 217–218, 247.
100. *Hyaku nenshi*, II, 596.
101. Ibid., p. 651. The San'yō and Kyushu subsidy orders also stipulated that, for the duration of the subvention, the appointment and dismissal of the president and vice-president would require the approval of the finance minister. Ibid., pp. 572, 602, 605.
102. Ibid., pp. 645, 653.

103. *Tetsudō senjin roku,* pp. 305–306; *Hyaku nenshi,* II, 662.

104. *Tetsudō senjin roku,* p. 356.

105. See *Kōgaku hakushi Shiraishi Naoji den,* ed. Dō Hensankai (By the Editor, 1943), pp. 77–108.

106. "Jūyaku kachō ichiranhyō."

107. *Tetsudō senjin roku,* pp. 57, 337; Sugiyama, "Kigyō no zaimu-tōshi katsudō," p. 72.

108. "Nihon no kaisha ni mo . . . korekara wa sō-shihainin o oku hitsuyō ari: San'yō tetsudō kaisha sossen shite kettei," reprinted in *Shinbun shūsei Meiji hennenshi,* ed. Dō Hensankai, 15 vols. (By the Editor, 1936), IX, 33.

109. Ushiba himself was appointed managing director of the San'yo in 1898 and chairman of its board in 1904. *Tetsudō senjin roku,* p. 57.

110. The phrase is Chandler's, although on the page cited he uses it in reference to stockholders in a "managerial enterprise." Chandler, p. 10.

111. Hoshino, "Nippon tetsudō (1)," p. 100.

112. Tagawa-shi, ed., II, 912–913.

113. Ishii, pp. 136–138, 147.

114. Adachi, p. 180.

115. *Tetsudō iken zenshū,* pp. 374–378, 387–389, 419–427, 458–476, 489–519.

116. Ibid., pp. 377–378.

117. See Wada Hiroshi, "Shoki gikai to tetsudō mondai," *Shigaku zasshi* 84.10:31–52 (October 1975).

118. *Hyaku nenshi,* II, 414; *Nihon tetsudōshi,* I, 829.

119. Kōbun Ruiju, 13th ser., Vol. L, cited in *Hyaku nenshi,* II, 564–565.

120. Ibid.

121. Ibid.

122. *Nihon tetsudōshi,* I, 735.

123. *Hyaku nenshi,* II, 566.

124. "The Protection of Railway Operations," *Japan Weekly Mail,* 17 May 1890, p. 495.

125. *Hyaku nenshi,* II, 414.

126. Ibid., p. 608.

127. *Kyū-tetsu nijū nenshi,* ed. Kyūshū Tetsudō Kabushiki Kaisha Sōmu-ka (By the Editor, 1907), pp. 27–28.

128. Memorial from President Hotta Masayasu of the Chikuhō Industrial Railway to Home Minister Saigō Tsugumichi, 14 May 1891, Tetsudō in Monjo, Chikuhō Kōgyō Tetsudō, Vol. I, no. 7, Transportation Museum Archives, Tokyo.

129. Memorandum from Inoue Masaru to the cabinet, 27 May 1891, ibid.

130. *Hyaku nenshi,* II, 639.

131. Ibid., p. 362.

132. Noda, *Nihon shōken shijō,* p. 98, "Corporate Finance of Railroad Companies," p. 88.

133. Harada Katsumasa and Aoki Eiichi, *Nihon no tetsudō: hyaku nen no ayumi kara,* Sanseido Books (Sanseidō, 1973), p. 46.

134. *Nihon tetsudōshi,* I, 961.

135. *Hyaku nenshi,* IV (1972), 222, 225.
136. Shimizu Keijirō, *Shitetsu monogatari* (Shunjūsha, 1930), p. 45.
137. *Hyaku nenshi,* II, 416–421, 426–429, 566–572, 602–605, 647–651.
138. Hoshino, "Nippon tetsudō (2)," pp. 17–18.
139. *Tetsudō kyoku nenpō* (1909), Appendix, pp. 43, 99; *Teikoku tetsudō yōkan,* 3rd ed. (Tetsudō Jihō Kyoku, 1906), p. 231.
140. Takizawa Naoshichi, *Kōhon Nihon kin'yū shiron* (Yūhikaku, 1912), p. 270.
141. *Nihon ginkō enkakushi,* ed. Dō Hensan-iin, 1st ser., 10 vols. (By the Editor, 1913), Vol. II, pt. 1, pp. 170–174. In its announcement of the measure, the bank actually designated 15 kinds of shares as authorized collateral, but 5 of them – N.Y.K., Tokio Marine Insurance, and 3 issues of Nippon Railway stock – it had in fact begun accepting before the announcement.
142. "Nihon kōgyō ginkō, dōsan ginkō oyobi nōgyō ginkō setsuritsu shushi no sō-setsumei," in *Nihon kin'yūshi shiryō: Meiji Taishō hen,* ed. Nihon Ginkō Chōsa Kyoku, 25 vols. (Ōkura Shō Insatsu Kyoku, 1955–1961), IV (1958), 1160; Patrick, p. 264, for total commercial bank loans.
143. Noda, *Nihon shōken shijō,* p. 195; Andō Yoshio, ed., *Kindai Nihon keizaishi yōran* (Tōkyō Daigaku Shuppankai, 1975), p. 53, for total national bank loans; Patrick, p. 264, for total commercial bank loans.
144. "Tetsudō kaiage ni kansuru chōsa-iin hōkokusho," in *Tetsudō iken zehshū,* p 40.
145. Ōkura Shō Kansa Kyoku, "Dai Jūsanji Ginkō eigyō hōkoku," 1890, in *Nihon kin'yūshi shiryō,* Vol. VII, pt. 1 (1960), p. 482.
146. *Meiji zaiseishi,* ed. Dō Hensankai, 15 vols. (Dō Hakkōsho, 1926–1928), XIV (1927), 942.
147. Directive from Watanabe to the Bank of Japan, 21 November 1892, Matsuo ke Monjo, 1st ser., Vol. LXXXII, no. 39, Finance Ministry Archives, Tokyo.
148. "Nihon ginkō enkaku teiyō (shuyō nisshi)," 1882–1905, in *Nihon kin'yūshi shiryō,* Vol. X (1957), Suppl., p. 181.
149. Noda, *Nihon shōken shijō,* p. 224.
150. *Hyaku nenshi,* II, 620; *Kyū-tetsu nijū nenshi,* p. 15.
151. Noda, "Corporate Finance of Railroad Companies," p. 98.
152. *Kyū-tetsu nijū nenshi,* pp. 22–23; Shibusawa Eiichi to Itō Hirobumi, 18 March 1893, in *Shibusawa denki shiryō,* IX, 6–7.
153. *Tetsudō kyoku nenpō* (1909), Appendix, pp. 22–46 passim.
154. "San'yō tetsudō kaisha," *Dai Nihon tetsudō zasshi* 9:20–21 (21 June 1890).
155. *Kyū-tetsu nijū nenshi,* p. 22.
156. *Honpō shasai ryakushi,* ed. Takahira Takao (Nihon Kōgyō Ginkō Chōsa Kakari, 1927), p. 3.
157. *Tetsudō kyoku nenpō* (1909), Appendix, pp. 22–46 passim.
158. *Sōken Matsumoto Jūtarō ōden,* ed. Matsumoto-ō Dōzō Kensetsukai (By the Editor, 1922), p. 30; "San'yō Tetsudō Kaisha no shasai boshū," *Tōkyō keizai zasshi* 666:394–395 (18 March 1893); *Tetsudō kyoku nenpō* (1909), Appendix, p. 24.
159. Kyūshū Tetsudō Kabushiki Kaisha, *Dai Jukkai hōkoku* (1893), p. 8, cited in Noda, *Nihon shōken shijō,* p. 90.

160. *Kyū-tetsu nijū nenshi,* p. 67; *Tetsudō kyoku nenpō* (1909), Appendix, p. 41.
161. "Kyūshū tetsudō hōkokusho," p. 278.
162. *Honpō shasai ryakushi,* pp. 12–16.
163. Sugiyama, "Kabushiki kaisha seido," pp. 122–123.
164. *Honpō shasai ryakushi,* pp. 13–16; Noda, *Nihon shōken shijō,* p. 130.
165. Kyūshū Tetsudō Kabushiki Kaisha, *Dai jūikkai hōkoku* (1894), p. 14, cited in Noda, *Nihon shōken shijō,* p. 95.
166. Noda, *Nihon shōken shijō,* pp. 93, 96.
167. *Teikoku tetsudō yōkan,* p. 151; "Shasaiken hikiuke jinmeihyō," 31 March 1895, in *Chikuhō kabunushi jinmeihyō,* p. 12.
168. Yamamura, "Revised View," pp. 173–178.
169. Ibid., p. 175.
170. Ibid., p. 173.
171. Yamamura, "Entrepreneurship, Ownership, and Management," p. 241.
172. Ibid., p. 243.
173. Kazuo Sugiyama, "Trade Credit and the Development of the Cotton Spinning Industry: Its Role and Background," in Nakagawa, ed., pp. 62–63.
174. On the raising of loan capital by the early British railways, see Reed, pp. 69–72.
175. On bank financing of German railways, see, for example, Richard Tilly, "Germany, 1815–1870," in Cameron et al., p. 179.
176. See Sugiyama, "Meiji 30 nendai," pp. 155–157, for the railway holdings of leading institutional investors in the early to mid-1900s.
177. Yamamura, "Entrepreneurship, Ownership, and Management," p. 262.
178. Chalmers Johnson, *MITI and the Japanese Miracle: The Growth of Industrial Policy, 1925–1975* (Stanford, Stanford University Press, 1982), p. 240.
179. See note 77 above.
180. Nakamura, p. 111.
181. Ibid., p. 110.
182. Chandler, p. 9.
183. Nakamura, p. 111.
184. Chandler, p. 9.
185. Noda, "Corporate Finance of Railroad Companies," p. 100.
186. On the pioneering of modern business management by railways in the United States, see Chandler, pp. 79–187.

6. Kagami Kenkichi and the N.Y.K., 1929–1935: Vertical Control, Horizontal Strategy, and Company Autonomy, by William D. Wray

I am grateful to Ishida Reiko for research assistance on this paper. I would also like to thank members of the Japanese Business History Society and the Economics Faculty Seminar at Tokyo University for helpful suggestions.

1. I have not treated here the issue of government-business relations (that is, the degree of company autonomy vis-à-vis the government). Even though government aid sometimes placed certain restrictions on company auton-

omy, however, shipping firms fought to retain a high degree of managerial autonomy within the framework of most subsidy programs.

2. In this respect, history influenced historiography, for British merchants and officials from Singapore and Malaya were among the more vocal witnesses before the British Imperial Shipping Committee. British shipping in this area suffered severe competition in the 1930s from the Shipping Department of Mitsui Bussan (the Mitsui Trading Company). This firm's shipping, which is outside the scope of the present study, can more accurately be characterized as part of a vertically integrated operation than can the case of the N.Y.K. Sometimes, however, British views of the Mitsui type of zaibatsu vertical integration were applied uncritically to other zaibatsu. For contrasts in the shipping operations of Mitsui Bussan and the N.Y.K., see my "NYK and the Commercial Diplomacy of the Far Eastern Freight Conference, 1896–1956," in Tsunehiki Yui and Keiichiro Nakagawa, eds., *Business History of Shipping: Strategy and Structure* (University of Tokyo Press, 1985), pp. 279–311.

3. Terai Hisanobu, *Kaiun no saiken* (Shichiyōsha, 1948), p. 91.

4. In my *Mitsubishi and the N.Y.K., 1870–1914: Business Strategy in the Japanese Shipping Industry* (Cambridge, Council on East Asian Studies, Harvard University, 1984), pp. 489–490, I used the label *horizontal* for the N.Y.K.'s business activity outside its zaibatsu, such as with Mitsui Bussan or cotton spinners. I contrasted this with *vertical* relations or *top-down* controls within the zaibatsu. This follows the definition in *Thirty-Eighth Report of the Imperial Shipping Committee: British Shipping in the Orient* (1939), #317, that an "important source of strength behind the Japanese shipping competition is the high degree of organization, in part vertical (Zaibatsu), in part horizontal (Rengokai [that is, the Cotton Spinners Association]), which characterizes the economic life of Japan." In the present study, I have used the term *horizontal* to refer to a company's relations with other firms in its own industry, rather than to describe, as I did in my book, its relations with other industries outside its zaibatsu.

5. *O.S.K. 80 nenshi* (Osaka, 1966), p. 27.

6. Terai Hisanobu, *Shio no michihi* (Gotō shoten, 1953), p. 59.

7. Nakagawa Keiichirō, *Ryōtaisenkan no Nihon kaiungyō*, Vol. I of *Nihon kaiun keieishi* (Nihon Keizai Shinbunsha, 1980), p. 47–109.

8. Wakimura Yoshitarō, "Sengo ni okeru Nippon Yūsen Kabushiki Kaisha," *Keizaigaku ronshū* 5.1:183 (June 1926).

9. Iwai Ryōtarō, *Kagami Kenkichi den, Katō Takeo den* (Tōyō Shokan, 1955), pp. 129–131; interview with Harada Kenjirō, former N.Y.K. director, 14 June 1974; N.Y.K. Kabunushi sōkai gijiroku, 29 May 1919; *N.Y.K. 70 nenshi* (Dōshahen, 1956), p. 675; *OSK 80 nenshi*, pp. 764–765.

10. Sugiyama Kazuo, *Kaiungyō to kin'yū*, Vol. IV of *Nihon kaiun keieishi* (Nihon Keizai Shinbunsha, 1981), pp. 125–128 (hereafter, Sugiyama); Asahara Jōhei, *Nihon kaiun hattenshi* (Chōryūsha, 1978), pp. 270–275; *Shibusawa Eiichi denki shiryō* (Ryūmonsha, 1958), Vol. 51, pp. 391–437; "Taishō 13 Yūsen naifun," in Ōtani Noboru Kankei Bunsho, Tokyo University, Faculty of Economics, Shiryō Shitsu.

11. It is sometimes said that a 3-man committee of Iwasaki Koyata, Gō Seino-suke, and Shibusawa Eiichi appointed Shirani. See Sugiyama, pp. 127–128. However, Shirani's son, Shirani Mitsuru, told me that Iwasaki made the appointment. Personal communication during interview with Shōda Shūhei, N.Y.K. director, 16 September 1975.
12. Sugiyama, pp. 157–158.
13. If we designated the N.Y.K.'s pre-1914 business results as 10 on a scale of 10, results for the 1920s by comparison would rate about a 4, though, with the pre-1914 subsidization rate, the figure would be closer to 6.
14. Nakagawa, *Ryōtaisenkan*, p. 138.
15. Ibid., pp. 133–137; Asahara, pp. 258–261. For details on the overseas lines and conferences, see *Wagasha kakukōro no enkaku*, ed. NYK Kamotsu-ka (1932); and Wray, "Commercial Diplomacy."
16. N.Y.K. Torishimariyakukai gijiroku #982, 11 March 1927 (Hereafter NYK-TG).
17. NYK-TG#1017, 21 December 1928; *Chōsen Yūsen Kabushiki Kaisha 25 nenshi* (Seoul, Dōshahen, 1937), pp. 205–206, 270.
18. NYK-TG#1031, 20 November 1929; *Nisshin Kisen Kabushiki Kaisha 50 nenshi* (Dōshahen, 1941), pp. 211–216, 265–269, 326; Asahara, pp. 261–262, 332.
19. For an account of Mitsubishi's management structure through late Taisho, see Hidemasa Morikawa, "The Organizational Structure of the Mitsubishi and Mitsui Zaibatsu, 1868–1922: A Comparative Study," *Business History Review* 44.1:62–83 (Spring 1970).
20. Mishima Yasuo, ed., *Mitsubishi zaibatsu*, in *Nihon zaibatsu keieishi* (Nihon Keizai Shinbunsha, 1981), pp. 94–106, 212–238.
21. Ibid., p. 51.
22. For the analogy, see Suzuki Mosaburō, *Zaikai jinbutsu tokuhon* (Shunjūsha, 1937), p. 100. On the insurance companies, see *Tōkyō Kaijō 80 nenshi* (Tōkyō Kaijō Kasai Hoken Kabushiki Kaisha, 1964), pp. 419–422; and Suzuki Sakae, ed. *Kagami Kenkichi-kun o shinobu* (1949), p. 268. For further comments on analogies with the Restoration during this period, see my "Asō Hisashi and the Search for Renovation in the 1930s," *Papers on Japan* 5:65–67 (1970).
23. Mishima, ed., *Mitsubishi*, p. 51. For Kagami's experience in London see Inagaki Shōsaburō, ed., *'Kagami-shi no shuki' to 'taieichū no hōkoku oyobi ikensho'* (Tōkyō Kaijō, 1951). Yamashita Kamesaburō notes that the event that symbolized Kagami's transformation from simply a man of insurance to a leader of the business world as a whole was a speech he gave in 1920 at the Industrial Club just after his return from a tour of the West. He spoke of trends in the world economy to luminaries of the business world and to the entire Cabinet. Yamashita Kamesaburō, *Shizumitsu ukitsu* (Yamashita Kabushiki Kaisha Hishobu, 1943), II, 12–13.
24. One account notes that Kagami as an individual (and not as a representative of Tokio Marine) was the second largest stockholder in the Mitsui Trust Co. in 1924. His 1.9% share was worth over half a million yen. See Asajima Shōichi, "Senzen ni okeru shintaku kaisha keiei no tokushitsu," *Keiei shigaku* 9.3:6 (June 1975).
25. Suzuki Mosaburō, *Nihon zaibatsu ron* (Kaizōsha, 1934), pp. 85–89.

Junnosuke Inouye, *Problems of the Japanese Exchange, 1914–1926* (London, Macmillan, 1939), p. 213, remarked that "the finance of the Japanese shipping trade is in the hands of a small section of the Japanese marine insurance companies."

26. Kimura Tsuyoshi, *Jinbutsu zaibatsu shi Mitsubishi, Sumitomo sono ta hen* (Jitsugyō no Nihonsha, 1956), p. 62; *Ekonomisuto*, 21 August 1938, p. 37; Iwai Ryōtarō, *Mitsubishi kontsuerun tokuhon* (Shunjūsha, 1937), p. 297.

27. Iwai, *Kagami*, pp. 129–131; Iwai, *Mitsubishi*, pp. 308–309; *Kaiji ihō*, 22 September 1919, p. 2 [hereafter *KI*]; and NYK Kabunushi Seimeibo.

28. NYK-TG#1024, 17 May 1929. On Kagami as a director prior to 1919, see Asahara, pp. 308–309.

29. Nakagawa, *Ryōtaisenkan*, p. 137; and Terai, *Shio*, p. 81.

30. Most Japanese stocks had a par value of ¥50. When companies decided on a capital stock increase they had stockholders pay for their shares in installments (4 in the N.Y.K.'s case, with each installment covering the value of one-quarter share, or ¥12.5). For further discussion of this issue, see Steven Ericson's chapter in this volume. The N.Y.K. carried out a large capital stock increase after the war but had received only the first installment prior to the recession. After that, they did not call in the remaining 3 installments. Thus stockholders' lists contain both old and new shares. See Table 5.

31. NYK-TG#1024, 17 May 1929; *KI*, 22 July 1929, p. 11; and Sugiyama, p. 160.

32. U.S. Foreign Economic Administration, Enemy Branch, "Administration of the Property of the Imperial Household of Japan," EA-17, September 1945. Ministry of Finance, taken from the Federal Record Center, Suitland, Maryland, especially pp. 40–42.

33. Opinion given by Yoneda Fujio, former official in the Ministry of Communications. Interview, 6 June 1974.

34. Wray, *Mitsubishi and the NYK*, pp. 243, 478–479; Ōtani Noboru nikki, 1 and 2 November 1929. Tokyo University Economics Faculty, Shiryō Shitsu. Ōtani's diary runs from 1906 to 1954 with several years missing. It is principally a log of events written in a diary book with one page per day. He generally avoids presenting his own opinions or discussing controversial issues. [Hereafter Ōtani Diary].

35. Asahara, pp. 329–330. For suggestive comments by Prince Konoe Fumimaro about the Emperor's personal concern with stock prices, see Gordon Mark Berger, *Parties Out of Power in Japan, 1931–1941* (Princeton University Press, 1977), pp. 268–269.

36. See esp. *KI*, 3 June 1929, p. 11; *Kaiun geppō*, June 1929, p. 55; and Iwai, *Mitsubishi*, p. 310. This was a good short-term deal for the Imperial House, for the new share price had fallen to ¥17.8 by August 1929 and to ¥8.3 by July 1930, remaining at that level for more than a year. See *KI*, 19 August 1929, p. 12; 14 July 1930, p. 12; and 17 August 1931, p. 12.

37. Terai, *Shio*, p. 81; NYK-TG#1050, 27 March 1931; *KI*, 29 July 1929, p. 2; and 3 February 1930, p. 2.

38. Nakagawa Keiichirō, "Ryōtaisenkan no Nihon kaiun," in Nakamura Takafusa, ed., *Senzenki no Nihon keizai bunseki* (Yamakawa Shuppansha, 1981), pp. 256–260; Asahara, pp. 326–328. For a fuller analysis, with excellent data,

of the O.S.K.'s New York line, see Tatsuki Mariko, "Kaiun fukyō to teikisen no gōrika: Ōsaka Shōsen no ke-su," *Shakai keizai shigaku* 52.3:1–33 (August 1986), esp. pp. 7–18.

39. Ōtani Diary, January to March 1931, esp. 26 and 27 March; NYK-TG#1050, 27 March 1931; *Kaiun geppō,* April 1931, pp. 1–9; *Kaiun,* May 1931, pp. 6–9; *KI,* 6 April 1931, p. 3 and 13 April 1931, p. 11; Asahara, pp. 333–340. The N.Y.K.'s subsidiary, the Kinkai Yūsen Kaisha, was added as a third signatory to the agreement on 6 April. Later, on 30 May, it worked out an agreement on lines, ports, and pooling with the O.S.K.'s Kita Nihon Kisen. See Asahara, pp. 337–338, and *Kita Nihon Kisen Kabushiki Kaisha 25 nenshi* (Otaru, Dōsha, 1939), p. 84.

40. Nomura Jiichirō, *Waga kaiun 60 nen* (Kokusai Kaiun Shinbunsha, 1955), p. 111. See also Murata Shōzō, "Yūsen shachō to shite no Kagami-san no omoide," in Suzuki, ed., *Kagami,* p. 52; and Terai, *Shio,* p. 82.

41. Ōtani Diary. Ōtani and Murata then went to secure the approval of Kagami, who discussed the matter on the phone with Yamashita during their meeting.

42. Ōtani Diary, 7 April 1931; *KI,* 13 April 1931, p. 11.

43. Ōtani Diary, 19 April 1931.

44. Asahara, pp. 354–355; Nakagawa, *Ryōtaisenkan,* pp. 137–139.

45. Asahara, pp. 255, 353–354; Nomura, p. 112; *KI,* 27 September 1920, p. 2; and NYK-TG#830, 9 April 1921.

46. KI, 5 June 1922, p. 4.

47. Itō Yonejirō, *Nihon on kaiun* (Hōbunkan, 1922), pp. 256–275; Sugiyama, pp. 76–122; Yamashita, II, 12.

48. Ōtani Diary, 10 April 1931; *Kaiun geppō,* May 1931, pp. 40–41, and August 1931, pp. 60–61. For comments by Ōtani and Murata on the labor situation, see *KI,* 27 April 1931, p. 3; and for discussion of the response of the non-main-line companies (*shagaisen*) to the accord, see *Kaiun,* May 1931, pp. 56–64; and *Kaiun geppō,* April 1931, pp. 10–15.

49. Masaru Udagawa and Seishi Nakamura, "Japanese Business and Government in the Inter-war Period: Heavy Industrialization and The Industrial Rationalization Movement," in Keiichiro Nakagawa, ed., *Government and Business,* Vol. V of *The International Conference on Business History* (University of Tokyo, 1980), pp. 83–100; Asahara, p. 354.

50. Yoneda Fujio interview.

51. Ōtani Diary, 30 March 1931; *Kaiun geppō,* April 1931, pp. 45–46.

52. Nakagawa Masau, "Kōtsū jigyō no gōrika," in Kazamatsu Shintarō, ed., *Kōtsū jigyō no gōrika* (Nihon Kōtsū Kyōkai, 1931), pp. 230–231; Ōtani Noboru, "Kaiun jigyō no gōrika," in Kazamatsu, pp. 1–31, esp. pp. 9, 15.

53. *KI,* 27 April 1931, p. 3; Ōtani Diary, 30 March 1931, and 4 April 1931.

54. John Swire & Sons Archive, School of Oriental and African Studies, University of London, JSSII 2/11, Butterfield & Swire to Alfred Holt & Co., 28 October 1932. (Hereafter JSS)

55. The quotation is from John K. Fairbank, Edwin O. Reischauer, and Albert M. Craig, *East Asia: The Modern Transformation* (Boston, Houghton Mifflin

Co., 1965), p. 506. Cf. Keiichiro Nakagawa, "Japanese Shipping in the Inter-war Period," unpublished paper presented at the Japan Forum, Harvard University, May 1979, p. 31. One rough estimate for the 1970s was that Mitsubishi supplied only 10% of N.Y.K. freight; Shōda Shūhei interview.

56. Wray, *Mitsubishi and the NYK*, pp. 457–466; Mishima, ed., *Mitsubishi*, pp. 334–337.

57. Nakagawa, "Japanese Shipping," p. 8; Iwai, *Mitsubishi*, p. 212. On the connection between Murata's shipbuilding plan and Mitsubishi, see Shiba Kōshirō, "Fuku shachō jidai," in *Murata Shōzō Tsuisōroku*, ed. Itō Takeo (O.S.K., 1959), pp. 68–70.

58. Ōtani Diary, 26 February 1931.

59. Sugiyama, p. 148; *KI*, 7 November 1932, p. 2. For further background on this financing, see Sugiyama Kazuo, "Shipbuilding Finance of the *Shasen* Shipping Firms: 1920's–1930's," in Yui and Nakagawa, eds., *Business History of Shipping*, pp. 255–272; and "Senkanki no senpaku kenzō to kin'yū," in Nakagawa Keiichirō, ed., *Ryōtaisenkan no Nihon kaiji sangyō* (Chūō Daigaku Shuppanbu, 1985), pp. 103–160.

60. Yoneda Fujio interview.

61. Sumitomo sold these shares in 1934. See *KI*, 20 August 1934, p. 10. See also Asahara, p. 266; and *OSK 80 nenshi*, p. 643.

62. The timing can be inferred from *KI*, 10 August 1931, p. 12. The purchase may also have been a shrewdly calculated investment, since O.S.K. shares were selling at only half of par value.

63. The following is based on *KI*, 19 December 1932, p. 7. The projected authorized capital stock of the new firm was to have been ¥200 million; Asahara, p. 357.

64. *Seattle Times*, 25 October 1932. GN President's Subject File 7606#3. Great Northern Railway Company Records. Minnesota Historical Society. The basic source for this exposé is Murata's account, "Yūsen shachō," pp. 49–57. In it he gives 11 November as the date for the exposé, which Asahara, pp. 353–362, follows. The actual date was 11 December. The initial newspaper stories appeared prior to 11 November, and most later discussion took place in December. In his diary, Ōtani reports being besieged by phone calls on 11 December as a result of the article. Cf. *Fūtō no hibi: Shōsen Mitsui 100 nenshi*, ed. Nihon Keieishi Kenkyūjo (Mitsui-OSK Line, 1984), p. 214.

65. *Zaikai bukko ketsubutsu den* (Jitsugyō no Sekaisha, 1936), I, 442–445.

66. Statements from newspaper interviews reprinted in *KI*, 19 December 1932, p. 8. For a negative view of the German experiment, see Lars U. Scholl, "Shipping Business in Germany in the Nineteenth and Twentieth Centuries," in Yui and Nakagawa, eds., *Business History of Shipping*, pp. 208–209.

67. *The Japan Advertiser*, 22 December 1932, in JSSII 2/11 (from Japan); *Fūtō no hibi*, p. 216; Interview with Kikuchi Shōjirō, late N.Y.K. chairman, 13 December 1982.

68. For discussion, see *KI*, 7 November 1932, p. 2; 5 December 1932, p. 2; and 19 December 1932, p. 2.

69. The following account of the breakdown of talks in December is taken from

Murata and Asahara (note 64) and Nomura, pp. 110–116; Terai, *Shio,* pp. 80–83; Teratani Takeaki, *Kaiungyō to kaigun,* Vol. III of *Nihon kaiun keieishi* (Nihon Keizai Shinbunsha, 1981), pp. 18–21; Nakagawa, *Ryōtaisenkan,* pp. 139–140; and *KI,* 19 December 1932, p. 7.

70. For comments on the lack of harmony following this merger, see *Zaikai,* 15 August 1974, pp. 104–109.
71. Ōtani Diary, 26 December 1932. *Tokyo Nichinichi,* 22 December 1932.
72. Terai, *Shio,* p. 80.
73. Yoneda Fujio interview.
74. Asahara, p. 358.
75. Nomura, p. 165. On Yoneda, see Teratani, p. 20.
76. Ōtani Diary, 8 November 1932, and 14 December 1932.
77. Suzuki, *Zaikai,* p. 260. For further comments on Hori by Ogura, Ōtani, and Murata, see *Hori Keijirō o tsuikairoku* (Osaka: Dō Hensankai, 1949), pp. 16–20, 26–30, 252–258. See also Okada Eitarō, "YūShō gappei no hanashi, sono ta," in *Ōta Heigorō tsuisōroku* (Osaka, Dō Kankokai, 1967), pp. 68–70; and *Fūtō no hibi,* pp. 211–214.
78. Letter from Ōtani (Singapore) to President Kondō Renpei, 20 July 1915, and trade reports by Ōtani from Southest Asia in the author's personal possession.
79. Hugh T. Patrick, "The Ecomomic Muddle of the 1920s," in James W. Morley, ed., *Dilemmas of Growth in Prewar Japan* (Princeton University Press, 1971), p. 256.
80. JSSII 2/12 (from Japan), 7 February 1933.
81. *KI;* Asahara, pp. 359–360. O.S.K. shares usually traded at about ¥10 below those of the N.Y.K. *Fūtō no hibi,* pp. 216–217.
82. *Shuyōkoku senzen kaiun joseishi,* ed., Kaiji Sangyō Kenyūjo (1969), pp. 4, 44; Teratani, pp. 22–34; Mitsubishi Economic Research Bureau, *Japanese Trade and Industry* (Macmillan, 1936), pp. 468–475.
83. JSSII 2/12 (from Japan), 31 March 1933. Cf. JSSII 2/11 (from Japan), 28 October 1932 and 23 December 1932.
84. JSSII 2/12 (from Japan), 7 February 1933.
85. Ōtani Diary, 11 to 14 December 1932.
86. *Tokyo Nichinichi,* 15 December 1932, in JSSII 2/11 (from Japan), p. 3.
87. Memorandum from Kagami to Finance Minister Takahashi Korekiyo, 1 July 1933, Shōwa zaiseishi shiryō, series 3, Vol. 66, no. 19. Finance Ministry Archives.
88. On Kikuchi, see Nitta Naozō, *Kikuchi Kyōzō ōden* (Osaka, 1948), pp. 293–303. The following account is taken from *NYK 70 nenshi,* pp. 617–638; and Sugiyama, pp. 128–129, 162. I have omitted several directors who served only for a year or two between 1924 and 1935, for they played only minor roles and do not reflect any trends in the composition of the board.
89. NYK-TG#1030, 1 November 1929.
90. Nomura, pp. 220–222; Harada Kenjirō interview; *Terai Hisanobu* (N.Y.K. Nai Denki Hensan Iinkai, 1965), pp. 129–145.
91. Murata, "Yūsen shachō," p. 54; and Asahara, p. 358.

92. Ōtani Diary; Kagami Kōhei interview. Also, the Board met very infrequently during 1932. NYK-TG.
93. Terai, *Shio*, pp. 80–82. Terai made these comments despite the fact that he owed his return to the N.Y.K. to Kagami's strong backing. Interviews with Harada Kenjirō and Kikuchi Shōjirō.
94. Udagawa and Nakamura, pp. 89–91.
95. Comments by former N.Y.K. President Ariyoshi Yoshiya in Sakaguchi Akira, *Mitsubishi* (Chūō Kōronsha, 1964), pp. 148–149.
96. Chalmers Johnson has commented on zaibatsu interest in "easing competition through mergers" in the 1930s. *MITI and the Japanese Miracle: The Growth of Industrial Policy, 1925–1975* (Stanford, 1982), p. 111. Yet, some of his examples—Mitsubishi Heavy Industries and Sumitomo Metals—were mergers *within* zaibatsu. Mitsubishi Iron and Steel and a Mitsui-controlled firm joined in the Japan Steel merger, but neither was a leading firm within its own zaibatsu. Mergers between major direct subsidiaries of different zaibatsu were rare. The Ōji Paper Co., which Johnson mentions, is one exception.
97. For examples of these, see Chalmers Johnson, *Japan's Public Policy Companies* (Washington, American Enterprise Institute for Public Policy Research, 1978), pp. 25–74.
98. Alfred D. Chandler, Jr., *The Visible Hand* (Cambridge, Harvard University Press, 1977), pp. 9–10.
99. For many other examples of this shift, see Morikawa Hidemasa, *Nihon keieishi* (Nihon keizai shinbunsha, 1981). The number of cases discussed by Morikawa suggests that we can apply the term *managerial capitalism* to Japan.
100. In the words of Kikuchi Shōjirō, interview.
101. With the N.Y.K.'s checkered history, its business operations outside the Mitsubishi zaibatsu and Mitsubishi's relatively small ownership share in it suggests that the N.Y.K. was atypical and that we cannot extend these generalizations to the direct subsidiaries of the Mitsubishi zaibatsu in the 1930s. Yet, the extent to which these direct subsidiaries and their postwar successors may have gained autonomy in management, first in the evolution from the 1930s to the mid-1960s, when the postwar groups stabilized, and then in the new opportunities arising from changes in industrial structure, between 1970 and 1985, is a subject that remains largely unexplored.

7. Noguchi Jun and Nitchitsu: Investment Strategy of a High-Technology Enterprise, by Barbara Molony

Place of publication is Tokyo unless otherwise noted.

1. Chalmers Johnson, *MITI and the Japanese Miracle: The Growth of Industrial Policy, 1925–1975* (Stanford, Stanford University Press, 1982), p. 23.
2. Hoshino Yoshirō, "Noguchi Jun to gijutsu no kakushin," *Chūō Kōron* 80. 928:359–365 (February 1965), p. 360.
3. Denka Rokujūnenshi Hensan Iinkai, *Denka rokujūnenshi* (Denki Kagaku

Kōgyō KK, 1977), p. 87; Nakamura Chūichi, *Nihon kagaku kōgyōshi* (Tōyō Keizai Shinbunsha, 1959), p. 24; Shimotani Masahiro, "Hensei ryūan, sekkai chisso kōgyō to denki kagaku kaisha no seiritsu: wagakuni kagaku kōgyō ni okeru dokusen keieishi," *Ōsaka Keidai ronshū* 106:25–53 (July 1975), p. 30.

4. Kuriyama Toyo, *Gendai Nihon sangyō hattatsushi: Denryoku* (Gendai Nihon Sangyō Hattatsushi Kenkyūkai, 1964), pp. 54–62.

5. Yoshioka Kiichi, *Noguchi Jun* (Fuji Intanashiyonaru Konsarutanto, 1962), Chapter 2; Denka Rokujūnenshi, p. 87; Fukumoto Kunio, ed., *Noguchi Jun wa ikite iru: jigyō supiritto to sono tenkai* (Fuji Intanashiyonaru Konsarutanto, 1964), pp. 15–18.

6. Yoshioka Kiichi, p. 59.

7. Nihon Ryūan Kōgyō Kyōkai, *Nihon ryūan kōgyōshi* (Nihon Ryūan Kōgyō Kyōkai, 1963), p. 50.

8. Katagiri Ryūkichi, *Hantō no jigyō-ō, Noguchi Jun* (Tōkai Shuppansha, 1939), pp. 184–185.

9. L. F. Haber, *The Chemical Industry 1900–1930: International Growth and Technological Change* (Oxford, Clarendon Press, 1971), p. 88; Ōshio Takeshi, "Nippon Chisso Hiryō KK ni yoru hensei ryūan seizō kigyōka no katei," *Keizai ronshū* 26:253–271 (March 1977), p. 260. The young men's license acquisition created quite a stir in financial circles in Japan; see Yoshioka Kiichi, pp. 70–71.

10. Yamamoto Tomio, *Nippon Chisso Hiryō jigyō taikan* (Osaka, 1937), pp. 438–439 (this is the official company history); Matsushita Denkichi, *Kagaku kōgyō zaibatsu no shinkenkyū* (Chūgai Sangyō Chōsakai, 1938), p. 65.

11. Ōshio Takeshi, "Nippon Chisso Hiryō KK," p. 260; Katagiri Ryūkichi, p. 42; Fukumoto Kunio, p. 24; Yamamoto Tomio, p. 439.

12. Katō Takeo, quoted in Yoshioka Kiichi, p. 73. Ōshio Takeshi, "Nippon Chisso Hiryō KK," p. 262, also notes that Nitchitsu should more properly be considered related to the Iwasaki family rather than to the Mitsubishi company.

13. Katagiri Ryūkichi, pp. 31–33; pp. 40–43. Birthplace ties were important to Nakahashi, according to Ichikawa Seiji; Ichikawa Hōmei, *Ichikawa Seiji den* (Ōsaka, Bunshindo, 1974), p. 60.

14. Shimotani Masahiro, "Nippon Chisso Hiryō KK to takakka no tenkai," *Ōsaka Keidai ronshū* 112:94–124 (July 1976), p. 98; Katagiri Ryūkichi, pp. 26, 248.

15. The degree of Noguchi's independence from Mitsubishi decision makers has been debated. While few of his biographers mention his consulting with Board members before making important decisions, they often state that he asked for approval from Nitchitsu's leading shareholders. Satō Kanji contends that Noguchi was a Mitsubishi man; other writers stress Noguchi's independence of Mitsubishi. Satō Kanji, *Hiryō mondai kenkyū* (Nihon Hyōronsha, 1930).

16. Matsushita Denkichi. In particular, Nitchitsu borrowed ¥500,000 from the Hypothec Bank in 1910. By then, Nitchitsu's debts exceeded reserves, making it highly vulnerable and therefore potentially dependent on Mitsubishi. That Noguchi avoided falling into dependency on the zaibatsu

bank was the result of careful planning and not a little luck.

17. Shimotani Masahiro, "Nippon Chisso Hiryō KK," p. 98; Yoshioka Kiichi, p. 75; Ōshio Takeshi, "Nippon Chisso Hiryō KK," pp. 263–265; Denka Rokujūnenshi, pp. 92–93.

18. Shimotani Masahiro, "Nippon Chisso Hiryō KK," p. 98.

19. Yoshioka Kiichi, pp. 82–83; Yamamoto Tomio, pp. 445–446.

20. Sengoku Mitsugu, head of the Railroad Board during its control of Nitchitsu's facilities, was originally a scientist at Mitsubishi Mining who later became known as a conduit for political contributions from Mitsubishi to the Kenseikai. Yoshioka Kiichi, p. 101.

21. Yamamoto Tomio, p. 446.

22. Yamamoto Tomio, pp. 451–455; Yoshioka Kiichi, p. 102. Shareholders were not alone in reaping the rewards of high profits; white-collar workers received bonus shares in the company, and long-time blue-collar workers received watches.

23. Shimotani Masahiro, "Nippon Chisso Hiryō KK," pp. 102–103; p. 107. For an explanation of the strike at Kagami in 1918, see Katagiri Yasuo, "Kagami kōjō no omoide," in Kamata Shōji, ed., *Nippon Chisso shi e no shōgen,* (Tōkyō Shinku Sabisu, 1979), VIII, 72–77.

24. Shimotani Masahiro, "Nippon Chisso Hiryō KK," pp. 102–103.

25. Yoshioka Kiichi, p. 106, praises Noguchi particularly strongly. Of course, Noguchi was not the only employer with such a reputation. Hitachi's Ōdaira Namihei and Shibaura's Kishi Keijirō also created working environments remembered fondly by their employees. I am indebted to Professor Morikawa Hidemasa for this observation.

26. As a joint-stock company, Nitchitsu relied heavily on its shareholders for capital. Noguchi frequently requested increases in authorized capital stock from his fellow stockholders. Each time capitalization was increased, the company's total worth increased. Because shares in Japanese corporations were issued by the company at a percentage of their par value, shareholders' initial payments were lower than the par value of the stock. Whenever Nitchitsu needed additional capital, shareholders could be expected to pay additional installments toward total par value. Paid-up capital, then, was often less than the authorized capitalization of the company; all shares were paid up to their par value when paid-up capital equaled total capitalization. Purchasing shares of Nitchitsu stock was an excellent investment through most of the period of expansion before and during World War I. Stock-market prices for Nitchitsu shares were consistently at least 20% above par value, and dividend payments averaged between 10% and 30% of par throughout the war, jumping to 104% in 1920 before resuming more normal rates. With such high return on investment, shareholders might be expected to pay requested installments readily. Apparently they did, and also responded favorably to each additional stock offering.

27. Yamamoto Tomio, p. 457.

28. L. F. Haber, pp. 205–206; p. 208. The Japanese government also funded ammonia research at the Special Nitrogen Research Laboratory at the Tokyo

Industrial Research Laboratory. Research was slow, but Yokoyama Būichi and Shibata Katsutarō eventually perfected a method later used by Shōwa Hiryō to make ammonia. Nihon Ryūan Kōgyō Kyōkai, pp. 129–131.

29. Management at both Mitsui (Makita Tamaki) and Sumitomo (Suzuki Masaya) expressed great interest in ammonia manufacture, and were willing to invest quite heavily in the chemical. The high cost of their chosen method of production impeded their progress, however. Morikawa Hidemasa, *Zaibatsu no keiei shiteki kenkyū* (Tōyō Keizai Shinposha, 1980), p. 205; Nihon Ryūan Kōgyō Kyōkai, p. 60.

30. Nihon Ryūan Kōgyō Kyōkai, pp. 60, 64; Nissan Kagaku Shashi Hensan Iinkai, *Hachijūnenshi* (Nissan Kagaku Kōgyō, 1969), p. 80.

31. Hashimoto Jūrō, "1920 nendai no ryūan shijo," *Shakai keizai shigaku* 43.4:386 (1978).

32. Yoshioka Kiichi, pp. 125–132; Yamamoto Tomio, p. 458.

33. Yoshioka Kiichi, pp. 133–134. Noda Utarō, communications minister in the Hara Cabinet, had ruled that electricity generated in Miyazaki prefecture should be transmitted outside the prefecture for the benefit of the surrounding areas. The change benefiting Noguchi permitted retention of electricity in Miyazaki, where he could use it.

34. Yoshioka Kiichi, p. 138; Yamamoto Tomio, p. 460. Kudō Konogi and Hashimoto Hikoshichi, later important scientists at Nichitsu—Hashimoto discovered the mercury catalyst later found to be responsible for Minimata disease—oversaw adaptation of Minamata's plant to the new technology. Kagami's plant was sold to Dai Nihon Hiryō in October 1927.

35. Shimotani Masahiro, "Nitchitsu kontsuerun to gōsei ryūan kōgyō," *Osaka Keidai ronshu* 114:58–89 (November 1976), p. 67.

36. Hiroyuki Itami, Tadao Kagona, Hideki Yoshihara, and Akimitsu Sakuma, "Diversification Strategies and Economic Performance," in Kazuo Sato and Yasuo Hoshino, *The Anatomy of Japanese Business* (Armonk, M. E. Sharpe, 1984), p. 323.

37. Yoshioka Kiichi, p. 151; Shimotani Masahiro, "Nippon Chisso Hiryō KK," p 112.

38. Hashimoto Hikoshichi, who discovered the mercury catalyst, was, ironically, mayor of Minamata when mercury poisoning came to light in the 1960s; Yoshioka Kiichi, p. 205.

39. Kobayashi Hideo, "1930 nendai Nippon Chisso Hiryō Kabushiki Kaisha no Chōsen no shinshutsu ni tsuite," in Yamada Hideo, *Shokuminichi keizaishi no shomondai* (Ajia Keizai Kenkyūjo, 1973), p. 163. Given their response to complaints in the 1970s, there is little to suggest that the company would have hesitated to develop the patent in any case.

40. Kobayashi Hideo, p. 150; p. 167. Electricity cost just 1/2 sen per kilowatt-hour at Hungnam.

41. Satō Kanji, pp. 122–126; Nihon Ryūan Kōgyō Kyōkai, p. 100. The Sherman Antitrust Act prevented American firms from joining the cartel. Japan was a target because it was the only major agricultural nation that failed to

408 Notes to Pages 244–248

produce enough to satisfy its own market and was, at the same time, not a colonial market dominated by a mother country.

42. Yoshioka Kiichi, pp. 189–190.

43. Suzuki Tsuneo, "Nihon ryūan kōgyō no jiritsuka katei,"; *Shakai keizai shigaku* 43.2:66–91 (1978), p. 73; Hashimoto Jūrō, "1920 nendai," p. 59. Mitsubishi Trading Company had exclusive rights to import American ammonium sulfate from U.S. Steel and Barrett. While imports of German fertilizer by Mitsui increased, there was little increase in imports of American fertilizer by Mitsubishi. Because the trade in American fertilizer was limited to Mitsubishi on the Japanese side and was dominated by U.S. Steel on the American, we have only a limited sample from which to extrapolate conclusions. Mitsubishi claimed to be losing 40 yen per ton on its contracted sales of U.S. Steel's ammonium sulfate after 1922, but this may be insufficient explanation for the loss of the American product's market share. Mitsubishi Shōji Kabushiki Kaisha, ed., *Ritsugyō bōekiroku* (Tokyo, 1958), p. 470.

44. Kondō Yasuo, *Ryūan: Nihon shihonshugi to hiryō kōgyō no gaikan* (Nihon Hyōronsha, 1950), p. 154.

45. Kondō Yasuo, pp. 156–157.

46. Ōshio Takeshi, "Fujiwara-Bosch kyōteian to Nihon no ryūan kōgyō," *Keizai kenkyū* 49–50:45–65 (1978), p. 47.

47. Kondō Yasuo and Nihon Ryūan Kōgyō Kyōkai both take this position, which overlooks some of the complex aspects of ammonia imports as well as the attempts by firms related to Mitsui and Mitsubishi to import production technology.

48. Ōshio Takeshi, "Fujiwara-Bosch," pp. 50–52.

49. Morikawa Hidemasa, p. 173; pp. 206–209, p. 220; Mikami Atsufumi, "Kyūzaibatsu to shinkō zaibatsu no kagaku kōgyō: Sumitomo Kagaku to Shōwa Denkō o chūshin to shite," in Yasuoke Shigeaki, ed., *Zaibatsu kenkyū* (Nihon Keizai Shinposha, 1979), pp. 148–158; Watanabe Tokuji, *Gendai Nihon sangyō hattatsushi: Kagaku kōgyō* (Gendai Nihon Sangyō Hattatsushi Kenkyūkai, 1968), pp. 448–453.

50. Hashimoto Jūrō, "Ryūan dokusen no seiritsu," *Keizaigaku ronshū* 45.4:44–68 (1980), pp. 61–62.

51. Nihon Ryūan Kōgyō Kyōkai, pp. 118–120.

52. Kobayashi Hideo, p. 144.

53. Kamoi Yu, *Noguchi Jun* (Tōkōsha, 1943), pp. 216–217.

54. Yoshioka Kiichi, pp. 124–125.

55. Sang-chul Suh, *Growth and Structural Change in the Korean Economy* (Cambridge, Council on East Asian Studies, Harvard University, 1980), pp. 9–10. The Corporation Law limited investment in industry in Korea because the Japanese initially feared Korean industries would undersell the still-developing Japanese industries. A strengthening of the Japanese industrial economy may also have permitted lifting of the 1911 regulation.

56. Andrew Grajdanzev, *Modern Korea* (New York, Institute of Pacific Relations,

1944), pp. 133–134. The earliest estimates of projected generation of 57,000 kw. were revised upward in the 1920s to 2.25 million.

57. Hatade Isao, *Nihon no zaibatsu to Mitsubishi* (Rakuyū Shobō, 1978), pp. 228–229; Nihon Ryūan Kōgyō Kyōkai, p. 153.

58. Morita Kazuo, "Noguchi Jun o Fusenkō Kaihatsu," in Takanashi Kōji, ed., *Noguchi Jun o Tsuikairoku* (Ōsaka, Noguchi Jun Tsuikairoku Hensankai, 1952), pp. 383–389; Yoshioka Kiichi, pp. 153–154; Hoshino Yoshirō, p. 363.

59. Yoshioka Kiichi, pp. 155–156, 167; Fukumoto Kunio, p. 60; Nakamura Seishi, "Kyōdai denryoku kagaku konbinato no kensetsu," in Morikawa Hidemasa, et al., *Nihon no kigyōka* (Yuhikaku, 1978), III, 64.

60. Noguchi Jun, "Nihonkai ni kiriotoshita Fusenkō no suiden jigyō," in Shinogi Itsuo, ed., *Chōsen no denki jigyō o kataru* (Seoul, Chōsen Denki Kyōkai, 1937), p. 116.

61. Shimooka declared, "Zaibatsu are absolutely out of the question. A new person like Noguchi would be better." Fukumoto Kunio, p. 63. I am indebted to Peter Duus for his suggestion (21 April 1983) that Shimooka's personal aversion to the Mitsubishi-connected politician Katō Takaaki may also have affected the Political Affairs Officer's decision.

62. Noguchi Jun, p. 117. Even after the split with Mitsubishi, Iwasaki Hisaya still held 2.8% of Nitchitsu shares (1935). The shares bought by the Iwasaki family constituted, in any case, a greater part of Nitchitsu's capital than the short-term (though important) loans from Mitsubishi Bank. Shimotani Masahiro, "Nitchitsu kontsuerun," p. 64; Watanabe Tokuji, p. 381.

63. Noguchi Jun, p. 117.

64. Nakamura Seishi, p. 69; Yoshioka Kiichi, pp. 167–168.

65. Nihon Ryūan Kōgyō Kyōkai, p. 99; Shimotani Masahiro, "Nitchitsu kontsuerun," p. 73.

66. Yoshioka Kiichi, p. 231; Kamoi Yū, p. 210; Kariya Susumu, "Kayaku kōjō," *Kagaku kōgyō* (January 1951), p. 80; Shimotani Masahiro, "Nitchitsu kontsuerun," p. 67.

67. Kushida Manzō at the Mitsubishi Bank balked at underwriting the ¥10 million anticipated start-up costs for Hungnam; Katagiri Ryūkichi, p. 65.

68. Yoshioka Kiichi, p. 181. So little rain fell in the summer of 1930 that the reservoir filled to only 40% of capacity, and Hungnam-based scientists lamented that "one millimeter (of rain) is worth 10,000 yen."

69. Watanabe Tokuji, p. 360.

70. Ugaki Kazushige, "Noguchi Jun o omou," in Takanashi Koji, ed., *Noguchi Jun o tsuikairoku*, p. 39; Yoshioka Kiichi, p. 178; Matsushita Denkichi, p. 152.

71. Suh, pp. 162–163.

72. Ugaki Kazushige, p. 42.

73. Imai Raijirō, "Denki tōsei to denryokukai no genzai to shōrai," in Shibuya Reiji, *Chōsen no kōgyō to sono shigen* (Seoul, Chōsen Kōgyō Kyōkai, 1937), pp. 328–331; Grajdanzev, p. 135.

74. Ugaki Kazushige, p. 44; Yoshioka Kiichi, pp. 233–234.

75. Ōshio Takeshi, "Chōshinkō kaihatsu o meguru Nitchitsu to Mitsubishi no tairitsu ni tsuite," *Shakai kagaku tōkyū* 89:167–185 (1985), p. 176.
76. Yoshioka Kiichi, p. 234. Aichi Bank substituted short-term loans for long-term loans.
77. Katagiri Ryūkichi, pp. 102–106.
78. Ōshio Takeshi, "Chōsen Chisso Hiryō Kabushiki Kaisha no shūeki ni kansuru ichikosatsu," *Keizai Kenkyū* 72 (1985), pp. 117–123.
79. Tamaki Masaharu, "Hungnam kōjō to Chōsen no daikibo hatsuden," *Kagaku kōgyō* (January 1951), p. 43. Yoshioka Kiichi, p. 240. The Chōsen Electric Transmission Company (Chōsen Sōden Kaisha, a national-policy company) transmitted 1/2 of Changjin's output to distant cities like Seoul. It was established in 1934 with Noguchi Jun as president and Kubota Yutaka as managing director.
80. *Chōsen Ginkō: Shokeisansho* (Seoul, Chōsen Ginkō), Vols. XLIII–LXVIII, 1930–1943, set incomplete, unpaginated.
81. Katagiri Ryūkichi, pp. 84–85.
82. For information about Katō's desire to assert his independence of the Ministry of Finance, I am indebted to Karl Moskowitz, interview, 31 July 1981.
83. Katagiri Ryūkichi, p. 98. For example, the Industrial Bank of Korea lent the money for the sardine plant near Hungnam.
84. Suh, pp. 162–163.
85. Katagiri Ryūkichi, p. 211.
86. Matsushita Denkichi, p. 84; Yoshioka Kiichi, pp. 229–231; Kamoi Yū, p. 210; Kariya Susumu, p. 80.
87. Kariya Susumu, p. 80.
88. Explosives were initially sold to industrial customers and then increasingly to government agencies to build the Korean economic infrastructure necessary for strategic reasons and to use in the development of Manchuria and North China. Kariya Susumu, p. 81; Katagiri Ryūkichi, p. 223; Kamoi Yū, p. 30.
89. Arnold Krammer, "Fueling the Third Reich," *Technology and Culture* 19.3: 395 (July 1978).
90. Watanabe Tokuji, p. 513; Kamoi Yū, p. 327; Hoshiko Toshiteru, "Chōsen ni okeru sekiyu jigyō," in Shibuya Reiji, ed., *Chōsen no kōgyō to sono shigen*, pp. 364–367.
91. Noguchi was neither the only entrepreneur nor the Navy the only government agency interested in developing synthetic fuel and increasing refinery output of crude oil. Other oil suppliers enjoyed government support for unprofitable projects, notably Imperial Oil (Teikoku Sekiyu KK), Japan's largest wartime oil producer. General Headquarters, Supreme Commander for the Allied Powers (GHQ-SCAP), Historical Monograph No. 41, "The Petroleum Industry" (1952), p. 11.
92. James C. Abegglen and George Stalk, Jr., *Kaisha, The Japanese Corporation* (New York, Basic Books, 1985), pp. 189–190.
93. Yasuo Okamoto, "The Grand Strategy of Japanese Business," in Kazuo Sato

and Yasuo Hoshino, *The Anatomy of Japanese Business* (Armonk, M. E. Sharpe, 1984), p. 312.

94. Chalmers Johnson traces this development in Chapters 3, 4 and 5 of *MITI and the Japanese Miracle.*

95. Sheridan Tatsuno, *The Technopolis Strategy: Japan, High Technology, and the Control of The Twenty-first Century* (New York, Prentice Hall, 1986), pp. 5–10.

8. *"Scientific Industry": Strategy, Technology, and Entrepreneurship in Prewar Japan, by Michael A. Cusumano*

1. Mochikabu Kaisha Seiri Iinkai, ed., *Nihon zaibatsu to sono kaitai* (Hara Shobō, 1951 and 1973), II, 469, 473. (Note: All places of publication are Tokyo unless noted. Publishers are not listed if they are identical to the author or editor.)

2. For biographical data on Ōkōchi see Ōkōchi Kinen Kai, ed., *Ōkōchi Masatoshi: hito to sono jigyō,* and Nakagawa Keiichirō and Yui Tsunehiko, eds., *Keiei tetsugaku keiei rinen* (Daiyamondo, 1969–1970), II, 161–165.

3. See, for example, Miyake Haruteru, *Shinkō kontsuerun tokuhon* (Shunshūsha, 1937); "Yakushin-suru Riken Kontsuerun" in *Tōyō keizai,* January 1937 Special Issue, pp. 177–196; Tamaki Hajime, *Nihon zaibatsu shi* (Shakai Shisōsha, 1976); Udagawa Masaru, *Shōwa shi to shinkō zaibatsu* (Kyōikusha, 1982); and the publications of Chō, Ōkōchi Akio (no relation to Ōkōchi Masatoshi), and Ōno cited in this chapter.

4. Itakura Kiyonobu and Yagi Eri, "The Japanese Research System and the Establishment of the Institute of Physical and Chemical Research," in Shigeru Nakayama, ed., *Science and Society in Modern Japan* (Cambridge, MIT Press, 1974), pp. 161–163, 168; and Andō Yoshio, *Nihon no rekishi* (Shogakukan, 1976), XXVIII, 306–307.

5. Itakura and Yagi, pp. 189–194.

6. Quoted in Ibid., pp. 191–192. This passage is taken from Rikagaku Kenkyūjo, "Zaidan Hōjin Rikagaku Kenkyūjo setsuritsu keika gaiyō."

7. Nakagawa and Yui, p. 163.

8. Itakura and Yagi, pp. 193–194.

9. Nakagawa and Yui, p. 163; Andō, p. 307.

10. Saitō Ken, "Riken Sangyō-dan no keisei," *Keiei shigaku* 17.2:50 (July 1982).

11. Hideomi Tuge, *Historical Development of Science and Technology in Japan* (Kokusai Bunka Shinkokai, 1961), p. 117.

12. Tuge, pp. 107, 116–117, 132.

13. Tomonaga and Yukawa are cited in The Institute of Physical and Chemical Research, *Riken* (Wakō-shi, Saitama-ken, 1982), p. 1.

14. Since the yen was not readily convertible into dollars between the mid-1930s and 1949, I have not included conversion figures for these years. The average value of the yen was about 2 per dollar until it declined to about 3 per dollar in 1934.

15. *Tōyō keizai* January 1937 Special issue, p. 180, and Saitō, p. 54.

16. Saitō, p. 70, Table 13.
17. *Tōyō keizai,* 12 September 1942, p. 16, and Itakura and Yagi, p. 196.
18. "Nōson no kōson-ka" and "Nōson no kōgyō" are reprinted in Chō Yukio, ed., *Jitsugyō no shisō* (Chikuma Shobō, 1964), pp. 310–322.
19. Chō also reprints this essay (pp. 273–309).
20. Ōkōchi Masatoshi, *Moteru kuni Nihon* (Kagaku-shugi Kōgyōsha, 1939), pp. 1–3, 83–91.
21. *Ōkōchi Masatoshi: hito to sono jigyō,* pp. 367–369, provides a complete listing of Ōkōchi's 33 publications.
22. Ōkōchi Masatoshi, "Shin-shihon-shugi kōgyō to kagaku-shugi kōgyō," in Chō, pp. 276–278, 292–297. See also Ōkōchi's *Kōgyō keiei sōron* (1936), pp. 49–68.
23. "Shin-shihon-shugi kōgyō to kagaku-shugi kōgyō," p. 278.
24. Quotation from "Shin-shihon-shugi kōgyō to kagaku-shugi kōgyō" in Ōkōchi Akio, "Kagaku-shugi kōgyō," in Kawashima Takeyoshi, ed., *Kokumin keizai no shoruikei* (Iwanami Shoten, 1968), p. 761.
25. Ōkōchi Akio, pp. 763–764; and Ōno Hideji, "Shinkō zaibatsu no shisō," in Chō Yukio and Sumiya Kazuhiko, eds., *Kindai Nihon keizai shisō shi* (Yūhikaku, 1971), II, 121.
26. Ōkōchi Akio, p. 767.
27. Quoted in Ōno, p. 124. See also Saitō Ken, "Hōkoku yōshi: shiryō," Table 4. This is an unpublished collection of quotations and other data for a lecture at the 18th annual meeting of the Business History Society of Japan on 6 November 1982. Table 4 consists of Ōkōchi's references to the Haber patent while he served in the upper house of the Diet.
28. Morikawa Hidemasa, *Zaibatsu no keiei shiteki kenkyū* (Tōyō Keizai Shimpōsha, 1980), pp. 170–171, and Atsufumi Mikami, "Old and New Zaibatsu in the History of Japan's Chemical Industry: With Special Reference to the Sumitomo Chemical Co. and the Showa Denko Co.," in Akio Okochi and Hoshimi Uchida, eds., *Development and Diffusion of Technology: Electrical and Chemical Industries* (University of Tokyo Press, 1980), pp. 210–211.
29. See Morikawa, pp. 169–175; Mikami, pp. 204–207; Tamaki, pp. 429–430; and Yoshioka Kiichi, *Noguchi Jun* (Fuji Intaanashonaru Konsarutanto Shuppanbu, 1962), pp. 125–130.
30. "Shin-shihon-shugi kōgyō to kagaku-shugi kōgyō," p. 283.
31. Ōno, pp. 116–117.
32. Quoted in Ōkōchi Akio, p. 771.
33. See "Shihon-shugi kōgyō to kagaku-shugi kōgyō," in Chō, pp. 299–302.
34. Ōno, pp. 127–128.
35. Ibid., p. 125. See also *Moteru kuni Nihon,* pp. 125 and 151.
36. Ōno, p. 157.
37. Quoted in Ōkōchi Akio, pp. 771.
38. Ōno, pp. 107–108.
39. Ōkōchi Akio, p. 768.
40. See "Nōson no kōson-ka" and "Nōson no kōgyō," in Chō, as well as *Kōgyō*

keiei sōron, pp. 105–126, Ōno, pp. 113–114, and *Nōson no kōgyō to fukugyō* (Kagakushugi Kōgyōsha, 1937), pp. 63–73.

41. Ushiyama Keiji, "Ōkōchi Masatoshi to 'Nōson no kōgyō-ka,'" in *Nōmin-sō bunkai no kōzō* (Nōgyō Sōgyō Kenkyūjo, 1975), pp. 232–233, 239–241. Balance sheets and profit-and-loss statements of various Riken companies can be found in Tōyō Keizai Shimpōsha, *Kabushiki kaisha nenkan.*
42. Saitō, p. 51.
43. Ibid., p. 52, and *Kabushiki kaisha nenkan* (1927), provide lists of top executives.
44. *Kabushiki kaisha nenkan* (1940), p. 135.
45. Saitō, p. 61.
46. Tamaki, p. 442.
47. Ushiyama, pp. 234–236.
48. Saitō, pp. 59–60. The productivity estimate comes from Ōkōchi's *Nōson no kikai kōgyō,* p. 10.
49. Ushiyama, pp. 234–236.
50. Quoted in Nakagawa and Yui, p. 164.
51. Saitō, pp. 56–59; Miyake, p. 334; and *Tōyō keizai,* January 1937 Special issue, pp. 182–183.
52. This discussion is based on Fuji Intaanashonaru Konsarutanto Shuppan-bu, *Kagiri naku yakushin-suru Riken Kōgaku,* pp. 10–40.
53. See *Kabushiki kaisha nenkan* (annual).
54. Saitō, pp. 67–68, and Ōno, p. 126.
55. *Tōyō keizai,* 27 April 1940, pp. 109–110.
56. *Tōyō keizai,* 7 June 1941, pp. 41–43.
57. *Kabushiki kaisha nenkan* (1942), p. 104.
58. See Takahashi Makoto, "The Development of Wartime Controls," *Developing Economies* 5.4:648–665, and Takafusa Nakamura, *The Postwar Japanese Economy: Its Development and Structure* (University of Tokyo Press, 1981), pp. 3–20.
59. Capitalization figures are from *Nihon zaibatsu to sono kaitai,* Vol. II.
60. Interview with Maeda Riichi (Yokohama), 21 May 1982.
61. Maeda Riichi, "Pisuton ringu no kenkyū," in *Jidōsha gijutsu shō* 1.11 (1941), Part I, pp. 1–7, and Part II, pp. 19–24. Maeda refers to Nippon Piston Ring under "Method A" and Riken under "Method B."
62. Interview with Miyazaki Shōkichi, Mitsutoyo Manufacturing Company (Tokyo), 10 February 1981.
63. *Tōyō keizai,* 20 January 1946, pp. 7–8.
64. *Nihon zaibatsu to sono kaitai,* II, 17.
65. Ibid., p. 72. See also Itakura and Yagi, p. 196.
66. Itakura and Yagi, p. 196.
67. See Rikagaku Kenkyūjo, "Rikagaku Kenkūjo yōran," published annually.
68. *Ōkōchi Masatoshi: hito to sono jigyō,* pp. 379–381.
69. See Tasugi Kyō and Mori Junji, *Seisan kanri kenkyū* (Yūgendō, 1960), a standard Japanese text on production and operations management by two

professors from Kyoto University and Osaka City University, respectively, pp. 41–45.

70. See Morikawa Hidemasa, *Zaibatsu no keiei shiteki kenkyū* (Tōyō Keizai Shimpōsha, 1980), and "Zaibatsu-kei shihon no kakuritsu to zaibatsu no shisō," in *Kindai Nihon keizai shisō shi* (1969), I, 265–273.

71. Saitō Ken provides a summary of these views in "Ōkōchi Masatoshi ni okeru keiei rinen no keisei," in *Keiei Shi Gakkai Dai Jū-Hachi Kai Taikai hōkoku shū*, pp. 1–4 (6 and 7 November 1982). Among authors cited in the present article, Ōkōchi Akio (no relation to Ōkōchi Masatoshi), Ōno Hideji, and Chō Yukio concentrate on the postive sides of Ōkōchi. Saitō refers to Ōtsuka Hisao and Nakamura Seishi as business historians who have been critical of Ōkōchi.

72. See Saitō Ken, "Ōkōchi Masatoshi no hatsugen."

9. Afterword: The Writing of Japanese Business History, by William D. Wray

1. Aoki Masahiko, "The Japanese Firm in Transition," in Kozo Yamamura and Yasukichi Yasuba, eds., *The Political Economy of Japan*, Vol. I, *The Domestic Transformation* (Stanford University Press, 1987), p. 268. The other two prerequisites listed by Aoki are a cooperative ideological stance shared by management and employees (usually discussed under the rubric of enterprise unions) and protection from unfriendly takeovers.

2. *Japanese Yearbook on Business History* 1:178 (1984). (See note 24 of my Introduction to this volume.) Yasuoka Shigeaki, "The Early History of Japanese Companies," Ibid., 3:1–25 (1986); and "Capital Ownership in Family Companies: Japanese Firms Compared with Those in Other Countries," in Okochi Akio and Yasuoka, eds., *Family Business in the Era of Industrial Growth* (University of Tokyo Press, 1984), pp. 1–32.

3. Miyamoto Matao and Hiroyama Kensuke, "The Retreat from Diversification and the Desire for Specialization in Kōnoike: Late Meiji to Early Shōwa," *Japanese Yearbook on Business History* 1:104–130 (1984). Beyond the issues mentioned here, in assessing performance in the Meiji period, it should be noted that Kōnoike lost substantial assets in the currency changes during the Restoration years. However, even Sumitomo came close to bankruptcy at the time.

4. Lee Smith, "Japan's Autocratic Managers," *Fortune*, 7 January 1985, pp. 56–65.

5. Morikawa Hidemasa, "Comments," in *Family Business*, pp. 36–37.

6. For two examples, involving the Sumitomo Bank and NEC, see (1) *Nihon keizai shinbun*, 28 December 1987, p. 40, 5 January 1988, p. 5, 11 January 1988, p. 44, *Keiei keizai*, 3 March 1988, pp. 32–36; and (2) *Keizaikai*, 26 April 1988, pp. 22–26, *Nikkan Kōgyō Shinbun*, 27 May 1988, p. 9.

7. Aoki, "Firm in Transition," pp. 269–270.

8. Michael A. Cusumano, *The Japanese Automobile Industry: Technology and Management at Nissan and Toyota* (Council on East Asian Studies, Harvard University, 1985), pp. 262–307.

9. The N.Y.K.'s late chairman, Kikuchi Shōjirō, illustrated the role of both middle-level strategist and one-man autocrat. In the 1950s, while only an assistant division chief (*fuku-buchō*), he spearheaded the company's postwar strategic transformation (towards more diversified shipping services), but in the 1970s he acted briefly as an autocratic president, forcing a partial withdrawal from tanker operation over the almost unanimous opposition of his top management. See Ariyoshi Yoshiya, *Half a Century in Shipping* (Tokyo, Tokyo News Service, 1977), p. 100; and *Kikuchi Shōjirō ikōshū* (Nippon Yūsen Kabushiki Kaisha nai, 1985), pp. 286–289. The career of NEC's former chairman, Kobayashi Kōji, offers a rough parallel to Kikuchi in the sense of youthful innovation, a commitment to middle management, and charismatic authority. He enhanced the firm's middle management through a structural reform giving autonomy to enterprise divisions, while his charisma and stature in the firm derive from his role in developing innovative technology in the 1930s and from his articulation of company strategy through the slogan "C&C," Computers and Communications. See Enomoto Satoshi, "Nippon Denki no kigyō senryaku to jigyō-busei soshiki henkaku," *Shōken keizai* 157:166–200 (September 1986); Kobayashi Kōji, *Watakushi no rirekisho* (Nihon Keizai Shinbunsha, 1988), pp. 114–119; and *Nippon Denki saikin 10 nenshi: Sōritsu 80 shūnen kinen* (Dōsha shashi hensan shitsu, 1980), pp. 5–15. Kobayashi has written numerous books in Japanese extolling this slogan and his managerial philosophy. In English, see *Computers and Communications: A Vision of C&C* (Cambridge, MIT Press, 1986).

These two leaders differed in their manner of leaving office. Partly because of illness, Kikuchi resigned early enough to ensure a smooth succession. Kobayashi's longevity as chairman led to disputes with the company president. Despite his age (81), Kobayashi remains active as honorary chairman, a post he accepted in 1988 and which created an additional tier above the organizational structure that has recently emerged in many Japanese companies, one with 3 top positions—chairman, vice-chairman, and president. See note 6 above.

10. The motivation for group membership has been much debated by economists. In the prewar period, the profits of zaibatsu firms were on average higher than those for independents. However, in recent decades the reverse has been true, with group firms having lower profits. In an excellent analysis, Nakatani Iwao has argued that the main function of group membership is to act as a complex mutual insurance scheme, which applies to lessening risks in both new ventures and cases of financial trouble. Nakatani Iwao, "The Economic Role of Financial Corporate Grouping," in Aoki Masahiko, ed., *The Economic Analysis of the Japanese Firm* (Amsterdam, North-Holland, 1984), pp. 227–258.

11. Aoki, "Firm in Transition," p. 279.

12. A case can be made that the *degree* of mutual holding today depends very much on the liberalization fears of the 1960s. Even so, the increase that occurred then built on the group-reconstruction initiatives of the city banks in the 1950s. The banks themselves experienced direct continuity from the

prewar period because the Occupation did not touch them. And mutual stockholding within zaibatsu had already emerged as a growing trend by at least the mid-1930s.

13. James R. Bartholomew, "Science, Bureaucracy, and Freedom in Meiji and Taishō Japan," in Tetsuo Najita and J. Victor Koschmann, eds., *Conflict in Modern Japanese History: The Neglected Tradition* (Princeton University Press, 1982), pp. 295–341.

14. Aoki, "Firm in Transition," pp. 266, 264.

15. The above account is taken from ibid., p. 281; and especially, Aoki Masahiko, "Aspects of the Japanese Firm," in Aoki, ed. *Economic Analysis,* pp. 16–23. There have been few studies in English analyzing the financing of Japanese firms from the nineteenth century to World War II. Though overly simple, I would venture the following periodization scheme: (1) from the 1890s to about 1910, equity was the main source of financing in Japanese firms; (2) in a second stage, lasting until the early 1920s, internal reserves accumulated rapidly and in some cases exceeded the value of stockholders' equity; (3) beginning in the mid-to-late 1920s, debt, especially bonds at first, was used to finance technological innovation. This last stage clearly foreshadowed the postwar reliance on debt. See ibid., p. 31.

16. Though statistically significant in some years, these reserves were still small relative to the main distorting factor in the ratio, which was land recorded at acquisition value despite a 4-fold increase in price by the date of Aoki's survey.

17. Calculated from my *Mitsubishi and the N.Y.K., 1870–1914: Business Strategy in the Japanese Shipping Industry* (Council on East Asian Studies, Harvard University, 1984), pp. 433–440, especially p. 433. (There I treat pensions as separate from business reserves.) Cf. Aoki, "Aspects of the Firm," p. 22.

18. For succinct summaries of this model, see Alfred D. Chandler, Jr., *The Visible Hand: The Managerial Revolution in American Business* (Harvard University Press, 1977), pp. 1–12; and "Managers, Families, and Financiers," in *Managerial Enterprise,* pp. 35–50. For an analysis of the importance of transaction costs, see Oliver E. Williamson, "The Modern Corporation: Origins, Evolution, Attributes," *Journal of Economic Literature* 19.4:1537–1568 (December 1981).

19. This second contrast is addressed explicitly in Chandler's "Response," in *Managerial Enterprise,* pp. 67–68; the first is drawn from several examples in the following discussion.

20. Aoki, "Aspects of the Japanese Firm," pp. 27–29; and "Firm in Transition," 282–286.

21. Daitō Eisuke, "Recruitment and Training of Middle Managers in Japan, 1900–1930," in *Managerial Enterprise,* pp. 169–175.

22. *Japan Times,* 1 September 1987, p. 4; *Asahi shinbun,* 31 August 1987, p. 1; *Matsushita Denki Bōeki 50 nen no ayumi: Kaden bōeki no paonia o mezashite,* ed. Dō 50 Nenshi Hensan Iinkai (Osaka, Matsushita Denki Bōeki Kabushiki Kaisha, 1985). On Hitachi: from 29 December 1987, *Nikkan kōgyō shinbun,* p. 1; *Nihon keizai shinbun,* p. 8. For background, see Sakamoto Kazuichi and

Shimotani Masahiro, eds. *Gendai Nihon on kigyō gurupu* (Tōyō Keizai Shinpōsha, 1987).
23. Daitō, "Middle Managers," pp. 159-169.
24. Morikawa Hidemasa, "Business History of the Zaibatsu," unpublished book manuscript, pp. 342, 326-327, 373-376.
25. Yui Tsunehiko, "The Organization and Development of Large Industrial Enterprises in Japan from 1885 to 1940," unpublished paper, pp. 43-46 (corrected pagination).
26. Williamson, "The Modern Corporation," pp. 1555-1556.
27. The definitions are from ibid., p. 1547n18.
28. As reported by Morikawa Hidemasa in "Summary of Concluding Discussion," in *Managerial Enterprise*, p. 287.
29. I have commented on this issue briefly in "Shipping: From Sail to Steam," in Marius B. Jansen and Gilbert Rozman, eds., *Japan in Transition: From Tokugawa to Meiji* (Princeton University Press, 1986), pp. 248-270.
30. For a brief reference to debates about the role of trading companies in connection with issues discussed here, see *Managerial Enterprise*, p. 287.
31. Chandler, "Managers," pp. 47-48; cf. Yonekura Seiichiro, "The Emergence of the Prototype of Enterprise Group Capitalism: The Case of Mitsui," *Hitotsubashi Journal of Commerce and Management* 20.1:63-104 (December 1985), pp. 86-88.
32. *Kengyō kaiko* (Mitsubishi Denki Kabushiki Kaisha, 1951), pp. 301-308; Mitsubishi Shōji Kabushiki Kaisha, ed. *Ristugyō bōeki roku* (Dōsha, 1958), pp. 197-198; *Mitsubishi Shōji shashi* (Dōsha, 1986), I, 221-224; conversations with Professor Yui Tsunehiko. For further discussion of trading-company marketing for electrical firms, see Hasegawa Shin, "1920 nendai no denki kikai shijō," *Shakai keizai shigaku* 45.4:34-63 (1979).
33. *Kengyō kaiko*, p. 123. Historians have studied the zaibatsu-dissolution issue by examining the policymaking process during the Occupation, the long-term effects the program had on the degree of competition, and the extent to which operating companies regrouped in the 1950s, but there has been little attention given to the shock of the dissolution of the two big trading companies on their business partners.
34. For the former case, see my "Japan's Big Three Service Enterprises in China, 1896-1936," in Peter Duus, Ramon H. Myers, and Mark Peattie, eds., *Japan's Informal Empire in China* (Princeton University Press, 1989), pp. 57-58 (tentative). Some details on the latter are in "Abrogation of Restrictive Contracts of Japanese Firms in International Trade," SFE-196, 1947, US National Archives and Japanese Ministry of Finance, Financial History Office.
35. One determinant of Nitchitsu's structure may have been that the technology of the chemical industry made it more inclined than other industries toward vertical integration. On the concept of such integration as "selective," that is, more likely to occur in certain industries, see Williamson, "The Modern Corporation," pp. 1564-1565; and Chandler, "Managers," pp. 48-49.
36. Chandler, "Managers," pp. 49-50. On the concept of the internal capital market, see Williamson, "The Modern Corporation," p. 1558.

37. Cusumano, *The Japanese Automobile Industry*, p. 268. On technological convergence, see Nathan Rosenberg, "Technological Change in the Machine Tool Industry, 1840–1910," *Journal of Economic History* 23.4:414–443 (December 1963).

38. *Nihon keizai shinbun*, 19 November 1987, p. 13. See also Suzuki Jūshirō, *Henshin suru Shin Nittetsu: fukugō keiei no hōto o saguru* (Nikkan Shobō, 1987); and *Gendai Nihon no kigyō gurūpu*.

39. This last venture includes, among other categories, amusement parks and retirement homes.

40. Chandler, "Managers," pp. 54–60; Jurgen Brockstedt, "Family Enterprise and Rise of Large-Scale Enterprise in Germany [1871–1914]: Ownership and Management," in *Family Business*, pp. 240–241.

41. Peter L. Payne, "Family Business in Britain: An Historical and Analytical Survey," in *Family Business*, pp. 180–181, cites some examples from the shipbuilding industry.

42. Chandler, "Managers," pp. 50–54; Leslie Hannah, "Visible and Invisible Hands in Great Britain," in Alfred D. Chandler, Jr., and Herman Daems, eds., *Managerial Hierarchies: Comparative Perspectives on the Rise of the Modern Industrial Enterprise* (Harvard University Press, 1980), p. 64.

43. W. Mark Fruin, "A Typology of Prewar Japanese Enterprises, 1885 to 1930," unpublished paper. Though the British and Japanese marketing systems differed, they both seem to have had a strong position in their economy relative, say, to Germany and the United States. Perhaps this deserves study. Furthermore, although it may appear inappropriate to compare Britain and Japan because of their different levels of development, structurally it makes sense, for, as Minami Ryoshin contends, "the fundamental pattern of development in Japan . . . was the traditional course of industrialization followed by England, and not the course followed by the later developing European economies." *Power Revolution in the Industrialization of Japan: 1885–1940* (Tokyo, Kinokuniya, 1987), p. 342.

44. Some comparison between Japanese trading companies and British marketing agents can be found in Yonekawa Shin'ichi and Yoshihara Hideki, eds., *Business History of General Trading Companies* (University of Tokyo Press, 1987).

45. Barry Supple, "A Framework for British Business History," in Supple, ed., *Essays in British Business History* (Oxford, Clarendon Press, 1977), pp. 14–17. From Supple's figures I calculate the average annual increase in real consumer expenditure as roughly 1.5% between 1870 and 1914.

46. Ibid., pp. 14, 12.

47. Chandler, "Managers," p. 54. See my *Mitsubishi and the N.Y.K.*, pp. 460–464, for the complex demand-pull structure that the government triggered through shipping subsidies starting in the late 1890s.

48. Francois Crouzet, as quoted in Alfred D. Chandler, Jr. and Herman Daems, "Introduction: The Rise of Managerial Capitalism and its Impact on Investment Strategy in the Western World and Japan," in Daems and Herman van

der Wee, eds., *The Rise of Managerial Capitalism* (Louvain, Leuven University Press, 1974), p. 1. Cf. Chandler, "Managers," p. 54.

49. Hannah, "Visible and Invisible Hands," pp. 65, 55–56.
50. Leslie Hannah, *The Rise of the Corporate Economy*, 2nd ed. (London, Methuen, 1983), p. 106.
51. Leslie Hannah, "A Pioneer of Public Enterprise: The Central Electricity Board and the National Grid, 1927–1940," in Supple, ed., *Essays*, pp. 223–225.
52. Hannah, *Corporate Economy*, pp. 119, 90–122; Chandler, "Managers," pp. 52–53.
53. Payne, "Family Business in Britain," pp. 196–197.
54. Supple, "Framework," pp. 17–18; Leslie Hannah, "Central Electricity Board," p. 226n13, *Corporate Economy*, pp. 120–121, and "Government and Business in Britain: The Evolution of the Modern Relationship," in Nakagawa Keiichiro, ed., *Government and Business* (University of Tokyo Press, 1980), p. 120.
55. Edwin Green and Michael S. Moss, *A Business of National Importance: The Royal Mail Shipping Group, 1902–1937* (London, Metheun, 1982); Katsura Yoshio, *Sōgō Shōsha no gen'ryū: Suzuki Shōten* (Nihon Keizai Shinbunsha, 1977), pp. 169–193.
56. Leslie Hannah, "Comments," in *Government and Business*, p. 104. For background on increasing industrial concentration in this period, see Kozo Yamamura, "The Japanese Economy, 1911–1930: Concentration, Conflicts, and Crises," in Bernard S. Silberman and H. D. Harootunian, eds., *Japan in Crisis: Essays in Taishō Democracy* (Princeton University Press, 1974), pp. 299–328.
57. Hannah, *Corporate Economy*, pp. 116–117.
58. Kozo Yamamura, "Japan's Deus ex Machina: Western Technology in the 1920s," *Journal of Japanese Studies* 12.1:65–94 (Winter 1986), pp. 91–92.
59. Hasegawa, "1920 nendai," pp. 40–49, 62–63.
60. See, for example, Kenneth Pyle, "Advantages of Followership: German Economics and Japanese Bureaucrats, 1890–1925," *Journal of Japanese Studies* 1.1:127–164 (Autumn 1974).
61. For comments on this background and the related history of the German firm, see Hans Jaeger, "Business and Government in Imperial Germany, 1871–1918," in *Government and Business*, pp. 146–149; and Steven B. Webb, "Tariffs, Cartels, Technology, and Growth in the German Steel Industry, 1879 to 1914," *Journal of Economic History* 40.2:309–329 (June 1980). Chalmers Johnson, *MITI and the Japanese Miracle: The Growth of Industrial Policy, 1925–1975* (Stanford University Press, 1982), pp. 103, 106, 108, touches on these issues briefly, but further study of them may strengthen his arguments pertaining to this period.
    The concept "organized capitalism" should not be confused with the term "organized entrepreneurship" frequently used by Japanese business historians. The latter refers to alliances primarily among, and initiated by, private

firms, though they were often aided by the government-controlled Yokohama Specie Bank.

62. This point is emphasized in Shinomiya Masachika, "Senzen no jidōsha sangyō: sangyō seisaku to Toyota," *Keieigaku kenkyū ronshū* (Seinan Gakuin Daigaku) 3.61–86 (June 1984); Yakushiji Taizo, "The Government in a Spiral Dilemma: Dynamic Policy Intervention Vis-a-Vis Auto Firms c.1900–c.1960," in Aoki, ed., *Economic Analysis,* pp. 265–310.

63. An example of the more conventional contrast, which emphasizes inappropriate U.S. regulation, is the U.S. export trading companies, promoted by the government under a 1982 law. The Federal Reserve Board, which oversees these enterprises, penalizes them for third-country transactions, one of the linchpins of Japanese trading-company practice. Senator John Heinz, *Japan Times,* 27 December 1987, p. 16. For a descriptive account of Japanese government policies in the 1950s which set a legal context for trading-company business methods, see Yasumuro Ken'ichi, "Sōgō Shōsha: tsūshō sangyō seisaku no shiten kara," in Keiei Shi Gakkai dai 23 kai taikai hōkokushū, November 7–8, 1987, pp. 129–136.

The quotas discussed here were, of course, "voluntary export restraints" formally imposed by the Japanese government on Japan's auto industry. But, they can still be termed "American policy." They were implemented only because, in their absence, Japan judged, America would take steps deemed more Draconian. In effect, this was a kind of American policy exercised by proxy through the Japanese government. U.S. law inhibited the American government from taking unilateral action. For an account of the interplay between law and bargaining tactics in this case, see Michael W. Lochmann, "The Japanese Voluntary Restraint on Automobile Exports: An Abandonment of the Free Trade Principles of the GATT and the Free Market Principles of United States Antitrust Laws," *Harvard International Law Journal* 27.1:99–157 (Winter 1986).

64. Yasuba Yasukichi, "Anatomy of the Debate on Japanese Capitalism," *Journal of Japanese Studies* 2.1:63–82 (Autumn 1975); Germaine A. Hoston, *Marxism and the Crisis of Development in Prewar Japan* (Princeton University Press, 1986).

65. Hoston, *Marxism,* pp. 186–187, 287.

66. In two findings of particular importance, Nakamura argues that the Matsukata deflation's impact on the growth of tenancy has been exaggerated and the economic recovery in the early 1930s owed less to military spending than has usually been assumed. See Nakamura Takafusa, *Economic Growth in Prewar Japan* (Yale University Press, 1983), pp. 54–58, 244–248.

67. See, for example, Ōishi Ka'ichirō, "Kadai to hōhō," in Ōishi, ed., *Nihon teikokushugi shi,* Vol. I, *Dai ichiji taisenki* (Tokyo Daigaku Shuppankai, 1985), pp. 1–20.

68. Hoston, *Marxism,* pp. 76–94.

69. See the bibliography of Johannes Hirschmeier, *The Origins of Entrepreneurship in Meiji Japan* (Harvard University Press, 1964).

70. Matsumoto Hiroshi, *Mitsui zaibatsu no kenkyū* (Yoshikawa Kōbunkan,

1979), pp. 4-5; Ōishi, "Kaidai to hōhō," pp. 8-9; and Ishii Kanji, *Nihon keizai shi* (Tokyo Daigaku Shuppankai, 1976), pp. 235-242. This last work provides a succinct summary of the prewar debate on capitalism and imperialism.

71. This subdivision is sometimes used informally for other periods, but its semi-technical application to the industrial-capital stage accommodates the Koza-ha emphasis on Japan's backwardness. These terms are so pervasive among Japanese scholars that a Westerner preparing an article for Japanese translation has to be aware of them to avoid confusion for the translator.

72. Hoston sees in Uno's ideas an early version of Immanuel Wallerstein's world-systems approach for analyzing world capitalism. *Marxism*, pp. 285-287, 318n50.

73. Space permits only a brief reference to these stages. For a rigorous theoretical approach by an Uno supporter, see Robert Albritton, *A Japanese Reconstruction of Marxist Theory* (London, Macmillan, 1986), pp. 74-94.

74. Ibid., p. 78.

75. Ibid., p. 88. My use of these quotations violates the Marxist distinction between "theory" and "analysis," but since, in practice, the two become blurred, my point stands.

76. "Introduction: Approaches to Business History," in Supple, ed., *Essays*, p. 1; Nakagawa Keiichirō, "Introduction," *Japanese Yearbook on Business History* I.vii (1984).

77. See, for example, Takeda Haruhito, "Shihon chikuseki (3): zaibatsu," in Ōishi, ed., *Teikokushugi*, pp. 246-247, who draws on Morikawa and Yasuoka.

78. *Nihon kin'yū shihon bunseki* (Tokyo Daigaku Shuppankai, 1965).

79. *Mitsubishi Sha shi*, available privately at the time of Shibagaki's research but since published by Tokyo Daigaku Shuppankai, 1980-1982.

80. Shibagaki, *Kin'yū shihon*, p. 17.

81. See the historiographical summaries in Mishima Yasuo, ed. *Mitsubishi zaibatsu* (Nihon Keizai Shinbun Sha, 1981), p. 15; Matsumoto, *Mitsui zaibatsu*, p. 6; and Ōishi, "Kadai to hōhō," p. 15.

82. Shibagaki Kazuo, *Nihon shihonshugi no ronri* (Tokyo Daigaku Shuppankai, 1971); Nishikawa Hiroshi, *Nihon Teikokushugi to mengyō* (Minerva Shobō, 1987); and the review of the latter by Takamura Naosuke, *Shigaku zasshi* 96.12:96-97 (December 1987).

83. Chandler, *Visible Hand*, pp. 9-10; Morikawa, "Summary of Concluding Discussion," pp. 284-285. Chandler's definitions do not necessarily imply development through stages. Furthermore, they are "ideal-types," to be distinguished from the dominant types of Uno's stages, which in Marxist theory are regarded as "material-types." See the difference between these two as well as the concept of "average-types," which stress what countries have in common, in Albritton, *A Japanese Reconstruction*, pp. 87-89.

84. These stages appear in Ishii, *Nihon keizai shi*, pp. 157-160, though the framework of his discussion differs somewhat from the question posed here.

85. Matsumoto, *Mitsui zaibatsu*, pp. 2-4, 369-397.

86. Hashimoto Jurō *Dai kyōkōki no Nihon shihonshugi* (Tokyo Daigaku Shuppankai, 1984), pp. 14-15, 299-380.

87. Yasuoka Shigeaki, *Zaibatsu keisei shi no kenkyū* (Kyoto, Minerva Shobō, 1970).

88. The following is taken from "Sengo keiei shi no shuppatsu ten: Zaibatsu kaitai" [interview with Wakimura Yoshitarō], *Business Review* (Hitotsubashi University) 31.2:88–98 (October 1983); Nakagawa Keiichirō, "Wakimura Sensei no hito to gyōseki," in *Wakimura Yoshitarō chosakushū*, Vol. I (Nihon Keiei Shi Kenkyūjo, 1976), pp. 1–16. A case can be made that Miyamoto taught business history earlier than Wakimura, but his courses were usually regarded as commercial, not business, history.

89. Nakagawa Keiichirō, "Organized Entrepreneurship in the Course of the Industrialization of Prewar Japan," in H. Nagamine, ed., *Nation-Building and Regional Development: The Japanese Experience* (Nagoya, Maruzen Asia, 1981), pp. 55–76.

90. For Wakimura's latest work on oil, written in 1982 at age 82, see "Ryō-taisenkan no Yusōsen," in Nakagawa Keiichirō, ed., *Ryōtaisenkan no Nihon kaiji sangyō* (Chūō Daigaku Shuppankai, 1985), pp. 253–279.

91. For background on this incident, see my "The Japanese Popular Front Movement, July 1936–February 1938," *Papers on Japan* (Harvard University, East Asian Research Center) 6.102–142 (1972); and, for Wakimura's position within Tōdai's Economics Faculty, see Byron K. Marshall, "Academic Factionalism in Japan: The Case of the Tōdai Economics Department, 1919–1939," *Modern Asian Studies* 12.4:529–551 (October 1978).

92. Ōtsuka was a popular professor whose ideas, interestingly, are remembered fondly by a large number of businessmen scattered among different Japanese companies. The impact of a partially Marxist-oriented university education on businessmen who emerged as leaders between the 1960s and the 1980s remains an important but unstudied issue.

93. For additional points, see Nakagawa Keiichirō, "Keiei shigaku no hōhō to mondai," in Keiei Shi Gakkai, ed., *Keiei shigaku no 20 nen: kaiko to tenbō* (Tokyo Daigaku Shuppankai, 1985), pp. 5–21.

94. In relation to this last point, a common perception among Marxist historians in Japan is that, though the first generation of Japanese business historians (most of whom emerged just a few years after Nakagawa) knew Marxism, today's younger ones lack even that familiarity.

95. Alexander Gerschenkron, *Economic Backwardness in Historical Perspective* (Harvard University Press, 1962), esp. Chapters 1–3.

96. See P. K. O'Brien, "Do We Have a Typology for the Study of European Industrialization in the XIXth Century?" *Journal of European Economic History* 15.2:291–333 (Fall 1986), esp., pp. 304–328.

97. Minami, *Power Revolution*, pp. 340–350.

98. Nakagawa, "Introduction," p. viii.

99. See, especially, *Kindai Nihon to Igirisu shihon: Jādein Maseson Shōkai o chūshin ni* (Tokyo Daigaku Shuppankai, 1984).

100. Yoshi Tsurumi, *Japanese Business: A Research Guide with Annotated Bibliography* (New York, Praeger, 1978), p. 119.

101. Yonekawa Shin'ichi, "Recent Writing on Japanese Economic and Social History," *Economic History Review* 38.1:107–123 (February 1985), p. 113.
102. This work is *Kōhon Mitsui Bussan Kabushiki Kaisha 100 nenshi,* ed. Nihon Keiei Shi Kenkyūjo (Unpublished, 1978), 2 vols. The early unofficial history of Mitsubishi Shōji, *Ritsugyō bōeki,* written by a former company executive, Tanaka Kanzō, has had a somewhat different experience. Yoshihara Kunio, *Sogo Shosha: The Vanguard of the Japanese Economy* (Tokyo, Oxford University Press, 1982), p. 91, suggests this work is not confidential but is hard to obtain. Actually the reverse is true. Many business historians in Japan have their own photocopy, some of which circulate in samizdat form.
103. See, for example, *Zen Nihon Kaiin Kumiai 40 nenshi,* ed. Nihon Keiei Shi Kenkyūjo, (Dō Kumiai, 1986). The IBM Japan history is forthcoming.
104. For useful comments on companies and their materials, see Tatsuki Mariko, "Business Archives and Research for Business History in Japan," in Nakagawa Keiichirō and Yui Tsunehiko, eds., *Organization and Management, 1900–1930* (Tokyo, Japanese Business History Institute, 1983), pp. 194–199. For a handbook on company histories aimed partly at potential graduate assistants, see Nihon Keiei Shi Kenkyūjo, ed., *'Kaisha shi' nyūmon* (Nikkan Shobō, 1984). This work contains useful bibliography and would be a good reference for a graduate seminar in the West.
105. Donald Coleman, "The Uses and Abuses of Business History," *Business History* 29.2:141–156 (April 1987), p. 142.
106. Jeffrey P. Mass, "Introduction," in Mass, ed., *Court and Bakufu in Japan: Essays in Kamakura History* (Yale University Press, 1982), pp. xvi–xvii.
107. Nagahara Keiji, "Reflections on Recent Trends in Japanese Historiography," *Journal of Japanese Studies* 10.1:178–179 (Winter 1984).
108. Leslie Hannah, review article in *Economic History Review* 35.4:639 (1982); and as quoted in Coleman, "Uses and Abuses," p. 141.
109. Morikawa Hidemasa, "Report of the Long-term Trends of the Business History Society of Japan," *Japanese Yearbook on Business History* 1.131–149 (1984), pp. 132–133, 143.
110. For this second approach, see W. Mark Fruin, *The Modern Corporation and Enterprise System in Japan,* forthcoming.
111. For bibliography on the topics discussed in this section, see my *Japan's Economy: A Bibliography of its Past and Present* (New York, Markus Wiener, 1989); Yonekawa Shin'ichi, "The Development of Chinese and Japanese Business in an International Perspective: A Bibliographical Introduction," *Business History Review* 56.2:155–67 (Summer 1982), and "Recent Writing;" *Keiei shigaku no 20 nen;* and the annual "Reports" section in the *Japanese Yearbook on Business History.*
112. Fruin, "Typology."
113. For assessments of company histories in shipbuilding and steel, see Shiba Takao, "Zōsen kigyō no shashi ni tsuite no ikkōsatsu," *Keiei shigaku* 22.3:90–104 (October 1987); and Okazaki Tetsuji, "Tekkō kigyō shi no ikkōsatsu," *Keiei shigaku* 22.1:62–70 (April 1987). Yonekura Seiichirō is working on the steel industry through Harvard and Hitotsubashi universities. For the

electrical industry, see Richard Rice, "Hitachi: Japanese Industry in an Era of Militarism, 1937–1945," PhD dissertation, Harvard University, 1974.

114. See note 32 above. On trading company histories, see Maeda Kazutoshi, "Sōgō shōsha no shashi ni kansuru ikkōsatsu," *Keiei shigaku* 23.1:52–66 (April 1988).

115. Kikkawa Takeo, "Functions of Japanese Trade Associations before World War II: The Case of Cartel Organizations," in Yamazaki Hiroaki and Miyamoto Matao, eds., *Trade Associations in Business History* (University of Tokyo Press, 1988), pp. 53–86 (comments included).

116. Uekusa Masu, "Industrial Organization: The 1970s to the Present," in Yamamura and Yasuba, eds., *Political Economy*, pp. 475–481; and *Sangyō soshiki ron* (Chikuma Shobō, 1982), pp. 179–224; Kozo Yamamura, "Joint Research and Antitrust: Japanese vs. American Strategies," in Hugh Patrick, ed., *Japan's High Technology Industries: Lessons and Limitations of Industrial Policy* (University of Washington, 1986), pp. 171–209.

117. Ronald Dore, *Flexible Rigidities: Industrial Policy and Structural Adjustment in the Japanese Economy, 1970–1980* (Stanford University Press, 1986), pp. 73–77.

118. For recent studies of the interwar years, see Hashimoto Jurō and Takeda Haruhito, eds., *Ryōtaisen kanki: Nihon no karuteru* (Ochanomizu Shobō, 1985).

119. See, especially, *Puroto kōgyōka no jidai: Seiō to Nihon no hikaku shi* (Nihon Hyōronsha, 1985).

120. The latter version is criticized by David Herlihy, a medieval historian, in his review of a book by Peter Kriedte, *Business History Review* 59.3:530–531 (Autumn 1985). For a more general critique by a business historian, see D. C. Coleman, "Proto-Industrialization: A Concpt Too Many," *Economic History Review* 36.3:435–448 (August 1983).

121. O'Brien, "Typology," p. 324. This paper views the concept of proto-industrialization more favorably than do the authors cited in the previous note, and in pp. 297–304 provides bibliography on recent works.

122. Saitō Osamu, "Scenes of Japan's Economic Development and the 'Longue Durée'," in Erich Pauer, ed., *Silkworms, Oil, and Chips . . . Proceedings of the Economics and Economic History Section of the Fourth International Conference on Japanese Studies*, Japan Seminar, University of Bonn, 1986, pp. 15–27.

123. Ibid.; quotations are from pp. 20–21.

124. Ibid., p. 22.

125. Coleman, "Proto-Industrialization," p. 447; Herlihy, review, p. 531.

126. In view of Chandler's emphasis on the role of railways in influencing the structure of U.S. companies, in comparisons, geographical factors should be given more weight in explaining developments in the organization of Japanese firms.

127. See my comments on the *kitamaesen*, traders and shipping enterprises from northwest Japan, in "Shipping: From Sail to Steam."

128. O'Brien, "Typology," p. 302, my emphasis.

129. Coleman, "Proto-Industrialization," p. 446.
130. Richard J. Smethurst, *Agricultural Development and Tenancy Disputes in Japan, 1870–1940* (Princeton University Press, 1986); Nakamura Masanori, *Kindai Nihon jinushisei shi kenkyū* (Tokyo Daigaku Shuppankai, 1979). See also Mihashi Tokio, *Nihon nōgyō keiei shi no kenkyū* (Minerva Shobō, 1979), which has a concluding chapter on modern agricultural business.
131. These topics are suggested by Fruin, "Typology;" see also his *Kikkoman: Company, Clan, and Community* (Harvard University Press, 1983).
132. Uchida Hoshimi: *Tokei kōgyō no hattatsu* (Hattori Seikō, 1985), *History of the Japanese Clock and Watch Industry*, Vol. I, *Osaka Watch Incorporated* (Hattori Seiko, 1986), Vol. II, *Wall Clocks of Nagoya, 1885–1925* (Hattori Seiko, 1987); David Landes, *Revolution in Time: Clocks and the Making of the Modern World* (Harvard University Press, 1983), pp. 338–360.
133. Yamaguchi Kazuo and Ishii Kanji, eds., *Kindai Nihon no shōhin ryūtsū* (Tokyo Daigaku Shuppankai, 1986).
134. (Nihon Keizai Hyōronsha, 1978–1979), 13 vols.
135. *Kindai Nihon kaiun seisei shiryō,* ed. by Nihon Keiei Shi Kenkyūjo, (Nippon Yūsen Kabushiki Kaisha, 1988).
136. On these developments, see Teratani Takeaki, *Nihon kōwan shiron josetsu* (Jichōsha, 1972); and Yamamoto Hirobumi, ed., *Kōtsū, Un'yu no hattatsu to gijutsu kakushin: rekishiteki kōsatsu* (Kokusai Rengō Daigaku, 1986).
137. Kandatsu Haruki, *Sangyō kakumei-ki ni okeru chiiki hensei* (Ochanomizu Shobō, 1987).
138. Ōishi Ka'ichirō, ed., *Kindai Nihon ni okeru jinushi keiei no tenkai: Okayama-ken Ushimado-chō Nishi-Hattori-ke no kenkyū* (Ochanomizu Shobō, 1985).
139. Ishii, *Kindai Nihon to igirisu shihon.*
140. The main proponent of this argument is Kawakatsu Heita. See his "International Competition in Cotton Goods in the Late 19th Century: Britain vs. India & East Asia," in *The Emergence of a World Economy, 1500–1914: Papers of the IX. International Congress of Economic History,* ed. Wolfram Fischer, et al. (Stuttgart, Franz Steiner Verlag Wiesbaden GmbH, 1986), pp. 619–643; for the intra-Asian trade, see Sugihara Kaoru, "Patterns of Asia's Integration into the World Economy, 1880–1913," in ibid., 709–728. [Both these papers appeared in *Shakai keizai shigaku* 51.1 (1985).] For Ishii's response to Kawakatsu, see his "Ishin henkaku no kiso katei: taigaiteki keiki to 'henseikae'," *Rekishigaku kenkyū* 560.138–148 (October 1986), especially pp. 138–140. See also Sugiyama Shin'ya, *Japan's Industrialization in the World Economy, 1859–1899* (London, The Athlone Press, 1988).
141. Yasuoka, *Zaibatsu keisei shi;* Nakase Toshikazu, *Sumitomo zaibatsu keiei shi kenkyū* (Ōtsuki Shoten, 1984); Hatakeyama Hideki, *Sumitomo zaibatsu seiritsu shi no kenkyū* (Dōbunkan, 1988). See also Yui Tsunehiko, "Yasuda Shōten no keiei to shihon chikuseki," *Keiei shigaku* 20.1:1–35 (April 1985); and the more popular work by Kobayashi Masaaki, *Seishō no tanjō: mō hitotsu no Meiji Ishin* (Tōyō Keizai Shinpōsha, 1986), which treats the business origins of many of the zaibatsu.
142. Chōginshi Kenkyūkai, ed., *Henkakuki no shōnin shihon: Ōmi shōnin Chōgin*

no kenkyū (Yoshikawa Kōbunkan, 1984). See also the popular book by Ogura Eiichirō, *Ōmi shōnin no keiei* (Kyoto, Sanburaito Shuppan, 1988), which went through ten printings in its first month. The recent success of Itō Chū, which traces its ancestry back to Ōmi merchants, in overtaking Mitsubishi Shōji as the general trading company with the largest sales, is likely to encourage more attention to early merchant traditions which developed independently of government ties.

143. For a recent study of wartime business, see Mishima Yasuo, ed., *Dai niji taisen to Mitsubishi zaibatsu* (Nihon Keizai Shinbunsha, 1987). This, however, does not examine the transition referred to here. For works on the steel industry which do, see Yonekura Seiichirō, "Sengo Nihon tekkōgyō shiron: sono renzokusei to hirenzokusei," *Business Review* (Hitotsubashi University) 31.2:67–87 (October 1983); and Inayama Yoshihiro, *Watakushi no Tekkō Shōwa shi* (Tōyō Keizai Shinpōsha, 1986).

144. An analysis of the effects of the purge on the managerial system also seems overdue.

Entrepreneurs: and use of high technology, 230; Noguchi as typical, 259

Equilibrium within firms, 323; examples of upset, 323–324

Ericson, Steven J., 5, 14, 121–182, 350–351, 365; chapter summarized, 8–10; on a firm's equilibrium, 323; topics suggested by, 369–370

Essential Industries Labor Management Ordinance, 77, 78–79, 84

Explosives, 410n88. *See also* Munitions

Exports, of silk, 6, 7

Factory councils: and labor disputes, 71; and binding arbitration, 71; Welfare Ministry vs. Zensanren on, 72–73

Factory Law, the, 55–57; 1911 version, 56; opposition to, 56–57; eventual acceptance of, 61

Families: commercial role of wealth of, 10; control of firms by, 334–335

Family firm: management of, 320; and industrial structure, 333–339; influence of British, 334, 335

Fanuc, 320

Fertilizer Distribution Improvement Regulations, 244–245

Fertilizers, 15; Noguchi's work on, 233; calcium cyanamide, 233; ammonium sulfate, 235; international cartels for, 243–244; made in Korea, 250

Feudalism, in theories of Japanese capitalism, 345, 346

Fifteenth National Bank, 9, 10; shares of Nippon Railway, 135–136, 177; on holdings in railways, 179, 392n38

Fijimoto Billbroker Trust, 42

Financial panic of 1890. *See* Panic of 1890

Financiers, as directors, 39–40

Financing: of early joint-stock companies, 124; role of speculation, 126–127; government subsidies, 163–165; Central Bank discounts, 166–170, 177; retrenchment, 170–171; preferred stock and corporate bonds, 171–176; of O.S.K. and N.Y.K., 209–213; of Nitchitsu, 231–235, 238; of Korean projects, 251, 254–255; of Riken, 274–275, 304, 310; by sale of patents, 276–277; periodization scheme of, 416n15; use of foreign capital in Japan and Britain, 341

Firms, Japanese: aspects of, 318–324; ownership of, 318; dominance by owners, 319–320; role of strong founder-executives, 320–321; autonomy of, 321–322;

group membership, 322, 415n10; Aoki's models of, 323–324; organization in large-scale (Chandler's model), 324–333; trading companies and vertical integration, 330; and industrial structure, 330; family control of, 334; compared to Britain's, 335–339, 418n43; other comparisons, 340–344; rise of new (1920s–1930s), 341

Fishlow, Albert, 142

Ford, Henry, 272, 288, 313, 326

Foreign personnel (*oyatoi gaijin*): salaries of, 29; limitations of, 30

Fourth National Bank of Niigata, 133, 177

France: and silk industry, 93; and Tomioka project, 98–101, 386n20; departure of French staff, 99; production of ammonia in, 239

Fruin, Mark, 3

Fuji Cotton Spinning, 48

Fujita, 10, 32; top management in, 39

Fujita Denzaburō, 138, 147; progressive policies of, 150

Fujiwara-Bosch Agreement, 245–247

Fujiwara Ginjirō, 42, 66, 245–247

Fujiyama Aiichirō, 49

Fujiyama Raita, 42, 45, 49

Fujiyama Tsuneichi, 232–233; Noguchi left by, 236

Fukoku Industries, 290, 304, 310

Fukumoto Motonosuke, 39

Fukuoka coal mines, 181

Fukuzawa Yukichi, 32

Furukawa Shōji, 32, 39, 43, 233, 301

Furukawa Ichibei, 39

General Chemical Corporation, 239

General Electric, 15, 342

General Motors, 321, 344

Germany: style of investment banking in, 179–180; shipping industries in, 206, 215; production of ammonia in, 239; and the Fujiwara-Bosch agreement, 245–247; synthetic fuels in, 258; Imperial Institute for Physics in, 273; capitalism in, 280, 313; "sweet-potato-root" in, 299–300; family control of firms in, 334–335; dyes in, 337; industrial organization compared to Japan's, 340; protective tariffs of, 342

Gerschenkron, Alexander, 355–356

Glycerine, Noguchi's manufacture of, 257

Gō Seinosuke, 63–64, 69, 83; on shipping merger, 206–207

Goddard, Henry, 29

Labor *(continued)*
69; "statist" concept of, 75, 77; integration of agencies concerned with, 77–78;
at Tomioka, 106, 110–111, 112; troubles
in N.Y.K., 188, 207; at Nitchitsu, 237.
See also Labor unions
Labor Council (Kinrō Kyōgikai), 82
Labor Management Ordinance 81, 82;
inspectors under, 84
Labor Union Bill, 62; campaign against,
62–63
Labor unions: in U.S., 22; legislation on,
54; and Zensanren, 54; vs. "paternal
care," 56; "company" unions, 58; opposition to, 59; issues in the 1930s, 62–70;
defeat of Union Bill, 63; significance of
Zensanren, 64–65; and "Japanese-style"
compromise, 69
Land, for railways, 157–158
Landholders, as investors in railways, 138
Liberalism: in stage theory, 347; cotton
manufacturing in stage of, 350
Life-insurance companies, as shareholders,
134
London Naval Conference, 63

MacArthur, Gen. Douglas, 372
McCallion, Stephen W., 5, 89–118; chapter
summarized, 6–8
Machinery: Riken as producer of, 290;
single-function vs. universal tools, 299
Maebashi, 104
Maeda Masana, 7
Maeda Riichi, 308; on quality of piston
rings, 308–309
Magnesium production, "sweet-potato-root"
style, 300
Magoshi Kōjirō, 49
Magoshi Kyōhei, 45, 49
Management: and labor policy, 20; M-
Form vs. U-Form, 328; intensity of in
Japan, 329
Managerial hierarchies in Japan; and the
Chandler model, 325; and lack of verti-
cal integration, 326
Managers: engineers as, 17, 152–153; of rail-
roads, 146–155; of San'yō, 147–151; of
Kyushu, 151; former public officials as,
151–152; professional middle manage-
ment, 153; and ownership of firms, 319;
Chandler model on, 325. *See also* Salar-
ied managers
Managing directors (*senmu torishimari-
yaku*), 40–41

Manchurian Incident, 277; and boycott of
Japanese goods, 205
Manufacturing groups, 326
Marxism, 422n94; on control by owner-
ship, 12; on capitalism, 313; ideology in
Germany, 342–343; and business his-
tory, 344–353; effect of dominance of,
346; stage theory, 346–348; continued
influence of, 348–349; and regional vari-
ations in historiography, 352–353; on
proto-industrialization, 365
Mass, Jeffrey, 360
Masuda Takashi, 34, 38, 233
Matsukata Kōjirō, 43
Matsukata Masayoshi, 7, 103, 104, 109, 124;
on railway construction, 144; on nation-
alization, 156
Matsumoto Gaku, 65
Matsumoto Hiroshi, on Mitsui Bussan, 352
Matsumoto Jūtarō, 40, 134, 147–148, 153,
182
Matsuoka Komakichi, 64, 66, 69
Matsushita, 320, 326, 327
Mechanization: in silk reeling, 111–112,
114–115; in imitation of Tomioka, 116
Meiji period, 45; management during,
329–330
Meiji Life Insurance Co., 134
Meiji regime: silk industry under, 89; and
Tomioka Filature, 91; cotton spinning
under, 121–122; railways under, 122,
132; and the Industrial Revolution, 366
Meiji Restoration, Kōza-ha vs. Rōnō-ha on,
345
Mercantilism, in stage theory, 347
Merchants, as investors in railways, 139
Merger of N.Y.K. and O.S.K., 213–219; proposal, 213–215; support for, 215–217;
opposition to, 217–218; leak of, 218;
economic context of, 220–222; and management of N.Y.K., 222–224
Mergers, Japanese: takeovers of bankrupt
firms, 340; trend toward horizontal concentration, 340; negotiations for rationalization, 340–341; Johnson on, 404n96.
See also Cartels
Mie Cotton Spinning Co., educated personnel in, 34
Miki Takeo, 354
Military, the: influence on labor, 54–55;
and Ordinance on Labor Management,
75; increased influence over labor, 75–
76, 84; orders from, 285; Ōkōchi's relation to, 314
Minamata: Nitchitsu plant at, 236, 237,
241; after the war, 261

Nakagawa Keiichirō, 353; organizer of Business History Society, 355; editor of journal, 356
Nakahashi Tokugorō, 234; Noguchi a protégé of, 235; as president of Nitchitsu, 235, 236
Nakamigawa Hikojirō, 12, 13, 38, 42, 50, 144, 147–148, 182; investment policies of, 148–149; rebellion against, 149–150; career of, 150–151; on land acquisition, 157–158
Nakamura Masanori, 369
Nakamura Takafusa, 121, 180, 181, 345, 420n66
Nakamura Yamamura, 121
Nakanishi Ken'ichi, 128
Nakatani Iwao, 415n10
Nan'yō Kaiun kaisha (South Seas Shipping Co.), 226
Narahara Shigeru, 148, 151
National Council of Federated Industrial Organizations, 64
National Federation of Industrial Organizations. *See* Zensanren
National General Mobilization Council, 78, 83
National General Mobilization Law, 74, 78
Nationalization: of railways, 127, 156; opposition to, 156–157; and the Railway Construction Law, 160–161; advocated for shipping, 206
NEC (Nippon Electric Company), 333, 415n9
New Economic Order, 73
New Japan Steel, 333
New York: O.S.K.'s express line to, 202–204; export of raw silk to, 204
Nichi-Man (Japan-Manchuria), magnesium in, 301
Niigata, 112
Nihon Kangyō Ginkō. *See* Japan Hypothec Bank
Nikkeiren, 64
Nippon Carbide Company, 233
Nippon Chisso Hiryō, 234
Nippon Kōkan, 225
Nippon Piston Ring, 309
Nippon Railway Company, 135; shareholders of, 135–136, 137; managers of, 147; government subsidies to, 163; additional shares, 171; and bank loans, 177
Nippon Soda, 283
Nishikawa Hiroshi, 350
Nishina Yoshio, 276
Nishio Suehiro, 63
Nishiwaki Kunisaburō, 133

Nissan, 341; salaried managers in, 44; as "new" zaibatsu, 283; use of piston rings, 308–309, 314
Nisshin Kisen (China-Japan Steamship Co.), 193, 225
Nitchitsu (Nippon Chisso Hiryō; Japan Nitrogenous Fertilizers), 17, 19, 229–268, 283, 332, 374; as "new zaibatsu," 230; investment strategy of, 231; financing of, 231–235, 238, 405n16, 406n22, n26; labor concerns of, 237–238; after World War I, 238–243; diversification of, 241–243, 256–259; cartels and cooperatives, 243–248; Korean subsidiaries of, 254; conclusions, 259–263; autonomy of, 321, 322; and vertical integration, 332, 417n35; as new firm, 341
Nitrogen Deliberative Association (Chisso Kyōgikai), 245
Nitrogen Engineering Corporation (NEC), 283
Nobeoka, chemical plant at, 241, 257
Noda Kichibei, 40, 170, 176
Noda Utarō, 206–207
Noda Masaho, 161
Noguchi Jun, 15, 18, 229–268; as innovative entrepreneur, 231–238, 272, 283; career of, 232–238; financing of license for calcium cyanamide, 233–234; manufacture of ammonium sulfate, 235–236, 403n15; after World War I, 238–243; Korean production by, 241, 248–251; diversification by, 241–243; and the Fujiwara-Bosch agreement, 245–247; and Ugaki, 252–256; strategic diversification, 256–259; conclusions, 259–263; as strong founder-executive, 320, 322
Nomura (bank), 304
Nomura Jiichirō, 205, 218
Northern Kyushu, 63
"Nōson no kōgyō" (Industry in rural villages; Ōkōchi), 278
"Nōson no kōson-ka" (The industrialization of rural villages; Ōkōchi), 278
Nouveaux riches family businesses, 47
N.Y.K. shipping line (Japanese Mail Steamship Co.), 11, 351; during World War I, 13–14; and Mitsubishi, 16, 184, 202, 322; salaried managers as directors, 37, 38; early history of, 187–188; compared to O.S.K., 188–192; vertical dimension of, 193–199; and Kagami Kenkichi, 196–199; early moves of Kagami as president, 200–206; agreement with O.S.K., 204–205; merger with O.S.K., horizon-

Harvard East Asian Monographs

21. Kwang-Ching Liu, ed., *American Missionaries in China: Papers from Harvard Seminars*

22. George Moseley, *A Sino-Soviet Cultural Frontier: The Ili Kazakh Autonomous Chou*

23. Carl F. Nathan, *Plague Prevention and Politics in Manchuria, 1910–1931*

24. Adrian Arthur Bennett, *John Fryer: The Introduction of Western Science and Technology into Nineteenth-Century China*

25. Donald J. Friedman, *The Road from Isolation: The Campaign of the American Committee for Non-Participation in Japanese Aggression, 1938–1941*

26. Edward Le Fevour, *Western Enterprise in Late Ch'ing China: A Selective Survey of Jardine, Matheson and Company's Operations, 1842–1895*

27. Charles Neuhauser, *Third World Politics: China and the Afro-Asian People's Solidarity Organization, 1957–1967*

28. Kungtu C. Sun, assisted by Ralph W. Huenemann, *The Economic Development of Manchuria in the First Half of the Twentieth Century*

29. Shahid Javed Burki, *A Study of Chinese Communes, 1965*

30. John Carter Vincent, *The Extraterritorial System in China: Final Phase*

31. Madeleine Chi, *China Diplomacy, 1914–1918*

32. Clifton Jackson Phillips, *Protestant America and the Pagan World: The First Half Century of the American Board of Commissioners for Foreign Missions, 1810–1860*

33. James Pusey, *Wu Han: Attacking the Present through the Past*

34. Ying-wan Cheng, *Postal Communication in China and Its Modernization, 1860–1896*

35. Tuvia Blumenthal, *Saving in Postwar Japan*

36. Peter Frost, *The Bakumatsu Currency Crisis*

37. Stephen C. Lockwood, *Augustine Heard and Company, 1858–1862*

38. Robert R. Campbell, *James Duncan Campbell: A Memoir by His Son*

39. Jerome Alan Cohen, ed., *The Dynamics of China's Foreign Relations*

40. V. V. Vishnyakova-Akimova, *Two Years in Revolutionary China, 1925–1927*, tr. Steven I. Levine

41. Meron Medzini, *French Policy in Japan during the Closing Years of the Tokugawa Regime*

42. *The Cultural Revolution in the Provinces*

43. Sidney A. Forsythe, *An American Missionary Community in China, 1895–1905*

44. Benjamin I. Schwartz, ed., *Reflections on the May Fourth Movement: A Symposium*

45. Ching Young Choe, *The Rule of the Taewŏn'gun, 1864–1873: Restoration in Yi Korea*

46. W. P. J. Hall, *A Bibliographical Guide to Japanese Research on the Chinese Economy, 1958–1970*

47. Jack J. Gerson, *Horatio Nelson Lay and Sino-British Relations, 1854–1864*

48. Paul Richard Bohr, *Famine and the Missionary: Timothy Richard as Relief Administrator and Advocate of National Reform*

STUDIES IN THE MODERNIZATION OF THE REPUBLIC OF KOREA: 1945–1975